2116

THE
RANDOM HOUSE
HANDBOOK

UNIVERSITY OF CALIFORNIA, BERKELEY **Frederick Crews**

THE RANDOM HOUSE HANDBOOK

RANDOM HOUSE • NEW YORK

Copyright © 1974 by Random House, Inc.

Library of Congress Cataloging in Publication Data
Crews, Frederick B
  The Random House handbook.
  1. English language—Rhetoric. 2. English
language—Grammar—1950–   I. Title.
PE1408.C715   808'.042   73-13640
ISBN 0-394-31065-9

Manufactured in the United States of America

Designed by James M. Wall

Cover created by John Murello

First Edition
987654321

June 1973, p. 59. Copyright © 1973 by the American Jewish Committee. Reprinted by permission of the publisher.

JOHN H. SCHAAR, excerpt from "The Case for Patriotism," *American Review*, No. 17, pp. 61–62. Reprinted by permission of the author.

ALIX KATES SHULMAN, excerpt from "The War in the Back Seat," *Atlantic*, July 1972, p. 50. Copyright © 1972 by Alix Kates Shulman. Reprinted by permission of Curtis Brown, Ltd.

PAUL SIGMUND, excerpt from "Princeton in Crisis and Change," *Academic Transformation*, by David Riesman and Verne Stadtman. Copyright © 1973 by Carnegie Foundation. Originally published in *Change*. Reprinted by permission of McGraw-Hill Book Company.

KENNETH M. STAMPP, excerpt from *The Era of Reconstruction, 1865–1877*. Copyright © 1965 by Alfred A. Knopf, Inc. Reprinted by permission of Alfred A. Knopf, Inc.

CALVIN TRILLIN, excerpt from "No Telling, No Summing Up," *The New Yorker*, 11 June 1966, pp. 118, 121. © 1966 The New Yorker Magazine, Inc. Reprinted by permission of the publisher.

LIONEL TRILLING, excerpt from "Sincerity and Authenticity." Reprinted by permission of Harvard University Press.

ELLEN WILLIS, excerpt from "The Fantasy of the Perfect Lover," *New York Review of Books*, 31 Aug. 1972, p. 7. Copyright © 1972 by The New York Review. Reprinted by permission of International Famous Agency, Inc., and the author.

TOM WOLFE, excerpt from *The Pump House Gang*. Copyright © 1968 by Tom Wolfe. Copyright © 1966 by the World Journal. Reprinted by permission of Farrar, Straus & Giroux, Inc.

WILLIAM ZINSSER, "Frankly, Miss Dodds," *Atlantic*, Apr. 1973, p. 94. Copyright © 1973 by William K. Zinsser. Reprinted by permission of the author.

Excerpt from "The President's Palace Guard," *Newsweek*, 19 Mar. 1973, p. 24. Copyright Newsweek, Inc. 1973. Reprinted by permission of the publisher.

Entry from *The Random House College Dictionary*. © Copyright, 1968, 1973 by Random House, Inc. Reprinted by Random House, Inc.

For Betty

To the instructor

Composition texts tend to fall into two categories, which might be called the Big Book and the Little Book. The Big Book impersonally sets forth the rules of "good English" and persuasive writing, and it usually includes information about such various matters as linguistics, logic, etymology, poetics, business letters, and the art of passing an exam. The Little Book speaks intimately to the student as a person who needs some assistance in composing essays. Necessarily, however, its advice is fragmentary; a reader can't turn to the index with any expectation of finding a reference to the specific problem that's troubling him.

The Random House Handbook attempts to combine the virtues of both texts without sharing their drawbacks. Like the Little Book, it is a personal statement from one essayist to others; its emphasis falls, not on unbending laws of correctness, but on a writer's options and on the difference between mechanical and lively prose. Yet it is also a reference work, dealing in great detail with the questions that affect young writers *as* writers. Instead of touching on every subject connected with "English," I have tried to give students an extensive guide to current opinion about diction, syntax, punctuation, and idiomatic expressions.

The *Handbook* deals with standard English, not as the best of all dialects, but simply as the one that most educated people expect to find when they read an essay. My attitude is pragmatic: I want students to use the language creatively without alienating their readers. Much of my advice, especially in the 795-entry Index of Usage, rests not only on personal taste but on a comparative study of recent authorities. The book to which I am most indebted is Roy H. Copperud's *American Usage: The Consensus,* a work which recognizes that normal contemporary practice should overrule scholars' whims.

The order of my chapters is intended to minimize the mere avoidance of errors while highlighting a writer's opportunities and responsibilities. In fact, however, the chapters can be assigned in any sequence that fits an instructor's plans. Since some teachers leave their students free to use a handbook on their own, I have explained some of the book's uses below. Further information about the individual chapters, along with a key to the Exercises, can be found in a manual which is available gratis to instructors.

To the student

This is a book for would-be essayists, most of whom find themselves members of an unloved course known as Freshman English. The inside word about Freshman English is that it's entirely concerned with error-hunting, that it penalizes originality, and that the key to success in it is to humor the instructor in his pet peeves. Although these rumors are generally false, they die hard, for they comfortably lay the blame for bad prose on the reader instead of the writer. The trouble is that they also help to bring about such prose. Believing that "English" demands a hypocritical kind of essay, some students never allow themselves to meet the real challenge of being a writer.

We all know what a writer is: it is someone who uses written words to reach out toward other people, trying to communicate part of his experience and also perhaps to win agreement to some idea that matters to him. The fact that he happens to be enrolled in a course may affect his task in numerous ways, but if this fact becomes the main consideration, he ceases to be a writer and is merely a survivor or a casualty of Freshman English. In order to help prevent such a result, I call attention to the essayist's freedom to be himself. To a large extent this is a book about a writer's necessary struggle to find his own voice by resisting clichés, half-truths, and prefabricated patterns of organization.

Yet a writer may also have to observe certain norms in order to gain a hearing for his ideas. Even though some of "the rules" shift from one decade to the next, at any given point they are taken seriously by nearly all educated readers. I have tried, not to dictate a purist attitude toward language, but to indicate the phrases and constructions that would be likely to cause trouble for you. You may have good stylistic reasons for writing colloquially, but at least you ought to know when you're doing so.

Because a student is asked almost overnight to become an essayist, my book starts by considering what essays are, how they are organized, and what the essayist's relation to his reader ought to be. Someone who has at least a rough competence in forming grammatical sentences can profitably read the first six chapters in order. Other readers may want to begin with later chapters that treat usage and mechanics. Those who aren't sure of the meaning of grammatical terms should turn directly to Chapter Seven, and then go to the chapters covering the problems they want to work on first.

For advice and encouragement I am grateful to Elizabeth Crews, James B. Smith, Richard Ohmann, George McMichael, Richard Larson, and, above all, June Smith of Random House, who has edited my book with enthusiasm, self-sacrifice, and extraordinary keenness of judgment.

Frederick Crews
October 1973

CONTENTS

I. A WRITER'S WORK

II. STYLE

4 WORDS

5 SENTENCES

II. USAGE

IV. MECHANICS

A WRITER'S WORK

1 THE ESSAY

YOU AND YOUR READER

If you're like most students entering a composition course, you arrive with a mixture of hope and apprehension. The hope is that the course will help you to put your thoughts into written words with greater precision and effect. The apprehension is that nothing of the sort will happen and that you'll have to go through a painful, humiliating ordeal. Essays, you know, will be required of you on short notice. Will you be able to write them at all? Looking ahead, perhaps you experience a feeling that assails every writer from time to time—the suspicion that words may fail you. (And if words fail you, the teacher will fail you, too.)

It may seem odd at first that "putting your thoughts into words" should be so challenging. Since childhood, after all, you've been speaking intelligible English. When you converse about things that matter to you, the right words often come to your lips without forethought. Again, in writing letters to friends you scribble away with confidence that you'll be understood. But in writing essays you find yourself at a disadvantage. You know that your prose is expected to make contact with a reader's feelings and carry him along with a developing idea of your own, but you don't have a clear idea of who this reader is. Instead of exchanging views with someone who can see your face, interpret your gestures, and tell you when a certain point needs explanation or support, you have to assume a non-existent relationship and keep on writing. It's almost like composing love letters "to whom it may concern" and mailing them off to "Occupant" or "Boxholder."

This is the normal situation of every essay-writer, but it is temporarily altered in a composition course. There you do get to know your reader, the instructor, in a certain limited way, and you can gradually develop some ease as you become familiar with his judgments. Unlike the mythical "general reader," this one will tell you what he likes and dislikes in your work; he'll even keep reading and commenting when he's bored. Nowhere else are you likely to get the systematic, prolonged encouragement and criticism he will offer. Thus the composition course poses a unique opportunity: if the teacher's opinions are sound and if you take them in the right spirit, you can spend these weeks discovering what other readers, the anonymous ones, would think about your writing, and you can strengthen the habits that make for a good reception.

But the course holds a risk as well as an opportunity. The risk comes directly from that first anxiety about having nothing to say. You'll quickly learn that there *are* ways of getting words onto paper even when you're confused, and if you're not careful you may begin writing mechanically. Instead of exploring your mind and trying to communicate what you believe, you may begin serving up ingredients you think the instructor wants to see. An essay, you tell yourself, has to have an introduction, a body, and a conclusion—and you forget that it's supposed to be interesting. You allot one prominent topic sentence to every paragraph, but the paragraphs, instead of moving forward, just stand there like abandoned temples to the god of the essay. Your prose acquires unity, coherence, emphasis—and acid indigestion. You've simply stopped trying to say what you mean.

The irony about "giving the teacher what he wants" is that this isn't what he wants at all. No teacher I've ever met has preferred an imitation essay to the real thing. Teachers often dwell on technical aspects of the essay because these are important and discussible, but what they want above all is that you be yourself in prose. And if you look at the classic essayists, the ones who are held up for your admiration in the course, you'll find that they haven't followed any routine formula. Some of them, in fact, seem to be outrageously indifferent to paragraph unity, logical transitions, and so forth.

What each of them has instead is his own strong voice that makes us want to listen and believe.

There is no simple way to acquire your voice as an essayist. It's largely a matter of critical rewriting, of refusing to be satisfied with the clichés and awkward phrases that crowd your mind when you're facing a blank page. A composition course and a handbook can show you the general difference between prose that convinces and prose that doesn't, but only you know what is clamoring for expression in your mind. The essential thing is to keep pressing toward clarity, trying to meet the reader's expectations while remaining in touch with your feelings.

WHAT AN ESSAY DOES

The kinds of writing you will do in other courses — exams, reports, term papers, perhaps a senior thesis — all resemble the essay in some respects and call upon the same techniques of persuasion. But the essay is a looser form than any of these; it lends itself to a special combination of personal opinion and reasoning, of intimacy and objectivity.

An *essay* can be defined as a *fairly brief piece of nonfiction that tries to make a point in an interesting way:*

1. *It's fairly brief.* Some of the classic essays by Montaigne and Bacon occupy only a few paragraphs, but essays generally fall between about three and twenty typed pages. Under that minimum, the development of thought that typifies an essay would be difficult to manage. Above the maximum, people might be tempted to read the essay in installments like a book. A good essay makes an unbroken experience.

2. *It's nonfiction.* The essayist tries to tell the truth; if he describes a scene or tells a story, we presume that he's doing his best to capture reality.

3. *It tries to make a point . . .* An essay characteristically tells or explains something, or expresses an attitude toward something, or supports or criticizes something — an opinion, a person, an institution, a movement. A poem or a novel may also do these things, but it does them incidentally. An essay is directly *about* something called its *topic* (see p. 21), and its usual aim is to win sympathy or agreement to the point or *thesis* (see p. 22) it is maintaining.

4. *. . . in an interesting way.* When you write an answer to an "essay question" on an exam, you don't pause to wonder if the reader actually *wants* to pursue your answer to the end; you know you'll succeed if you concisely and coherently satisfy the terms of

the question. But a full-fledged essay tends to be read in another way. Its reader could agree with every sentence and still be displeased. What he wants isn't just true statements, but pleasure and truth combined. In both cases, to be sure, you have to employ *rhetoric;* that is, you have to *choose and arrange your words for their maximum effect on the reader.* The difference is that the reader of an exam tends to brush aside the rhetoric in his search for correct remarks. The rhetoric counts for more in a genuine essay, where maintaining the reader's involvement has to be an uppermost consideration.

Perhaps the whole idea of rhetoric strikes you as manipulative and insincere. Why can't a writer just say what he means? But rhetoric and sincerity needn't work at cross-purposes, and whenever they do the rhetoric comes out sounding all wrong. Your job isn't to deceive the reader, but merely to draw him toward accepting your thesis by making dramatic use of the steps that led you to accept it yourself. Insincerity enters the picture only if you don't believe what you're saying.

The essayist, then, harmonizes reason and rhetoric, trying to be at once lively, fair, and convincing. He must:

tell the truth ⟶	but first make people interested in hearing it;
write with conviction ⟶	but consider whether the ideas will stand up under criticism;
supply evidence ⟶	but not become a bore about it;
be purposeful ⟶	but not follow such a predictable pattern that the reader's attention slackens.

HOW AN ESSAY SOUNDS

The way an essay sounds—the quality of feeling it conveys—is called its *tone.* Depending on your personality and the effect you want to create, you can be formal or informal, sober or whimsical, assertive or pleading, straightforward or sly. But the essay's general function, to present and support opinion, tends to rule out certain tones. Consider these three passages:

A. Yes, you CAN stop drinking! I tell you it's really possible! The fact that you're reading these words means that you have the MOTIVA-TION, the WILL POWER, to make the change now—*today!*—and to STAY ON THE WAGON *FOREVER!!* Think and believe, *I am just as good as everybody else! I don't NEED that bottle!* It's really true. You have more potential than the HYDROGEN BOMB! Just take yourself in hand *today*, and by tomorrow you'll start feeling like a NEW PERSON—the person that you really are inside!

B. While it has seemed probable that addiction to alcohol is at least in part due to the development of physiological tolerance to the drug, there have been to date no clear demonstrations that alterations in the blood level of alcohol alone (without concomitant experiential factors of taste and ingestion) were sufficient to produce a lasting enhancement of alcohol preference subsequent to treatment. Here we report a method capable of producing a lasting enhancement of alcohol preference without concomitant oral stimulation. . . .

This enhancement of preference has been achieved by prolonged passive infusion of alcohol into the stomach of rats. After recovery from surgical preparation, the rats were placed in a Bowman restrainer cage to adapt for 24 hours. After this initial period each rat was connected to a pump . . .[1]

C. Some alcoholic patients, however, if properly approached can be engaged in the attempt to discover what lies back of the alcoholic compulsion, what great anxiety drives them to this suicidal comfort. That it arises from external life difficulties is an alibi no alcoholic patient gives to a psychiatrist who has won his confidence. Troubles there are in the world, to be sure, and some insoluble problems that would vex the soul of the most enduring, but it is not these, or at least not these alone, which impel alcoholic solution. (If it were so, we should all become alcoholics.) No, the victim of alcohol addiction knows what most of his critics do not know, namely, that alcoholism is not a disease, or at least not the principal disease from which he suffers; furthermore, *he knows that he does not know* the origin or nature of the dreadful pain and fear within him which impel him, blindly, to alcoholic self-destruction. It is like some poor beast who has been poisoned or set on fire, and runs blindly into the sea to court one death in fleeing another.[2]

You can see at once that Passage A wasn't taken from an essay. It seizes us and gives us a series of hysterical jolts, as if we had no minds of our own and had to be bullied into obeying the writer's will. This prose simply gives orders—reminding us that essays, even impassioned ones, tend to be less direct and blaring than this. Something must be placed between writer and reader: a subject they both can contemplate while each party retains a certain independence.

Passage B is a scientific report. Here we have nothing *but* objectivity—reminding us that essays deal in personal opinion. As a presentation of findings this excerpt is competent and efficient. An essayist, however, would have stepped forward and expressed an attitude of some sort. *Facts are facts*, says the report. *Here is what interests me*, says the essay.

Only Passage C can be called fully essayistic (it comes, in fact, from an essay-chapter). Like B, it deals mostly with what the author considers to be verified truth. The truth, however, is enlivened in this case by the author's felt presence. Without ever mentioning himself, he offers broad statements that are evidently his personal views, and he establishes a bond of general human identity with his reader: *If it were so, we should all become alcoholics.* His rhetoric moves with a certain verve that is missing from Passage B. Look at the inverted sentence structure, the dramatic pause for a parenthesis, the emphatic *No*, and the vivid metaphor at the end. Every good essay has something of this animation, for the essay is above all an expression of sensibility and judgment, held out by one individual for the sensibility and judgment of another.

But this is not to say that every essay has to sound like Passage C. Look at this paragraph from Tom Wolfe's essay about surfers in Southern California:

Well, actually there is a kind of back-and-forth thing with some of the older guys, the old heroes of surfing, like Bruce Brown, John Severson, Hobie Alter and Phil Edwards. Bruce Brown will do one of those incredible surfing movies and he is out in the surf himself filming Phil Edwards coming down a 20-footer in Hawaii, and Phil has on a pair of nylon swimming trunks, which he has had made in Hawaii, because they dry out fast—and it is like a grapevine. Everybody's got to have a pair of nylon swimming trunks, and then the manufacturers move in, and pretty soon every kid in Utica, N.Y., is buying a pair of them, with the competition stripe and the whole thing, and they never heard of Phil Edwards. So it works back and forth—but so what? Phil Edwards is part of it. He may be an old guy, he is 28 years old, but he and Bruce Brown, who is even older, 30, and John Severson, 32, and Hobie Alter, 29, never haired out to the square world even though they make thousands. Hair refers to courage. A guy who "has a lot of hair" is courageous; a guy who "hairs out" is yellow.[3]

Here the essayist borrows his tone and even his vocabulary from what he is describing. The surfers' mentality as Wolfe understands it is restless, action-oriented, one-dimensional, and so is Wolfe's prose. Note the flat, colloquial sentences, studded with terms like *back-and-forth thing, guys, incredible, so what,* and *haired out.* The key word seems to be *and:* instead of subordinating one idea to another, Wolfe flattens his sentences into strings of coordinate clauses, as if every thought were just as meaningful or meaningless as the last. The offhand tone is keyed to the surfers' odd combination of prolonged adolescence and effortless genius for making money.

The opposite extreme may be represented by the controlled, almost ceremonious prose of James Baldwin, whose tone is always one of high seriousness:

> The cathedral at Chartres, I have said, says something to the people of this village which it cannot say to me; but it is important to understand that this cathedral says something to me which it cannot say to them. Perhaps they are struck by the power of the spires, the glory of the windows; but they have known God, after all, longer than I have known him, and in a different way, and I am terrified by the slippery bottomless well to be found in the crypt, down which heretics were hurled to death, and by the obscene, inescapable gargoyles jutting out of the stone and seeming to say that God and the devil can never be divorced. I doubt that the villagers think of the devil when they face a cathedral because they have never been identified with the devil. But I must accept the status which myth, if nothing else, gives me in the West before I can hope to change the myth.[4]

Baldwin, the black author seeking to define his identity in a "white" civilization, constructs his sentences with solemn deliberation, repeatedly shifting between Chartres cathedral and himself as he builds to a conclusion. Abstract and "important" words like *power, glory, obscene,* and *inescapable* urge us to share the writer's mood as he develops his antitheses: white versus black, God versus devil, spires and windows versus *the slippery bottomless well.*

Of course it isn't necessary to write with either Wolfe's studied casualness or Baldwin's studied gravity. Most essay prose has a "middle" tone, an air of speaking directly *to* an intelligent reader in a normal voice. Such a tone still allows plenty of room for the author's individuality to come through. Look, for example, at this paragraph by E. M. Forster:

> In search of a refuge, we may perhaps turn to hero-worship. But here we shall get no help, in my opinion. Hero-worship is a dangerous vice, and one of the minor merits of a democracy is that it does not encourage it, or produce that unmanageable type of citizen known as the Great Man. It produces instead different kinds of small men — a much finer achievement. But people who cannot get interested in the

variety of life, and cannot make up their own minds, get discontented over this, and they long for a hero to bow down before and to follow blindly. It is significant that a hero is an integral part of the authoritarian stock-in-trade today. An efficiency-regime cannot be run without a few heroes stuck about it to carry off the dullness—much as plums have to be put into a bad pudding to make it palatable. One hero at the top and a smaller one each side of him is a favourite arrangement, and the timid and the bored are comforted by the trinity, and, bowing down, feel exalted and strengthened.[5]

Here the writer's tone, like his theme, is forthright and democratic, yet it does reach both "up" and "down" for special effects. Words like *refuge, trinity*, and *exalted* are slightly "high"; they embody the love of pretension that makes people into hero-worshipers. But other phrases puncture these balloons: *stuck about it, a bad pudding*, etc.

Taken together, Forster's words constitute *irony*. That is, with certain language he seems to go along with a pretense (*the Great Man*), but with other language he shows that he hasn't been fooled (*that unmanageable type of citizen*). The inconsistent words jostle against either other mischievously:

> . . . and, *bowing down*, feel *exalted* and *strengthened*.

We sense something amiss with an exaltation and a strengthening that result from a bowing down. Forster's ironies, however, aren't so conspicuous that they detract from his general air of openness. What they contribute is a certain droll detachment, a hint that the skeptical private mind can enjoy the absurdity of the public world.

Is Forster's tone more successful than Wolfe's or Baldwin's? Not necessarily. Each writer has found a style that suits his temperament and purpose, and each would be handicapped if he were made to write like the others.

(More specific problems of tone are raised in Chapters Three and Four.)

MODES OF THE ESSAY

Every essay, it is often said, belongs to one of four types:

1. *Exposition*. The writer presents information, explaining something to his reader: "The Evolution of the Potato Chip"; "Chile's Economy Since the Fall of Allende."

2. *Description.* The writer evokes a place, object, or character: "Riverside Under the Smog"; "A Man After My Own Heart: Christiaan Barnard."

3. *Narration.* The writer tells a (supposedly true) story about himself or others: "My Crusade Against Pop-top Cans"; "Last Clambake at Chappaquiddick."

4. *Argument.* The writer tries to convince people that they should agree with his position on some issue: "Right and Wrong Ways to Fight Inflation"; "Abolish the Murderer, Not the Death Penalty."

You may find it useful to practice writing in each of these modes in turn, but the main thing to be said about them is that they rarely appear alone. Essays tend to shift between the modes — telling stories to buttress arguments, describing something prior to explaining its function, and so forth. What bears study is the way a good essayist pleases his reader by calling on all the resources he can muster.

Here, for example, are some paragraphs from an essay-chapter by Kenneth Stampp called "Abraham Lincoln: The Politics of a Practical Whig." The title leads us to anticipate an exposition (of Lincoln's politics), and we get it. But see how the exposition is laced with argument:

> Unfortunately Lincoln's admirers have often operated on the assumption that to call him a politician is somehow to degrade him; they reserve that label for his congressional critics.
>
> This attitude toward Lincoln reflects a curious American attitude toward politics. As Richard N. Current has observed: "Among Americans the words *politics* and *politician* long have been terms of reproach. Politics generally means 'dirty' politics, whether the adjective is used or not. Politicians, then, are dirty politicians unless they happen to be statesmen, and in that case they are not politicians at all." Lincoln himself contributed to this unpleasant image when, early in his career, he described politicians as "a set of men who have interests aside from the interests of the people, and who . . . are, taken as a class, at least one long step removed from honest men."
>
> And yet Lincoln's own much-admired statesmanship was based on a solid foundation of political talent and experience. He ranked loyalty to party high among human virtues; he understood the techniques of party management; he knew when to concede and when to hold firm; and he had a most sensitive feeling for trends in public opinion. Lincoln was an ambitious man — his ambition, said his former law partner, "was a little engine that knew no rest" — and he thoroughly understood that public office does not seek the man, but the man seeks the office. Accordingly, Lincoln was, from his early

manhood, openly available, unblushingly eager for any office to which he could win appointment or election. Early in 1860, when the greatest prize of all seemed within reach, he confessed to a friend with disarming candor, "The taste *is* in my mouth a little." He won the prize, and his masterful performance during his years as President has rarely been equaled and never surpassed. Under the most trying circumstances he presided over a Cabinet of prima donnas, held together his loosely organized party, and repeatedly outmaneuvered a dangerously powerful opposition party. "If Abraham Lincoln was not a master politician," wrote one of his admiring contemporaries who knew the meaning of the word, "I am entirely ignorant of the qualities which make up such a character. . . . No man knew better . . . how to summon and dispose of political ability to attain great political ends."

This is the man, it has often been made to appear, who approached the problem of postwar reconstruction without giving a thought to the political consequences of his plans. It was his innate generosity, his inner tenderness, and nothing else, that impelled him to extend to the South his generous terms, while selfish, scheming politicians in Congress cried out for vengeance. Nothing could be farther from the truth; nothing could more distort the character of the man.[6]

Stampp throws out a challenge to Lincoln's "admirers," whose discomfort with politics has made them sentimentalize their hero. By pausing over the meaning of *politics* and *politician*, producing evidence that Lincoln was a politician even in his best moments, the author disputes the cliché that may have warped our own idea of Lincoln. He is simultaneously giving information, winning a debate, and fostering a new attitude toward his subject.

Here is the opening of an essay that will prove to be largely expository. But instead of saying, in effect, *Here is my problem and now here's my solution*, the author begins with two paragraphs of narrative that arouse the reader's memories and curiosity:

Spring 1963. The signs of change in American higher education were everywhere. The civil rights struggle in the South had aroused students and professors from their post-McCarthy torpor. In May, "Bull" Connor set his police dogs on peaceful protesters in Birmingham, Alabama, and thousands of young people resolved to dedicate the summer to civil rights activity. The first Peace Corps volunteers were applying to graduate schools as their two-year hitches ended. A new organization called the Students for a Democratic Society (SDS) was publicizing its Port Huron statement, which called for greater participatory democracy in American life. Opposition to the threat of nuclear war had spawned disarmament organizations on American campuses, and the National Student Association took a directly political stand for the first time in its history when its national congress voted to support nuclear disarmament. And at Princeton? On May 6, 1963, there was a pantie raid on a neighboring women's college, which prompted the *New York Times Magazine* to publish an article on spring fever among college students.

Spring 1970. On Thursday, April 30, President Nixon announced the Cambodian intervention. At a mass meeting held in the Princeton Chapel immediately following the speech, students and faculty in attendance voted overwhelmingly in favor of a university strike. On Saturday a "Multimedia Rite of Protest" at the chapel led 190 students to turn in their draft cards and resulted in the formation of the Princeton Union for National Draft Opposition. On Sunday, the Council of the Princeton University Community, with representatives from nearly all sectors of the university, drew up a carefully worded resolution allowing a series of options to students wishing to suspend class activity, encouraging student participation in national electoral politics through the newly organized Movement for a New Congress and recommending a two-week pre-election recess in the fall. The next day, the Assembly of the Princeton University Community voted 2,000 to 1,500 in favor of the council-sponsored resolution over a more radical proposal. In the succeeding weeks the Movement for a New Congress and the Union for National Draft Opposition spread nationwide, and the Princeton Plan for a preelectoral recess in the fall was widely imitated. In June, the seniors boycotted the annual alumni parade and dedicated the graduation exercises (at which songwriter Bob Dylan received an honorary degree) to various forms of antiwar activity.

How did the sleepy "preppy"-dominated conservative bastion of 1963 become a major center of student political upheaval in 1970? And why did this transformation take place without the violence and division that shook similar universities elsewhere?[7]

And storytelling can sometimes be a direct means of argument, as in this paragraph by Erich Heller advocating "literary responsibility":

What to us has become so deeply questionable was a certainty for Confucius. When once his disciples asked him what he would do first if he had to administer a country, he answered: "The first would be to correct language." "Surely," they said, "this has nothing to do with the matter. Why should language be corrected?" The Master's answer was: "If language is not correct, then what is said is not what is meant; if what is said is not what is meant, then what ought to be done remains undone; if this remains undone, morals and arts will decay; if morals and arts decay, justice will go astray; if justice goes astray, the people will stand about in helpless confusion. Hence language must not be allowed to deteriorate. This matters above everything." What a grand definition of the writer's social responsibility, and what confident faith in the very correspondence between language and reality, and therefore between literature and life! Shall we ever regain the confidence of both this definition and this faith? It is the very condition of literary responsibility, and on it depends the future of our liberal education.[8]

And sometimes a narrative is so consistent in its theme that the writer never has to draw an explicit "moral." Here, as a final example, is a paper I received in a freshman English course. It appears at first to be sheer story and not an essay at all, but the last two paragraphs, without directly stating a thesis, bring everything into focus:

"You should fix everyone's coffee or tea. You know, add the sugar, etc., and pour it. If the meat is hard to handle, you should cut it for the patient," instructed my predecessor. "After you've passed out the trays, you feed Irene and Molly."

"That's Granny Post in there. She's 106. Even though she's not particularly senile, she's lost her teeth and must be fed with a giant eyedropper." I discovered just how clear Granny Post's mind was when I tried to feed her. The dear old lady wasn't hungry and spat it back at me.

After that first day at the convalescent hospital, I was on my own. Irene was eager to please and partially fed herself, but I dreaded feeding Molly. She was blind and pitifully thin. "I'm sick. I'm sick," she'd cry. "Don't make me eat any more. Please, I'm sick."

"But Molly, you've got to eat so you can get well. Come on, one more bite. Here, hold my hand. It's not so bad." And I'd coach one more bite down her before gathering the sixty trays onto their racks and wheeling them back to the safety of the kitchen. The rest of the evening I cleaned the coffee pot, set up the breakfast trays, scoured sinks, and mopped the floors. I didn't mind sitting on the floor scrubbing at the oven or making the juices and sandwiches for the evening nourishment. It was when I confronted the elderly people on the other side of that kitchen door that I became nervous and awkward.

In a few weeks I mastered the hospital routine, the names of most of the patients, and their idiosyncrasies.

Opposite the kitchen was what was fondly called "the ward." Dora, a small, white-haired woman who was continually nearly slipping out of the bottom of the wheelchair to which she was tied, was the ringleader of this group. She cussed up a storm at anyone who came near her and perpetually monotoned, "What can I do? Tell me, what can I do?" May accompanied her with "Put me to bed. I want to go to bed." One evening as I entered with dinner, the woman across from Dora was gaily slinging her waste matter about the room, especially at anyone who threatened to come near her. A nurse and some aides calmed her down.

As far as the two sisters in room twelve were concerned, they were traveling on a huge ocean liner. When I brought their trays, they always asked, "How long till we get to port?" or "I'm sorry. We can't eat today because we're seasick."

John mumbled perpetually about the batty ladies in the TV room. He liked his smokes and his sports magazine.

Mr. Harrison fed a stray cat that stayed outside his sliding-glass door. He loved his cat and I gave him leftovers to feed it. One day a car rushed down the hill and struck his cat. Mr. Harrison told me his cat ran away, but it would come back as always. He stood at his door watching for it.

There were two Irenes. Dora advanced to feeding herself so I began feeding Ethel Irene. Ethel Irene was small, roly-poly, and had gray-black hair cut short like a little boy's. She liked to joke and use large words. Sometimes when she grasped for a word, it just wouldn't come and great big tears would form in her eyes. She liked sunshiny days and the sound of birds singing. She liked me to sing to her, too. Always clamped tightly in her hand was the buzzer to call the nurse. It was Ethel Irene's lifeline. Occasionally it fell out of her hand and she became so frantic she couldn't speak, only pointing and crying.

I tried to regard the other Ethel as just one of the many patients to whom I delivered food. When I brought dinner, I fixed Ethel's tea, cut her meat, and tucked in her napkin. Then I'd clearly shout, "Enjoy your dinner." But instead of letting me leave, she'd pull me down to her and in a low, halting voice struggle out, "I like you. Can I kiss you?" It became increasingly difficult to leave Ethel. She'd refuse to release my arm, purposely eat slowly so I was forced to return just to retrieve her tray, and cry when I succeeded in making my exit. To avoid upsetting her, I began sneaking into the room to take her tray or sending someone else. If she realized the deception, she'd let out an anguished cry and begin sobbing. I couldn't bear to pass Ethel's room and see her arms reaching out for me.

Many of the patients were lonely like Ethel and starved for attention. Some were on welfare and had few or no relatives. Most were just forgotten.

Ethel's son visited one day. Roaring drunk, he first tried to get fresh with me and then stomped into the kitchen demanding food.

Molly had visitors once, too. When I reached work and dropped by to see Molly, two or three of her relatives were standing about her. Molly was breathing laboriously, her nose and mouth were attached to an oxygen tank. She'd often pleaded with me to leave her in peace to die. She was dying now. The relatives left shortly. Molly's bed was empty when I returned the next day.

I worked in the convalescent hospital only sixteen hours a week for eight months. The old people remained there twenty-four hours a day for months or years, depending on how "lucky" they were. They were fed, diapered at night, and sponge-bathed in the morning. But what they needed most . . .

The age is gone when three generations occupy the same house. Young people want a life of their own.

My parents are nearly fifty now.

The other members of my class were hard on this paper when I showed it to them. They commented:

"She hasn't told us the context."
"Dick and Jane dialogue . . . choppy sentences."
". . . weak transitions."
"It's too detached—just a lot of facts, and then she changes the subject at the end."
"The paragraphs are too short."
"What is it supposed to be about, anyway?"
"She says *coach* when she means *coax*."
"*Monotone* isn't a verb."
"I found a run-on sentence in paragraph 15."

Some of these objections are true, but all of them miss the compassion and control that outweigh any number of small defects in this essay. The memorable description of Ethel Irene and her "lifeline" buzzer, the understated recounting of Molly's death, seem like reality itself. And the apparent disorganization covers a subtle and effective movement in which the reader lives through the writer's own ordeal of first learning her chores, then coping with the patients' oddities, then facing the ultimate fact of death, and finally turning her thoughts to her own parents, who "are nearly fifty now" and may someday be like Molly and Mr. Harrison. Will she look after them in their senility? The abrupt ending leaves us troubled, not only by grotesque and tender images from the convalescent hospital, but also by conflicting feelings toward parents who deserve our care but who threaten to invade "a life of [our] own."

The essay is a free and open form. In subsequent chapters I will tell you how to proceed when you don't yet know what to say, and I'll talk about methods of presenting a case for your opinions. But remember that one rule trumps all others: *if it feels right, try it.* One sign of a good writer's work is that it makes its readers willing to set aside their checklist of expectations and simply listen, lending themselves to a confident voice. Although this is what the essay is supremely suited for, no handbook or teacher can make it available to you. Study the "rules," then—and be prepared to discard them whenever they seem to prevent you from taking your reader where you feel he must go.

EXERCISES

I. How would you characterize the tone of each of the following passages? Pick out specific uses of language that contribute to this tone.

A. Perhaps that was going to be the only discovery of the trip: mesquite in Hartley County. The drive merely pointed up two things that I had already known: the brush thrives, and the small towns wither, their sap draining into the cities year after year. In my own hometown, population 2,000, there was an old man named Taylor who lived in a mansion just across a sudan field from our house. His fortune was made, and he spent his time reading. When I went to bed at night I could see the light in his library window, and when I awoke in the morning it would often still be burning. At four in the afternoon he drove down the hill in his Packard and got his mail. In the junkpiles behind his house were piles of book-catalogues, mostly English. He was, I suppose, the village intellectual, a figure of yesteryear—defunct now like Buffalo Bill. His successors have all gone to the city: the brainy, the imaginative, the beautiful, even the energetic. None of them can find much reason for staying in the towns.[9]

B. History, if viewed as a repository for more than anecdote or chronology, could produce a decisive transformation in the image of science by which we are now possessed. That image has previously been drawn, even by scientists themselves, mainly from the study of finished scientific achievements as these are recorded in the classics and, more recently, in the textbooks from which each new scientific generation learns to practice its trade. Inevitably, however, the aim of such books is persuasive and pedagogic; a concept of science drawn from them is no more likely to fit the enterprise that produced them than an image of a national culture drawn from a tourist brochure or a language text. This essay attempts to show that we have been misled by them in fundamental ways. Its aim is a sketch of the quite different concept of science that can emerge from the historical record of the research activity itself.[10]

C. Like most courses in writing, Daily Themes demands that its students "show, not tell"—show through dialogue and description, rather than tell by pronouncement or plot summary. "Telling" written in the margin of a daily theme is severe criticism, and so is "Summing up" —trying to explain what should have been revealed in the action by tacking on what is meant to be a pregnant last sentence. The most vivid event in the memory of one Daily Themes veteran is a lecture by Nangle that ended with the evils of "summing up." Nangle appealed to the class, almost poignantly, not to submit to him any more themes that ended with the sentence "He walked away in disgust." Wearily leaning over the lectern, he tried to make clear how many themes he had read over the years that ended that way, and how many he was likely to read in the future, no matter how many appeals he made. At that thought, he walked away in disgust.[11]

II. Reread the essay on pp. 13–15. Briefly explain how the author could have used the same subject matter to write essays consisting mainly of (a) exposition and (b) argument.

NOTES

1. J. A. Deutsch and H. S. Koopmans, "Preference Enhancement for Alcohol by Passive Exposure," *Science*, 179 (23 Mar. 1973), 1242.
2. Karl Menninger, *Man Against Himself* (1938; rpt. New York: Harvest, n.d.), pp. 146–147.

3. Tom Wolfe, *The Pump House Gang* (New York: Farrar, Straus & Giroux, 1968), pp. 33–34.

4. James Baldwin, *Notes of a Native Son* (Boston: Beacon Press, 1955), p. 174.

5. E. M. Forster, *Two Cheers for Democracy* (New York: Harcourt Brace Jovanovich, 1951), pp. 72–73.

6. Kenneth M. Stampp, *The Era of Reconstruction, 1865–1877* (1965; rpt. New York: Vintage, n.d.), pp. 29–30.

7. Paul Sigmund, "Princeton in Crisis and Change," *Change*, Mar. 1973, p. 34.

8. Erich Heller, "Literature and Political Responsibility: Apropos the 'Letters of Thomas Mann,'" *Commentary*, July 1971, p. 54.

9. Larry McMurtry, *In a Narrow Grave* (1968; rpt. New York: Simon and Schuster, 1971), pp. 88–89.

10. Thomas S. Kuhn, *The Structure of Scientific Revolutions*, International Encyclopedia of Unified Science, II, 2, 2nd ed. (1962; rpt. Chicago: Univ. of Chicago Press, 1970), p. 1.

11. Calvin Trillin, "No Telling, No Summing Up," *The New Yorker*, 11 June 1966, pp. 118, 121.

COM2-POSING

From time to time every essayist gets the pleasant feeling that he knows exactly what to write about, what to say, and how to say it. When this mood arrives, you don't want to pause for advice about method; you just begin writing. If you can keep going until a whole draft is finished, *then* you can look back and see whether you really did have an inspiration. Even if something is gravely wrong with the draft, at least it has cost you little effort and is likely to be salvageable in some way.

More often, however, the feeling of inspiration leaks away after a paragraph or two, and you wonder how you could have been so confident about a project that has scarcely begun. And still more often, you have no such illusion in the first place. Especially if you're being asked to write one essay after another on topics that you haven't previously considered, you need to have some procedures for getting your bearings and ensuring that your very limited time won't be wasted on false leads and unworkable plans.

It may be useful, then, to review the usual, "uninspired" stages of composing and the questions a writer should put to himself at each point. The stages overlap somewhat even for the most methodical essayist. The point isn't to do everything in precise order, but to master certain difficulties sooner or later before you submit a final version of your essay.

CHOOSING A TOPIC AND A THESIS

The first and most important problem you face as an essayist is what topic to write about and what position to take. In order to choose wisely, you must have a clear sense of the differences between a *subject area*, a *topic*, and a *thesis*:

Subject Area

A *subject area* consists of a broad range of possible issues; it defines the boundaries within which you will find your actual topic. Assignments in a composition course are typically stated in terms of subject areas. Thus, if you're asked to "describe a personal experience," or "discuss an issue of civil liberties," or "write a paper about Book Four of *Gulliver's Travels*," you've been given subject areas, not topics. A subject area is usually much too large to be taken as a topic in itself.

Some students, however, hope to save time and effort by turning an assignment directly into a topic. Asked to write about civil liberties, the student immediately pulls out a sheet of paper and christens it with his title:

CIVIL LIBERTIES

Well, that's settled, he thinks; *I'm two words closer to being finished*. But in fact he has wandered into a maze. How is a brief essay going to say something conclusive about civil liberties in general? The title will glare down reproachfully at the text, reminding the reader of everything that's being left undiscussed.

Topic

The *topic* of an essay is its specific subject: the question to be answered or the material to be covered. Usually, but not always, the essay's title directly announces its topic:

The Right to Privacy
Should Criminals Go Free on Technicalities?
Wiretapping: The New National Pastime

All three of these title-topics come from the subject area of civil liberties, and all three are defined narrowly enough to permit the writer to say something meaningful.

Thesis

The *thesis* is the main point of the essay, the one main idea to which all others should be subordinate. If the topic is a question, the thesis is the answer. It ought to lend itself to statement in one clear sentence. Thus, in the three sample papers about civil liberties, the theses might be:

The right to privacy, broadly conceived, is the most fundamental of civil liberties in a democracy.

Known criminals shouldn't be excused from punishment because of technical errors in the way they were arrested and tried.

When government officials eavesdrop on innocent citizens and routinely tap one another's phones, everyone's constitutional liberties are threatened.

Finding a Thesis

Finding a topic and finding a thesis aren't really separate processes. You can't be sure that any topic will be a good one until you've decided on a point to make about it. If a given topic "just doesn't interest" you, the chances are that you haven't made a proper search for a thesis. Topics in themselves tend to be inert, but they come alive when you've isolated definite questions that require answering.

Suppose you've been asked to write an essay about sports. You groan with annoyance: you have nothing to say about sports. But is this really true? Possibly, but perhaps your apparent lack of interest is really a *disagreement* with popular attitudes toward sports. Your instructor didn't forbid you to take a skeptical attitude, did he? If you press on toward a thesis you might end with an argument like one of these:

A GENERATION OF SPECTATORS

Looking around you at a generation raised on televised Superbowls and weekly "classic" golf tournaments, you see that the cult of sports is producing, not healthy, athletic citizens, but passive consumers of fantasy.

SHOULD THE OLYMPICS BE ABOLISHED?

Yes, you say. Instead of helping to overcome nationalism, cheating, and violence, the Olympics tend to encourage them.

MARK SPITZ: AMERICA'S GNAWING TOOTHACHE
To your mind, the transformation of Spitz from an amateur athlete
to a million-dollar "property" sums up everything that's wrong with
the American approach to sports.

But of course your essay doesn't *have* to be anti-sports. You could
narrow the topic to a favorite sport of your own, finding your thesis
in an opinion that you believe to be well founded:

THE BIG SERVE
Recounting the famous matches between the agile, wily Bobby Riggs
and Jack Kramer, who perfected the booming service that now domi-
nates tennis, you show that the "big serve" has simplified the game,
eliminating the drama of back-court rallies.

THE COACH MAKES THE DIFFERENCE FOR UCLA
Players like Alcindor, Wicks, and Walton look unstoppable, you say,
but they don't explain UCLA's success in basketball. They were drawn
to UCLA by John Wooden's coaching, and this coaching is the real
reason why his teams have won so consistently over the years.

Note that all these papers contain a thread of *argument*—that is,
they defend one position against possible alternatives to it. Your
thesis doesn't have to be openly antagonistic to individuals or institutions, but it should represent a commitment of some sort, a
stand that requires support in the body of your essay.

trial thesis If you've tentatively arrived at a topic, see how many questions you
can ask about it, and treat the answer to each question as a *trial
thesis*, a possible argument around which to organize the essay. In
each case, ask yourself whether the question-and-answer is (a) plausible enough to be made convincing; (b) sufficiently challenging;
and (c) within your reach, given the limitations on your time, your
access to pertinent information, and the anticipated length of the
essay.

What you need is a complete idea—a problem and its solution,
or a manifesto and its defense, or a discovery and its meaning, or a
fragment of life and a reason for making it known. Think ahead to
your probable conclusion: is it a point that most people already
believe? If so, it's going to be especially difficult for you to make it
interesting. Is it an assertion that will still look dubious after you've
exhausted the available number of pages? In that case you should
scale down your plans. Your job isn't to revolutionize a reader's
whole way of looking at things, but to show him the grounds for

believing something he might well have concluded himself if he'd found the evidence you'll offer. Instead of trying to demonstrate how much you know or to snuff out every conceivable objection to your case, you should write an essay that seems rounded off in its own terms.

Try to judge the approximate amount of work you'll need to do in order to be convincing. Would you have to master a whole new discipline? Can you interpret the question in a way that will allow you to bring in personal observations and knowledge? If research is necessary, do you know where to start looking? How reliable are the sources you've already located? Can you frame your argument by contrasting your way of looking at the problem with somebody else's? Above all, don't settle on a thesis until you've made sure that some genuine, indisputable information will be available to support your case. Knowing that you have facts on your side will help you to do without the rhetoric of bogus certainty, obfuscation, and space consumption.

NOTES

Making Use of Notes

The best way to discover a thesis is to find it in your notes, which you've been jotting down ever since you began searching for a topic. I don't mean that somewhere among your notes you'll find the thesis already fully developed. That may happen once in a while, but more often a thesis emerges from a *clash* of notes. An idea that looked good on Tuesday may need modifying on Thursday. Certain insights pull you toward one conclusion, but certain others make you feel cautious about it. Your notes amount to a dialogue with yourself, a continual record of possible assertions, examples, hints, and objections. The essential fact about serviceable notes is that, taken together, they contain a more complicated, subtle view of the topic than you're likely to have in mind at any given moment. Even if you formed your thesis at the outset and were only taking notes to collect evidence for it, you can check the thesis against the notes to make sure that you still agree with yourself.

from notes to thesis   If you have trouble finding even one trial thesis to work with, use your notes to stimulate your thinking. Remember that it's impossible to think about one unitary thing; to think is to establish relationships. The way to get off dead center is to juxtapose a potential topic against something else or to break it into parts. Check your dictionary's entries for key terms suggested by the topic, and see whether those definitions lead to new material. What does the topic resemble? What is most nearly opposite to it? Comparisons and contrasts don't have to govern the eventual structure of your essay, but they can sharpen your focus as you continue to take notes. As you get closer to a final thesis your notes can become more pointed and detailed, amounting in effect to trial paragraphs for the essay itself.

But perhaps your topic is still too unfocused and needs to be defined more narrowly. Start listing *particular instances* you'd like to write about, even if you don't yet know how they will fit in; perhaps you'll see in these instances the broad principle you've been looking for. Again, try to catch yourself *censoring* certain possible ideas. If you want to take a position but find yourself shying away from it because it embarrasses you, consider it again and write down everything that comes to mind. Perhaps you can fashion a lively argument by putting your reader through the same process of facing unwelcome truths that you yourself are undergoing. Asked, for example, to write about democracy or the idea of civilization, you may find yourself stymied by the suspicion that the term *democracy* has become meaningless, or that *civilization* is the value system of the nation possessing the largest bombs. Instead of trying to muffle such thoughts, see whether you can make a case for them.

Still another way to discover ideas is to talk with other people about the subject area or topic, taking notes on whatever promising leads emerge from the conversation. In debate with someone else you may be pressed into making an exceptionally clear formulation that hadn't occurred to you before.

notes for analysis   If your task is to analyze a text, reread it as many times as you can, marking all passages (in your own copy) that look significant for any reason. Then take notes on the basis of these preliminary indications. If one part of the text looks thematically connected to another part, try to define the connection and see whether you haven't begun to solve certain problems of interpretation. If things *don't* add up, ask yourself why not. Perhaps you've found a real inconsistency of attitude on the author's part. An especially useful exercise is to take one passage that seems typical or important and to write about it at random, allowing your mind to play freely with it. What you say about this one passage may prove to be true of the whole work, and you may be able to use some of this close analysis in your final essay.

Notes Are Only a Tool

A large part of good notetaking consists in knowing when to stop. Some writers, anxious to postpone composition as long as possible, seem to develop an unnatural fondness for the notes themselves. Instead of taking down the selective facts and ideas that he'll need for the one essay at hand, the note fetishist copies out whole pages, amassing an impressive-looking stack of cards or sheets. This stack reassures him that he possesses great knowledge—yet it's never quite enough for him to begin writing. And indeed it isn't, for he's been collecting the makings of an almanac, not an essay. If he ever gets around to writing, his concern shifts from acquiring knowledge to not wasting it: he dumps his entire hoard of information on the reader's head with a tacit *"That'll* hold you!" He has forgotten that notes are only aids to composition, not documents having meaning in themselves.

Form of Notes

Since your notes are for no one's eyes but your own, they can take any form you please. They can be written on index cards, slips of paper, or large pages. They can employ all sorts of eccentric abbreviations whose meaning is known only to you. They can, if you like, include obscene snarling at authors who didn't anticipate your views. But the notes must give you all the information you'll need, and do so with accuracy.

If all your notes consist of ideas of your own, you don't have to be systematic in the way you handle them. But for some essays, and especially for a research paper (pp. 376–395), you'll be taking notes on books and articles by other writers, and such notes do require certain precautions. (These are explained in detail on pp. 354–357.)

ORGANIZING AND OUTLINING

Avoiding the Obvious

Once you have a thesis and a body of supporting information or ideas, your last job before writing is to organize your thoughts in a coherent, effective order. If you bear in mind the reader's wish for clarity, economy, and dramatic interest, you will often find a structure already implicit in your thesis. For example, if you intend to write an expository essay that relies heavily on description, you could begin with an arresting detail, then supply its context and gradually unfold your main ideas, and finally return to some specific scene whose meaning has now been made clear. Your reader, instead of feeling overwhelmed by sheer description or sheer argument, would sense a pleasant balance between the two. Again, if you're going to write a problem-solving essay, your organization might be some variant of the most obvious one in which the problem is stated, evidence is presented, and a conclusion is drawn. Insofar as this is what the reader expects, you would do well to surprise him a little— for instance, by slightly delaying the statement of the problem, or by presenting the conclusion near the beginning instead of at the end, or by conducting a running debate with some proponent of a rival idea. The point is that you're not just organizing your thoughts, but organizing them *for* somebody who may or may not want to give you a fair hearing. He needs some coaxing, and your job of organizing consists essentially in deciding how he can become both involved and satisfied.

Use and Abuse of Outlines

The traditional tool of organizing is the outline. It can be a very powerful tool if properly used, but you should realize that a superficially conceived outline can actually be a hindrance to good writing. Your neatly indented and numbered headings can give you a false sense of control over materials you haven't quite mastered. Instead of allowing yourself to be carried forward by your sentence-to-sentence reasoning, and instead of intuiting how you ought to handle the doubts and objections that your argument raises at each difficult point, you can persist with your outline, "logically" mimicking a sense of purpose. Most formula-essays are ponderously "well organized," with the main points protruding like elbows from sleeves. You can almost hear the writer sighing as he finishes section II.C. and gathers himself up to tackle section III.A. What's needed is just the reverse, a movement that simply flows in a seamless, absorbing way. If you have that movement, you can even get away with an occasional digression; if you don't have it, your outline isn't going to intercede for you to plead your good intentions.

Now, this isn't to cast doubt on outlining as a useful procedure, but only to remind you that the functional units of your essay are sentences and paragraphs, not outline headings. Rightly used, an outline isn't an inflexible program but a means of keeping a sense of proportion and direction as you work your way through one paragraph and prepare a transition to the next. You should always be ready to depart from the outline in minor ways or to replace it altogether if you find that it's forcing you to write inhuman prose.

Thus, in a paper contrasting two sets of ideas, your outline may dictate an overorganized "ping-pong" structure:

X
Yes, but Y
To be sure, but X
Perhaps, but then Y
On the other hand, X
In conclusion, X and Y

Long before finishing such a paper you will feel oppressed by its monotony. Don't trudge grimly through to the end, but make a new, less symmetrical outline that reflects the differing importance of the various points. Your mind, after all, isn't a metronome. If it seems that way to a reader, the reason is that you've been outlining instead of thinking.

The writer who can spin out whole paragraphs without pausing, however, may be the one who stands most in need of an outline. He has developed the knack of making small transitions, hooking one sentence into the next, picking up a theme from the end of one paragraph and using it to launch the opening of his next paragraph. Yet his elegant prose may arrive nowhere at all. Lacking a total plan, the writer becomes an impressionist who merely sounds purposeful and ends by exasperating the reader with his inability to make a case.

Scratch Outline

You may find yourself most comfortable with the so-called *scratch outline*, which is simply a list of phrases or sentences consecutively naming the major points you intend to make. This leaves you free to devise the individual paragraphs as you arrive at them in context, giving you a chance to exercise a sense of variety and rhetorical opportunity that's less available at the outline stage. Again, you may want to combine a scratch outline with references to your notes, reminding yourself of the right place to insert examples, quotations, and footnotes.

Full Outline

If your paper is to be long and intricate, or if you simply want to be sure of every step in advance, you may prefer a more complete outline that will show the intended subordination of minor ideas to major ones. It doesn't matter whether you use a *topic outline*, with brief phrases for each heading and subheading, or a *sentence outline*, in which the points are spelled out. You can even combine these types as you please.

When you subordinate, however, make sure that each subheading has at least one partner—no *I* without *II*, no *A* without *B*. Subheadings are for *divisions* of larger points. If you have a lonesome *A* in a draft outline, work it into the larger category.

WRONG.
I. Significance of *The Tempest*
   A. Autobiographical
II. Character of the Late Romances

BETTER:
I. Autobiographical Significance of *The Tempest*
II. Character of the Late Romances

In addition, you should always check a draft outline to make sure that all the subheadings under a given heading logically contribute to it. Don't try to tuck in irrelevant items just because you want to get them out of the way.

    Here is a relatively uncomplicated outline for an essay defending the private automobile:

IS THE CAR ALL THAT BAD?

Thesis: **If it is properly restricted and improved, the private automobile can still make a valuable contribution to American life.**

I. Justified Complaints Against the Automobile
   A. Traffic congestion
   B. Smog
   C. Energy waste
   D. Danger

II. Defects Can Be Remedied
   A. Regulate traffic: tolls, taxes, car pools, mass transit
   B. New smog-control devices
   C. Limit horsepower, vary propellants
   D. Require safety features

III. Continued Benefits
   A. Individual travel for vacations, certain businesses
   B. Dispersal of population
   C. Cars foster initiative, individualism

IV. Conclusion: On Balance, the Car Retains Its Usefulness

    And here is a more detailed outline for an essay criticizing several Supreme Court rulings about obscenity:

A SETBACK FOR FREEDOM

Thesis: **The Supreme Court's obscenity rulings of 21 June 1973 jeopardize free speech.**

I. Former Guidelines
   A. One national standard of obscenity
   B. Only works "utterly without redeeming social value" could be prosecuted
   C. Expert judgment was consulted

II. The New Rulings
   A. Community standards replace the national one
   B. States must list forbidden acts
   C. Work "taken as a whole" must have "serious" value
   D. Courts must follow the views of "the average person"

III. Objections to New Rulings
   A. "Average person" is no judge of artistic seriousness
      1. "Average person" said for decades that abstract painting "wasn't art"
      2. "Average person" thought that Joyce's classic fiction was obscene
   B. Rulings are dangerously vague
      1. A person could go to jail in one community for doing what another community might welcome
      2. States and communities given overlapping jurisdiction
   C. Chilling effect on free speech
      1. Fear of arbitrary prosecution limits expression
      2. Monetary inducement to address only the "safest" audience

IV. Conclusion: The Rulings Shouldn't Stand

THE FIRST DRAFT

A first draft almost never comes easily, and everyone has to develop his own way of unblocking himself and getting something, however crude, onto the page. Since the great enemy of the first draft is uncertainty, you will find your work much less awesome if you've done a sound job of taking notes, finding a thesis, and outlining. Knowing that you have a clear and interesting point to make, knowing that the paragraph you're struggling with now will be followed by others whose main ideas are already there in your outline, you can talk back to that little demon who keeps saying, *You're stuck, you're stuck, you're stuck . . .*

Some people can compose only at night; others, only before breakfast; still others can't sit down, or need to have a radio blaring, or can write for two hours a day and not a minute more. How you compose is nobody's business but your own. Maybe you should start with a later paragraph if the introductory one looks too forbidding. If you're worried about losing inspiration in the middle of a sentence, you can compose in a form of shorthand, keeping your mind on the continuity of thoughts instead of on the words. Instead of writing, you may find it easier to talk into a tape recorder and then transcribe the better parts. Whether you write or dictate, don't be afraid to include too much, and don't be embarrassed by minor imperfections. What matters is that you get the draft finished—and that you understand how much more work remains to be done afterward.

REVISION

Resistance to Revision

Unpracticed writers usually harbor both of the following opinions: *I will never be able to say what I mean* and *What I've just written will suffice, because it's mine.* One of these ideas succeeds the other as a first draft limps toward completion. The writer is so relieved to find the page before him no longer empty that he draws a protective curtain across it: *I have suffered enough: here are my precious thoughts, exactly as they flowed from my brain.* And so he insulates himself from advice about revision. Having discovered that he isn't completely inarticulate, he prefers not to ask whether people will be likely to accept what he has written.

Another way of characterizing this defensiveness is to say that a writer invests *himself* in his first draft. He doesn't see it as a collection of sentences and paragraphs, more or less intelligible and persuasive, but as an expression of his inner worthiness. What he feels, of course, is a normal dread of rejection, but his way of coping with the feeling is to fantasize that his work has already been approved. Every writer, no matter how experienced he may be in coping with his own unconscious tricks, is temporarily swept up in this false success. A novice may differ from a veteran only in being less willing to descend from the clouds and begin rereading with a critical eye.

He retains a magical attitude as long as he can, and then abandons all interest in his production.

Because the creative demands of the first draft are bound to interfere somewhat with your concern for the reader's opinion, revision is indispensable. Without necessarily abandoning any of your first-draft ideas, you've got to cultivate some skepticism toward them. To revise is to see your essay as public property, a case that has to stand or fall on its merits. Instead of overrating your words and then forgetting them, you change the nature of your investment; what you finally admire is the way you've made the argument, not the fact that you're the one who made it.

Revising for Clarity

Resistance to revision often takes the form of a faith that one's thoughts are clear, whether or not they've been given adequate expression. The writer can't understand how the reader failed to grasp his point:

"But I *said* that!"
"Where did you say it?"
"Right here! Umm . . . well, I thought I said it. At least I knew what I
    meant to say."

But what good does an unfulfilled intention do? Though the writer may think his difficulty in communicating is technical and minor — a small matter of his not having done full justice to his thoughts — he really hasn't accepted the minimum terms of rational exchange: the only thing that counts is what is there.

Experienced authors will tell you, furthermore, that revision is often their best means of finding out what they wanted to say. This may seem like a strange remark after all the emphasis I've put on planning and organization, but it's true nonetheless. Composition is a continual struggle against a wish to keep your familiar bearings, and originality is possible only when this struggle has been won. In order to challenge a reader you must first suffer a little disorientation yourself. Sometimes the habit of thinking in clichés prevails over every contrary effort until a slight change of wording allows a suppressed idea to burst through. As the anthropologist George Devereux has said of his own work:

> In correcting the first draft of a scientific manuscript, I deliberately look for ambiguously worded passages, whose obscurity is usually due to the presence of some still latent and pre-conscious supplementary insight. I also realize that my occasional — highly puzzling and sometimes quite exasperating — inability to express clearly, on the

first try, some seemingly simple idea, is nearly always due to the sub-liminal stirrings of some additional, still repressed insights. Hence, whenever this happens to me, I stop struggling with syntax and seek to discover instead precisely what suppressed idea is trying to force its way into the "simple" statement I *consciously* seek to make. I stumbled upon some of my best ideas in this manner.[1]

Revising for Tone

One of the most important advantages of revision is the effect it can have on an essay's tone. Because a writer is friendless in the first stages of composition, he can be subject to the disorders of solitude. Is anyone going to listen to him? Suppose everyone is already against him! Without realizing it, he may start betraying a certain bitterness and frenzy. When he senses the weaknesses of his argument, he resorts to bluster and innuendo, implying that those who disagree with him have the lowest of motives. Now he emphatically declares open questions to be closed. By the time he has made it through one draft, he may be mired in sarcasm and defiance.

Revision can correct this tendency because it puts the writer into a measure of contact with his audience. Paranoia thrives on ig-norance of the "enemies" whose malice it anticipates; the less a writer actually knows about his readers, the freer he is to impute bad motives to them. In a sense, though, a writer *becomes* a typical reader as he revises, preferring clear prose to unclear, sound logic to faulty, openness to deception, generosity to insinuation, and poise to hys-teria. There's nothing mysterious or unreasonable about these tastes, and as you come closer to satisfying them you get a better sense of the effect your essay is going to produce.

A WRITER'S CHECKLIST

Whether you write only two drafts or several more, there are certain questions—discussed in various chapters of this book—that you must ask yourself before reaching the final, submitted version:

1. Have I kept to the point and made a plausible, economical case for my thesis? [CHAPTER TWO]
2. Have I included all *essential* material from my notes and outline? [CHAPTER TWO]
3. Have I met objections to my case? [CHAPTER THREE]
4. Is my logic correct? [CHAPTER THREE]

5. Is my tone appropriate and consistent? [CHAPTERS THREE, FOUR, and FIVE]
6. Do all my words mean what I think they mean? [CHAPTER FOUR]
7. Have I avoided euphemisms, clichés, jargon, and circumlocutions? [CHAPTER FOUR]
8. Is my language sufficiently vivid and lively? [CHAPTER FOUR]
9. Is my sentence structure sufficiently varied, and does it reflect my meaning? [CHAPTER FIVE]
10. Are my paragraphs internally coherent and effectively organized? [CHAPTER SIX]
11. Have I made smooth and effective transitions from paragraph to paragraph? [CHAPTER SIX]
12. Does my introductory paragraph draw the reader's curiosity and sympathy? [CHAPTER SIX]
13. Does my concluding paragraph have the necessary rhetorical force? [CHAPTER SIX]
14. Is my grammar correct? [CHAPTER SEVEN]
15. Is my usage idiomatic at every point? [CHAPTERS EIGHT and NINE]
16. Is my punctuation correct, and does it make my meaning clear? [CHAPTER TEN]
17. Are my words all correctly spelled? [CHAPTER ELEVEN]
18. Are my capitals, italics, abbreviations, and numbers all handled correctly? [CHAPTER TWELVE]
19. Have I made use of available library resources? [CHAPTER THIRTEEN]
20. Have I fairly and accurately documented quotations and ideas that need acknowledgment, and have I kept to a consistent, intelligible style of documentation? [CHAPTER FOURTEEN]

THE FINAL COPY

No matter how many changes you've made from draft to draft, the paper you eventually hand in should bear no signs of agony. A few last-minute changes, carefully and clearly inserted, may prove necessary, but any page with more than a few additions or deletions should be retyped. Try to standardize all aspects of essay *form*, so that the *substance* of your argument comes through clearly.

The following advice is routine, and can be followed wherever your instructor doesn't specify something different:

1. Use standard-sized (8½ × 11″) paper. If your essay is hand-written, choose paper with widely spaced lines. If it is typewritten, use unlined paper of ordinary weight, not onionskin.

2. Write in dark ink or type with a black ribbon that isn't faded. Whether writing or typing, use only one side of the paper.

3. You can have a title page with the title (not underlined or placed in quotation marks) centered from the sides, and beneath it your name, the course number, and perhaps the date and the instructor's name. This information can also be placed on the first page instead of on a title page. If you do have a title page, it's a good idea to repeat the title alone at the top of the first page. (For capitalization in titles see p. 328. You can, however, put your whole title in capital letters.)

4. Allow ample margins: approximately 1½″ at the top and left, and 1″ at the right and bottom. Your right margin needn't be perfectly even. Remember that a handwritten paper should leave just as much marginal space as a typed one.

5. You can leave the first page unnumbered, but all other pages should have Arabic numerals in the upper right-hand corner.

6. Leave at least a triple space between the title and the first line.

7. Double-space the whole paper except for the notes, which can be single-spaced if you aren't writing for publication.

8. Don't put extra spaces between paragraphs, but indent the first line of each paragraph five type-spaces or, in a handwritten paper, about an inch.

9. If your notes are at the foot of each page (see pp. 363–364), be sure to allow ample space for them. A line running across about one-third of the page should separate those notes from the text above.

10. If you have to revise on the final copy, put a line through all material you intend to omit. For inserted material, put a caret (∧) at the point of insertion and type or write the correction directly above it.

11. If possible, make a carbon copy of your submitted paper or have it duplicated, and retain this copy until you get the original back. Teachers have been known to mislay a student paper now and then.

EXERCISES

I. Comment on the suitability of each of the following topics for a five-page essay:

    a. World Peace
    b. Should the United States Sell Arms to Underdeveloped Countries?
    c. Geological Evidence and the Noah Story
    d. The Old Testament
    e. My Life
    f. How to Translate a Press Conference into English

II. Within each of the following subject areas, write (1) a possible topic for an essay; (2) a title for the essay; and (3) a thesis statement:

    a. Ecology
    b. Drug laws
    c. An important public event that has affected you

III. For any one of the three papers envisaged in Exercise II, write a possible outline. Use the outline form you would prefer in your own composing.

NOTE

1. George Devereux, *From Anxiety to Method in the Behavioral Sciences* (The Hague: Mouton, 1967), p. 207.

3 BEING REASON-ABLE

When an essayist wants to make a point, he can't say to his reader *Believe it because I told you* or *Believe it or else*. Readers aren't easily frightened, and they rarely take things on faith. The essayist has to appeal to common sense, showing that his thesis rests on sound reasoning about facts. The reader, to be sure, can always question the writer's evidence or interpret it differently or raise counterarguments that the writer has ignored; nothing can be definitively proved within the scope of an essay. But this makes it doubly important for the writer to have a generally reasonable manner. By making modest claims, by being frank about uncertain points and missing evidence, and by raising objections before the reader does, he can show that he has nothing to hide. His *air* of reliability is more compelling than any single argument he can make.

Clearly, the writer needs to have logic on his side—both *inductive* logic, by which a general statement is inferred from a set of particulars, and *deductive* logic, by which one statement is inferred from the relation between two other statements, called *premises:*

PREMISE:
• No Boy Scout would trip an old lady.

PREMISE:
• Ralph trips old ladies just for fun.

CONCLUSION:
• Ralph is no Boy Scout.

Such a *syllogism* or formal chain of deductive reasoning is said to be *valid* if the conclusion strictly follows from the premises and *invalid* if it doesn't. There is no necessary relation between true conclusions and valid ones; you could stumble onto a true conclusion through faulty reasoning, or validly derive a false conclusion from false premises. One thing is certain, however: an essayist can't afford to make conspicuous procedural errors. In a reader's eyes, bad logic "invalidates" even the truest conclusion.

But this doesn't mean that an essay should consist of interlocked valid syllogisms in which every step is tediously labeled. No one wants to read prose like this:

> If it were true that Americans are capable of learning from history, we would long ago have ceased to fight foreign wars. In fact, however, such wars persist, and thus we see that Americans are incapable of learning from history. Taking this conclusion as a premise, then, and reflecting that the Great Depression belongs to history, we arrive at the inference that Americans are incapable of learning from the Great Depression.

Instead of lecturing us in such humorless fashion, good essayists tell stories, paint scenes, and say things that we instantly recognize as true to experience. When they do build a case deductively, it doesn't have the self-conscious tidiness of this passage. Of the two necessary premises that imply a conclusion, one is usually left unstated; it's an idea we're expected to take for granted. The writer skips along at the advancing edge of our awareness, trusting our intuitive sense of logic and trying to be interesting as well as convincing.

It isn't necessary to memorize new principles in order to play fair as an essayist. Although some of the following reminders could be stated in formal logical terms, they really amount to the standards of reasonableness that you already apply as a reader. You know that you feel insulted when you find sloppy thought or deceptive claims or coercive rhetoric in someone else's writing. All you need do is mentally change places with your own reader, crediting him with skeptical intelligence and asking yourself how you can meet his questions openly.

1. **Put your evidence where it counts**

An essayist who is arguing a point has to support that point with
other statements—facts or reasons—that his reader is likely to accept as true. The old cliché, *The facts speak for themselves*, still describes the ideal rhetorical situation, even though facts really speak
only for someone who has unearthed them and put them in the
strategically right place.

Your sense of proportion and your tact should decide what evidence you choose to submit. The rule of thumb is that you ought to
support the assertions that are debatable and vital to your argument. Ask yourself where you *must* be convincing, and resist the
temptation to make use of a fact simply because you went to the
trouble of learning it. When you toss it in irrelevantly you're only
confessing that it's a recent acquisition. An excess of minor details
can make for confusion about your main point.

But when the point is a central one, you have to demonstrate that
you're in touch with "the facts." A student writer, for example,
wanted to show that Shakespeare uses the character of Laertes to
put Hamlet into bold relief. This argument required that he first
establish that Hamlet and Laertes are paired in significant ways:

> We need only abstract Laertes' five brief appearances in order to see
> that he and Hamlet are meant to be taken as parallel figures. In Act I,
> scene 2, Laertes asks the King for permission to return to France; in
> the same scene we learn that Hamlet has asked the King for permis-
> sion to return to Wittenburg. In Laertes' second appearance he re-
> proaches his sister for her receptivity to Hamlet; Hamlet later gives a
> comparable lecture to Gertrude. Hamlet's loss of a father through
> murder is mirrored by Laertes' loss of Polonius to Hamlet's own
> sword, and in Act IV, scene 1, Laertes reappears with the Hamlet-like
> idea of killing his father's murderer. Again, Laertes' cries of grief at
> Ophelia's funeral are travestied by Hamlet, who leaps after him into
> the grave. And in Laertes' fifth appearance in Act V, he and Hamlet
> square off for a duel of offended sons—and the result of the scene is
> that both of them die and both are avenged. Laertes, we might say,
> scarcely exists apart from Hamlet. Superficially, at least, they harbor
> the same desires and grievances, love the same woman, behave alike,
> and are drawn into a single fate at the end.

This is a useful factual paragraph, setting up an opportunity for
the writer to show how Hamlet's character stands out from Laertes'.
That point too will require ample evidence, but we already know
that the writer has a firm grasp of his materials and a respect for
precise detail.

When you're building an argument on a quarrel with some other presentation or belief, your evidence should be concentrated at the points of disagreement. Look at the following paragraphs from an essay called "The Dangers of Early Schooling" by Raymond Moore and Dennis Moore. The authors begin by recognizing that most people take for granted the desirability of getting children into school as soon as possible. They note, however, that no real evidence has ever been brought forward to show that this is true, and they allude to "an impressive body of research indicating that the late starter generally does better through school than the child who starts early."[1] Then they begin questioning the chief assumption of the authorities they must overrule if their own view — that children should be kept out of school until they are seven or eight — is to prevail:

> Advocates of early schooling usually start from two well-proved points: the fact of incredibly rapid growth in the child's intelligence between birth and age five, and the need for the child's social development to keep pace with his intellectual maturity. But then they go on to make unfortunate twin assumptions: that a child's intelligence can be nurtured by organizing it, and that brightness means readiness for the world of schooling. In short, their happy vision is that early schooling offers the best garden for a child's budding intelligence and developing social awareness.
>
> These assumptions, however comforting or promising, are contradicted by clear-cut experimental evidence. A wealth of research has established that one of a child's primary needs in these formative years is for an environment free of tasks that will tax his brain, and an equally important need is for a setting that provides warmth, continuity, and security. That normal school experience does not successfully meet these needs has been established by three different kinds of studies: those that compare early and later school entrants; those that explore important but little understood changes in the young child's brain; and those that compare the effectiveness of parents and teachers in the development of young children. All three lines of investigation point to a common conclusion: early schooling, far from being the garden of delights its advocates claim, may actually be a damaging experience.[2]

This passage doesn't present evidence, but it explains where the evidence is going to come and why. The authors then survey the studies that cast doubt on early schooling — studies of reading ability, intelligence scores and school grades, physical development, maternal deprivation, and so forth. The "impressive body of re-

search" makes a striking contrast with what seems to be sheer prejudice on the other side.

2. Be skeptical about facts and figures

An inexperienced writer is liable to be too impressed by statistics.
You should know that figures dealing with even the most seemingly neutral matters—the crime rate, the price of an airplane, the increase or decrease of smog over a city—are subject to manipulation
and error. Some imposing studies, especially those financed by lob-
bies, are biased from the start. A news report in a liberal paper may
differ remarkably from a conservative paper's coverage of the same
event. And experts can honestly disagree without having any self-
interested motives. Even when the facts are indisputable—a movement of troops, a change in climate—their interpretation can introduce new openings for debate. Was the movement "offensive" or
"precautionary"? Is pollution to blame for the rise in temperature?
As an evaluator and presenter of evidence you've got to be skeptical. Where have the so-called facts come from? Are they up to date?
Can the source be precisely cited? Could contrary "facts" be located
elsewhere? Choose your emphasis prudently, making allowance for
reasonable doubts and putting weight only on the facts that seem
unassailable.

A writer who can show the difference between figures and reality
is in a good position to win his reader's confidence. Thus Paul A.
Carter, in an essay asserting the importance of small-town life in
the 1920's, questions the meaning of a famous statistic:

> Those employed by the Bureau of the Census for the decennial count-
> ing of the American people discovered that in 1920, for the first time
> in the Republic's history, more than 50 percent of the American pop-
> ulation was definably urban.
>
> Half-truths in history probably outnumber the outright whop-
> pers. This particular statistic has been interpreted ever since as mark-
> ing a great watershed in American history, as the moment when the
> long opposition between the country bumpkin and the city slicker
> entered its final phase. Thomas Jefferson's agrarian faith that those
> who labor in the earth are the chosen people of God had apparently
> lost out to Alexander Hamilton's vision of the rich, the well born, and
> the able presiding over an industrial America. The "roar" of the Roar-
> ing Twenties seemed to be the roar of urban traffic and industry.
> According to a music critic writing in 1929, even the preindustrial
> human rhythms of jazz had become "caught up in the incessant
> movement of the machine, pounding not only in our ears but also

continuously in our consciousness . . . with its unrelieved tension." Except for a few nostalgic rallyings — the Scopes trial in Dayton, Tennessee, or the defeat of Al Smith — the rural America of the founding fathers is supposed to have lost its hold on the American imagination after 1920.

The half-truth in the 1920 statistic lay in the census-takers' definitions of "rural" and "urban" populations as those inhabiting towns of less than 2,500 people and those inhabiting towns of more. By an act of mathematical magic resembling Whitehead's fallacy of misplaced concreteness, a community of only 2,499 souls became a benighted village, while 2,501 residents made a cosmopolis. Such figures make the urban hegemony look less convincing. And in fact, gazing away from Manhattan's Great White Way any night during the decade following 1920, one could have seen wide, dark stretches of the continent where the roar of the Twenties was muted indeed; where life was lived by a rhythm in which there was no faintest echo of jazz.[3]

3. Don't allude to further proofs that aren't forthcoming

An occasional *etc.* or *and so forth* is harmless enough, especially if you really could extend your list. But you shouldn't boast that your argument is stronger than you've let on:

- Examples could be multiplied indefinitely.
- With sufficient space, I could show how this pattern is confirmed a thousand times over.

Provide the necessary examples without recourse to bluffing, and no one will doubt your sincerity.

4. Quote and summarize succinctly and accurately

Direct quotation, accurately transcribed and attributed, is one of the standard means of presenting evidence. Remember, though, that excessively lengthy quotations can sap the vitality of your argument. Quote only passages whose exact wording is useful for your purposes, and don't allow quoted material to take up so much space that it crowds your own argument. The dominant voice in your essay ought to be your own.

The rule that all quotations and summaries should be checked against the original is doubly important for material that you're using as a foil to your own ideas. Nothing is more embarrassing than to be caught misquoting a passage that you've triumphantly pronounced to be inadequate, yet a glance at the letters-to-the-editor in any journal will show you that this happens to many an experienced author and famous scholar. Get in the habit of assuming that your quotations and summaries need correction.

Perhaps the strongest temptation an essayist must resist is that of distorting an opponent's argument. It's all too easy to put your emphasis on the weakest part of his case or to rephrase it so as to make it appear self-evidently absurd. Then, presumably, your own ideas can prevail unchallenged. Instead of having to deal with serious objections, you have manufactured what's known as a *straw man* — a harmless manikin that will topple with the slightest push.

This, needless to say, is poor ethics — but it's also poor rhetoric. Your sarcasm and mock outrage will almost certainly show a perceptive reader that you've been tampering with the facts. And suppose no one does notice the deception. In the act of making things easy for yourself, you've made them boring for others. If the holder of a contrary view is *this* stupid, they think, why has anyone bothered to refute him? The more lopsided your victory over the straw man, the deader its rhetorical effect.

When readers decide that they're being presented with a straw man, they're apt to turn stubborn and resist the author's whole case, even if it's a sound one. Examine your own response to this passage, which introduces a sensible and incisive essay about ecology:

> Man's occupance of the earth is everywhere under attack by environmentalists and conservationists. Man is harassed for using nature's resources, for building dams, for exterminating bothersome species, for disposing of his refuse, for using the waters, for cultivating the topsoil, and for just being present. One gets the impression from this cacophony that nature has been contrived for all species of life except man.[4]

If we had no other source of information than this author, we would gather that environmentalists bully ("harass") their fellow men not for abusing nature, but "for just being present" on the earth. The environmentalist position appears to be that the human species should move to a different planet altogether or to execute itself as a collective criminal. *Is* this what environmentalism is about? To ask the question is to answer it — and then a rebuttal begins to gather force in your mind. If you go over the passage closely, you see that every sentence contains a gross exaggeration. The author's strategy has backfired, and the rest of his argument — trenchant, challenging, and well worth considering — may not get a fair hearing. Like many another writer who wants to dispose of opposition in advance, this one has turned *himself* into the reader's straw man.

5. Anticipate objections

A writer who is unsure of his position will want to erase contrary arguments from his mind. The thought of a strong objection rattles him. If the doubter were right, all his drudgery would prove to have been wasted. And so he forges ahead with his affirmative points, perhaps laying special stress on them in the hope of forbidding dissent. But readers are an inquisitive lot. If you try to suppress objections, you run the risk of making them appear weightier than they really are. Finding no discussion in your essay of the question in his mind, the reader may assume that you couldn't have answered it if you'd tried.

When you've settled on the outlines of your argument and are convinced that you could defend it, you still have the job of showing that this is so. Your best course is to raise the doubts yourself and meet them actively through *refutation* or *concession*. If a contrary argument strikes you as superficially attractive but valueless, you should refute it—that is, give the reader a good reason for rejecting it. If the argument makes sense but isn't fundamentally damaging to you, you should concede it and show why your main point still holds true.

Thus Jacques Barzun, in an essay advocating capital punishment, meets one of his opponents' chief arguments by granting it and trying to show that it doesn't address the real issue:

> I readily concede at the outset that present ways of dealing out capital punishment are as revolting as Mr. Koestler says in his harrowing volume, *Hanged by the Neck*. Like many of our prisons, our modes of execution should change. But this objection to barbarity does not mean that capital punishment—or rather, judicial homicide—should not go on. The illicit jump we find here, on the threshold of the inquiry, is characteristic of the abolitionist and must be disallowed at every point. Let us bear in mind the possibility of devising a painless, sudden and dignified death, and see whether its administration is justifiable.[5]

By recognizing the counterargument Barzun reduces its force, and by setting it to one side he deprives the abolitionists of a major point and implies that his own case is less "emotional" than theirs.

Think carefully, though, before building a whole argument on a series of refutations. The essay can turn out to be excessively defensive, dry, and overorganized, with a hypnotic swinging from negative to positive and a tone of superiority: "Watch me knock over the opposition!" Try to meet objections without becoming preoccupied with scorekeeping.

6. Don't slip from *may* to *is*

Watch to see that you haven't expressed more certainty than you feel and can justify. A common vice is to introduce an idea swathed in *perhaps, conceivably,* or *let us suppose,* and then, when the novelty has worn off, to treat it like an established truth. The mere fact that readers have become familiar with your notion doesn't make it less controversial in their eyes. And whenever you're hesitating between *possibly* and *surely,* choose the former. It makes no enemies, and it can help to win you some respect for your judiciousness. Writers who slightly understate their case, allowing readers to divine that *these conclusions and more* are warranted by the evidence, are considerably better off than writers who beg for leaps of faith.

7. Observe the difference between analogies and proofs

A useful but often misleading way of making a point is to argue that the matter at hand is like some other matter. If A resembles B, and if certain consequences follow from A, then comparable consequences follow from B. This sounds impressive, but there's a catch: A and B may be *un*like in crucial respects, and a reader who sees this will have freed himself from the power of your analogy.

Suppose, for example, that you wanted to argue against democratic reforms in the leadership of a political party. The party, you might say, is just like an army: it's vast and complex, it has battles to wage, and it will be held responsible for the outcome. Would a wise general share his command, allowing himself to be overruled at every point? An army led in this fashion would be easily defeated. Just so, you conclude, the party must preserve its central leadership and chain of command. What have you really proved by this analogy? Nothing. At best you've made your point in a vivid way, and this is all to the good. A shrewd opponent, however, could make you suffer for your "militaristic" conception of a nonmilitary organization whose strength lies in popular sentiment. Every analogy, even the most telling one, provides such openings for rebuttal.

Analogies can serve you well if you bear in mind that they only illustrate, never prove. They are simply extended metaphors (pp. 75–80). Perceiving the point at which the metaphor ceases to be effective, you can sometimes turn dissimilarities to your advantage. Here, for example, is a radical who doubts whether the Keynesian idea of "fine tuning" the economy can solve the chronic problems of capitalism:

> Fine tuning doesn't do much good when the tubes are weak; but economists these days are much like the TV audience in that they don't understand how the set works. Where that analogy breaks down, and uncomfortably, is that TV-watchers can call in a repairman; but the economist *is* the repairman.[6]

By pointing out the limits of his own analogy, the author underlines his main point, that liberal economists are less wise and competent than you might have thought.

8. Don't sneer

Sarcasm, the heaping of abusive derision on some person or idea, has no place in effective writing. Unless a reader already shares your position, he isn't going to be interested in seeing you stomp and mutilate your victims. The more disgust or ridicule you express, the more doubts you raise about your good faith. Why aren't you going about the business of building your case? By trying to make a fool of someone else, you give the impression of serving up a scapegoat to the reader instead of inviting his attention to your own argument.

Thus a student, asked to comment on C. Wright Mills' essay "The Structure of Power in American Society," wrote:

> Isn't this the same C. Wright Mills who wrote a book praising his dear friend, the tyrant Fidel Castro? What an "expert" on democratic institutions! Mills really should have written us an essay about the structure of power in Cuba, where things are so simple that even a totalitarian brain like his could understand them. As for *this* essay, it scarcely deserves commentary. As soon as you remember that Mills was a far-out leftist, you can predict everything he would say.

The writer's *ad hominem* attack (see point 14 below) succeeds only in exposing his unwillingness to address the content of Mills' essay, which may in fact be biased in the way he implies. We'll never know, because his sarcasm makes his own bias so apparent that we distrust anything further that he might say.

9. Don't emphasize your candor

Phrases like *to speak frankly, in all candor, Let's be forthright about this*, and *I am compelled to confess* tend to backfire. They make the reader suspect that you've only just now decided to see whether a little honesty will serve your purposes. In fact, though, an outcropping of one of these phrases is usually a sign of bad faith on the writer's part: the rest of the sentence may prove to be *less* candid than usual.

10. Avoid insincere praise

Unless you're striving for an ironical effect, don't pretend to an exaggerated respect for people with whom you're disagreeing. It's one thing to be civil, but something else again to indulge in fulsome praise. Some writers do this as a way of taking back the hostile implications of what they're about to say. They bow in reverence before the renowned and nearly infallible so-and-so, and then start hurling verbal tomatoes at him; the nastiness that's just been denied is now unleashed. If you regularly find such contradictions in your work, you probably have what's loosely known as an authority problem. In successive drafts you can work toward a more measured tone, erasing the signs of inconsistency.

11. Don't lose control of your feelings

Student prose sometimes conveys a defiant, passionate obscurity, a sense of misplaced urgency. The writer cares, but he doesn't quite know what he cares about. The frustrations of composing redouble his feelings, and finally, like the chivalrous Don Quixote who couldn't locate any dragons to slay or maidens to rescue, he strikes out at anything that reminds him of a suitable target. Here, for example, is a paragraph by a talented student:

> Our government insulates us from the violence it sanctions. The people we fight are not human. Their humanity is disguised by bloodless terminology. Only through personal accounts which we are usually protected from do statistics melt, leaving bleeding, seared human beings. Our governmental superstructures have become so complex and attenuated that their main purpose has been lost. They are for humanity. We fight for ideologies and neglect the individuals beneath these superstructures.

This is intense prose, but we're not sure, after reading six sentences, whether we've been told six things or one. The author is furious with the government for disguising people's humanity, and he wants to show us the contrast between abstract terminology and real, suffering people. But he himself is flailing at abstractions, at unspecified "statistics," "superstructures," and "ideologies"—the plural needs explaining. "The people we fight are not human": this is too close to being ambiguous. Our "governmental superstructures . . . are for humanity." Really? For all humanity? What is a superstructure, and how can it become "attenuated"? And are "the people we fight" identical with "the individuals beneath these superstructures"? Like a cry of pain, the excerpt stirs our attention and sympathy but tells us nothing that we could weigh as being true or false.

A celebrated passage from George Orwell, dealing with roughly the same subject, can give you an idea of what the student's paragraph was striving toward but not achieving:

> In our time, political speech and writing are largely the defence of the indefensible. Things like the continuance of British rule in India, the Russian purges and deportations, the dropping of the atom bombs on Japan, can indeed be defended, but only by arguments which are too brutal for most people to face, and which do not square with the professed aims of political parties. Thus political language has to consist largely of euphemism, question-begging and sheer cloudy vagueness. Defenceless villages are bombarded from the air, the inhabitants driven out into the countryside, the cattle machine-gunned, the huts set on fire with incendiary bullets: this is called *pacification*. Millions of peasants are robbed of their farms and sent trudging along the roads with no more than they can carry: this is called *transfer of population* or *rectification of frontiers*. People are imprisoned for years without trial, or shot in the back of the neck or sent to die of scurvy in Arctic lumber camps: this is called *elimination of unreliable elements*. Such phraseology is needed if one wants to name things without calling up mental pictures of them.[7]

Here we have clarity, assurance, and detail. Instead of merely talking about "bloodless terminology," Orwell supplies examples of it, shockingly juxtaposed against the realities it purports to describe. Instead of shaking his fist at intangible "superstructures," he names the policies and events that have been prettified. Is he less angry than the student who wrote of "bleeding, seared human beings"? Probably not, but his use of real examples gives him a chance to be both vivid and fair.

12. Watch out for absolute generalizations

In daily life we have to play the averages and assume that what we already know will enable us to meet and understand new events, and in conversation we're usually unconcerned with exceptions. "It never rains here in the summer," we say, or "Nobody ever learned anything from a correspondence course." It's understood that we're speaking in an approximate manner. But an argument in writing should be more responsive to small differences. If you mean *most* or *usually*, don't write *all* or *always*. *Rarely* and *never* aren't synonyms; neither are *hardly anybody* and *nobody*. Reaching for the absolute term may gratify your wish to have done with the subject once and for all, but it leaves you open to attack as a shallow thinker. If you feel undecided between two degrees of inclusiveness, choose the one that's less assertive and less open to disproof.

The risk of false generalization is especially great when a group isn't modified at all: "New Englanders are stingy." Does this mean all or only some New Englanders? The difference becomes critical if the generalization is being used to determine whether a given New Englander is stingy. Prejudice against individuals often takes the form of assigning them a trait that supposedly covers their group. The person making the judgment doesn't think to ask himself whether he means to include every last member, and if pressed he would almost certainly admit that he didn't. Meanwhile, though, he doesn't really see the individual standing in front of him; all he sees is a type.

In argumentation, one usual source of false generalizing is over-confidence in the writer's own experience. If the question is whether the human species has an aggressive instinct, the writer may feel inclined to look in his heart and say either yes or no. In doing so, he's making two common blunders: his sample of one is obviously too small, and he's making no allowance for possible bias. If the person being studied were anyone but himself he'd be more cautious. Somehow, though, we all tend to assume that we know ourselves, and we find it hard to believe that what seems true for us won't serve for everyone else. A foreign-born student writes, "The idea that immigrants want to become 'Americanized' is contradicted by all experience" (translation: "I, for one, don't want to be Americanized"). Another student writes, "Professors actually enjoy making students suffer" (translation: "I had an ugly experience in History 10"). Personal experience can have a great anecdotal value, but only if it's recognized *as* personal experience and not as a basis for generalization.

Especially in their opening paragraphs, many essays indulge in vague throwaway comments that aren't meant to be demonstrable. They're simply a way of leading into the one problem that will be treated carefully. Used in moderation, these passing remarks are harmless enough; the reader takes them for what they are, a bit of throat-clearing. But they become a serious problem as soon as rhetorical emphasis is laid on them. If the main argument of your essay rests on a proposition like "The West is guided by Christian morals," or "The purpose of evolution is to create a higher form of man," or "The decay of our culture has been accelerating every year," you're being naïve. How is anyone going to confirm or disprove such a gas bubble? An astute reader won't even try; he'll simply decide that you have a weakness for overstatement.

13. Beware of catch-all explanations

Consider this paragraph:

> The decline of the Roman Empire has been variously ascribed to libertinism and luxury, to the advent of Christianity, and to an overextension of military commitments. Some scholars have even resorted to misty theories about inevitable cycles of development and senility, as if every civilization followed the same laws. Now, however, we can put aside all such fantasies. Recent analysis of Roman earthenware has shown that highly toxic quantities of lead were being absorbed into the Romans' daily diet. The Roman Empire was literally poisoned to death.

Is this good reasoning? No, because the writer hasn't succeeded in doing away with the explanations that he intends to replace with his new one. For all we know, all five ideas may be partially right. Furthermore, the single fact that Romans were eating lead doesn't entail the intangible "decline of the Roman Empire." This paragraph illustrates a widespread tendency to favor new ideas simply on the grounds of their newness; it's a matter, once again, of overrating one's own discoveries without considering that they too could be challenged or assigned a minor place.

Remember that two events or conditions can be associated in time without being related as cause and effect. Perhaps this seems self-evident, but most of us become superstitious when partisan feelings or pet beliefs are involved. Democrats claim that Republican administrations "cause" economic recessions; Republicans call their rivals "the war party" because most wars have erupted when Democrats were in power; and mystics of various kinds support their faith by arguing that their dreams were fulfilled or that some good result followed the performance of a ritual. We all yearn for certainty, and we all relax our skepticism on a few points where the will to believe overrides every other motive. The trouble comes with expecting others to share our superstitions. On the whole they won't do so without being shown a better reason than mere temporal sequence between the supposed cause and effect.

A natural, but illegitimate, way of urging the inevitability of your position is to frame it with clearly unacceptable alternatives:

> In this crisis the President could, as he told the people, have done nothing at all, thus allowing the enemy to enslave our allies. Or he

could have retaliated with our whole nuclear arsenal, endangering the planet. That would have been shamefully reckless. Fortunately for the cause of civilization and peace, a middle course was found. By bombing only carefully selected targets and using conventional weapons, the President demonstrated once again that he is a man of forethought and moderation.

In order to represent this as valid reasoning, you would have to begin by stating, "Only one of the following three alternatives was open to the President." This proposition would appear very unlikely. The writer hopes that you'll pick up the emotional force of his rhetoric and count yourself thankful to be still alive, without thinking too precisely about his logic.

14. Don't evade the question

No one would subscribe to the following as a respectable bit of reasoning:

PREMISE:
• If X, then Y.

PREMISE:
• Z.

CONCLUSION:
• Therefore, who cares about X and Y?

This, however, is roughly what goes on in question-evading. Faced with a difficult or embarrassing problem, the writer simply changes the subject. Thus an editorial in a student newspaper might say:

> The Kittredge Hall Five are charged with setting fire to the Dean's office and blowing up the ROTC building. In the eyes of the power-mad people who run this university, such actions constitute violence and must be punished. But what exactly does "violence" mean when the word is spoken by these paternalistic liberals? Didn't they support the violence of the Vietnam war? And doesn't this campus stand on Indian territory that was seized by violence? People whose whole way of life is violent have no right to accuse others of violence!

In one sense you might say that this is "good rhetoric": by diverting attention from one issue to another one that the writer feels righteous about, it serves as a smokescreen to cover the accused. The judges are being transformed into defendants, at least for the duration of one editorial. Nevertheless, there's something sleazy about the passage: a careful reader will see that terms are being redefined in a loose, self-serving way, and that the original issue is being quietly dropped instead of settled or discussed.

Frequently, as in this example, question-evading takes the form of *ad hominem* (Latin 'to the man') argument. That is, a position or action is rejected on the grounds that the wrong person or party is in favor of it. Instead of addressing the merits of a question, the writer indulges in guilt-by-association:

> Comrade A claims that the Soviet government should abolish the censorship of literature. In order to decide this matter, let us recall that Comrade A has long been an apologist for American imperialism and bourgeois revisionism.

> Should we extend medical insurance to every citizen? I find it interesting that subversives have been trying for many years to get this legislation enacted.

> The oil and highway lobbies are doing everything in their power to defeat this anti-pollution initiative. If you believe in ecology, that should be all you need to know in order to decide how you're going to vote.

You can see that an argument needn't smear one individual in order to be *ad hominem*. All that's necessary is a channeling of interest from the idea itself to a prejudice about the people or faction supporting it.

15. Avoid prejudgments

You're *begging the question* or indulging in *circular reasoning* if you treat a debatable idea as if it had already been proved or disproved. Sometimes this happens in the very posing of the problem. Consider these two questions:

A. Is it a wise policy to let hardened criminals out of prison prematurely so that they can renew their war on society?
B. Does society have the right to take the victims of poverty and inequality and lock them up indefinitely, brutalizing them in the name of "rehabilitation"?

Writers A and B are addressing the same issue, but each of them has settled it in advance. The word *prematurely* already contains the idea that many convicts are released too soon, and other terms — *hardened criminals, renew their war* — reinforce the point. For writer B there's no such thing as a criminal in the first place. When "victims" have been "brutalized," it isn't hard to decide whether the brutalization should be prolonged. The trouble is that both A and B, in their eagerness to sweep away objections, have shown at the outset that their "investigations" will be phony. If you want to engage your reader's mind, you have to pose a genuine question, not a question-and-answer.

When a writer takes the correctness of his position for granted, his prose tends to sound either smug and cliché-ridden, or frantic, or both at once. He may go through the logical motions of arguing, but what he's actually doing is rallying the faithful, those who already agree with him and are as closed-minded as he is.

Here is a long passage dealing with the question of whether public school systems can make good use of "free school" ideas. The author, Jonathan Kozol, is himself a leading advocate of unstructured teaching, but in this article he asks whether real freedom is compatible with the nature and purpose of the public schools:

In an unjust nation, the children of the ruling-classes are not free in any way that matters if they are not free to know the price of pain and exploitation that their lives are built upon. This is a freedom that no public school in the United States can willingly give children. Businessmen are not in business to lose customers; public schools do not exist to free their clients from the agencies of mass-persuasion. "Innovative schools" with "open-structured" classrooms speak often about "relevant learning-processes" and "urban-oriented studies," but the first free action of such a class of honest children in an un-manipulated, genuinely open classroom in a segregated school within an all-white suburb, would be to walk out of class, blockade the doors and shut down the school building. School serves the state; the interest of the state is identified, for reasons of survival, with the interests of industrial dominion. The school exists to turn out manageable workers, obedient consumers, manipulable voters and, if need be, willing killers. It does not require the attribution of sinister motives, but only of the bare survival instincts, to know that a monolithic complex of industrial, political and academic interests of this kind does not intend to build the kinds of schools which will empower pint-sized zealots to expropriate their interests. It is in the light of considerations such as these that all innovations, all liberal reforms, all so-called "modern" methods and all new technologies ought to be-scrutinized: Do they exist to free consumers, to liberate citizens, to inspire disagreement, inquiry, dissent? Or do they exist instead to quiet controversy, to contain rebellion and to channel inquiry into accepted avenues of discreet moderation? Is it conceivable that public schools can serve at once the function of indoctrinating agent and the function of invigorating counterfoil? I find this quite improbable and view with reservations of the deepest kind such genteel changes as may appear to offer broader liberties to captive children.[8]

This is an impassioned piece of writing, and to some people it might seem persuasive and even eloquent. Before the first sentence is over, though, Kozol has begun prejudging. The United States is casually described as "an unjust nation" — as compared to what others? The "price of pain and exploitation" is mentioned but not explained. All freedoms but one are judged valueless — in whose eyes? And is it true that the children of the unspecified "ruling-classes" generally go to public schools? Kozol has jammed a series of questionable, if perhaps defensible, ideas into the crannies of his prose, as if to forbid us an opportunity to disagree about any of them.

Instances of question-begging occur throughout the paragraph:

> . . . public schools do not exist to free their clients from the agencies of mass-persuasion.

(To call students "clients" is to dispose in advance of the possibility that their freedom will be respected.)

> "Innovative schools" with "open-structured" classrooms speak often about "relevant learning-processes" and "urban-oriented studies" . . .

(The sarcastic quotation marks are a giveaway.)

> The school exists to turn out manageable workers, obedient consumers, manipulable voters and, if need be, willing killers.

(Other, more benign purposes are excluded without discussion. If Kozol's description is accurate, the main question of his essay — whether the schools can be truly free — appears ridiculous. Should we strive for "innovative" ways to produce "willing killers"?)

> Is it conceivable that public schools can serve at once the function of indoctrinating agent and the function of invigorating counterfoil?

(To impart one ideology is "indoctrinating"; to impart the author's is "invigorating.")

I . . . view with reservations of the deepest kind such genteel changes as may appear to offer broader liberties to captive children.

(When children are defined as captives, anyone would harbor "reservations" about their liberties. Once again the author's triumph is too easily earned.)

In a certain limited sense Kozol's paragraph is "logical." His essential argument could be stated in two interlocked syllogisms:

PREMISE:
• Public schools exist either to free people or to enslave them.

PREMISE:
• Public schools can't possibly exist to free people.

CONCLUSION:
• Public schools exist to enslave people.

PREMISE:
• All reform of the public schools serves the fundamental purpose of those schools.

PREMISE:
• The fundamental purpose of the public schools is to enslave people.

CONCLUSION:
• All reform of the public schools serves to enslave people.

These deductions are valid but they are also absurd, for they rest on wildly dogmatic premises that seem to settle in advance *all* questions about the reform of our institutions. The more "logical" Kozol becomes, the more his radicalism sounds like a snobbish refusal to concern himself with public education.

The lesson here, and the point of this chapter, is that reasonableness in prose can't be simply a matter of going through certain motions. However many valid syllogisms you string together to prove that captives aren't free, you're still not thinking. Being reasonable means showing concern for what you don't yet know. It means aiming for a level of difficulty where the choice between one idea and another is really open, not fixed by a gross contrast between right and wrong. Reaching for certainty, you should also show an awareness of uncertainty, modulating your tone as you find yourself on stronger or weaker ground.

EXERCISES

I. Suppose you wanted to write an essay against tenure (the guarantee of job security after a probationary period) for college professors. The main traditional defense of tenure, you know, has been made on grounds of academic freedom: tenure is needed to protect free inquiry, which otherwise might be stifled by meddlesome politicians and businessmen. Cushioned by tenure, the argument goes, professors can pursue ideas wherever they lead. In two or three paragraphs, write a summary of an essay that would confront this argument and propose reasons why tenure ought to be abolished.

II. The following passage was written by a member of a cooperatively owned grocery store who believes that the store's board of directors should take stands on political issues. What kind of reasoning is illustrated in this passage? Write a paragraph explaining possible objections that might be made by an opponent.

> Some people will tell you that the Co-op has no business siding with one political faction against another, since its only business is to provide food at bargain prices. But where can we draw the line between "political" and "nonpolitical" today? To breathe is now a political act, since political decisions determine whether or not the air we breathe is going to make us sick. Or consider the fact that lettuce these days can be highly toxic because of poisonous sprays. To eat a salad has become a totally *political* act, an act of solidarity with the growers against the farm workers and ecologists. Isn't it ridiculous, then, to complain about "politicization" of the Co-op? The only serious question to be answered is whether the Co-op's politics should be progressive or reactionary.

III. Study the following passage by Adolf Hitler, and write an analysis of it in which you discuss (a) the handling of abstract generalization, and (b) the use of evidence. Could the same style of reasoning be used to reach exactly opposite conclusions? If so, indicate how.

> No more than Nature desires the mating of weaker with stronger individuals, even less does she desire the blending of a higher with a lower race, since, if she did, her whole work of higher breeding, over perhaps hundreds of thousands of years, might be ruined with one blow.
>
> Historical experience offers countless proofs of this. It shows with terrifying clarity that in every mingling of Aryan blood with that of lower peoples the result was the end of the cultured people. North

America, whose population consists in by far the largest part of Germanic elements who mixed but little with the lower colored peoples, shows a different humanity and culture from Central and South America, where the predominantly Latin immigrants often mixed with the aborigines on a large scale. By this one example, we can clearly and distinctly recognize the effect of racial mixture. The Germanic inhabitant of the American continent, who has remained racially pure and unmixed, rose to be master of the continent; he will remain the master as long as he does not fall a victim to defilement of the blood.[9]

NOTES

1. Raymond S. Moore and Dennis R. Moore, "The Dangers of Early Schooling," *Harper's*, July 1972, p. 58.
2. Moore and Moore, pp. 58–59.
3. Paul A. Carter, "Of Towns and Roads, Three Novelists, and George McGovern," *Columbia Forum*, Spring 1973, pp. 10–11.
4. Amos H. Hawley, "Ecology and Population," *Science*, 179 (23 Mar. 1973), 1196.
5. Jacques Barzun, "In Favor of Capital Punishment," *The American Scholar* (Spring 1962), p. 182.
6. Doug Dowd, "Watch Out: Prosperity Is Just Around the Corner (Again)," *Ramparts*, Mar. 1971, p. 36.
7. George Orwell, "Politics and the English Language," *A Collection of Essays* (Garden City, N.Y.: Anchor, 1954), pp. 172–173.
8. Jonathan Kozol, "The Open Schoolroom: New Words for Old Deceptions," *Ramparts*, July 1972, p. 41.
9. Adolf Hitler, *Mein Kampf*, trans. Ralph Manheim (Boston: Houghton Mifflin, 1943), I, p. 286.

STYLE ||

WORDS
4

Diction, or the choice of words, is obviously a central element in every writer's style. Although good diction is partly a matter of trial and error, of tinkering with sentences until they sound right, it's also a matter of following certain general preferences that readers and writers tend to share. Those preferences underlie the following suggestions for using diction effectively in your own writing:

1. Make use of your dictionary

The first principle of diction is that you have to know the exact meanings of the words you choose. This means that you should own and make continual use of a dictionary. It will tell you the definitions of unfamiliar words, and it can settle most questions of spelling, alternate forms, pronunciation, capitalization, and syllable division. These, of course, are matters of correctness, not style, but to some extent the dictionary can also help you to make subtler judgments. Above all, you can use the dictionary to increase your

60

working vocabulary: the more words you know, the more precisely and confidently you can write. When you come across a new word, or an old word that's being used in an unfamiliar way, don't scurry past it with a sense of discomfort, but routinely look it up.

Your dictionary ought to be small enough to be easily handled and large enough to answer nearly all your questions about *denotation* (the primary meanings of words) and at least some of your questions about *connotation* (finer shadings of meaning). For these purposes you should probably have a recent "college" edition of a reputable dictionary such as *The Random House College Dictionary*, *The American Heritage Dictionary of the English Language*, or *Webster's New Collegiate Dictionary*. Such dictionaries are good source books not only for words but also for abbreviations, symbols, biographical and given names, places and population figures, weights and measures, names and locations of colleges, and principles of usage. And to a limited extent, varying considerably from one dictionary to the next, they will tell you which words belong to standard English and which ones are regarded as colloquial, dialect, or slang.

To see what a dictionary can and can't do, look at Random House's entry under *fabulous:*

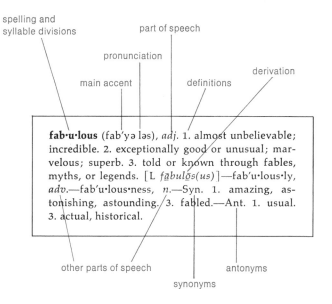

spelling and syllable divisions

part of speech

pronunciation

derivation

main accent

definitions

fab·u·lous (fab'yə ləs), *adj.* 1. almost unbelievable; incredible. 2. exceptionally good or unusual; marvelous; superb. 3. told or known through fables, myths, or legends. [L *fābulōs(us)*]—fab'u·lous·ly, *adv.*—fab'u·lous·ness, *n.*—Syn. 1. amazing, astonishing, astounding. 3. fabled.—Ant. 1. usual. 3. actual, historical.

other parts of speech

synonyms

antonyms

The entry shows, in the following order:

- how the word is spelled and the points where syllable divisions occur (*fab-u-lous*);
- where the main accent falls (*fab'*);
- how the word is pronounced: the pronunciation key at the bottom of every pair of pages reveals, among other things, that ə = *a* as in *alone*;
- the part of speech (adjective);
- three definitions (*not* in order of acceptability);
- the word's derivation from the first three syllables of the Latin (L) *fabulosus*;
- an adverb and a noun stemming from the main word;
- synonyms (words with nearly the same meaning) of definitions 1 and 3;
- antonyms (words with nearly the opposite meaning) of definitions 1 and 3.

Thus, if you as a writer had turned to *fabulous* to check its spelling, or to see where it can be hyphenated at the end of a line, or to check a possible meaning, or to find whether it can be used as an adverb (*he did it fabulous*), this entry would have helped you.

What *wouldn't* it have done? It wouldn't have told you how *fabulous* is pronounced in various nonstandard dialects, or how it came down to modern English by way of old French, or its earliest known use in an English sentence, or its relation to the slang adjective *fab*. It wouldn't have told you, if for some reason you wanted to know, that the Latin *fabulosus* is itself derived from *fabula* 'story' and that *fabulous* is related in origin to *affable*, *fib*, and *ineffable*. And it wouldn't have provided several meanings of *fabulous* that were once standard and are still available to writers: "fond of relating fables or legends," "celebrated in fable or myth," "unhistorical," "absurd, ridiculous." For this information you would have to consult a more specialized dictionary (p. 353).

Above all, this dictionary entry won't tell you whether all three of its definitions of *fabulous* are currently regarded as "good usage" by people who dislike clichés and distortions of established meanings. You can see that definition 3 is closest to the Latin root and that definition 1 looks like a reasonable extension of 3, but you aren't told that most authorities have reservations about definition 2. Yet this may be what you as an essayist most need to know. The main work of a college dictionary is to tell you how a word is actually used by contemporary speakers, not whether you should use all those senses in formal writing. In a clear case such as that of *ain't* or *irregardless*, the dictionary will warn you off with the label *nonstandard*; but most choices you face are more difficult, and the dictionary can't help you. It's therefore good to have on hand a special dictionary of usage such as Roy H. Copperud's *American Usage: The Consensus*, which says of *fabulous*:

Criticized by Bernstein, Evans, and Fowler as a vogue word for *incredible, astounding, astonishing*, and the like. The original sense, it is pointed out, was *mythical, legendary;* that is to say, relating to a fable. The faddish use of the word is found mostly in advertisements, where it may be applied to anything from girls to typewriters. This sense is recognized as standard, however, by American Heritage, Random House, and Webster.[1]

Writers are sometimes advised to use a *thesaurus* (a dictionary of synonyms and antonyms) as a way of avoiding repetitiousness in their prose. But there is a danger here. Synonyms are rarely exact, and the thesaurus won't indicate fine differences of meaning. The risk of inaccuracy or faulty tone is great when you borrow unfamiliar terms. It's important not only to build your vocabulary, but also to keep new words out of your writing until you've seen how other writers use them.

2. Suit your words to the occasion — and to yourself

Broad distinctions can be made between standard and nonstandard English and between relatively formal and relatively informal terms (see pp. 62 – 63 and 172 – 174). Generally speaking, most essay prose occupies a "middle" level of diction, with words like *face* appearing more often than words like *visage* and *mug*. A technical paper may require somewhat "higher" diction than an autobiographical sketch, but formal diction loses its effectiveness as soon as it begins sounding pompous. You should try to sound like yourself in everything you write.

It's foolhardy to mix levels of diction without good reason, as in this sentence: *Fielding's exquisite employment of peripeteia makes manifest that he could do a classy job.* Here the slangy words pointlessly clash with the stuffy ones. But sometimes mixed diction can be used to good effect, making for intended irony or humor. The boxing reports of A. J. Liebling, for example, had a formal elegance that was purposefully "above" the fight game, and they juxtaposed literary references and colloquialisms:

> I do not know what took place in Mr. Moore's breast when he saw him get up. He may have felt, for the moment, like Don Giovanni when the Commendatore's statue grabbed at him—startled because he thought he had killed the guy already—or like Ahab when he saw the Whale take down Fedallah, harpoons and all.[2]

And James Herndon's style in his books about education is pitched deliberately "below" the administrative jargon of the school officials who see achievers, nonachievers, and intolerables, but never human "kids":

> There had always been kids in school who were smart—that is, the school said they were smart, they could be shown to have been smart at some time in their lives on the school's own tests—but who did not do well in school, who got bad grades and who were a pain in the ass. Naturally they annoyed the school. Smart kids who got good grades were O.K., and dumb kids who got bad grades were O.K., but smart kids who got bad grades weren't O.K., since the implication was that they were deliberately rejecting advantage, the whole notion of winning, the very virtue of the school.[3]

Both Liebling and Herndon use *mixed diction* to detach themselves from what they're describing. You, however, may want to aim at an entirely different effect. The point isn't to imitate one writer or another, but to keep an open mind about what constitutes acceptable diction, and discover what feels right for yourself.

3. Avoid euphemisms

A *euphemism* is an unnecessarily formal synonym, like *domicile* for "house" or *expectorate* for "spit." Euphemisms always sound pretentious, and usually they're intended to disguise something unpleasant or embarrassing. In a letter to owners of 1972 Torinos and Rancheros, for example, the Ford Motor Company mentioned that the rear axle bearings on some of those cars were suspected of faulty design. "Continued driving with a failed bearing," the letter advised, "could result in a disengagement of the axle shaft and *adversely affect vehicle control*" (emphasis added). Just *how* inconvenienced you would be when your rear axle dropped onto the road, the authors preferred not to say.

You're probably familiar with such euphemisms as *memory gardens* (cemeteries), *human resources development* (unemployment), *negative population growth* (fewer people), *relocation centers* (concentration camps), *inoperative* (false) *statements*, and *limited duration protective reaction retaliatory strikes* (unprovoked bombing). The effort at prettification in these instances has a commercial or political motive that gradually gets forgotten as the phrase catches on. A good many terms that are now regarded as normal, such as *realtor* (real estate salesman) and *defense* (armaments), began as euphemisms but can't be regarded as such any longer; a euphemism is only a euphemism so long as the word it attempts to replace is still dominant.

The rule is that you should prefer simple and ordinary words to

euphemism	for
abode	house
altercation	fight
commence	begin
concept	idea
deceased, passed away, departed	dead
dichotomy	difference, opposition
differential	difference
directive	order
epistle	letter
esthetic	pretty, beautiful
facility	building
formulate	say, state
gender	sex
individual	person
initial	first
libation, liquid refreshment	drink
limited	small
locate	settle, find
major	large, important
marginal	small
offspring	child
optimum, optimal	best
partake of	share, eat
party	person
patron	customer
peruse	read
presently	now
proceed	go
proposition	proposal, idea
remains	corpse
reside, residence	live, house
settle	pay
societal	social
state	say
transpire	happen, occur
usage, utilize	use
verbalize	say, put in words
verdict	opinion
visitation	visit

ceremonious ones unless you have some special reason (such as a wish to be ironical) for sounding arch. On p. 65 is a sampling of common euphemisms. Every word in the left column has a legitimate function, but it's a euphemism when it replaces the word on the right.

4. Avoid clichés

A cliché is an expression so overworked that it has become an automatic way of getting around the main business of writing, which is to suit each word to the meaning at hand. The habitual user of clichés—the person who describes money as *filthy lucre*, whose indifference to language comes *from the bottom of his heart*, and whose meaning is lost *like a needle in a haystack*—brands himself as a lazy writer. He selects phrases like jukebox tunes, allowing them to drown out whatever he meant to say. And sometimes he even confesses his laziness by inserting *so to speak* or *as the saying goes*, as if it helped to confess his embarrassment.

Some clichés, like *gilding the lily* and *a Procrustean bed*, are based on misquotations or on allusions whose meaning isn't widely known. Others are intelligible but deadeningly monotonous. When the reader sees *nuclear*, he knows that *holocaust* will follow; what is *foreseeable* must of course be the *future*; a *mixture* is *heady*, *praise* is *unstinted*, and so on. The resultant prose is a *far cry* from being a *sure winner* in the *minds and hearts* of readers *from every walk of life*.

It's fairly easy, in the process of revision, to catch gross clichés such as *cut the Gordian knot, conspicuous by its absence, eat one's cake and have it too*, and *a miss is as good as a mile*. More insidious are harmless-looking pairs of "inseparable" adjectives and nouns (*supreme moment, vicious circle, vital role*) and the pat phrases that lend pseudo-importance to one's rhetoric (*it stands to reason, far be it from me, in a very real sense, in the last analysis*). Such handy expressions are *a snare and a delusion*, for they are *part and parcel* of recognizably weak prose.

Now and then, like the owner of a VW bus who first thought to paint NO LEFT TURN UNSTONED on the back panel, or like the student who wrote on a course-evaluation form, *At the end of the hour I feel like oinking for more pearls*, you can twist a cliché into a new and temporarily humorous form. But bear in mind that twisted clichés can soon become clichés themselves: *praise with faint damns, less there than meets the eye*.

No list of clichés can ever be all-inclusive, for a cliché is born whenever a phrase becomes too predictable. The following clichés (all cited in Bergen and Cornelia Evans' *Dictionary of Contemporary American Usage*) are only a *drop in the bucket*, but they will give you a *bellyful* of expressions that are *dead as a doornail:*

agree to disagree
apple of one's eye
as the crow flies
avoid like the plague
baker's dozen
battle royal
bee in one's bonnet
beyond the pale
dyed in the wool
eat one's heart out
eternal verities
face the music
far from the madding crowd
feather one's nest
feel in one's bones
few and far between
get up on the wrong side of bed
give the devil his due
grin and bear it
handwriting on the wall
head over heels
heave a sigh of relief
high and dry
hit below the belt
hit the nail on the head
horse of a different color
in the same boat
innocent as a newborn babe
irons in the fire
keep a stiff upper lip
know the ropes
lap of luxury
last but not least
lay one's cards on the table
leave in the lurch
let the cat out of the bag
light as a feather
live from hand to mouth
lock, stock, and barrel
mad as a hatter
make no bones about it
man after my own heart
milk of human kindness
move heaven and earth
neither rhyme nor reason
new wine in old bottles
nip in the bud

no love lost
not wisely but too well
one foot in the grave
out of the woods
picture of health
pillar of the church
play with fire
pull one's weight
put one's foot down
radiantly happy
rain or shine
read between the lines
rest on one's laurels
risk life and limb
rule the roost
screw up one's courage
seamy side of life
sell like hot cakes
set one's heart on
seventh heaven
shadow of one's former self
ships that pass in the night
short and sweet
sight for sore eyes
silver lining
skeleton in the closet
skin of one's teeth
smell a rat
snake in the grass
soft place in one's heart
speak of the devil
square peg in a round hole
stew in one's own juice
stitch in time
straight from the shoulder
stung to the quick
swear like a trooper
sweat of one's brow
take by storm
take to one's heels
tempest in a teapot
there's the rub
tilt at windmills
toe the mark
token of esteem
twinkling of an eye
untold wealth

voice crying in the wilderness	whip hand
wages of sin	with a vengeance
walking on air	with bated breath
water under the bridge	without rhyme or reason
wave of optimism	work one's fingers to the bone
weather the storm	worth its weight in gold
wedded bliss	wrong side of the tracks

It isn't necessary to memorize all clichés or to eliminate them entirely from your prose. Both tasks would be impossible. The clichés to watch out for are the ones that recur in your work as all-purpose filler.

5. Avoid jargon

Technical terms have technical uses, and there's no need to apologize for them if the technical meaning is the one you must have. There are important differences between *liquidity* and *cash, ego* and *self, kinship structure* and *family.* Jargon proper occurs when the term from ordinary language would have conveyed all that's really meant.

The user of *sociologese,* for instance, not only writes *sociological* when he means "social"; he also uses *upwardly mobile* for "ambitious" and *parameters* for "borders." If two things resemble each other, he sees them *on a continuum,* draws a *correlation* between them, and describes one as *a function of* the other. In his world people don't do things, they indulge in *behavior,* taking *orientation* from their *peer groups.*

As for the user of *psychologese,* he thinks that every pattern is a *syndrome,* that vanity shows *a big ego,* that hostility means *getting rid of aggressions,* and that a strong interest in anything amounts to an *obsession* or *fixation.* In sad people he detects a *death wish;* in happy ones, *manic* tendencies. But he himself, luckily, is *adjusted,* although he does face the *trauma* of paying income tax or waking up in the morning.

Advertising, journalism, business, and bureaucracy also exert warping effects on diction. If you find yourself writing about *pay hikes* and *Russ subs;* if your writing is full of *probes, vows, tolls, blazes, slates,* and *boosts;* if you feel possessed by the urge to say *inks the contract, gets the nod,* and *OK's the pact,* then you have a desperate case of *journalese. Bureaucratese,* in contrast, shows up in *breakthroughs, dialogue, decision-making process, brainstorm, viable, massive* (meaning "not small"), *maximize, finalize, potential* as a noun, *air* as a verb, *priorities, profiles,* and so on. Journalese is breezy, concrete, and cryptic to a fault; bureaucratese is self-important and abstract.

For a choice sample of bureaucratese, look at these paragraphs written by the president of an American university:

> It is reasonable to assume that graduate education in the United States developed on undergraduate college campuses because its presence was somehow synergistic with respect to the higher education enterprise. The most important factor was probably the presence of a cadre of scholars engaged in the learning pursuit, both with neophytes and on their own. In addition, libraries, laboratories, and skilled artisans were available.
>
> For half a century or more, the whole clearly exceeded the sum of the parts, whether considered from the viewpoint of quality, cost effectiveness, or a combination of both. Now, however, the proliferation of graduate programs on the individual campus, the increase in the number of campuses providing graduate education, the current oversupply of these graduates, and the seeming inflexibility of many people with advanced degrees calls into question the synergism argument in favor of graduate education on the country's campuses.[4]

Note the redundancy in this passage (*campus* and *campuses* occur three times in one sentence), the abstractions, the unnecessarily fancy words (*synergistic, cadre, neophytes*), the use of nominal forms in place of adjectives (*the higher education enterprise, the learning pursuit, the synergism argument*), and the impersonal tone. Nothing is *happening* here; no one is doing anything to anybody. Instead we have ghostly states: a factor was a presence, libraries were available, the whole exceeded the sum, the proliferation calls into question the synergism . . . The ratio of rhetorical noise to information is so high that you probably had some difficulty concentrating on the argument.

Politics, too, has its expanding store of jargon. A generalissimo may be called either *a running dog of the imperialist oppressors* or *a staunch friend of the American way of life*, depending on the writer's affiliation. The epithets are opposite in meaning, but they both express the same contemptuous attitude toward language. The jargon sets off either a stink bomb or a perfumed mist; in either case the idea isn't really to describe, but to manipulate and deceive.

Less obviously, you may notice that the difference between *propaganda* and *consciousness-raising*, or between *mobilization* and *incitement*, is entirely political. An army invades a neighboring country; this is *liberation* if it's your army, *conquest* if it's your country. You may, of course, feel strongly that one of these nouns is accurate. When the habitual user of political jargon says something true, however, he is right only by accident; he would have used the same flag-waving terms in any case.

6. Don't strain the function of words

English has always been indulgent toward coinages, extensions of meaning, and *back formation* of verbs (as in *drowse* formed from *drowsy*, *diagnose* from *diagnosis*). But most new terms disappear after a short while, and a weakness for them may imply that you're too susceptible to fads. It's better to draw your main vocabulary from words that have a history; the evocativeness of good prose comes in part from our lifelong acquaintance with the range of possible meanings.

Many of the words that sound cheap to educated readers have a common feature: they belong to one part of speech but are being used as another. Sometimes a suffix such as *-wise* has been hastily added to turn a noun into an adverb: *policywise*, *differentiationwise*, *atrocious usagewise*. More often a noun is appropriated as a verb (to *author* a book), a noun becomes an adjective (a *fun* party), an adjective becomes a noun (the *feline*) or adverb (she did it *first-rate*), a verb becomes a noun (a long *quote*, an effective *rewrite*), and so forth.

The use of nouns as adjectives deserves special mention in the age of bureaucratese. Standard English allows some latitude for such attributive nouns, as they're called, but officials have a way of jamming them together in a confusing heap. The governor of a large western state, for example, not long ago proposed what he called a *community work experience program demonstration project*. This row of attributive nouns was meant to describe, or perhaps to conceal, a policy of getting welfare mothers to pick up highway litter without receiving any wages.

7. Avoid circumlocutions

Although you needn't squeeze every phrase into the smallest possible number of words, you should be on the lookout for circumlocutions—that is, pointlessly roundabout expressions. Nearly every paragraph of a first draft usually contains some words that can be stripped away without any sacrifice of meaning. Finding *advance planning*, for example, in one of your sentences, you should ask whether *advance* says anything not contained in *planning*. No; so out it goes. *Share in common* fails the same test and should be reduced to *share*; *deliberate lie* becomes *lie*, *pair of twins* becomes *twins*, *adequate enough* becomes either *adequate* or *enough*, and so on. The revision makes for a cleaner, more purposeful effect.

Some internally redundant circumlocutions, with the unnecessary words printed in italics, follow:

absolutely nothing	one *specific* case, one *definite* reason
arrive *on the scene*	
betwixt and between	part *and parcel*
check *up*, end *up*, head *up*, open *up*, pay *up*	period *of time*
	personal friend
circle *around*	pervade *the whole*
close proximity	really *and truly*
collect *together*, combine *together*, assemble *together*	regress *back*
	repeat *the same*
contributing factor	*self*-confessed
dead bodies	*separate and* distinct
deflect *away*	shuttle *back and forth*
diametrically opposite, *completely* opposite, *polar* opposites	skirt *around*
	small *in size*, large *in size*
	start *in*
disappear *from view*	strangle *to death*
disregard *altogether*	surround *on all sides*
end product, *end* result	throughout *the whole*
equally as good	to the north*ward, to the* northward
extremely immoderate	*total of* ten
final completion, *final* conclusion	traverse *across*
	true fact
funeral obsequies	universal *the world over*
living incarnation	until *such time as*
new innovation	visit *with*
one and the same	*ways and* means
one *particular* example,	

A few of these phrases would be meaningful in certain contexts (He was *small in size* but not in courage), but for most purposes the italicized words are implicit and should be dropped.

Not all circumlocutions are redundant. Some are merely vague, and others, like *as a matter of fact* and *to make a long story short*, are simply ways of getting from one sentence to the next, or perhaps of making a short story long. Others, like *in connection with* and *as regards*, are ways of pointing to a relationship without specifying what it is. Still others lend fake dignity to sentences by jamming them with nouns: instead of *he was kind* we get *he was of a kindly nature*, and *it was unusual* is exalted to *it was of an unusual character* or *it was unusual in nature* or *it had a tendency to be unusual*. Writers who prefer such phrases rarely use simple, active, transitive verbs like *meet*, *destroy*, and *arouse*; their choices are *make contact with*, *render inoperative*, and *give rise to*. In place of *because* they write *due to the fact that*; and in their prose things are never *certain*, they're *beyond the shadow of a doubt*. You can see that circumlocution and cliché are overlapping topics.

In order to develop an aversion to circumlocutions, you might try to use as much padding as you can in one gruesome paragraph. For example:

> As far as the wolf was concerned, Little Red Riding Hood was basically a person who was acting, rightly or wrongly, on the hypothesis that by dint of exhibiting a tendency to girlish charm, so to speak, she might play a leading role in militating against being devoured. The contributing factors, by and large, that entered the area of concern that indicated a less sanguine conclusion had the effect, frankly speaking, of rendering inconsequential whatever ambitions the diminutive lass might have possessed in terms of establishing truly positive relations with a beast who was one of such a disputatious and unpredictable nature. It stood to reason that with respect to a simple-type female along the lines of herself, and with a viewpoint toward clarifying for a certainty the premises that might take effect should the wolf succeed in giving grounds for apprehension, Little Red Riding Hood felt strongly impelled toward the posing of a query serving the purpose of allowing the wolf to give expression to his intentions in a forthright manner and to the fullest extent. In this instance, however, things soon came to the point that further speculation either pro or con, as the case may have been, was reduced to zero — as, to make a long story short, was our heroine herself.

8. Avoid vague and insincere intensifiers

In conversation most of us use words like *basically, certainly, definitely, incredibly, intensely, of course, perfectly, positively, quite, really, simply*, and *very* without pausing to worry about their meaning, if any. These terms bolster our morale as we pick our way through a maze of half-formed ideas; their actual sense is *maybe* or *I hope*. Our friends have to forgive us for talking this way, so that they in turn can be forgiven. But written prose is expected to convey fully realized thoughts, and readers are impatient with authors who include intensifiers just for their reassuring sound. If you mean *very* you can write it without apology, but first make sure you do mean it; most of the intensifiers in a typical first draft deserve to be pruned away.

While we're talking we don't hunt for adjectives to express the exact degree of our enthusiasm or dismay. We veer toward the extremes of *fantastic, terrific, sensational, fabulous*, and *awful, horrible, terrible, dreadful*. In print these words are often doubly inaccurate: they misrepresent the writer's true mood and they violate their own proper meaning. Something *fantastic* should have to do with fantasy; *dreadful* means "inspiring dread." Don't write *I am awfully glad* or *It was terribly thoughtful of him to come* — unless the one who came was Dracula.

9. Avoid unnecessary negatives

When you find many negative statements in an early draft, look to see how many of them can be recast in positive form. Invariably you'll discover that some of them are secret affirmations that have been couched negatively so as to make an impression of judicious caution: *There is no reason not to suppose*, etc. Such constructions are acceptable if they're used sparingly, but some writers make a vice of them. The problem is that negative statements are harder to follow than positive ones. A succession of them makes for a pallid, weaseling effect. Sometimes the writer as well as the reader gets tripped up by negatives: *The fact that psychologists did not themselves find the key to such symbols until the twentieth century does not rule out the possibility that a great novelist might not have intuited their meaning on his own.* If you have the patience to untangle this sentence, you'll find that it says the opposite of what the writer intended.

10. Beware of unrelieved abstraction

Language that names tangible impressions or specific things is called *concrete: dog, bush, Chicago, red.* Words characterizing general qualities, classes of things, or relationships is called *abstract: canine, vegetation, urban, color.* The line between concrete and abstract sometimes depends on the context, but you needn't worry about fine distinctions; what matters is the relative sharpness or vagueness of your habitual prose.

Although young writers are often urged to "be concrete," there's no need to feel that you're writing badly when your abstract terms are precisely conveying what you mean to say. The most accomplished writers don't hesitate to write abstractly when they want to get from the mere fact of a thing to its significance. Look, for example, at the way this paragraph, written by Frank Conroy, gracefully moves between exact description and general principles:

> The greatest pleasure in yo-yoing was an abstract pleasure — watching the dramatization of simple physical laws, and realizing they would never fail if a trick was done correctly. The geometric purity of it! The string wasn't just a string, it was a tool in the enactment of theorems. It was a line, an idea. And the top was an entirely different sort of idea, a gyroscope, capable of storing energy and of interacting with the line. I remember the first time I did a particularly lovely trick, one

in which the sleeping yo-yo is swung from right to left while the string is interrupted by an extended index finger. Momentum carries the yo-yo in a circular path around the finger, but instead of completing the arc the yo-yo falls on the taut string between the performer's hands, where it continues to spin in an upright position. My pleasure at that moment was as much from the beauty of the experiment as from pride. Snapping apart my hands I sent the yo-yo into the air above my head, bouncing it off nothing, back into my palm.[5]

Should we criticize this author for relying on the abstract terms *pleasure, dramatization, laws, geometric purity, enactment of theorems, idea, energy, momentum,* and *nothing?* Frank Conroy's paragraph succeeds because he has been able to show precisely how his intellect was engaged by the abstract properties of a childhood toy. Like much good writing, this paragraph defines the poetry of ordinary things, and its general words are just as purposeful as its specific ones.

The real trouble with abstract language comes when a writer isn't quite sure what he wants to say; then he's tempted to use vague terms as hiding-places for his confusion. The effect is opposite to Conroy's simplicity and clarity. Instead of setting up a relation between detail and general laws, the writer typically buries himself in generalities, shutting off every opportunity for vividness. Given Conroy's theme, he might have written of *the illustration of various physical laws by the component elements of toys, the discipline of mastery of diverse techniques, and combined intellectual and esthetic satisfactions,* without describing the activity itself as Conroy does.

Here is what can happen when abstract language is unrelieved:

On the positive functional side, a high incidence of certain types of patterns is essential to our occupational system and to the institutional complex in such fields as property and exchange which more immediately surround this system. In relatively common-sense terms it requires scope for the valuation of personal achievement, for equality of opportunity, for mobility in response to technical requirements, for devotion to occupational goals and interests relatively unhampered by "personal" considerations. In more technical terms it requires a high incidence of technical competence, of rationality, of universalistic norms, and of functional specificity. All these are drastically different from the patterns which are dominant in the area of kinship relations, where ascription of status by birth plays a prominent part, and where roles are defined primarily in particularistic and functionally diffuse terms.[6]

Talcott Parsons, to be sure, does know what he's talking about, and he has good reason not to pause over concrete examples: the whole purpose of his essay is to isolate general laws. But was it necessary for him to lull his readers with those strings of prepositional phrases, those monotonous adjective-noun pairs, and those uniformly colorless terms? Excessively abstract prose is always noun- and preposition-ridden. Only eight of Parsons' 133 words are verbs, and they're all forms of the inert *be, surround, require*, and *play*. No action is visualized; no energy flows from subject to object; all we can discern are cloudy relationships. An incidence is essential to a and b, it requires scope for the valuation of c, for d of e, for f in response to g, for h to i and j relatively unhampered by k. It also requires a high incidence of l, of m, of n, and of p . . . *What* did the man say?

If your prose is needlessly abstract you may also get caught in unintended metaphors (see point 12) and in misplaced agency. *This area of concern*, you may write, *plays a role in the formation of the high mortality of cancer*. But can an area play a role, and can an area of concern be in any sense a cause of disease? For that matter, how are we to understand the formation of a mortality? The abstract nouns, looped together by prepositions, blur the causal relations they're supposed to explain. Worst of all, once you've written such a sentence you may imagine that you've actually said something, and on this quicksand foundation you may build the rest of your argument.

11. Don't use logical terms unless you mean them

Words like *proof, refutation, validity, premise*, and *conclusion* have technical meanings that ought to be respected. It's true that good writers often use *valid* to mean *legitimate* or *correct*, as in *This is a valid proposal*. But when you mean *rebut* or *challenge*, you shouldn't write *refute;* a refutation is a disproof, not a mere disagreement. Similarly, a *premise* is meaningful only in relation to a conclusion it will yield when it's combined with another premise. If you use it as a synonym of *idea*, you're once again displaying, not logic, but only a wish to sound logical. The abuse of logic also extends to more common words like *because, since, therefore, then*, and *thus*. These terms assert that one thing is the cause of another, and you shouldn't use them to mean anything less.

12. Make your metaphors vivid and appropriate

A *metaphor*, strictly defined, is an implied comparison, and a *simile* is an explicit one:

METAPHOR:

- George's hedgeclipper mind gives a suburban sameness to everything it touches.

(George's mind is compared to hedgeclippers, but without a term of comparison such as *like* or *as*.)

SIMILE:

- Like a patio rotisserie, George's mind always keeps turning at the same slow rate, no matter what is impaled on it.

(George's mind is explicitly likened to a rotisserie.)

In practice, you can see, the difference between metaphor and simile isn't very important. One kind of figure isn't necessarily more poetical or risky than the other. What does matter is whether the figures you use (I'll call them all "metaphors" for convenience) are clear and pertinent and helpful.

Although metaphors usually find their way into the driest paragraph, some writers prefer to keep them to a minimum. Ernest Hemingway's descriptions, for example, are intentionally flat and literal:

> Then there was the bad weather. It would come in one day when the fall was over. We would have to shut the windows in the night against the rain and the cold wind would strip the leaves from the trees in the Place Contrescarpe. The leaves lay sodden in the rain and the wind drove the rain against the big green autobus at the terminal and the Café des Amateurs was crowded and the windows misted over from the heat and the smoke inside. It was a sad, evilly run café where the drunkards of the quarter crowded together and I kept away from it because of the smell of dirty bodies and the sour smell of drunkenness.[7]

Hemingway writes vividly, but he wants his scene simply to be itself, and so he tries to do without metaphor.

At the other extreme is the style of Norman Mailer, who recklessly piles one figurative image onto another. Here, for instance, is Mailer describing Miami Beach:

> Over hundreds, then thousands of acres, white sidewalks, streets and white buildings covered the earth where the jungle had been. Is it so dissimilar from covering your poor pubic hair with adhesive tape for fifty years? The vegetal memories of that excised jungle haunted Miami Beach in a steam-pot of miasmas. Ghosts of expunged flora, the never-born groaning in vegetative chancery beneath the asphalt

came up with a tropical curse, an equatorial leaden wet sweat of air which rose from the earth itself, rose right up through the baked asphalt and into the heated air which entered the lungs like a hand slipping into a rubber glove.[8]

Some readers might object to this passage as lush and imprecise. Hauntings and a curse, vegetal memories, and ghosts of unborn flora seem a bit melodramatic when the literal subject is the history and climate of Miami Beach. What exactly is a *leaden sweat?* Isn't there something wrong with saying that *ghosts* came up with a *curse*, which was in fact a *sweat of air*, which once again *rose*, and rose into still more *heated air*, which now resembled a hand? Yet for many readers the daring of Mailer's total idea, and the vividness of images like the adhesive tape on pubic hair and the hand slipping into the rubber glove, override all such objections. The passage succeeds not only in itself, but as a prelude to the events that Mailer will describe later as the Republicans at their convention, like the developers who laid asphalt over the jungle, disregard the elemental, threatening social forces at work in 1968. Both sets of planners can have their way, Mailer implies, but both will be "haunted" by the growth they stifle.

Sometimes a writer finds a good metaphor, not in fanciful comparisons such as Mailer's, but in a literal object that seems already to embody what he wants to say. In the passage that follows, F. Scott Fitzgerald is telling of his return to New York, the capital of his imagination, after a long stay in Europe. Meanwhile two things have happened: the Empire State Building has been constructed and the 1929 Depression has struck. Alarmed by the dreadful human effects of the crash, Fitzgerald casts about for a way of explaining what has happened. Looking out from the roof of the Empire State Building, he fancies that the stock speculators must have been unnerved by this same experience:

From the ruins, lonely and inexplicable as the sphinx, rose the Empire State Building and, just as it had been a tradition of mine to climb to the Plaza Roof to take leave of the beautiful city, extending as far as eyes could reach, so now I went to the roof of the last and most magnificent of towers. Then I understood—everything was explained: I had discovered the crowning error of the city, its Pandora's box. Full of vaunting pride the New Yorker had climbed here and seen with dismay what he had never suspected, that the city was not the endless succession of canyons that he had supposed but that *it had limits*—from the tallest structure he saw for the first time that it faded out into the country on all sides, into an expanse of green and blue that alone was limitless. And with the awful realization that New York was a city after all and not a universe, the whole shining edifice that he had reared in his imagination came crashing to the ground.[9]

A good metaphor induces a sense of rightness even when the idea behind it is wrong. Fitzgerald is hinting that the Depression was caused by the Empire State Building: climbing to the top, New Yorkers saw that their city wasn't the endless universe they'd thought, and so they panicked. Needless to say, this wasn't one of the causes of the economic crash; indeed, the building wasn't even completed until two years later. Yet Fitzgerald has captured something *like* the experience of 1929, and his figure is appropriate on a deeper level. The crash came when, after stock shares had been wildly inflated and investors had borrowed far beyond their capacity to repay, an avalanche of doubt occurred. Wall Street couldn't indefinitely extend its fantasy of easy wealth. Instead of saying this in flat literal terms, Fitzgerald finds an object, the Empire State Building, that contains the paradox of dizzy ascent and a realization that dreams can't keep reality at bay forever.

A weak metaphor typically fogs up like a windshield, obscuring our view of the main idea. Compare these two figures from the same magazine:

> Technology has given Goliath a club so heavy he cannot lift it. And it has given every David a sling: mass communications.[10]

> The American landscape is littered with the hulks of federal social programs — launched amid noisy trumpetry from on high — which have subsequently been dismembered, truncated for lack of funds, or strangled by the problems they set out to conquer.[11]

The first of these images concisely embodies the author's whole argument, namely that technology has enhanced human freedom instead of constricting it. Warfare, his article maintains, is becoming obsolete because the destructive power of weapons is now too large for them to be used effectively for political ends; and mass communications have meanwhile given the ordinary man access to information and power he never possessed before. The image of David and Goliath epitomizes this case in two brief, unpretentious, but emphatic sentences.

What about the second example? Here is a self-conscious metaphor of a landscape covered with junk. It begins with an air of authority, but then new and inconsistent elements are rushed in to keep the sentence from sagging. Federal social programs, first likened to ships that were *launched* and are now *hulks*, are littering the whole *American landscape.* Ships in Kansas? And is a ship *dismembered*, much less *strangled?* The author seems to have forgotten that her image is an inanimate object. Does a ship, furthermore, *set out to conquer problems?* The whole sentence has an air of empty, confused grandeur.

The technical term to describe such a clash of figures is *mixed metaphor.* A mixed metaphor isn't a succession of distinct images, but an awkward inconsistency within an image that's still being developed. If one image is unmistakably finished, you're free to take up a new one; a truly mixed metaphor is one that can't be visualized without absurdity. Thus President Eisenhower once created a classic mixed metaphor when he remarked that *The Japanese have a tough row to hoe to keep their economic heads above water.* Thinking in clichés rather than in concrete images, the President called up a picture of farmers hoeing their rice paddies while neck-deep in water.

More mixed metaphors result from clichés, in fact, than from deliberate efforts at figurative expression. Most ordinary terms, and nearly all clichés, are *dead metaphors*—that is, they contain latent implications of an image but aren't usually intended to evoke it. When clichés are used in close succession, they revive each other and become mischievously vivid:

- The community should vomit up this moral question mark.
- Climbing to the heights of oratory, the candidate tackled the issue.

And sometimes a cliché-metaphor isn't exactly mixed, but just lamely abandoned:

- I would like to rattle all the skeletons in the current outlook.
- He had no intention of providing grist for this debate.

If you're going to *rattle skeletons* at all, they have to be in a *closet;* and *grist for the mill,* uninspired in itself, is made still more unacceptable by being left incomplete.

Test your sense of metaphor, finally, against the example of these sentences written by Greg Calvert and Carol Neiman:

> The wave of political reaction which has threatened to engulf the left since 1968 has certainly not been broken, and, although it only hovers in the wings of this study, the immediate concerns it generates occupy a stage front position in the minds of the authors. However, only a larger historical and theoretical context can begin to light the way beyond the impasse we face.[12]

Here the metaphors are themselves mostly clichés: *wave of reaction, hover in the wings, stage front position, light the way.* Reaching always for the nearest phrase, the authors create an image of a giant wave quivering at the side of a stage while *the immediate concerns it generates* (everything is suddenly abstract) *occupy a stage front position* (we're back in the aquatic theater after all). And what will *light the way?* Not a lamp, but a *context.* To light the way beyond an impasse, incidentally, makes as much sense as to turn left at a dead end. If you can get beyond it at all, it isn't an impasse. The authors simply aren't listening to the sense of the words they've chosen.

Metaphors, then, are as treacherous as they are useful. When you intend an abstract meaning, you have to make sure that your dead metaphors stay good and dead. And when you do mean to be figurative, see whether you're getting the necessary vividness and consistency. If not, go back to literal statement: it's better to make plain assertions than to litter your verbal landscape with those strangled hulks.

EXERCISES

I. Using your dictionary, establish the main differences of meaning between the following paired words. For each pair, write a sentence that makes use of the contrast between the two terms:

1. ample, excessive	6. bold, brash
2. policeman, cop	7. erotic, lustful
3. cunning, politic	8. impartial, indifferent
4. overhear, spy	9. simulate, fake
5. ecstatic, happy	10. opponent, enemy

II. Discuss the levels of diction in the following passage. Do you think the writer intended the effects he gets?

There are two faces to the drug problem. There is the drug problem itself. And there is the police-drug problem. The view that cops can stop people from taking dope is so childish that a kid of ten would be flunked for proffering it to a teacher in a school in a rational society. It just ain't so, Joe. Vide Prohibition.

The drug problem has increased in almost exact proportion to the amount of money that has been spent to police it. In the last five years the feds have increased funds to fight dope by nearly 1100 per cent to more than $791 million annually. The drug problem, by no accident, is now completely out of hand.[13]

III. Here is a fictitious letter parodying a certain "official" style. Pick out several examples of jargon in the letter, and comment on the way they convey or disguise meaning:

Dear Miss Dodds:

Thank you for your letter deploring the 14,000 fish deaths apparently related to thermal outflow into Long Island Sound from our nuclear power facility at Squaw Point. While the blame for this regrettable incident might most properly be ascribed to the fish, which swam closer to the Connecticut shore than is their normal habit, we believe that the ultimate solution must be found in terms of "the human element." Specifically, it is a task of public education in this era when customer demand for power markedly exceeds the deliverability capability of the electrical segment of the energy usage industry.

Do you ever stop to think, Miss Dodds, where the power comes from when you flick on your air-conditioner, your hair dryer, your cake mixer, your vacuum cleaner, and the myriad other appliances that enable you to live in "the lap of luxury" vs. the meager subsistence standard enjoyed by most of the peoples of the world? Until the American housewife is willing to go back to the egg beater and the broom, the utilities industry cannot be made the scapegoat for occasional episodes of ecological incompatibility.

Many consumers today advocate "zero growth" and a turning back of the clock to a simpler agrarian past. Quite frankly, if the rural American of 1900 had been as counter-oriented to the ongoing thrust of technology as certain romantic elements are in 1973, the outhouse would never have been supplanted by the flush toilet.

Very truly yours,

NORMAN R. HOWELL
Vice President for Consumer Relations
AFFILIATED UTILITIES COMPANY[14]

IV. Analyze the use of metaphor in the following passage, and comment on its effectiveness:

Academics, it has been said before, are very much like people who drive their cars by looking through their rear-view mirrors. Looking backward does offer certain satisfactions and provides splendid intellectual vistas, but it hardly brings into focus the best view of the road ahead. Academics may seem to bemoan the fact that the federals now hold the cards, and that they must do their bidding, however reluctantly. But the facts would appear to be otherwise: it is the federals who are at least trying to game-plan an extremely delicate future, while most academics remain on the sidelines, seized by fits of moral indignation about the felt deprivation of their intellectual autonomy. It would rarely occur to them that the federal planners would like nothing better than a showing of academia's own imaginative initiatives and social vision, if only they would gird themselves for that sort of resolve.[15]

V. Professor X describes himself as follows in a classified advertisement:

Sophisticated, debonair college prof., 35, recently divorced, with liberal values and classical tastes, seeks broadminded female companion for travel and cultural pursuits. Knowledge of vintage wines and modern verse desirable. Send photo. Box 307, NYR.

What do you think Professor X is really like? Write a paragraph describing him *vividly*, and then underline all the concrete diction you have used.

NOTES

1. Roy H. Copperud, *American Usage: The Consensus* (New York: Van Nostrand Reinhold, 1970), p. 97.
2. A. J. Liebling, *The Sweet Science* (New York: Viking, 1956), pp. 299–300.
3. James Herndon, *How to Survive in Your Native Land* (New York: Simon and Schuster, 1971), p. 122.
4. Norman Hackerman, "The Future of Graduate Education, If Any," *Science,* 175 (4 Feb. 1972), 475.
5. Frank Conroy, *Stop-time* (New York: Viking, 1967), pp. 114–115.
6. Talcott Parsons, "The Kinship System of the Contemporary United States," *Essays in Sociological Theory,* rev. ed. (1949, 1954; rpt. New York: Free Press, 1964), p. 191.
7. Ernest Hemingway, *A Moveable Feast* (1964; rpt. New York: Bantam, 1965), p. 3.
8. Norman Mailer, *Miami and the Siege of Chicago: An Informal History of the Republican and Democratic Conventions of 1968* (New York: Signet, 1968), pp. 11–12.
9. F. Scott Fitzgerald, *The Crack-up,* ed. Edmund Wilson (1945; rpt. New York: New Directions, 1956), p. 32.
10. Lewis M. Branscomb, "Taming Technology," *Science,* 171 (12 Mar. 1971), 973.
11. Constance Holden, "Community Mental Health Centers: Storefront Therapy and More," *Science,* 174 (17 Dec. 1971), 1221.
12. Greg Calvert and Carol Neiman, *A Disrupted History: The New Left and the New Capitalism* (New York: Random House, 1971), p. 8.
13. Charles McCabe, "Are We Wrong on Drugs?" San Francisco *Chronicle,* 18 May 1973, p. 41.
14. William Zinsser, "Frankly, Miss Dodds," *Atlantic,* Apr. 1973, p. 94.
15. G[eorge]. W. B[onham]., "The Decline of Initiative," *Change,* Apr. 1973, p. 16.

5 SEN-TENCES

"A sentence," wrote Henry Thoreau, "should read as if its author, had he held a plow instead of a pen, could have drawn a furrow deep and straight to the end." The image is memorable but not easily translated into practice, as Thoreau's own work reveals. *A Week on the Concord and Merrimack Rivers*, where this statement appears, is a peculiar example of verbal plowing, with more zigzags and arabesques than straight furrows. Thoreau's advice was probably directed at himself: he was trying to reform the bookish manner he had acquired at Harvard in the 1830's, and as yet he wasn't having much success. If he later became a master stylist, it wasn't simply by continual writing, but by progressively simplifying his prose—indulging in fewer quotations and reveries, exercising greater concreteness and sharper wit. Thoreau's sentences began approaching his ideal when he spoke directly to his countrymen instead of daydreaming in their presence.

Every student writer resembles the young Thoreau in one important way: he needs to fix a direction of improvement, a tendency that will run counter to his present weaknesses. Thoreau began with an affected, pretentious style and worked toward plainness; so should those students who write floridly. They ought to realize that a good sentence is an efficient act of communication and not just a gem on display. Some other students, however, write sentences that are too brief, with little or no subordination and a monotonous sameness of pattern from one sentence to the next. For these writers the direction of improvement should be toward greater complexity and flexibility.

Most of the things that can go wrong with sentences — blunders of "grammar" and spelling and punctuation, inappropriate word choices, illogic, vagueness, unfocused emotionalism — are treated in other chapters. There remains the general question of how you can *build* effective sentences by making real assertions, by placing emphasis where it's demanded by meaning, by being concise, and by striving for both variety and consistency. You will find that seemingly minor improvements — the moving of a clause from one position to another, a shift from the passive to the active voice, even a slight change in rhythm — can make the difference between drab sentences and pointed ones.

MEANINGFUL STATEMENT

Avoid Irrelevancy

A sentence is typically a single unified statement. Even if it consists of several independent parts linked by commas or semicolons, those parts ought to be logically related. Don't allow incompatible elements to weaken the whole:

- Computers, *whose memory capacity has been increasing rapidly in recent years*, would have had a major influence on the conduct of World War II if they had existed sooner.

The italicized clause has nothing to do with the point of the sentence; instead of simply registering that point, we have to juggle conflicting references to the 1940's and the 1970's. The sentence should be shortened and rearranged to bring out its conditional logic: *If computers had been available in time, they would have had a major influence on the conduct of World War II.*

Make Real Assertions

Try to avoid sentences that simply mark time between other statements, or that assert vague or self-evident truths:

- There are, of course, two sides to every question.
- It is interesting to consider this problem more closely.
- Let us remember that the full story won't be known until all the facts have been assembled.
- As inflation continues unchecked, prices are steadily rising.

Make every sentence count. "Filler" sentences naturally occur in first drafts as you feel your way toward meaning, but you should eliminate them after they've served their purpose.

Don't Hide Behind the Passive Voice

Passive verb forms (it *was done*) place emphasis on the action performed; *active* verb forms (he *did* it) distribute emphasis between the action and the performer. Both constructions have their place in good prose. The following sentence, for example, uses the passive for emphasis:

- The essential truth about Watergate *has been buried* under a mountain of incidental details.

The writer could as easily have said *A mountain of incidental details has buried the essential truth about Watergate*, but this would have been slightly less effective; he wanted to emphasize, not *what* has buried the truth, but *the fact that* it has been buried.

The passive, then, needs no apology when it expresses the writer's precise meaning. But habitual use of the passive is another matter. It makes for a colorless and sometimes ambiguous effect (see p. 202), and it disguises the relation between the doer and the thing done. This, in fact, is why the passive appears so often in bureaucratese (pp. 68–69). Those who don't want to accept responsibility for their actions or opinions have an intuitive fondness for the passive:

> Oil-storage depots and staging areas *were targeted* in today's limited sorties. Civilian zones *were* carefully *avoided*. Heavy antiaircraft and SAM missile reaction *was encountered* and appropriate countermeasures *were initiated*. Losses of aircraft and personnel, if any, *will be announced* at a subsequent briefing. From preliminary evaluation of photographic data it *is indicated* that thirty-four hostile bicycles and three Communist water buffalo *were rendered* inoperable.

Look over your own writing to see whether your passive constructions are defensible. Wherever the passive isn't conveying your meaning more accurately than the active would, you should abandon it.

Avoid Vague Predication

With few exceptions, every sentence has at least one *subject* and *predicate*—that is, something *spoken about* (the subject) and something that is *said about it* (the predicate):

	SUBJECT	PREDICATE
•	President Johnson	disliked his portrait.

	SUBJECT	PREDICATE
•	It	was, in his opinion, "the ugliest thing I ever saw."

	PREDICATE	SUBJECT	PREDICATE
•	Never had	he	seen anything that looked less like himself.

The predicate, as you can see, is the verb plus all its modifiers and complements.

Many "grammatical" sentences are weakened by a misalignment of meaning between the subject and predicate. This is especially likely to happen when the verb is a form of *to be*—when, that is, an equation is implied between the subject and a complement. Consider:

• The story of Joanna Burden, Joe Christmas, and Gail Hightower is one of the perils risked by those who defy the community's standards.

Here the subject, *story*, is equated with the complement, *perils*. Can a *story* be *perils?* Obviously not. The writer meant to say something like *The story . . . illustrates the perils . . .*

A related mistake occurs in this sentence:

• The meaning of *Light in August* deals with the lifelong psychological damage caused by racism.

The abstract subject, *meaning*, is said to *deal with* something. But again, can a *meaning deal?* No, it can only *be*. The writer could say *The meaning . . . is that . . .*, or, better:

• *Light in August* deals with the lifelong psychological damage caused by racism.

Alternatively:

• In *Light in August* Faulkner deals with the lifelong psychological damage caused by racism.

The same problem subtly undermines this sentence:

- The reason for legalizing marijuana is on the grounds of personal freedom.

This sounds almost right, but the predicate doesn't fulfill the promise of the subject, *reason*. If you say *The reason . . . is*, you have to state the reason directly, as in *The reason . . . is that the laws against marijuana violate personal freedom*. Otherwise you could say *The case for legalizing marijuana rests on the grounds of personal freedom*.

Sometimes the mismatch is contained entirely within the predicate:

- Those sadistic dog trainers have changed the qualities that made the dog "man's best friend" into a demon.

(Can *qualities* be changed into a *demon?* In order to bring his sentence into focus the writer would have to drop *the qualities that made*.)

Always reread your own sentences to make sure you haven't fallen into such awkwardness.

SUBORDINATION

Subordination, the placing of certain elements in modifying roles, is a fundamental principle of writing. Adjectives and adverbs, phrases of all types, and subordinate clauses all serve to specify or qualify words that have greater importance. There are, to be sure, ways of making a technically subordinate element more prominent than anything else in its sentence, but in general, subordination is the main device for indicating the difference between major and minor emphasis.

Subordinate to Avoid Monotony

Although it's impossible to write without using some degree of subordination, many students rely excessively on independent clauses to carry their meaning. The near-absence of modifying clauses and phrases gives their prose a clumsy, staccato effect, as if they were grudgingly answering questions instead of pursuing their thoughts. Compare these passages:

A. The AFL under George Meany has been accused of favoring an aggressive foreign policy. The accusation is entirely justified. But critics may not realize that there is nothing new about this. The first president of the AFL, Samuel Gompers, advocated American expansionism. Labor has tended to suffer under peacetime administrations and to prosper under wartime ones. Leaders of the AFL don't like to point this out in so many words. But they have consistently advocated a pugnacious American stand toward rival nations. They have probably been motivated by self-interest.

B. Although the AFL under George Meany has been justly accused of favoring an aggressive foreign policy, this is no break with the past; the union has advocated expansionism since the days of its first president, Samuel Gompers. Labor has tended to suffer under peacetime administrations and to prosper under wartime ones. While AFL leaders don't like to point this out in so many words, it is clear that self-interest underlies their pugnacity toward America's rivals.

Passage A, containing one subordinate clause (*that there is nothing new about this*), takes seven rigid sentences to say what Passage B says in three supple ones. The entire second sentence of A has been condensed in B into one subordinate word, *justly*. Where Passage A leaves the reader to decide which statements have prime importance, Passage B saves its independent clauses for the major ideas. And note, above all, that the choppiness of A is remedied in B, where one brief and straightforward sentence "paces" two complicated ones.

Subordinate to Show Which Is the Main Statement

In a set of consecutive sentences, some remarks are bound to be subordinate in meaning to others. They should be made syntactically subordinate as well. Thus, in Passage B above, the words *Although* and *While* allow us to see at once that a limitation is to be placed on a more important part of the sentence; the subordination helps us to locate the main assertion without difficulty.

The following pairs of sentences illustrate some of the details and relations that typically (though not always) belong in subordinate constructions. The sentences in the right column are more precisely focused, sparing us the trouble of deciding which idea is the main one.

	without subordination	with subordination
Time	The earthquake struck, and then everyone panicked.	Everyone panicked *when* the earthquake struck.
Place	William Penn founded a city of brotherly love. He chose the juncture of the Delaware and Schuylkill Rivers.	*Where* the Schuylkill River joins the Delaware, William Penn founded a city of brotherly love.
Cause	She was terrified of large groups. Debating was not for her.	*Because* she was terrified of large groups, she decided against being a debater.
Concession	He claimed to despise Vermont. He went there every summer.	*Although* he claimed to despise Vermont, he went there every summer.
Condition	She probably won't be able to afford a waterbed. The marked retail prices are just too high.	*Unless* she can get a discount, she probably won't be able to afford a waterbed.
Exception	The grass is dangerously dry this year. Of course I'm not referring to watered lawns.	*Except for* watered lawns, the grass is dangerously dry this year.
Purpose	The Senators moved to Texas. They hoped to find more enthusiastic supporters there.	The Senators moved to Texas *in search of* more enthusiastic supporters.
Description	The late Edward Steichen showed his reverence for life in arranging the famous exhibit, "The Family of Man," and he was a pioneer photographer himself.	The late Edward Steichen, *himself a pioneer photographer*, showed his reverence for life in arranging the famous exhibit, "The Family of Man."

Subordinate to Break up Lengthy Compound Sentences

Some writers, anxious to avoid a string of brief, abrupt sentences, loop independent clauses together with coordinating conjunctions. But the result isn't much of an improvement:

- The right to secede is very dubious, *and* perhaps it shouldn't be considered a right at all, *for* it threatens the existing order, *and* that order grants the right in the first place.

Subordinate clauses or phrases offer a way of getting some life into such a gabby sentence:

- Perhaps the right to secede, *dubious at best*, shouldn't be considered a right at all. Can the existing order grant a right *that threatens its own existence?*

(One difficult sentence has become two clear ones, thanks largely to the use of subordination.)

Choose an Appropriate Means of Subordination

The several means of subordination carry different degrees of emphasis:

1. Clauses tend to be most emphatic. but wordier (p.98)
2. Phrases tend to be less emphatic.
3. Words tend to be least emphatic.

Thus:

- Premier Chou listened *politely* as the President explained how Chinese dinners leave people hungry a half-hour later.

(The single adverb is unemphatic.)

- Premier Chou listened *with studied politeness* as the President explained how Chinese dinners leave people hungry a half-hour later.

(Emphasis is gained through use of a prepositional phrase.)

- Premier Chou, *whose politeness never wavered*, listened as the President explained how Chinese dinners leave people hungry a half-hour later.

(The subordinate clause is still more emphatic.)

- Although he had to listen to the President explain how Chinese dinners leave people hungry a half-hour later, *Premier Chou never allowed his politeness to waver.*

(The writer has decided to make the subordinate element into his main statement; it has now become an independent clause.)

Place Subordinate Elements Where They Will Convey Your Exact Meaning

Native speakers usually have a good intuitive sense of where to place adjectives and most adverbs. But because adverbs are more flexible in position than adjectives, they sometimes get involved in problems of awkwardness and ambiguity. Shadings of meaning are controlled by the position of an adverb:

* *Only* I can understand your argument.   [No one else can.]
* I can *only* understand your argument.   [I can't agree with it.]
* I can understand *only* your argument.   [But not your motives; *or* The arguments of others mystify me.]

You can see that carelessness about placement of adverbs can give a sentence an unintended emphasis.

Although most adverbs belong immediately before the words they modify, emphasis and sentence rhythm may sometimes dictate other positions if there's no danger of ambiguity. The placement of *sentence adverbs*—conjunctive adverbs like *therefore* and *however*—is especially flexible. Unlike other adverbs, sentence adverbs place a stress on the words that immediately precede them:

* I, *however*, refuse to comply.   [I contrast myself with others.]
* I refuse, *however*, to comply.   [My refusal is emphatic.]

In the initial and final positions, sentence adverbs are less emphatic and more diffuse in effect:

* *However*, I refuse to comply.
* I refuse to comply, *however*.

(The final position is the least emphatic of all.)

Some authorities recommend that sentence adverbs never be used in the initial position, but most people ignore this supposed rule. What you must avoid is a monotonous, automatic choice. Put your adverbs where they'll convey the particular modifying effect and the degree of stress required by your meaning.

The same advice applies to larger subordinate elements as well. It isn't enough to avoid the outright blunders of misrelated and dangling modifiers (pp. 194–197) that can destroy whole sentences. You also have to consider which of two "correct" positions most clearly expresses your meaning. The following sentences make quite different assertions:

- He decided to resume his career as an FBI informer *when the war was over*.
- *When the war was over*, he decided to resume his career as an FBI informer.

(In the first sentence the decision is said to be taken during the war; in the second sentence the decision is said to be taken after the war was over.)

The position you assign your subordinate elements won't usually make such a fundamental change of meaning as this, but it will always contribute something to the way the sentence is understood. You can usually discover which positions are emphatic by reading a sentence over, trying each alternative in turn. When in doubt, remember that:

1. Subordinate elements tend to gain emphasis whenever they appear in unexpected positions:

- *With heroic determination* he continued to stay afloat.

2. Main elements are usually most emphatic at the end of a sentence:

- In spite of the apparent hopelessness of his situation, *he somehow knew he would be rescued.*

3. Main elements are least emphatic when they appear neither at the beginning nor at the end:

- In spite of the apparent hopelessness of his situation, *he knew he would be rescued*, without being able to say how he knew it.

The position you assign a subordinate element can make for a subtle difference of connotation. Compare these sentences:

- A. *Although Patsy still loves Paul*, she has finally asked him to choose between her and his set of electric trains.
- B. Patsy has finally asked Paul to choose between her and his set of electric trains, *although she still loves him.*

In A, the subordinate clause occupies a subordinate position; it qualifies a main statement that literally has the last word. In B, the main statement is weakened by being placed first and then chipped away by the *although* clause. Instead of feeling that Patsy has made her decision once and for all, we wonder whether she hasn't already begun to change her mind.

Avoid Competing Subordination

A sentence can contain many subordinate elements if each of them is doing its own distinct job of qualifying the main statement. But subordinate clauses sometimes crowd each other awkwardly. Look at the way the independent clause gets trapped between qualifications in this sentence:

- *Although he was reluctant to accuse Patsy of sabotage*, Paul wondered why his toy freight train had exploded, *because he hadn't even been playing "munitions shipment" at the time, although he did have some gunpowder in the basement.*

Even though the statement is clear, the competing subordination makes a cluttered effect.

COORDINATION

Coordination, the linking of equally weighted elements, shows up chiefly in series, in comparisons and contrasts, and in repeated words and phrases.

Coordinate to Show That Ideas Belong Together

Compare the following passages:

A. Animals think, but they think *of* and *at* things; men think primarily *about* things. Words, pictures, and memory images are symbols that may be combined and varied in a thousand ways.[1]

B. Animals think *of* things. They also think *at* things. Men think primarily *about* things. Words are symbols that may be combined in a thousand ways. They can also be varied in the same number of ways. This can be said of pictures as well. The same holds true for memory pictures.

Passage B is an attempt to convey the meaning of Passage A without recourse to coordination. Two sentences have become seven, thirty-one words have become fifty-one, yet the longer passage is much harder to understand than the shorter one. The reason is that B lacks A's signals of coordinate structure—signals that immediately show us which ideas belong together.

In A we have:

1. Coordinate clauses:

Animals think,
    but
they think *of* and *at* things

2. Coordinate halves of a sentence:

Animals think, but they think *of* and *at* things
    ;
men think primarily *about* things

3. Coordinate prepositions:

of
    and
at

4. Coordinate nouns in a series:

words,
pictures,
    and
memory images

5. Coordinate past participles:

combined
    and
varied

6. A repeated word:

think
think
think

Each of these instances of coordination serves the author's meaning by putting related thoughts into sentence positions that make the relation immediately clear.

Balanced structures are especially prominent in *aphorisms* — that is, in memorable sentences conveying a broad truth:

- What is *written without effort* is in general *read without pleasure*. (Samuel Johnson)
- We must indeed *all hang together*, or, most assuredly, we shall *all hang separately*. (Benjamin Franklin)
- Democracy substitutes *election by the incompetent many* for *appointment by the corrupt few*. (George Bernard Shaw)

(For correct and faulty ways of assembling parallel constructions, see pp. 205–207.)

Repeat Words, Phrases, and Constructions for Emphasis

A repeated sentence element always draws attention. If the repetition is rhetorically meaningless, it constitutes *redundancy*, a distracting failure to get ahead with the essay's business. But there are many opportunities in a typical essay for effectively pointed repetition. Thus in the following sentences, which abound with coordinating devices, the name *Ottawa* is artfully plucked out from other names:

> Perhaps a visitor cannot truly understand the country until he has traveled from the genteel poverty of the Atlantic coast with its picturesque fishing villages and stiff towns through the Frenchness of sophisticated Quebec cities and rural landscapes, past the vigorous bustling Ontario municipalities and industrial vistas, over mile after mile of wheat fields between prairie settlements into the lush and spacious beauty of British Columbia; but he must also visit *Ottawa* and the House of Commons. *Ottawa* the stuffy, with its dull-looking houses, its blistering summer heat, its gray rainy afternoons; *Ottawa* the beautiful, on a snowy day when the government buildings stand tall and protective, warmly solid above the white landscape; on a sunny spring afternoon with the cool river winding below, and people moving easily through the clean streets, purposeful but not pushed. Even during the morning and evening traffic rushes, *Ottawa* seems to remain sane [emphasis added].[2]

In the first sentence *Ottawa* belatedly emerges as the key name among several; it gains importance by being weighted singly against all the "travelogue" references before the semicolon. In the second sentence (or deliberate sentence fragment) the name is used insistently and fondly. And the author exploits this effect in her final sentence, using the name yet again to reinforce her idea that Ottawa stands apart from the rest of Canada. This, clearly, isn't redundancy but calculated and successful rhetoric.

In the following passage the rhetoric is that of a debater, not a scene-painter, but here too repetition is effective:

> Are we returning to more rigid controls because our recent experience demonstrates that they are an effective method of stopping inflation? Hardly. Consumer prices rose . . .

Are we returning to more rigid controls because other experience demonstrates that controls are an effective method of stopping inflation? Hardly. The standard life-history of controls — documented time and again — is initial apparent success . . .

Are we returning to more rigid controls because economic reasoning demonstrates that they are an effective method of stopping inflation? Hardly. A few economists — John Kenneth Galbraith is the most prominent — argue that they are. But for two centuries and more, most economists have regarded controls as an attack on symptoms, not causes . . .[3]

Here the author's repetitions are like the authoritative pounding of a fist on a table. His insistence may seem excessive, but in context, with full paragraphs between the question-answer pairs, the passage conveys a balance between indignation and logic, rhetorical challenge and hard evidence.

Make Your Series Consistent and Climactic

The usefulness of a series can be destroyed not only by faulty syntax (pp. 271–272), but also by the inclusion of inappropriate items, especially at the end. You don't want to write, for example, *She gathers pears, apples, and assorted fruits;* the third category, *fruits,* overlaps with the first two. Nor should you toss in items of markedly different importance:

• Travelers in this part of the country fall in love with *the fields of waving grain, the infinite sky,* and *the deluxe jumboburgers.*

Such effects of anticlimax are good for a laugh, but embarrassing if the laugh is unintended.

If you aren't aiming at a comic letdown, the most important item in your series should always come last:

• He was prepared to risk everything — *his comfort, his livelihood,* even *his life itself.*

(Put *his life itself* in either of the other positions in the series and you'll see how important a climactic order is.)

CONCISENESS

The fewer words you can use without sacrificing part of your meaning, the better chance you stand of being attentively read. This is partly a matter of avoiding circumlocutions (pp. 70–72), but there are other means of economizing as well. Often the most effective way to achieve conciseness is to demote a clause to a phrase, or a phrase to a word.

Look at the way this sentence drags along:

• At the present time, the realities of nuclear diplomacy are such that the strongest countries, when they face each other, find that their enormous power leaves them no opportunity to make use of that power.

This is competent writing, but it has no snap to it. The two *that* clauses are like layers of wrapping paper between us and the main idea. Stripping the sentence to its grammatical core, we find an empty statement:

SUBJECT   VERB   COMPLEMENT
• realities   are   such

Evidently the sentence's meaning and its syntax aren't very well aligned. Three subordinate clauses and three prepositional phrases, each with its tiny burden of meaning, are trying to say something that could be put into one prepositional phrase and one independent clause:

• In the age of nuclear diplomacy, mutual strength is mutual weakness.

Now the sentence's meaning and syntax are in harmony:

SUBJECT   VERB   COMPLEMENT
• strength   is   weakness

Notice how clauses and phrases have been dissolved into smaller elements. A whole clause, *when they face each other*, has become a single word, *mutual*, and the repetition of that word in a balanced construction—*mutual strength is mutual weakness*—produces an aphoristic quality of terse, condensed meaning.

VARIETY

No one sentence pattern is right for all occasions, and one sentence creates the expectations against which the next sentence will be heard. Thus if you follow one complex and taxing construction with another one, you're probably subtracting emphasis from both of them; your reader needs a little breathing space before he'll grant you another extraordinary effort of attention. You have to pace yourself, either by reading your prose and listening for the spots where more variety is needed, or, second best, by systematically checking to see that one sentence pattern isn't crowding out all others.

Break the Monopoly of Declarative Sentences

Nearly all the sentences in a typical essay will be declarative, but an occasional question or, less frequently, an exclamation can vary the pattern. (For the classification of sentences by purpose, see p. 166.) One standard way of organizing a paragraph is to open with a question and then to supply a detailed answer. Thus Rachel Carson asks, "Why does the spider mite appear to thrive on insecticides?"[4] There are, she says, three likely reasons, and she proceeds to spell them out. Here the question is simply a blunt way of letting the reader know what issue the paragraph will address. But precisely because the question is a standard opening device, you should be careful not to overuse it.

You can also resort to an occasional *rhetorical question*, one that requires no answer. Once again you should be wary of overuse, for rhetorical questions can sound melodramatic. But observe the sensitive use to which Jason Epstein puts such a question as he considers his involvement with New York City:

> In desperate fantasy one thinks, at times, of escaping. From childhood there remains a faint memory, nearly lost, of a stream in a Northern forest: a stone dam, a trickling sluice, a hut of some sort where the dam-keeper lives. The loon cries over a lake, the pines stretch endlessly, black against the sky. And then one thinks of *The New York Times* on Sunday, five pounds of newsprint, a million-and-a-half copies a week. How many miles of forest, birds flung from their nests, the work of honey bees wasted, does our Sunday paper, thrown aside between breakfast and lunch, consume?[5]

This passage starts to make a sardonic turn after the third sentence, and the question completes that turn by linking the two previous thoughts—the fantasy of a forest escape and the reality of the Sunday *Times*—in a dawning realization that New York is devouring nature itself. The paragraph might well have ended with an exclamation point instead of a question mark, but that would have expressed outrage rather than ironic reflection.

If you do use exclamations in your own writing, use them seldom and only at moments of climactic emphasis. You may want to show that a certain idea is exciting, but you don't want to sound like a person who is constantly getting upset.

Vary the Order and Complexity of Sentence Elements

We have already seen (pp. 88–94) that a lack of subordination is one of the most common weaknesses of style. In technical terms, this means that *simple* and *compound* sentences—those containing no subordinate clauses—too often prevail over *complex* and *compound-complex* sentences, which do contain at least one subordinate clause apiece. (For the classification of sentences by structure, see pp. 166–167.) Although relentless use of any one sentence type can get monotonous, the inherent flatness of simple and compound sentences makes them especially tedious when placed in a row. The obvious remedy is to revise toward complexity wherever the meaning allows it.

But the cure for flatness needn't always be a recourse to subordinate clauses. Any sentence element that interrupts the ordinary sequence of subject-verb-object/complement can be a useful instrument of variety. Look, for instance, at Jason Epstein's sentences on p. 99. They make an impression of great flexibility, yet they contain only one brief subordinate clause: *where the dam-keeper lives*. Their range comes rather from three things: variation in sentence length (from nine to thirty-one words), many pauses for modifying phrases and elements in series, and *inversion*, the reversal of normal order:

MODIFYING PHRASE	SUBJECT	VERB	
• In desperate fantasy	one	thinks	

MODIFYING PHRASE		VERB	SUBJECT
• From childhood	there	remains	a faint memory

By delaying the subject, inversion makes for a certain formality and tension; the more postponement and complexity we feel, the surer we are that everything will fall exactly into place. Because inversions make an extra demand on our intelligence and memory, however, they ought to be played off against more straightforward patterns.

Another way to get variety is to write an occasional *suspended* (sometimes called *periodic*) sentence, in which an essential element is withheld until the end. Suspended sentences generally require greater concentration to be understood; the reader has to keep the unfinished core of meaning in mind as he passes through secondary elements:

- How many miles of forest, birds flung from their nests, the work of honey bees wasted, does our Sunday paper, thrown aside between breakfast and lunch, consume?

Until we get that final verb, the whole sentence remains in limbo. Again, look at this suspended sentence by Virginia Woolf:

And, what was even more exciting, she felt, too, as she saw Mr. Ramsay bearing down and retreating, and Mrs. Ramsay sitting with James in the window and the cloud moving and the tree bending, how life, from being made up of little separate incidents which one lived one by one, became curled and whole like a wave which bore one up and threw one down with it, there, with a dash on the beach.[6]

Here the suspended construction is intimately related to the author's meaning. As perceptions coalesce for Woolf's artist-heroine, the sentence that describes them picks up one leisurely phrase after another, gathers momentum, and becomes itself a wave that crashes in its final words.

To get an effect of suspension you don't always have to write a strictly periodic sentence, with part of the main clause reserved until the very end. The following sentence by Vladimir Nabokov is "suspenseful" in the extreme, yet its main clause is completed fairly early:

And I catch myself thinking today that our long journey had only defiled with a sinuous trail of slime the lovely, trustful, dreamy, enormous country that by then, in retrospect, was no more to us than a collection of dog-eared maps, ruined tour books, old tires, and her sobs in the night—every night, every night—the moment I feigned sleep.[7]

Here again structure and meaning are in harmony. The confession of Nabokov's Humbert Humbert is, like his whole personality, ingeniously devious. Look, for instance, at the way the phrase *with a sinuous trail of slime* interrupts a verb and its object, and notice how long it takes Humbert to get around to mentioning Lolita's sobs—as if he preferred to fix his mind on the nonhuman details that come earlier in the series. The last interruption, *every night, every night,* conveys anguish and remorse, yet in Humbert's prose even remorse is expressed with high style.

Elaborately suspended sentences are usually ambitious, cumulative, conclusive flights of rhetoric. Obviously, then, you shouldn't write many of them in a row. Intricate sentences in general, whether or not they employ suspension, deserve to be relieved by relatively brief and straightforward ones. Woolf's sentence, for example, follows this one: *The sky stuck to them: the birds sang through them.* And Nabokov lays his groundwork with *We had been everywhere. We had really seen nothing.*

CONSISTENCY

As I indicated in discussing tone (pp. 5–9), a reader expects an essayist to remain himself and not keep trying on styles like so many coats from a rack. Your sentence-by-sentence variety should be a variety within consistency. Because this consistency necessarily differs for every writer, not much practical advice about acquiring it can be given. In studying the following examples, however, you can get some sense of the way a good essayist, no matter how many sentence patterns he uses, always makes an impression of wholeness, of one mind confronting reality in a characteristic way.

Look first at the coldly bitter prose of Imamu Amiri Baraka (LeRoi Jones):

> Being a writer does not necessarily mean that a man will be singular. There are more bad writers than bad atomic scientists. Being sensitive means primarily that you do not like to see lynchings. But the vacuum behind such a circumstance can be, and usually is, immense. Men like Baldwin and Abrahams want to live free from such "ugly" things because (they imply) they simply cannot stand what it does to men.
>
> FACT: There is a racial struggle.
>
> FACT: Any man had better realize what it means. Why there is one. It is the result of *more* than "misunderstanding." Money is not simply something one gets for publishing novels or selling paintings.
>
> FACT: "People should love each other" sounds like Riis Park at sundown. It has very little meaning to the world at large.[8]

This passage is full of apparent defects: the emphatic capitals, the belittling quotation marks, the sentence fragment (*Why there is one*), and the succession of brief, harsh, disconnected sentences. But is Baraka trying to write gracefully and not succeeding? On the contrary, he is insisting on plainness as an ideological matter, a repudiation of "sensitive" people like James Baldwin who, in his opinion, have no stomach for "FACTS." The ugliness of this prose is pointed: the sentences stand apart from one another like those unpleasant truths that novelists and painters had better start facing. Baraka sounds very much like Ralph Waldo Emerson, another essayist who knew exactly what he meant and said it in cryptic, unyielding statements.

For a more relaxed style, examine these sentences by Pauline Kael:

> What those who believe in the perennial greatness of the Western may not have caught on to is that the new big Western is, likely as not, a studio-set job. What makes it a "Western" is no longer the wide open spaces but the presence of men like John Wayne, James Stewart, Henry Fonda, Robert Mitchum, Kirk Douglas, and Burt Lancaster, grinning with their big new choppers, sucking their guts up into their chests, and hauling themselves onto horses. They are the heroes of a new Western mythology: stars who have aged in the business, who have survived and who go on dragging their world-famous, expensive carcasses through the same old motions. That is the essence of their heroism and their legend. The new Western is a joke and the stars play it for laughs, and the young film enthusiasts react to the heroes not because they represent the mythological heroes of the Old West but because they are mythological movie stars. . . .
>
> . . . Wayne has a beautiful horse in this one—but when he's hoisted onto it and you hear the thud, you don't know whether to feel sorrier for man or beast.[9]

Kael writes with the mildly slangy air of an insider who can set us straight about Hollywood; she holds out an implicit promise of transforming us from naive "film enthusiasts" into hardened sophisticates who can see "the business" for what it is. Accordingly, her sentences are distinguished by a crisp, purposeful air. Although some of them are rather long, they have none of the suspended reflectiveness of Woolf's and Nabokov's constructions. A phrase like *a studio-set job* deliberately breaks the mood of *the perennial greatness of the Western*, and the active participles *grinning, sucking, hauling,* and *dragging* keep reminding us of the meaty figures behind the screen images. There is plenty of variety to Kael's sentence patterns, but note the scarcity of qualifying phrases; except for *likely as not*, the author never interrupts herself to make small adjustments of meaning. The gross truth about the movies, she seems to say, requires no embellishment: take it or leave it.

Finally, this passage from Willie Morris's *Yazoo* can illustrate a more intricate style:

> The most terrible burden of the writer, the common burden that makes writers a fraternity in blood despite their seasonal expressions of malice, jealousy, antagonism, suspicion, rage, venom, perfidy, competition over the size of publishers' advances—that common burden is the burden of memory. It is an awesome weight, and if one isn't careful it can sometimes drive you quite mad. It comes during moments when one is half asleep, or after a reverie in the middle of the day, or in the stark waking hours: a remembrance of everything in the most acute detail from one's past, together with a fine sense of the nuances of old happenings and the most painful reconsideration of old mistakes, cruelties, embarrassments, and sufferings, and all this embroidered and buttressed by one of the deepest of urges, the urge to dramatize to yourself about yourself, which is the beginning of at least part of the urge to create.[10]

If we pause to study this passage we can find some questionable features. Words like *rage, venom, perfidy, awesome*, and *mad* border on the histrionic, and the repetitions—four *burdens* in one sentence and three *urges* in another—might be considered excessive. Putting items in series comes so naturally to Morris that it almost seems like a tic instead of a useful device. His syntax, again, is relentlessly complicated, with only a minor respite in the middle sentence. Yet these features do make a consistent, purposeful effect. The author's sentences are "burdened" as if to match his idea about the burden of memory, and if they just barely survive the load, that too seems to be part of the point. The passage is written confidently, even daringly, and its assurance is contagious.

As you can gather from comparing Baraka, Kael, and Morris, no rule adequately covers the practice of all good writers. An essayist uses sentence patterns not only to make a point, but to make it in a certain manner that amounts to a personal signature. How can you get such effects yourself? Simply by writing often enough, and carefully enough, to acquire your own way of presenting reality.

SOUND

Avoid Distracting Repetitions of Sound

Unless you're after some special effect, don't make your reader conscious of rhymes (*the side of the hide*) or alliteration (*pursuing particular purposes*) or repeated syllables (*apart from the apartment*). These snatches of poetry usually result from an unconscious attraction that words already chosen exert on subsequent choices. Having written *the degradation*, you automatically write *of the nation* because the *-ation* sound is in your head.

Abstract, Latinate words — the ones that usually end in *-al*, *-ity*, *-ation*, or *-otion* — are especially apt to make for redundancy of sound. In Talcott Parsons' sentences on p. 74, for example, *functional*, *essential*, *occupational*, and *institutional* are too alike, and so are *equality*, *opportunity*, and *mobility*.

Knowing that repeated sounds draw attention, you can sometimes use them deliberately, as Mark Twain did in referring to

* the calm confidence of a Christian with four aces,

or as Thomas Paine did in writing

* These are the *times* that *try* men's souls,

or as Theodore Roosevelt did in advising his countrymen to

* Speak softly and carry a big stick.

In these examples the "poetic" quality goes along with a studied attempt to be aphoristic, to "make a phrase." What you must avoid is repetition that makes your words stand out for no apparent reason.

Listen for Sentence Rhythm

Without consciously realizing it, readers will be listening to your prose with what Robert Frost called the audial imagination. There is, as Frost perceived, a "sentence sound," or rather many sentence sounds, whose patterns are deeply fixed in our minds. "You may string words together without a sentence sound to string them on," Frost remarked, "just as you may tie clothes together by the sleeve and stretch them without a clothesline between two trees, but — it is bad for the clothes."[11]

The words in a "sleeve-tied" sentence pull against each other discordantly and oppressively. For instance:

- The subject of rhythm in speech or writing is one of those subjects which deal with complex sets of interrelationships between multiple but not altogether specifiable variables such as rise-fall patterns and the like, which makes it a sea-to-wave and wave-to-wave kind of thing.

There is a near-absence of significant pauses here; we have to plod ahead two or three words at a time, trying not to become dizzy. All the nouns, furthermore, have about the same degree of stress on their accented syllables, and there is no dramatic play between tight, emphatic phrases and phrases that are more extended. Read the sentence aloud and you'll hear its monotony.

Now compare this with the actual words of H. W. Fowler:

> Rhythmic speech or writing is like waves of the sea, moving onward with alternating rise and fall, connected yet separate, like but different, suggestive of some law, too complex for analysis or statement, controlling the relations between wave and wave, waves and sea, phrase and phrase, phrases and speech.[12]

Although the structure of this sentence is complex, we grasp it without much difficulty as it proceeds. Fowler's commas are like architectural supports that spare us the necessity of trying to carry the weight of the whole sentence at once. We see that one main clause is going to govern a sequence of phrases that will nudge us along *like waves of the sea*, and our voice pauses naturally on accented syllables: *like wavés of the séa, móving ónward*. These long, heavily stressed vowels make a pleasing contrast with harsher, more staccato phrases like *Rhýthmic spéech or wríting*. Fowler has illustrated his principle of complex relationship in the act of naming it—as, for example, in his "like but different" sets of three-word phrases:

- connected yet separate, like but different
- waves and sea, phrase and phrase, phrases and speech.

To return from Fowler's example to the first one is like going from navigation to seasickness.

For a quite different use of "sentence sounds," listen closely to this paragraph of Peter Matthiessen's about the Kilimanjaro area of East Africa. Matthiessen, in search of "the tree where man was born," comes across Maasai herdsmen at a pool:

> By the water's edge man squatted, worn rags pulled low over his brow against the sun. Manure smell, flies, the stamp and lowing of the herds, the heat. In the shallows a naked dancing boy darted and splashed. Then cloud shadow dimmed the water shine on his round head, and he turned black. In foreboding he paused; the water stilled,

and clouds gathered in the water. He picked at his thin body, one-legged in the evanescent pool that will vanish in summer like the haze of green on this burning land.[13]

This prose gains some of its force from a bunching of strongly accented syllables:

- wáter's édge mán squátted, wórn rágs púlled lów
- Manúre sméll, flíes, the stámp and lówing of the hérds, the héat
- a náked dáncing bóy dárted and spláshed
- Thén clóud shádow dimmed the wáter shíne on his roúnd heád, and he túrned bláck
- the wáter stílled, and cloúds gáthered in the wáter
- He picked at his thin bódy, one-légged in the evanéscent póol . . .

The jolting rhythm, accentuated by the shackled nouns *Manure smell*, *cloud shadow*, and *water shine*, is subtly loosened in the final clause, which comes closer to regular meter — that is, to an alternation of accented and unaccented syllables:

- that will vánish in súmmer like the háze of gréen on this búrning lánd.

Thus the paragraph as a whole accumulates tension and releases it like rain after thunder. The controlled uneasiness of Matthiessen's prose matches the vague ominousness of the scene: human life is precarious in this setting, and any change of weather seems to bear a threat of extinction.

The lesson here is that in reading and writing you should use your ears as well as your brain. The principles that go to make up a pleasing rhythm are too complex even to formulate, much less to turn into advice; but by reading good stylists you can pick up a general feeling for graceful and emphatic cadences.

EXERCISES

I. Each of the following sentences illustrates at least one weakness discussed in this chapter. Rewrite each sentence to remove the problem or problems.

1. There has been a strong reaction against science recently, and it probably has to do with some negative by-products of technology, and another reason may be the renewed quest for religious certainty.
2. The speaker, who wore a conservative blue suit, never did get around to saying what he meant by his title.

3. There is, in the history of American painting, one fact that is very interesting to note, and I am referring to the way in which American artists were extremely slow to develop anything that might remotely be characterized as a native style.

4. The motive for her visit dealt with a wish to see her father one last time.

5. At this point in time I think it would be useful to pause, stand back, and reflect that every problem has, as it were, two sides, and that, having examined one side of the problem under review, we might well turn our attention now to the other side of the problem.

6. Because the real-estate prices and taxes are high in this county, very few working-class people live here, since it would be hard for them to find property they could afford.

7. The explanation for her lateness was the time she spent in a traffic jam on the bridge.

8. Our conservation group has the purpose of maintaining a surplus of porpoises.

9. This plan is a tragedy for the country, an unprecedented catastrophe for the entire civilized world, and a disgrace to the party.

II. This passage lacks adequate subordination. Rewrite it, subordinating minor elements for emphasis and variety. You can merge sentences if necessary.

Hippocrates used garlic as a pharmaceutical. He used it to treat different diseases, and so did other early doctors. They believed that a plant or herb had a very penetrating odor so it must have a lot of therapeutic value. Tuberculosis and leprosy are not at all alike but garlic was used to treat both of them. There was a Roman naturalist named Pliny. He listed sixty-one diseases; garlic was supposed to cure them all. And he added the information that garlic has very powerful properties and you can tell this because serpents and scorpions are driven away by the very smell of it.

But don't think that only the ancients had such primitive notions. Some people today are just as sanguine. In the United States, garlic pills are sold in health-food stores, and they are supposed to have a salutary effect on arthritis. The pills have no medical sanction whatsoever. Afflicted Americans continue to buy them by the thousands. And the Russians are not above such medical hocus-pocus. A Soviet Union dispatch of April 4, 1965 shows this. Russian newspapers advised their readers to munch raw garlic so they would have a safeguard against contagion during an influenza epidemic. The epidemic was raging there at the time. There is no medical basis for eating garlic as a flu preventative—this is what most reputable doctors say—but they half seriously admit garlic's value. It forces people to keep their distance. This lessens the possibility of contagion.[14]

III. Write a paragraph or two analyzing the use of coordination in the passage by George Orwell on p. 49.

IV. The following passage lacks adequate sentence variety. Rewrite it to correct this weakness.

> Senator—now President—John F. Kennedy campaigned across West Virginia in the 1960 preferential primary. He saw at first hand the conditions existing in the coalfields of that state. The spectacle of mass misery and of mass surrender to it appears to have deeply impressed him. I say this because in the general election campaign he repeatedly referred to the hunger and depression he had seen there. West Virginia is not far from the great population centers of the Eastern seaboard where Mr. Kennedy grew up. It may be a cause for wonder that this inquisitive and well-educated young man could have been unaware of the deplorable situation in which the West Virginia highlander finds himself in the seventh decade of the twentieth century. The fact is that a million Americans in the Southern Appalachians live today in conditions of squalor, ignorance, and ill health. Those conditions could scarcely be equaled in Europe or Japan or perhaps in parts of mainland Asia.[15]

V. Copy out a few sentences by Baraka (p. 102) and a few by Morris (p. 104), and mark the heavily stressed syllables ('). Briefly discuss how each author's rhythm serves his mood and statement.

VI. Find a paragraph in your campus newspaper that looks deficient in several of the elements of effective sentence structure. Rewrite the paragraph and comment on the relevant differences between the two versions.

NOTES

1. Susanne K. Langer, "The Lord of Creation," *Fortune*, Jan. 1944, p. 140.
2. Edith Iglauer, "The Strangers Next Door," *Atlantic*, July 1973, p. 90.
3. Milton Friedman, "Monumental Folly," *Newsweek*, 25 June 1973, p. 64.
4. Rachel Carson, *Silent Spring* (1962; rpt. Greenwich, Conn.: Fawcett, n.d.), p. 224.
5. Jason Epstein, "Living in New York," *New York Review of Books*, 6 Jan. 1966, p. 15.
6. Virginia Woolf, *To the Lighthouse* (1927; rpt. New York: Harvest, 1955), p. 73.
7. Vladimir Nabokov, *Lolita* (1955; rpt. New York: Berkley, 1966), p. 160.
8. LeRoi Jones, *Home: Social Essays* (New York: Apollo, 1966), pp. 118–119.
9. Pauline Kael, *Kiss Kiss Bang Bang* (1968; rpt. New York: Bantam, 1969), pp. 53, 57.
10. Willie Morris, *Yazoo: Integration in a Deep-Southern Town* (1971; rpt. New York: Ballantine, 1972), p. 9.

11. Quoted by Lawrance Thompson, *Robert Frost: The Early Years 1874–1915* (New York: Holt, 1966), p. 434.

12. H. W. Fowler, *A Dictionary of Modern English Usage* (1926; rpt. n.p.: Oxford Univ. Press, 1937), p. 504.

13. Peter Matthiessen, *The Tree Where Man Was Born* (New York: Dutton, 1972), p. 193.

14. Adapted from Michael Field, *All Manner of Food* (New York: Knopf, 1970), pp. 4–5.

15. Adapted from Harry M. Caudill, *Night Comes to the Cumberlands* (Boston: Atlantic Monthly Press, 1963), p. xi.

PARA-GRAPHS

6

The most important unit of meaning in every essay is the paragraph. Sentences convey thoughts, of course, but an essay isn't a sequence of, say, eighty separate thoughts; it's rather a development of one central idea through certain steps. Those steps are paragraphs. Within an effective paragraph you'll find that the sentences support and combine with one another in various ways, making a single, complex, unfolding idea.

A writer who works from an outline will generally devote paragraphs to each of his outline subheadings (pp. 26–30). But this needn't always be the case. A paragraph is a unit of attention as well as a unit of meaning; it contains a certain amount of material that the reader is supposedly able to read and digest comfortably with one continuous effort. Instead of mechanically dividing the essay into paragraphs corresponding to outline categories, a good writer forms new units wherever he senses that major pauses are needed. In other words, he knows where he's going but he doesn't know exactly how many stops there will be along the way. One par-

112

agraph may cover several subheadings, or conversely, a subheading may require such intricate development that it requires more than one paragraph.

THE MANY USES OF THE PARAGRAPH

a paragraph can:

announce the topic
anticipate misunderstandings and objections
define a term
isolate a problem
solve a problem
launch a generalization
test a hypothesis
explain a cause
compare and contrast
raise an objection
concede a limitation
supply evidence
analyze a passage
give an illustration
tell a story
draw an analogy
describe something
announce a key transition
call for action
recapitulate and emphasize

In order to cover such a wide range of functions, paragraphs have to be flexible in length, in complexity, and in the degree of emphasis they carry. There are, however, certain general rules that can help you suit each paragraph to its purpose:

UNITY AND EMPHASIS

Pursue One Main Idea

A paragraph can, and usually should, contain sentences that *qualify* its central idea, but it should have no sentences that *stand apart* from that idea. Examine this well-organized (if notably dated) paragraph:

(1) Harry Robbins Haldeman is, as he once cheerfully put it, Richard Nixon's son of a bitch. (2) He sits 100 gold-carpeted feet down the hall from the Oval Office, glowering out at the world from under a

crew cut that would flatter a drill instructor, with a gaze that would freeze Medusa. (3) He is neither quite so forbidding as he looks nor quite so fierce as his reputation as the keystone of a Berlin wall around Mr. Nixon; he even has a sense of humor, about subjects other than the boss. (4) But he is the man who says No for the President of the United States, a mission he executes with a singleness of purpose and an authority that are respected — and feared — throughout official Washington. (5) "Bob Haldeman is probably the most powerful man in the country next to the President," says one ex-colleague — and he got that way because he spends more time next to the President than anybody else in government.[1]

Here the opening sentence clearly states the paragraph's main idea, which is that Haldeman is tough on behalf of the President. The other four sentences all bear directly on this assertion:

1. Haldeman is	TOUGH	ON BEHALF OF THE PRESIDENT
2. He is		close to the President
He is	fierce in aspect	
3. He is	not as fierce as he looks	
He even has	a sense of humor about subjects	other than the President
4. But he	says no	for the President
And he	does this with a respected purpose and authority	
5. He has	power	second only to the President's
And he got it by		being closer to the President than anyone else

(Suppose the paragraph had contained a further sentence: *Like another of the President's close advisers, Haldeman has a degree from UCLA.* This would have constituted a violation of paragraph unity.)

Be ruthless about keeping irrelevant material out of your paragraphs. No matter how interesting a statement may be, it will damage the whole paragraph if it doesn't advance or qualify the one central point.

The traditional way of ensuring unity is to see that each paragraph contains a *topic sentence* (sometimes called *thesis sentence*). Like the opening sentence of the sample paragraph above, the topic sentence plainly states the leading idea, showing both the reader and the writer himself what the whole paragraph ought to be about. The test for unity then becomes whether each subordinate sentence is adequately related to this main one. In a tightly organized, logical argument, the topic sentences of all the paragraphs sum up the writer's case, and a reader who scans those sentences can see at once where the essay is headed.

But you needn't become a fanatic about the topic sentence. In narrative and descriptive essays, where the logical subordination of elements isn't always apparent, topic sentences tend to be inconspicuous and sometimes completely missing. Some paragraphs, like this description of a rock dance by Albert Goldman, gain their unity from presenting one continuous experience and the reflections that follow from it:

> Magnetized by the crowd, impelled by the relentless pounding beat of the music, one is then drawn out on the floor. Here there is a feeling of total immersion: one is inside the mob, inside the skull, inside the music, which comes from all sides, buffeting the dancers like a powerful surf. Strangest of all, in the midst of this frantic activity, one soon feels supremely alone; and this aloneness produces a giddy sense of freedom, even of exultation. At last one is free to move and act and mime the secret motions of his mind. Everywhere about him are people focused deep within themselves, working to bring to the surfaces of their bodies their deep-seated erotic fantasies. Their faces are drugged, their heads thrown back, their limbs extended, their bodies dissolving into the arcs of the dance. The erotic intensity becomes so great that one wonders what sustains the frail partition of reserve that prevents the final spilling of this endlessly incited energy.[2]

This paragraph subjects us to the author's "total immersion" while we feel what he wants us to. It would have been much less engaging if he had thought his job was to present a thesis and defend it with arguments and examples. A paragraph must first of all be interesting, and any formal order gained at the expense of liveliness is a bad bargain.

Even in exposition and argument, you will occasionally find a good paragraph that deviates from the topic-sentence rule. Look ahead, for instance, to Alix Kates Shulman's paragraph on p. 127. The opening sentence seems to be a topic sentence for the whole, but the paragraph slips away and makes a strong, independent statement at the end. Shulman's paragraph has unity, not because it's a model of subordination, but because its thoughts simply fit well together as they develop.

If lack of unity were the only problem a writer of paragraphs had to watch out for, it could always be handled in revision. But real first-draft paragraphs usually call for so much sentence-by-sentence rewriting that a disunity of idea can pass unnoticed. Here, for instance, is a first-draft paragraph that you can recognize as faulty in various ways:

I don't believe that Christian civilization has succeeded because of all the wars we still have. This is my conclusion, and I think it is justified by a lot of evidence, but some people might disagree with it anyway. Since I want to convince everybody, I am going to set forth my reasons in detail, because otherwise some people might still disagree. This is why this paper is going to emphasize the mass murders, the witch trials, and the intolerance that completely and totally dominate the record of a religion of this type. In his book *The Pursuit of the Millennium* the author, Norman Cohn, gives many examples of the sort of behavior to which I am referring, but this tome unfortunately didn't discuss the wars alluded to in the first sentence of this paragraph.

In order to strengthen his individual sentences, this writer would have to work on such problems as faulty subordination, redundancy, circumlocution, and confusion of tenses. Yet if all the problems were solved the paragraph would still be flawed. In the first place, the writer hasn't made up his mind why he rejects Christian civilization. Is it because of "all the *wars* we *still* have" or is it because of "the mass murders, the witch trials, and the intolerance" of the *past?* The two reasons are compatible, of course, but the writer hasn't yet recognized that they *are* two reasons, and so he sends his paragraph off in two directions at once. And second, the paragraph trails away in its final sentence. The writer probably meant to say that *The Pursuit of the Millennium*, though it doesn't discuss the present age, corroborates his own idea about Christian barbarity. Instead, however, he seems to be adding an irrelevant criticism of the book, and we feel a loss of what little coherence the paragraph had mustered. The moral here is that disunity is the *first* problem to look for, before you waste any time improving sentences that don't belong in the paragraph at all.

Place the Main Idea Emphatically

Most paragraphs do contain topic sentences (p. 114), and most of these come right at the beginning. By placing the topic sentence first, a writer lets the reader see where he is going and what the logical function of the remaining sentences will be: all of them will either limit or defend the initial statement. There is no better way of ensuring that the essay's structure will be clear.

In some paragraphs, however, the topic sentence comes second, after a transitional, "tugboat" sentence that maneuvers the previous paragraph into a new alignment:

The statistics, then, paint a depressing picture. *Yet if we set aside the government reports and take the trouble to interview farm workers one by one, we find an astounding degree of confidence in the future. . . .*

This is still an emphatic position. Indeed, any position can become emphatic if you make a sharp, conspicuous turn as you begin the topic sentence; you can even build a paragraph inductively, taking the reader through a set of particulars and then presenting the conclusion that follows from them.

ADVANCING THE ARGUMENT

Write in Paragraph Blocks

A well-organized essay typically develops, not simply paragraph by paragraph, but in groups of paragraphs that address major points. Just as each paragraph usually has one primary sentence and an array of supporting ones, so the paragraph block has a "thesis" paragraph and one or more contributory ones. Subordination, in short, is just as important in the succession of paragraphs as it is in sentence structure (pp. 88–94). The following excerpt from a graduate student's paper about the English novelist E. M. Forster gives an indication of the way paragraphs of general assertion can be played off against paragraphs of evidence:

(1) Despite his general liberalism and tolerance, and despite his explicit support of women's rights, E. M. Forster allows a deep resentment of the female sex to pervade his novels. Most of his women are not the benign creatures that the critics speak of, but outright troublemakers who injure the major characters — usually men. Nearly every novel contains what I call a "crisis of chivalry," a situation in which the men are required to protect or defend women, and this crisis triggers the downfall of the male protagonist. One could say, of course, that the code of chivalry rather than womankind is to blame, but this doesn't work out in practice. The truth is that Forster was rarely capable of portraying a sympathetic female character, and that he regarded the chivalric code as rooted in female weakness and malice.

(2) Perhaps the best-known of Forster's "crises of chivalry" is the scene in *A Passage to India* in which Fielding rescues Adela from the angry crowd that awaits her after Aziz's trial. Fielding must stay beside Adela because of the chivalric demand that men protect women from violence, but in so doing he loses his friend Aziz and misses

their victory celebration. Aziz is offended by Fielding's absence, and from that point on their friendship (the most valued relationship in the novel) is spoiled by resentment and suspicion. Adela is regarded as the cause of all this; both Fielding and the narrator talk as if she were to blame for needing Fielding's protection in the first place.

(3) This note of blame directed at women is struck by comparable episodes in the other novels. In *Where Angels Fear to Tread*, the hero, Philip Herriton, is thwarted in his attempt to enjoy Italy and the comradeship of the engaging Italian, Gino, by his obligations to women. Here the "crisis of chivalry" is Philip's effort to rescue his sister-in-law, Lilia, from the hands of Gino, who is suspected of wanting to marry her for her money. Philip would like to befriend Gino, but his artificial role as Lilia's "protector" forces him to act as Gino's antagonist, and indeed as the antagonist of all that is human and appealing in Italy.

(4) Lucy Honeychurch is the young lady who needs protection in *A Room With a View*, and the necessity of her being kept away from George Emerson, who has been cast in the role of "seducer" by Lucy's puritanical female chaperone, prevents the friendship of George and Lucy's brother, Freddy. In *Howards End* the consequences of chivalrous behavior are disastrous in the extreme. Helen is the wronged maiden whose seduction by Leonard Bast must be avenged, and the crisis occurs when Charles Wilcox confronts Leonard and strikes him down with a sword. The consequences are that Leonard dies, Charles is imprisoned, and Henry Wilcox collapses—bringing the whole Wilcox family down with him. What this shows is that female mischief causes male disaster.

(5) Thus there is a contradiction, and a deep one, in Forster's treatment of women. In simple terms it is the contradiction between his advocating greater freedom for women and his "demonstration" that women aren't deserving of such freedom. In a more sophisticated sense, it is the incompatibility of Forster's *asserting*, in his theoretical passages, that the chivalrous mentality should be eliminated for the sake of the women whom it oppresses, and his *showing*, through the operation of his plots, that it should be eliminated for the sake of men, who are its real victims.

Here paragraph 1 states a thesis, paragraphs 2–4 support it with evidence, and paragraph 5 recapitulates, bringing the whole issue into sharper focus. Whether or not we agree with the argument, we appreciate the author's sense of proportion and command of facts. If each paragraph had asserted a new general idea and tried to defend it, the effect would have been weaker.

Don't Waste Full Paragraphs on Transitions

If your essay contains two large paragraph blocks in a row, and if you sense that you may be overtaxing the reader's patience and memory, you can separate the blocks with a brief paragraph of orientation:

> And now what has all this to do with the Dickens we already know? Why should he have occupied the last years of his life in concocting this sinister detective story?[3]

These sentences could easily have formed the opening of a larger paragraph, but the writer felt that a pause was needed between major parts of his essay.

As a rule, however, it's unwise to call much attention to the total design of your essay. The ideal is to keep the reader's interest focused on your argument, not on your problems of organization. Instead of forever promising what's to come and referring to what's just been proved, give each point the emphasis and position it deserves, and allow the reader to feel—not be told—that no step has been omitted. Full paragraphs that do nothing but announce how far the essay has come and where it will now be headed tend to produce more annoyance than gratitude.

Some good writers, I grant, violate this principle from time to time, but they sacrifice liveliness of tone when they do so. Judge for yourself, for example, whether the following paragraph—already considerably shortened from its first published version—sustains your interest:

> I have not put forward the matter of our culture's adverse opinion of narration in order to deal with it as in itself it deserves to be dealt with, but only to exemplify the kind of cultural phenomena which might properly come within our purview. But now that it is before us, it may appropriately be made to serve a further purpose, that of introducing a large and difficult subject—the ideal of authenticity as it relates to the modern theory of the mind, and in particular to that concept which is definitive of modern psychological theory, the unconscious.[4]

The author is an eminent man, and his topic is large and awesomely abstract; his paragraph does convey the weightiness of his task. The question, however, is whether or not he is losing momentum here. Our attention is drawn, not to his message, but to his effort to make a major transition look more casual than it is. He didn't raise an issue for one purpose. Do we care? The paragraph is like a tugboat maneuvering a gigantic ship into deep water. What we want is not this strenuous nudging and pulling, but a sense of the voyage itself.

CONTINUITY

Link Your Sentences Within Each Paragraph

A paragraph, for all its possible complexity, should make a single impression of developing thought. Its sentences should not only *be* related; they should also *feel* related. Most of those sentences ought to contain signals of *identity* or *transition* or both, so that a reader can easily see the kind of relation that's implied between one statement and its predecessor. The terms of identity assert that something already treated is still under discussion; the transitional words assert that the previous statement will be expanded or qualified in some way.

The signals of *identity* are chiefly *pronouns, demonstrative adjectives, repeated words and phrases*, and *omissions* that are understandable in the light of a previous sentence.

PRONOUNS:
* In the third round Miller sustained his precarious one-stroke lead. *He* teed off on Sunday knowing that eleven endorsement contracts hung in the balance.

DEMONSTRATIVE ADJECTIVES:
* The whole football team showed a significant improvement in reading and arithmetic scores. *This* result came as a surprise to everyone but the coach, who had volunteered to do the grading.

REPEATED WORDS AND PHRASES:
* Mayor Bradley's foremost concern is with rapid transit. It is a *concern* that is bound to be shared by those citizens who are not already asphyxiated.

OMISSIONS:
* The treaty placing a limited ban on nuclear tests has now been signed by 119 nations. More than a hundred [*nations*], including Togo and Burundi, have also subscribed to a nonproliferation treaty.

(For other examples of rhetorical identity, review the examples on pp. 96 – 97.)

The signals of *transition* consist of all the words and phrases that show *how* a statement will be built on the previous one. The types of transition, with a few examples of each type, are:

CONSEQUENCE:
* therefore, then, thus, hence, accordingly, as a result

LIKENESS:
* likewise, similarly

CONTRAST:
* but, however, nevertheless, on the contrary, on the other hand, yet

AMPLIFICATION:
* and, again, in addition, further, furthermore, moreover, also, too

EXAMPLE:
* for instance, for example

CONCESSION:
* to be sure, granted, of course, it is true

INSISTENCE:
* anyway, indeed, in fact, yes, no

SEQUENCE:
* first, second, finally

RESTATEMENT:
* that is, in other words, in simpler terms, to put it differently

RECAPITULATION:
* in conclusion, all in all, to summarize, altogether

TIME OR PLACE:
* afterward, later, earlier, formerly, elsewhere, here, there, hitherto, sub-
  sequently, at the same time, simultaneously, above, below, farther on,
  this time, so far, until now

Such signals shouldn't occur with great frequency, but they ought
to appear wherever the relation between two sentences wouldn't be
immediately clear without them. The following paragraph, which
isn't difficult to follow, "coasts" between its four (capitalized)
marks of transition:

I have little hope that my plea for patriotism will succeed, and much
anxiety that it will be heard by many as fatuous or wrong-headed.
Citizens would not need the argument, and noncitizens probably cannot hear it. STILL, I shall make the argument. I do so partly out of
blockheadedness, partly out of a wish to repay a welcome debt to
patriotic predecessors and contemporaries, and partly for two reasons
that might carry more weight. The FIRST REASON stems from my
affection and respect for fellow-citizens, and from my wish to see them
even more respectable than they are. We have lost patriotism. Although many count the loss small, and many others do not know it
has occurred, I believe that the loss is great. The SECOND REASON
stems from my wish to see a revitalized radical politics in this country,
and from my conviction that Susan Sontag is correct when she says
that "probably no serious radical movement has any future in America
unless it can revalidate the tarnished idea of patriotism." The radicals
of the 1960s did not persuade their fellow-Americans, high or low, that
they genuinely cared for and shared a country with them. AND no
one who has contempt for others can hope to teach those others. A

revived radicalism must be a patriotic radicalism. It must share and care for the common things, even while it has a "lover's quarrel" with fellow-citizens.[5]

In a well-constructed paragraph, marks of identity and transition tend to appear without any conscious design on the writer's part. If you keep a feeling for what your reader knows and needs to learn, the connective signals will usually fall where they belong. In rereading, however, you may find that you've neglected to reveal the linkage between certain pivotal sentences. Ask yourself what logical step has been taken without sufficient notice, and supply the word or phrase that will keep your sentences flowing.

Link One Paragraph to the Next

Most of your paragraphs ought to begin with sentences containing at least one indication of continuity with the foregoing paragraph. Exactly the same devices that make for internal paragraph unity can be called upon to hook one paragraph into the next one. In an essay by Lewis Mumford, for example, some paragraphs begin as follows:

- But at present these happy prospects are heavily overcast . . . [*But* and *these* show transition and identity].
- I shall not end on this negative note; but it is necessary . . . [*this* and *but* show identity and transition].
- But we are in the midst of other explosions . . . that will be just as fatal as long as they go in the present fashion . . . [*But* and *other* show transition; *the present* shows identity].
- Closer comparisons make our own achievements seem even more destitute . . . [*Closer* and *even more* show transition].
- Some of this attitude is doubtless left over from pioneer days . . . [*this* shows identity].
- I have of course intentionally, and doubtless grossly, caricatured the life of the representative American today . . . [the whole statement explicitly announces a transition].[6]

As in the case of individual sentences, a paragraph opener whose continuity is immediately apparent needn't spell out the connection. But the lesson, once again, is that you should extend your hand to the reader wherever you think he might stumble.

VARIETY

Vary the Length of Your Paragraphs

Paragraph length is partly a matter of convention and partly a matter of style. In newspaper reporting, where the main purpose is to communicate bits of information with a minimum of analysis, paragraphs consist of one, two, or three sentences at the most. Paragraphs of dialogue also tend to be short; most writers indent for every change of speaker. Some essayists—for example, Imamu Amiri Baraka (pp. 102–103)—use very brief paragraphs to emphasize that certain plain facts can't be overlooked. At the other extreme lie the immense fictive paragraphs of, say, James Joyce and William Faulkner—passages that disregard our sense of form so as to mimic the unending stream of a character's thoughts.

Most essayists, however, write paragraphs averaging 100–200 words in length, with two or three paragraphs to the typewritten, double-spaced page. If your own paragraphs regularly take up a whole page or more, they need to be scaled down to meet a reader's normal attention span. If they rarely contain more than three brief sentences, they're lacking in development and are probably making a simple-minded impression. Consider this passage:

> Yesterday I saw my little brother watching a horror movie on television. This made me think of how much television influences children.
>
> What can we do about this social disorder? My little brother was certainly not being improved by this experience. This is a serious problem.
>
> In other countries there is state control of television. This is a bad thing, yes. But it is also a good thing, because it prevents the above-mentioned damage to little minds that may not grow up to be as sophisticated as you and me.

Paragraph construction is only one of this writer's problems, but the mere size of his paragraphs is a handicap. He won't be able to fashion a thoughtful argument if he short-circuits his prose before it gets properly started. Each break sets him back to zero again, forcing him to raise a new topic without adequate preparation for it. He has, for example, completely forgotten to justify his belief that horror movies cause "damage to little minds," and he implies that the unspecified influence of television is itself a "social disorder." These paragraphs read like sketchy notes that haven't yet been sorted, much less developed for the eyes of a reader.

If the paragraphs in your first drafts go to the other extreme and seem to ramble interminably, you needn't be alarmed. It's easier in revision to cut paragraphs down to size than to puff them out with new material. Often you'll find that an unwieldy paragraph has shifted its topic somewhere near the middle, and that you need only mark a new paragraph there in order to retain most of your sentences. If you do this, however, make sure that both of the new paragraphs are tightly organized.

Establishing a middle-sized paragraph as your norm, you can depart from that norm with good effect. When your reader comes across a somewhat longer paragraph, he will know that he's being asked to deal with an exceptionally complex part of your argument. Occasionally you can insert a very short paragraph — a sentence or two, or even a purposeful sentence fragment — to make a major transition, a challenge, an emphatic statement, or a summary. The emphasis comes precisely from the contrast between such a paragraph and the more developed ones surrounding it.

Vary Your Sentence Structure

Variety of sentence structure within a paragraph is essential for sustaining your reader's involvement and pleasure. This matter is treated in the previous chapter (review pp. 99 – 102).

Move Between Generality and Detail

Paragraphs, like whole essays, should back up their main assertions with detail. Although there's nothing wrong with an occasional paragraph consisting entirely of general statements or entirely of particulars, in most paragraphs these elements should be juxtaposed. It isn't simply that the reader deserves to see the basis for your broadest remarks; it's also a question of avoiding monotony. A series of paragraphs like the following, excessively abstract one would make a suffocating effect:

> Fate, which can be defined as the destiny of a human being, can turn out to be either good or bad. There are probably two general interpretations of fate as this idea occurs in literature. One interpretation is that a person's fate is a direct consequence of the rightness or wrongness of his actions, while the other interpretation is that nothing can alter the pattern that was established at birth or even earlier.

Does the writer have any sense of fate, or is he just reciting what he's been told? By not getting down to examples he makes a vacant impression.

The author of the following paragraph has one general assertion to make about the amount of coastline in the United States. The assertion, though important to his argument, is obvious and even dull, but he enlivens it by combining precise statistics with a vivid and witty image:

> On the map, the simple fact is that we have plenty of seashore to go around. We are no landlocked Switzerland, but a nation of coasts. Even if all 210 million of us went to the beach in a legion, we could get wet together. To be precise, there would be 2.102 feet of ocean frontage for each of us — enough to wade in abreast, arm-in-arm, in a continental chorus line.[7]

Since topic sentences typically appear at the beginning of a paragraph, the transition from generality to detail often occurs after the opening sentence. Note the wealth of supporting material that follows a broad statement in this paragraph by Sonya Rudikoff:

> Although more marriages nowadays seem to be performed by clergymen, often hip ministers or "modern" rabbis, or, alternatively, very old-fashioned ones, their doctrine may not be part of anyone's daily life or conduct. The clergyman seems indistinguishable from the guests, and nothing prepares us for the moment when he steps forward in the garden and begins, all of a sudden, "Dearly Beloved . . .," or something of the sort. The Navajo or Hopi ceremonies, the dawn or midnight, garden or woodland nuptials, the Our Relationship sermons by the bridal pair, all borrow sanction and dignity from a sacramental tradition which is probably dropped as unceremoniously as possible after the ceremony. The couple married in the woods do not live by the law of the woods, the Hopi vows do not make a Hopi marriage in a modern California setting, the girl who circles seven times around the groom or the groom who stamps on a glass may ignore the imperatives of their actions, and their conduct after the marriage may bear no relation to the ceremony that made it; indeed, no rules of conduct for the future can be deduced from the ceremony. The couple is unlikely to say, as Thomas and Mary Ellwood did of their Quaker marriage in 1669: "We sensibly felt the Lord with us and joining us, the sense whereof remained with us all our lifetime, and was of very good service and very comfortable to us on all occasions."[8]

But an opposite movement, from the particular to the general, is also possible. Examine the following paragraph by Paul Goodman:

During the hearings on Vietnam before the Senate Foreign Relations Committee, Senator Thomas Dodd of Connecticut—who had been mentioned as Lyndon Johnson's choice for Vice President in 1964— was asked what he thought of the sharp criticism of the government. "It is the price that we pay," he said, "for living in a free country." This answer was routine and nobody questioned it. Yet what an astonishing evaluation of the democratic process it is, that free discussion is a weakness we must put up with in order to avoid the evils of another system! To Milton, Spinoza or Jefferson, free discussion was the strength of a society. Their theory was that truth had power, often weak at first but steady and cumulative, and in free debate the right course would emerge and prevail. Nor was there any other method to arrive at truth, since there was no other authority to pronounce it than all the people. Thus, to arrive at wise policy, it was essential that everybody say his say, and the more disparate the views and searching the criticism, the better.[9]

Goodman wants to make an abstract point about free discussion in a democracy, but instead of starting on that plane he tells a story and then draws us into examining its meaning. Our anger is stirred: the prominent Senator, the would-be Vice-President, has casually downgraded a precious right. By beginning with the anecdote about Senator Dodd, Goodman makes us more inclined to accept his own libertarian values.

BEGINNINGS AND ENDINGS

Make Your First Paragraph Count

The most important paragraph in an essay, though it is also likely to be the one containing the least information, is the opener. An experienced reader can usually tell after two or three sentences whether the writer has command of his material and is capable of making it interesting. Nothing much can be hoped from essays whose opening paragraphs begin with self-evident platitudes:

- Conservation is a very important topic now that everyone is so interested in ecology.
- One of man's greatest enemies is disease.

or with restatements of an assigned topic:

- It is interesting to inquire into the reasons for the emergence of fascist ideology after World War I.

or with laments over the difficulty of it all:

- A person like me, situated far from the scene in both space and time, faces an almost insuperable task in trying to assess the meaning of the Counter-Reformation. However, . . .

A good opening paragraph customarily accomplishes three things. It catches the reader's interest, it establishes the tone of the essay, and — usually but not always — it reveals the one central problem that's going to be addressed. Look at this beginning by Alix Kates Shulman:

> The revival of the forties and fifties is upon us. That Middle-American time of my youth is gaining its place in our historical imagination. Movies, essays, stories, novels, and the sheer passage of time have already begun transforming that era from banal to exotic. The record is being filled not only with nostalgia but with critical insight, as writing men of wit try to pin down those days. Nevertheless, something crucial is missing, for the reality being recorded about that era is essentially a male reality, the experience male experience. And until the female side is acknowledged and recorded, the era cannot even begin to emerge in perspective.[10]

This paragraph certainly could be strengthened: the first five sentences are constructed alike, the diction is somewhat repetitive, and little progress is made from the first sentence through the fourth. Yet the author does what needs doing. Her opening sentence gives us orientation and a promise of interesting details to follow; we can tell from the tone that this will be a no-nonsense essay, factual and critical in its emphasis; and the paragraph ends with a topic sentence for the whole essay, thus concluding one movement of thought and opening up a more ambitious one. Not very much has been said, but we have settled back and prepared ourselves for the rest.

Another opening succeeds in a quite different way:

> Old men, old women, almost 20 million of them. They constitute 10 percent of the total population, and the percentage is steadily growing. Some of them, like conspirators, walk all bent over, as if hiding some precious secret, filled with self-protection. The body seems to gather itself around those vital parts, folding shoulders, arms, pelvis like a fading rose. Watch and you see how fragile old people come to think they are.[11]

This essay, like the previous one, tries to tell the truth about a poorly understood aspect of American life, but its approach is anecdotal and descriptive rather than polemical. Though the author has managed to slip two statistics into her first two sentences, her opening paragraph is evocative, "poetical," alerting us to the prominence of her feelings in the paragraphs to come. Her fragmentary opening sentence, her early recourse to physical detail, and her free use of figurative language bespeak a less contentious relation to her material than Shulman's.

Perhaps the most common way to draw a reader into an essay is to use the first paragraph as bait. An alarming fact, a story, an opinion that flies in the face of received views—whatever the item, it teases the reader by its very refusal to say what the argument will be. We suspect that a writer who can start at the periphery of his topic in this way must have an unusual control over the total conception of his essay. Of course we could also suspect that the writer is simply being evasive or sloppy; much depends on the paragraph that follows this one. When used responsibly, though, the baited opener has the merit of stirring our thoughts and emotions before we have a chance to draw back and say, "Oh, is that the topic? I'm not interested in reading about *that*."

In the following opener J. Bronowski, writing about the uses of technology, doesn't even hint at his topic in the first paragraph, but arouses our curiosity in a way that he can exploit immediately afterward:

> We all know the story of the sorcerer's apprentice; or *Frankenstein* which Mary Shelley wrote in competition with her husband and Byron; or some other story of the same kind out of the macabre invention of the nineteenth century. In these stories, someone who has special powers over nature conjures or creates a stick or a machine to do his work for him; and then finds that he cannot take back the life he has given it. The mindless monster overwhelms him; and what began as an invention to do the housework ends by destroying the master with the house.
>
> These stories have become the epitome of our own fears . . .[12]

Ralph Ellison, in a celebrated quarrel with Irving Howe, startles us by beginning with angry challenges:

> First, three questions: Why is it so often true that when critics confront the American *as Negro* they suddenly drop their advanced critical armament and revert with an air of confident superiority to quite primitive modes of analysis? Why is it that sociology-oriented critics

seem to rate literature so far below politics and ideology that they would rather kill a novel than modify their presumptions concerning a given reality which it seeks in its own terms to project? Finally, why is it that so many of those who would tell us the meaning of Negro life never bother to learn how varied it really is?[13]

And Gay Talese opens his book on the Mafia by putting us inside the shoes, not of a main character, but of a doorman who wants no trouble:

> Knowing that it is possible to see too much, most doormen in New York have developed an extraordinary sense of selective vision: they know what to see and what to ignore, when to be curious and when to be indolent; they are most often standing indoors, unaware, when there are accidents or arguments in front of their buildings; and they are usually in the street seeking taxicabs when burglars are escaping through the lobby. Although a doorman may disapprove of bribery and adultery, his back is invariably turned when the superintendent is handing money to the fire inspector or when a tenant whose wife is away escorts a young woman into the elevator—which is not to accuse the doorman of hypocrisy or cowardice but merely to suggest that his instinct for uninvolvement is very strong, and to speculate that doormen have perhaps learned through experience that nothing is to be gained by serving as a material witness to life's unseemly sights or to the madness of the city. This being so, it was not surprising that on the night when the Mafia chief, Joseph Bonanno, was grabbed by two gunmen in front of a luxury apartment house on Park Avenue near Thirty-sixth Street, shortly after midnight on a rainy Tuesday in October, the doorman was standing in the lobby talking to the elevator man and saw nothing.[14]

The ingenuity of this paragraph consists in its subtle way of conferring a privilege on us. As real people in the path of the Mafia we would have to suppress our curiosity, see no evil; but in fact we are only reading a book, and now we can leave the doorman behind and learn what he would swear he hadn't witnessed.

Opening paragraphs are sometimes compared to a funnel: the reader's interest is supposedly caught by a very broad statement and then narrowed to the topic at hand. In fact, however, this is only one of many possible openings, and it is the one that most frequently turns stale. Composition teachers are all too familiar with superficially "well-organized" first paragraphs that sound like this:

The subject of psychotherapy is definitely one of the major issues of our time. In this democratic, post-Freudian age, we all have an interest in learning which kinds of therapy are more likely to work than other kinds. It is therefore very interesting to all of us when new books are published on this important subject. In this essay we shall examine two such books, respectively entitled *The Love Treatment* and *The Radical Therapist*. The thesis of the former is that sexual intimacy between therapists and patients may be beneficial, and the thesis of the latter is that therapy is all too often a reflection of social injustice. These are certainly challenging ideas. Six points in particular deserve to be made about them.

Compare this with Ellen Willis's opening paragraph on the same topic:

I am a sucker for psychology books, so when the paperback edition of *The Love Treatment* appeared on the rack at Woolworth's, I picked it up and leafed through it. Its premise, I discovered, was that the taboo on sexual intimacy between psychotherapists and their patients should be re-examined, not only because it was being broken all the time anyway but because in the right circumstances such intimacy might have therapeutic value. My immediate hostility to this idea — I'd heard any number of horror stories from friends who had slept with or been propositioned by their therapists — did not keep me from admiring its brilliance. Psychotherapy, as conventionally practiced, had proved a useful tool for exploiting women, and so had the ideology of sexual revolution — why not combine them? It didn't take much imagination — or excessive cynicism — to foresee the practical result of giving (mostly male) therapists a professional rationale for going to bed with their (mostly female) clients. After all, the argument that sex is therapeutic had been a favorite of amateur psychiatrists for years.[15]

Now, this might be considered too breezy a beginning for the purposes of most student papers. The author is deliberately slangy in her first sentence, and she makes no effort to get both of the assigned books within her sights. Her offhand, autobiographical manner is that of a typical piece in *The New Yorker* or *The Village Voice*.

Yet her paragraph accomplishes a good deal without seeming to labor over the obvious requirements of a book review. Note, for example, that instead of dutifully announcing the thesis of *The Love Treatment*, she manages to integrate it into a little story about herself. We've been told what we somehow had to learn, but the information has been put in an active setting. More important, the author has shown us that she's not in fact a "sucker" but a skeptic who can be counted on to resist the self-interested arguments of male therapists. This display of sophistication is what chiefly gives the paragraph its alertness. By voicing at the start the suspicions that many of her readers would harbor about *The Love Treatment*, Ellen Willis marks herself as having passed beyond cliché responses. We want to read further because we see that she cares about her subject and doesn't intend to let preconceptions keep her from dealing with it fairly.

End with a Strong Paragraph

The only general rules for writing a final paragraph are negative ones:

1. Don't launch a completely new topic.
2. Don't apologize.
3. Don't make a major concession or throw your whole thesis into doubt.

The reason for these warnings is that a reader comes away from the essay with the last paragraph in mind; it epitomizes the whole for him. If you end on a nervous or hesitant note, you're encouraging him to discount everything that has gone before.

Insofar as possible, a final paragraph should sound conclusive. In some cases it will in fact be the conclusion to the argument, deferred until this emphatic but perilously late moment. More often, though, the main point has already been stated, and the job of the final paragraph is to convey a *sense* of completion. This can entail a summarizing of what has been established, but such summaries are often stale; the reader suspects that the writer has simply run out of things to say. A good summary always restates the argument in some fresh manner, providing a vivid image or witty reflection, posing a further challenge, or returning to an idea, episode, or figure of speech that occurred near the beginning.

Sometimes the lift can come merely from the definiteness with which the writer epitomizes his case. Here, for instance, is the last paragraph of an essay by Nathan Glazer challenging the claims of the New Left:

> I view radicalism as a great reservoir of energy which moves the establishment to pay attention to the most serious and urgent problems, and tells it when it has failed. To a more limited degree, it is also a reservoir of potential creativity—a reaching for new solutions and new approaches. What radicalism is not, and what it can no long-

er be, is the great sword of vengeance and correction which goes to the source of the distress and cuts it out. There is no longer a single source, and no longer a single sword.[16]

Glazer is recapitulating the pros and cons reviewed in the body of his essay. He concedes much to radicals, but makes sure to end on his own keynote: the New Left has underrated the complexity of things. Instead of repeating what he has said before, he finds an image, "the great sword of vengeance and correction," and nicely turns it to his own uses in the final sentence.

Many persuasive essays make no explicit attempt to summarize, but instead merely leave us satisfied that the argument does hang together. Last paragraphs resemble first paragraphs in this respect: if the writer can get along without a direct thematic statement, he is showing, and imparting, confidence in the soundness of his case. This is why an anecdote often makes an effective ending:

> Somehow, as I think of all the faculty members who are getting leaves from the classroom these days to work out solutions to restlessness among students, it seems to me that the best commentary is contained in an old, now famous, Herblock cartoon. It was drawn when the late John Foster Dulles was incessantly engaged in missions outside Washington, D.C. It showed President Eisenhower sitting at the telephone saying: "Foster, don't just *do* something; *stand* there."[17]

And sometimes the anecdote is left unexplained, so that the reader will feel its significance for himself. Here are the two final paragraphs of Alfred Kazin's autobiographical volume, *Starting Out in the Thirties:*

> One day in the spring of 1945, when the war against Hitler was almost won, I sat in a newsreel theater in Piccadilly looking at the first films of newly liberated Belsen. On the screen, sticks in black-and-white prison garb leaned on a wire, staring dreamily at the camera; other sticks shuffled about, or sat vaguely on the ground, next to an enormous pile of bodies, piled up like cordwood, from which protruded legs, arms, heads. A few guards were collected sullenly in a corner, and for a moment a British Army bulldozer was shown digging an enormous hole in the ground. Then the sticks would come back on the screen, hanging on the wire, looking at us.
>
> It was unbearable. People coughed in embarrassment, and in embarrassment many laughed.[18]

History has outstripped the political and literary imagination: all the assumptions of the thirties have suddenly become irrelevant in view of the unknown horror that had been developing all along. The knowledge of what happened in the extermination camps couldn't be assimilated all at once, and Kazin's personal feelings are indescribable. In stopping his book at this awkward moment, he imparts to us his sense of paralysis and disbelief, and leaves us with his own postwar task of trying to comprehend the ultimate dehumanization.

Kazin's ending can serve as a reminder that final paragraphs don't have to follow the threadbare *Thus we have seen* formula; nor do they have to take an exalted or ceremonious tone. It's quite true that many excellent conclusions stand out from the rest of their essay by a certain heightening of intensity or formality; last sentences in particular often have a quality of compressed sureness, as Glazer's does. But what really matters about an ending is whether it carries a reader's sympathy through to the last word. If his parting thought is *So that's what it all means* or *What more is there to say?*, you've done your job. If, somewhere before that final word, he tells himself with a smirk, *Ah, yes, the customary ringing summary*, you've laid on the rhetoric of conclusiveness too thickly. Try to keep your reader guessing until the very end, so that he never feels that he can stop reading whenever he pleases.

EXERCISES

I. Find the irrelevant sentence that was inserted into the following paragraph, and explain why it doesn't belong there:

In 1886 Grinnell suggested in the pages of *Forest and Stream* that concerned men and women create an organization for the protection of wild birds and their eggs, its administration to be undertaken by the magazine's staff. Grinnell did not have to grope to name this organization. He had grown up near the home that the great bird painter, John James Audubon, had left to his wife and children at his death. As a boy Grinnell had played in an old loft cluttered with stacks of the red muslin-bound copies of the *Ornithological Biography* and boxes of bird skins brought back by Audubon from his expeditions. He had attended a school for small boys conducted by Lucy Audubon nearby. All his life he would remain an avid reader. Grinnell quite naturally called the new organization the Audubon Society.[19]

II. The following five sentences, presented out of order, belong to a paragraph by Wilson Follett. Rearrange them in what you take to be the best order, and briefly explain why you placed each sentence where you did:

(1) The right way is believed to be clearer, simpler, more logical, and hence more likely to prevent error and confusion.

(2) Despite the modern desire to be easy and casual, Americans from time to time give thought to the language they use — to grammar, vocabulary, and gobbledygook.

(3) And as on other issues they divide into two parties.

(4) Good writing is easier to read; it offers a pleasant combination of sound and sense.

(5) The larger, which includes everybody from the proverbial plain man to the professional writer, takes it for granted that there is a right way to use words and construct sentences, and many wrong ways.[20]

III. Turn back to the paragraph by John H. Schaar (pp. 121–122), where signals of *transition* are indicated by capitalized words. Make a list of the signals of *identity* (p. 120) you find in the paragraph.

IV. Study the following paragraph by Joseph Wood Krutch. Taking the sentences one by one, discuss their elements of *continuity* (both identity and transition):

(1) This is an appalling demonstration of the cruelty of nature, not much worse, perhaps, than many others, but seeming so just because of the huge size of the victim. (2) Perhaps the commercial slaughters of the whale are less cruel; but one curious fact does remain and illustrates a general law: killer whales do not exterminate the race of gray whales. (3) In fact, I doubt that there is a single known case in historical times where any large animal living in its native environment has been responsible for the extermination of any other. (4) Presumably during the great crises of evolution something of the sort did take place — when, for example, the advanced mammals all but exterminated the marsupials over almost the whole surface of the earth. (5) Something of the sort also happens when goats, dogs, and cats are

established by man on islands where nature had worked out no balance taking them into account. (6) But in general, live and let live is the motto — even of predators.[21]

V. Find, in your own writing for this or another course, two consecutive paragraphs that now strike you as deficient in some or all of the following: unity, emphasis, continuity, variety. Copy the paragraphs and then rewrite them to remove the problems you have isolated.

VI. Do you believe that amnesty should be granted to young men who avoided or resisted the draft at the time of the Vietnam war? Write what you consider effective *opening* and *concluding* paragraphs to an essay presenting your view on this issue.

NOTES

1. ''The President's Palace Guard,'' *Newsweek*, 19 Mar. 1973, p. 24.
2. Albert Goldman, ''The Emergence of Rock,'' *New American Review*, No. 3, p. 119.
3. Edmund Wilson, ''Dickens: The Two Scrooges,'' *Eight Essays* (Garden City, N.Y.: Anchor, 1954), p. 84.
4. Lionel Trilling, *Sincerity and Authenticity* (Cambridge, Mass.: Harvard Univ. Press, 1972), pp. 139–140.
5. John H. Schaar, ''The Case for Patriotism,'' *American Review*, No. 17, pp. 61–62.
6. Lewis Mumford, ''California and the Human Horizon,'' *The Urban Prospect* (New York: Harcourt, Brace, 1968), pp. 3, 4, 6, 8, 11.
7. Anthony Wolff, ''We Shall Fight Them on the Beaches . . . ,'' *Harper's*, Aug. 1973, p. 55.
8. Sonya Rudikoff, ''Marriage and Household,'' *Commentary*, June 1973, p. 59.
9. Paul Goodman, ''The Psychology of Being Powerless,'' *People or Personnel and Like a Conquered Province* (New York: Vintage, 1967), p. 344.
10. Alix Kates Shulman, ''The War in the Back Seat,'' *Atlantic*, July 1972, p. 50.
11. Sharon Curtin, ''Aging in the Land of the Young,'' *Atlantic*, July 1972, p. 68.
12. J. Bronowski, ''Science, the Destroyer or Creator,'' *The Common Sense of Science* (1955; rpt. New York: Vintage, n.d.), p. 136.
13. Ralph Ellison, ''The World and the Jug,'' *Shadow and Act* (1964; rpt. New York: Signet, 1966), pp. 115–116.
14. Gay Talese, *Honor Thy Father* (1971; rpt. Greenwich, Conn.: Fawcett Crest, 1972), p. 16.
15. Ellen Willis, ''The Fantasy of the Perfect Lover,'' *New York Review of Books*, 31 Aug. 1972, p. 7.
16. Nathan Glazer, ''The New Left and Its Limits,'' *Commentary*, July 1968, p. 39.
17. Robert A. Nisbet, ''Crisis in the University?'', *The Public Interest*, Winter 1968, p. 64.

18. Alfred Kazin, *Starting Out in the Thirties* (Boston: Little, Brown, 1965), p. 166.

19. Carl W. Buchheister and Frank Graham, Jr., "From the Swamps and Back: A Concise and Candid History of the Audubon Movement," *Audubon*, Jan. 1973, p. 7; one sentence added.

20. Rearranged from Wilson Follett, *Modern American Usage: A Guide* (New York: Hill & Wang, 1966), p. 3.

21. Joseph Wood Krutch, *The Forgotten Peninsula: A Naturalist in Baja California* (1961; rpt. New York: Apollo, 1970), p. 177.

USAGE

A REVIEW OF GRAMMAR 7

The advice given throughout this book, and especially in Chapters Eight and Nine, won't make much sense to you if you don't know the meaning of terms like *gerund*, *past participle*, and *subjunctive mood*. Even if you do, you may want to sharpen your memory of the principal parts of certain verbs, or of distinctions between types of pronouns, or between restrictive and nonrestrictive clauses. The following review is offered, then, as a resource which you can either read straight through or consult when necessary.

PARTS OF SPEECH

Definitions of the parts of speech are notoriously difficult. Most of the traditional formulas (*a noun is the name of a person, place, or thing*) imply that the dictionary meaning of a word will tell you what part of speech it is. But is *dictionary* a noun in the previous sentence? Its function is plainly adjectival. (Most grammarians would call it an *attributive noun*—a noun in an adjectival position.) You can see that matters are far from simple.

The word *hard*, for example, has four quite separate functions in the following four sentences:

1. The ball was hard.
2. He tried hard.
3. "Hard" is a versatile word.
4. The vessel was hard by the starboard bow.

Hard is clearly an adjective in (1) and an adverb in (2). In (3) it has become a noun—or strictly speaking a *nominal*, a word lacking the normal features of a noun but occupying a noun's position. As for (4), *hard* might there be considered an adverb, as in *The vessel remained hard by;* but its real function is to form part of the compound preposition *hard by*, with *bow* as its object. Memorizing "the" part of speech of *hard* isn't enough; a word's function in a given sentence takes precedence over its usual classification.

Completely adequate definitions of the parts of speech would have to be both *inflectional* (taking note of how words belonging to certain parts of speech can have their endings changed) and *positional* (listing all the sentence positions that each part of speech can occupy). Thus, a noun is a word that can change its ending or inflection in certain characteristic ways (*girl, girl's, girls, girls'*) that are unavailable to words like *to*, *sad*, and *the;* but it is also a word that can occupy certain sentence positions and no others. In the sentence *Philo will fall in _____ with anything so long as it is a girl*, the blank can only be filled by a noun.

Whether or not you could list all the sentence positions the parts of speech can fill, you do recognize those positions intuitively as a speaker of English, and I will take that knowledge for granted below. My definitions will follow those of linguists, but without aiming at exhaustiveness.

Nouns

A noun is a word that can be inflected to become either plural or possessive or both; these are the only inflections it can take. Thus, both *series* and *hat* are nouns, even though *series* can't be inflected for the plural. *He* can become possessive, but since it also has an object form *him*, it can't be a noun.

In the following sentences, nouns are marked with N:

N   N   N
Stanley ran quickly to the *barricade* and tossed two rotten *eggs* at the passing
N   N   N   N
dignitary from *Washington*. They landed on *target* and made quite a *mess* of
N   N   N   N   N   N
his *forehead*. Our *hero's contribution* to the *cause* of *peace* and *brotherhood* was

outstanding.

A noun can function as:

a subject (p. 159)
a direct object (p. 161)
an indirect object (p. 162)
a complement (p. 162)
an object of a preposition (p. 156)
an appositive (p. 163)
a subject of an infinitive (p. 150)
an object or complement of an infinitive (p. 150)
an object of a participle (p. 150)
a subject of a gerund (p. 151)
an object of a gerund (p. 151)
part of an absolute phrase (p. 164)
a possessive (*Stanley's*)
a term in direct address (*Stanley, come here!*)

A word or group of words functioning as a noun but not usually regarded as a noun is called a *nominal*. Thus, in the sentence *He thought
of leaving*, the final word is a nominal (in this case a gerund): it
functions as the object of a preposition but isn't usually considered
a noun.

Nouns have traditionally been classified as either *concrete* (having
physical existence) or *abstract* (lacking physical existence).

CONCRETE:
• barricade, egg, forehead

ABSTRACT:
• contribution, cause, peace, brotherhood

A *proper* noun is a name (*Stanley, Washington*); a *common* noun
isn't a name (*barricade, peace*).

Verbs

A verb is a word that can be inflected to form some or all of the following: past tense (*walked*), present participle (*walking*), and past
participle (*walked*). Verbs have traditionally been identified as words
expressing action or being. But *action* and *being* aren't verbs, and
neither are such action-packed words as *earthquake* and *rushing*. A
word with the inflectional features of a verb is truly a verb when it

occupies certain sentence positions that we all recognize as characteristic of verbs. Thus, *iron* has the necessary inflectional features *ironed, ironing, ironed,* but we intuitively recognize that it doesn't occupy a verb position in the sentence *The iron is hot.* Compare *She ironed the dress; She was ironing; Iron the dress!* We recognize that in all three sentences the word is doing a verb's work.

In the following passage the verbs are marked with v:

          v   v

"I *have decided* to become a guru," *declared* Norbert. "Many years of study
                  v   v
and self-denial *will be involved,* but the world *stands* in need of my services.
                                v
Once certified as an adept, I *will bestow* advice upon everyone seeking
                        v
enlightenment. People *will come* to know me as 'Norbert the Hierophant of

Daly City.'"

principal parts The principal parts of a verb (that is, the forms from which all its tenses are composed) consist of its infinitive (without *to*), its past form, and its past participle. Every verb is either *regular* or *irregular* according to the way it forms its past tense and past participle. *Regular* verbs simply add *-d* or *-ed: hike, hiked, hiked; talk, talked, talked. Irregular* verbs change their form more radically: *smite, smote, smitten; swim, swam, swum.*

Here are the principal parts of some common irregular verbs and a few regular ones that cause trouble. Where more than one form is given, all are permissible. If you don't find one of your own problem verbs here, consult the dictionary; it gives principal parts for all verbs.

infinitive	past tense	past participle
awake	awaked, awoke	awaked, awoke, awoken
be	was, were	been
bear (carry)	bore	borne
bear (give birth to)	bore	born
beat	beat	beaten, beat
begin	began	begun
bend	bent	bent
beseech	beseeched, besought	beseeched, besought
bind	bound	bound
bite	bit	bit, bitten
bleed	bled	bled
blow	blew	blown

infinitive	past tense	past participle
break	broke	broken
bring	brought	brought
build	built	built
burst	burst	burst
buy	bought	bought
catch	caught	caught
chide	chided, chid	chided, chidden, chid
choose	chose	chosen
cling	clung	clung
clothe	clothed, clad	clothed, clad
come	came	come
creep	crept	crept
deal	dealt	dealt
dig	dug	dug
dive	dived, dove	dived
do	did	done
drag	dragged	dragged
draw	drew	drawn
dream	dreamed, dreamt	dreamed, dreamt
drink	drank	drunk
drive	drove	driven
eat	ate	eaten
fall	fell	fallen
fit	fitted, fit	fitted, fit
fly	flew	flown
forget	forgot	forgotten, forgot
freeze	froze	frozen
get	got	gotten, got
give	gave	given
go	went	gone
grow	grew	grown
hang (an object)	hung	hung
hang (a person)	hanged	hanged
hew	hewed	hewed, hewn
hide	hid	hidden, hid
kneel	knelt, kneeled	knelt, kneeled
knit	knit, knitted	knit, knitted
know	knew	known
lay (put)	laid	laid
lead	led	led
lean	leaned, leant	leaned, leant
lend	lent	lent
lie (recline)	lay	lain
light	lighted, lit	lighted, lit
lose	lost	lost

infinitive	past tense	past participle
mow	mowed	mowed, mown
pay	paid	paid
prove	proved	proved, proven
put	put	put
quit	quit, quitted	quit, quitted
rid	rid, ridded	rid, ridded
ride	rode	ridden
ring	rang	rung
rise	rose	risen
run	ran	run
saw	sawed	sawed, sawn
see	saw	seen
set	set	set
sew	sewed	sewed, sewn
shake	shook	shaken
shave	shaved	shaved, shaven
shear	sheared	sheared, shorn
shine	shone, shined	shone, shined
show	showed	showed, shown
shrink	shrank, shrunk	shrunk, shrunken
sing	sang, sung	sung
sink	sank	sunk
sit	sat	sat
slide	slid	slid, slidden
smite	smote	smitten
speak	spoke	spoken
speed	sped, speeded	sped, speeded
spring	sprang, sprung	sprung
stand	stood	stood
steal	stole	stolen
strew	strewed	strewed, strewn
strike	struck	struck, stricken
strive	strove, strived	striven, strived
swim	swam	swum
swing	swung	swung
take	took	taken
teach	taught	taught
tear	tore	torn
thrive	thrived, throve	thrived, thriven
throw	threw	thrown
tread	trod	trod, trodden
wake	waked, woke	waked, woke, woken
wear	wore	worn
wring	wrung	wrung
write	wrote	written

Note that some verbs have alternate forms of past participles, such as *drunken* and *sunken*, which are acceptable in adjectival positions (*a drunken fool*). The list gives only the forms acceptable for strictly participial use (*he had drunk too much*).

transitive and intransitive verbs In any given sentence, a verb is either *transitive* (taking at least one object) or *intransitive* (not taking an object):

TRANSITIVE:
• Norbert *disappointed* Wanda.

INTRANSITIVE:
• Norbert *was* a disappointment to Wanda.

In the second example, *disappointment* is not something acted upon by the verb; it is a predicate noun (p. 162) equated with the subject *Norbert*.

Some verbs can never be transitive (*be, loaf*, etc.), but many others can be used in both transitive and intransitive constructions:

TRANSITIVE:
• He *paid* a high price for it.

INTRANSITIVE:
• He *paid* dearly for it.

linking verbs An intransitive verb connecting a subject with a predicate noun or predicate adjective (p. 162) is known as a *linking verb*:

          LV   PRED N
Norbert *is* a devoted *fellow.*
          LV   PRED ADJ
He *has remained* monotonously *faithful* to his vows.

Typical linking verbs are *be, seem, appear,* and, when they take a complement, *act, feel, grow, look, remain, smell, sound,* and *taste.*

tenses The tense of a verb is the time it expresses. The tenses recognized by most grammarians are:

present
present progressive (action ongoing in present)
past
past progressive (action ongoing in past)
present perfect (past action regarded from the present)
past perfect (action completed before another past time)
future (action contemplated now)
future perfect (action regarded as completed from vantage of some future
   time)

The verb forms expressing these tenses are illustrated here for the active voice (see below) of the regular verb *walk* and the irregular verb *go:*

ACTIVE VOICE		
tense	person	
	I	*he, she, it*	*we, you (sing./pl.), they*
Present	walk	walks	walk
	go	goes	go
Present Progressive	am walking	is walking	are walking
	am going	is going	are going
Past	walked	walked	walked
	went	went	went
Past Progressive	was walking	was walking	were walking
	was going	was going	were going
Present Perfect	have walked	has walked	have walked
	have gone	has gone	have gone
Past Perfect	had walked	had walked	had walked
	had gone	had gone	had gone
Future	will (shall)* walk	will walk	will (shall) walk
	am going to walk	is going to walk	are going to walk
	will (shall) go	will go	will (shall) go
	am going to go	is going to go	are going to go
Future Perfect	will (shall) have walked	will have walked	will (shall) have walked
	will (shall) have gone	will have gone	will (shall) have gone

*For the choice between *will* and *shall*, see p. 259.

voice   The voice of a verb indicates whether the subject performs (is active in) or receives (is passive to) the action of the verb.

ACTIVE VOICE:
• Frankie *shot* Johnny.

PASSIVE VOICE:
• Johnny *was shot* by Frankie.

If a verb can ever be transitive (*she walked the baby*), it can also be passive (*the baby was walked*). The conjugation (formation of all tenses) of two verbs in the active voice has just been given. Here now are passive conjugations of the regular verb *shock* and the irregular verb *take:*

PASSIVE VOICE			
tense	person		
	I	*he, she, it*	*we, you (sing./pl.), they*
Present	am shocked	is shocked	are shocked
	am taken	is taken	are taken
Present Progressive	am being shocked	is being shocked	are being shocked
	am being taken	is being taken	are being taken
Past	was shocked	was shocked	were shocked
	was taken	was taken	were taken
Past Progressive	was being shocked	was being shocked	were being shocked
	was being taken	was being taken	were being taken
Present Perfect	have been shocked	has been shocked	have been shocked
	have been taken	has been taken	have been taken
Past Perfect	had been shocked	had been shocked	had been shocked
	had been taken	had been taken	had been taken
Future	will (shall) be shocked	will be shocked	will (shall) be shocked
	will (shall) be taken	will be taken	will (shall) be taken
Future Perfect	will (shall) have been shocked	will have been shocked	will (shall) have been shocked
	will (shall) have been taken	will have been taken	will (shall) have been taken

mood A verb's mood is the manner in which the action or state is conceived. English has three moods: the *indicative*, for making statements or asking questions; the *imperative*, for giving commands or directions; and the *subjunctive*, for special purposes discussed below.

INDICATIVE:
• I *ate* a banana.
• *Did* you *eat* a banana?

IMPERATIVE:
• *Eat* the banana!

SUBJUNCTIVE:
• If I *were* to eat a banana . . .

The indicative and imperative moods pose no problems of usage. But the subjunctive is tricky, for two reasons: it sometimes changes the form of the verb, and the circumstances in which it should be used at all are in dispute.

For all verbs except *be*, the subjunctive involves a changed form *only in the third-person singular*. Thus, the present active forms of *like* in the three moods are:

	indicative	imperative	subjunctive
I	like		like
you	like	like	like
he, she, it	likes		**like**
we	like		like
you	like	like	like
they	like		like

You can see that the one change is simply a dropping of the *-s* or *-es* from the indicative form of third-person singular. In the passive, the only subjunctive form occurring with any frequency in modern English is in the present tense:

INDICATIVE:
• he *is liked*

SUBJUNCTIVE:
• that he *be liked*

Be is made subjunctive in the following ways:

1. Where the indicative is *am*, *is*, or *are*, the subjunctive is *be*:

INDICATIVE:
• I *am* late; he *is* late; they *are* late

SUBJUNCTIVE:
• if I *be* late; lest he *be* late; that they *be* late

2. Where the indicative is *was*, the subjunctive is *were*:

INDICATIVE:
• if I *was* there [and possibly I was]

SUBJUNCTIVE:
• if I *were* there ⎱
• *were* I there ⎰ [but I'm not]

3. Where the indicative is *were*, the subjunctive is *had been*:

INDICATIVE:
• if they *were* there [and possibly they were]

SUBJUNCTIVE:
• if they *had been* there ⎱
• *had* they *been* there ⎰ [but they weren't]

4. Where the indicative is *have been*, the subjunctive is *had been*:

INDICATIVE:
- if you *have been* there [and possibly you have]

SUBJUNCTIVE:
- if you *had been* there ⎫
- *had* you *been* there ⎭ [but you haven't]

When should the subjunctive be used? Although at one time it was a flourishing part of daily usage, the subjunctive now survives only in limited kinds of statements:

1. Certain formulas such as:

as it were	heaven forbid
be it known	long live the Queen
be that as it may	the devil take it
come what may	the taxpayers be damned
God bless you	

2. Impossible or unlikely conditions:

- If I *were* on the moon now, I would tidy up the junk that has been strewn there.
- *Had he taken* that plane, he would be dead today.

(It is now archaic to use the subjunctive for simple conditions, as in: *If the weather be rainy, the game will be postponed.*)

3. *That* clauses expressing requirements or recommendations:

- The IRS requires that everyone *submit* his return by April 15.

4. *Lest* clauses (but these verge on the archaic):

- Lest it *be thought* that I am neglectful of my duties . . .

The subjunctive often sounds stilted even when doing its proper work, and some writers prefer to risk sounding ungrammatical: *If I was on the moon now*, etc. But distaste for the subjunctive shouldn't be carried that far. Note that precise use of the subjunctive can sometimes prevent ambiguity. Compare:

- It is important that everyone *loves* me.
- It is important that everyone *love* me.

If the writer means to express a *wish* for love, his meaning is made clear only in the second sentence, using the subjunctive.

In some cases you can get around the subjunctive by using one of the auxiliaries discussed next:

SUBJUNCTIVE:
• I demand that everyone *be* here at eight o'clock.

INDICATIVE:
• Everyone *must be* here at eight o'clock.

auxiliaries Certain words are called auxiliaries because they can combine with (or "help") other verb forms. Some grammarians regard *is, was, were, has, have, will have*, etc., as auxiliaries when they combine with participles of other verbs to make up the tenses. Other grammarians speak of the present progressive tense (*is throwing*), the past perfect tense (*had thrown*), etc. (see p. 145), and consider each form as one unit instead of breaking it down into components. The difference is unimportant. The unquestioned auxiliaries include *can, could, may, might, must, need, ought, shall, should*, and *would*:

• He *could* throw harder.
• He *must* throw harder.
• He *should* throw harder.

merged verbs A verb form combined with a preposition is sometimes called a merged verb: *check out, cave in*, etc. Note that merged verbs can easily be confused with verbs *followed by* a preposition. Compare:

• He *looked up* the number.
• He *looked up* the elevator shaft.

Or again:

• She *turned on* the switch.
• She *turned on* him in anger.

The first sentence in each pair contains a merged verb: *looked up, turned on*. In the other sentences, *up* and *on* are prepositions taking the objects *shaft* and *him*. You can tell the difference either by considering the unity of meaning in a merged verb — in the first sentence *look* is simply incomplete without *up* — or by noting a difference in voice stress. In the merged verbs *look up* and *turn on*, the words *up* and *on* receive more stress than they do when used as prepositions.

verbals Several forms derived from verbs are regarded as distinct grammatical entities: *infinitives, present participles, past participles*, and *gerunds*.

Infinitives Forms like *to become* and *to know* are called infinitives. They can stand alone or take subjects, objects, or complements:

SUBJECT:

                   S INF
* Norbert asked *Wanda* to concentrate on the One.

OBJECT:

                                 OBJ INF
* He was no longer concerned to gratify *Wanda*.

COMPLEMENT:

          S INF   COMPL INF
* He wanted *her* to become *enlightened.*

                        COMPL INF
* He wanted to be her *instructor.*

Note, in the first example, that *Wanda* appears to do double service as the indirect object of *asked* and as the subject of the infinitive *to concentrate*. Subjects of infinitives always appear in objective-case positions (pp. 151–152). For purposes of sentence analysis they are construed *as* subjects of infinitives, not as direct or indirect objects, objects of prepositions, etc. The whole infinitive phrase *Wanda to concentrate on the One* should be regarded as the direct object of *asked*. What did Norbert ask? He asked *Wanda to concentrate on the One.*

Infinitives can be either active (*to gratify*), passive (*to be gratified*), or progressive (*to be gratifying*).

Present participles A present participle is a word that ends in *-ing* and modifies a noun or pronoun. *Seeking* is a present participle in the phrase *everyone seeking enlightenment.*

Present participles can be active (*seeking*) or passive (*being sought*). They can stand alone (*Seeking, he found*) or take an object (*Seeking enlightenment, he found it*).

Past participles A past participle has the same function as a present participle, but it refers to a past action. It too can be active (*sought, having sought*) or passive (*having been sought*).

Gerunds In form a gerund is indistinguishable from a present or past participle, but in function it is always equivalent to a noun:

                     GER
* His first step will be *suppressing* [the suppression of] all desire.

Here are some further gerunds:

GER
1. *Debating* with Norbert is futile.
GER
2. He loves *contemplating* his merger with the universe.
GER
3. He will give *meditating* a try.
GER
4. He is tired of *having striven.*

In these sentences the gerund is by turns a subject (1), part of a direct object (2), an indirect object (3), and the object of a preposition (4). Note that a gerund, unlike a participle, never modifies another word. In the sentence *Debating with Norbert, Wanda grew angry,* you can tell that *Debating* is a participle by the fact that it modifies *Wanda.*

A gerund can have both a subject and an object:

S GER   OBJ GER
• *George's* deserting the *battlefield* came as a surprise.

(For the use of possessive forms in the subject of a gerund, see p. 198.)

Note that although infinitives, participles, and gerunds are called *verbals* (because they derive from verbs), they never function as verbs. In function they are either nominal, adjectival, or adverbial.

Verbals and verbs aren't always easy to tell apart. Compare:

• He *was throwing* harder.
• He began *throwing* harder.

(In the first sentence *was throwing* is a verb in the past progressive tense [p. 145]. But in the second sentence *throwing* is a gerund, serving as the direct object of the verb *began.* He began what? *throwing harder.*)

Pronouns

It used to be said that a pronoun takes the place of a noun. But the pronoun *it* in the previous sentence doesn't take the place of a noun; nor do the pronouns *nobody, none, no one,* and *anything.* All you can do is learn to recognize a pronoun when you see one.

Most, but not all, pronouns differ from nouns in their inflection for *case.* The case of a noun or pronoun reflects its sentence function. The three cases in English are *subjective, objective,* and *possessive:*

SUBJECTIVE:
- The *boy* went home. ⎤
- *He* went home.   ⎦ subject of verb

- He was the *boy*. ⎤
- The boy was *he*. ⎦ complement

OBJECTIVE:
- They punished the *boy*. ⎤
- They punished *him*.   ⎦ direct object of verb

- They taught the *boy* a lesson. ⎤
- They taught *him* a lesson.   ⎦ indirect object of verb

- They taught it to the *boy*. ⎤
- They taught it to *him*.   ⎦ object of preposition

- They wanted the *boy* to go. ⎤
- They wanted *him* to go.   ⎦ subject of infinitive

POSSESSIVE:
- the *boy's* hat ⎤
- *his* hat   ⎦ possession of noun

- the *boy's* departure ⎤
- *his* departure   ⎦ subject of gerund

As you can see, nouns change their form only in the possessive case, but some pronouns have different forms for all three cases.

Most pronouns function as nouns but take their meaning from an *antecedent* word or phrase. An antecedent is a sentence element to which a pronoun refers:

     ANTE PRO
the *play that* Harold saw

personal pronouns   These have case distinctions for subjective (*I* went), objective (to *me*, gave *me*), and possessive (*her* hat).

SINGULAR			
	subjective	objective	possessive
First Person	I	me	my, mine
Second Person	you	you	your, yours
Third Person	he	him	his
	she	her	her, hers
	it	it	its
PLURAL			
First Person	we	us	our, ours
Second Person	you	you	your, yours
Third Person	they	them	their, theirs

relative pronouns A word in a sentence is a relative pronoun only if it

a. introduces a subordinate clause (p. 164),
b. occupies a noun position; and
c. has an antecedent word or phrase in the same sentence.

Thus, *who* is a relative pronoun in the following sentence:

REL PRO
• Tom is a man *who* suffers withdrawal symptoms when his
  picture tube is away at the shop.

(*Who* introduces a subordinate clause, *who suffers withdrawal symptoms;* it occupies a noun position as the subject of the verb *suffers;* and it has an antecedent, *man.*)

The relative pronouns include *who, whom, whose, that,* and *which.* These same forms can serve other functions as well. In *that hat* and *I don't know which way,* for example, *that* and *which* aren't relative pronouns but demonstrative adjectives. *Who* is an interrogative pronoun in *Who cares?*

When a relative pronoun can be inflected for case (*who, whom, whose*), its case should be determined by its function within its own clause (see pp. 188–189).

interrogative pronouns These introduce direct and indirect questions. They include *who, whom, whose, which,* and *what.*

DIRECT QUESTION:
INT PR
Who could have predicted that Tom would put a set in every room?

INDIRECT QUESTION:
INT PR
I wondered *who* could have predicted it.

(Note that some interrogative forms, such as *why* and *when,* are considered either adverbs or conjunctions, but not pronouns, since they don't serve noun functions in their clauses.)

reflexive and ~~sive pronouns~~ These are *myself, yourself, himself, herself, itself, oneself, ourselves, yourselves, themselves* (never *theirself* or *theirselves*). These derivatives of the personal pronouns are used either for emphasis (intensive) or for indicating that the subject of a verb is also its object (reflexive).

INTENSIVE:
- She *herself* will drive the truck.
- For *myself*, I want no part of it.

REFLEXIVE:
- He admires *himself* unreservedly.
- We have done *ourselves* very little good.

demonstrative pronouns *This, that, these,* and *those* are called demonstratives because they single out (or "demonstrate") what they refer to:

- *These* are the good old days.
- I don't recognize *this* as your work.

Used adjectivally, these same words are called *demonstrative adjectives:*

- *These* days are the best we will ever see.
- *This* sculpture, consisting of a stack of soup cans on top of a motorcycle, is a powerful social statement.

reciprocal pronouns These express mutual relation: *each other, each other's, one another, one another's.* Although they always refer to at least two parties, they are always singular in form:

RIGHT:
- Wanda and Norbert compared *each other's* defects.

WRONG:
- Wanda and Norbert compared *each others'* defects.

Although some writers reserve *each other('s)* for two parties and *one another('s)* for more than two parties, the terms are really interchangeable.

indefinite pronouns An indefinite pronoun leaves unspecified the person or thing it refers to. The indefinite pronouns are:

all	both	everything	nobody	several
another	each	few	none	some
any	each one	many	no one	somebody
anybody	either	most	nothing	someone
anyone	everybody	much	one	something
anything	everyone	neither	other	such

Some of the indefinite pronouns can become possessive, but none of them can be inflected in any other way. They are considered indefinite pronouns only when they are not used as modifiers. *Any* is an indefinite pronoun in *any of you*, but it is an adjective in *any coat*.

Adjectives

Adjectives are words modifying nouns or pronouns. They can be altered to indicate degree, either by inflection (*wide, wider, widest*) or by addition of *more* and *most* or *less* and *least*. In general, adjectives of one syllable are made comparative and superlative by adding -*er* and -*est*, respectively; adjectives of more than two syllables take *more* and *most;* and adjectives of exactly two syllables can take either form:

positive degree	comparative degree	superlative degree
high	higher	highest
tough	tougher	toughest
happy	happier (more happy)	happiest (most happy)
beautiful	more beautiful	most beautiful
astounding	more astounding	most astounding

Some adjectives are compared irregularly:

positive degree	comparative degree	superlative degree
bad	worse	worst
good	better	best
far	farther, further	farthest, furthest
little	littler, less, lesser	littlest, least
many, some, much	more	most

When in doubt about comparisons, consult your dictionary.

If a word or group of words occupies the function of an adjective in a sentence, but isn't customarily regarded as an adjective, it is called an *adjectival:*

ADJL
- Her eyes had a *come-hither* look.

ADJL
- He was a *West Point* graduate.

Another name for *West Point* in the second sentence is an *attributive noun* — a noun serving as an adjective.

Adverbs

Adverbs are words that modify either verbs, adjectives, other adverbs, prepositions, phrases, clauses, or whole sentences. They typically express manner (*disgustingly*), degree (*very*), frequency (*seldom*), time (*now*), place (*there*), affirmation (*certainly*), negation (*not*), qualification (*however*), and logical relationship (*therefore*).

Most single-word adverbs end in -*ly*, but some important ones do not:

ahead
down
therefore
well (*etc.*)

Some adverbs are identical in form to adjectives:

better	late	much
close	loud	slow
fast	more	tight (*etc.*)

Thus you often have to distinguish an adverb from an adjective by its function alone:

       ADV
• You had *better* come.

(The adverb modifies the verb *had come*.)

       ADV   ADJ
• He was a *much better* player than Ralph.

(Here *better* modifies the noun *player*, and *much* modifies *better*.)

            ADV   ADV
• You are someone who buys *cheap* and sells *dear*.

(The adverbs modify *buys* and *sells*.)

    ADV   ADV   ADJ
• It went *clean* against my inclination to go *slow* in that *slow* zone.

(*Clean* modifies *went*. The first *slow* is an adverb modifying the infinitive *to go*; the second is an adjective modifying the noun *zone*.)

(For the position an adverb should occupy, see pp. 194–196.)

Prepositions

Prepositions are uninflected function words showing a relationship between a noun or pronoun (the object of the preposition) and another word or phrase in the sentence. A word commonly recognized as a preposition (*by, for, of, onto, to, without*, etc.) isn't truly prepositional in a given sentence unless it takes an object. Note how the presence or absence of an object affects the parts of speech marked in these examples:

- He looked *under* the *bridge.*
  PREP   OBJ PREP

- He dived *under.*
  ADV

- *Apart from* his *shyness*, nothing obstructed his career.
  PREP   OBJ PREP

- He stood *apart.*
  ADV

- The fighter came *to* the *arena.*
  PREP   OBJ PREP

- He came *to* after he had been knocked *out.*
  ADV   ADV

In many doubtful cases the disputed word is part of a merged verb such as *look up, carry away, come to, knock out* (see p. 149).

Prepositions can be made from strings of words: *by means of, by reason of, in front of, on account of, with respect to*, etc.

A preposition and its object, along with the modifiers of the object, is called a *prepositional phrase.*

Conjunctions

Conjunctions are uninflected function words that connect words, phrases, or clauses. They are customarily classified as *coordinating* conjunctions (joining words, phrases, or independent clauses), *subordinating* conjunctions (introducing subordinate clauses), and *correlative* conjunctions (joining matched pairs):

coordinating conjunctions			
and	nor		
but	or		
for	yet		

subordinating conjunctions			
after	before	so (that)	when
although	how	that	whenever
as	if	though	where
as if	in order that	till	wherever
as long as	provided (that)	unless	while (*etc.*)
because	since	until	

correlative conjunctions			
both . . . and			
either . . . or			
neither . . . nor			
not only . . . but also			

Note that *either* and *neither* sometimes serve as indefinite pronouns, as in *Neither of us could go.*

Some grammarians include *conjunctive adverbs* among conjunctions. The function of these words is intermediate between those of adverbs and conjunctions: they simultaneously modify a phrase or statement and indicate its logical relationship to a previous one.

conjunctive adverbs	
also	moreover
besides	nevertheless
consequently	nonetheless
furthermore	similarly
however	then
indeed	therefore
likewise	thus

Interjections

Interjections have traditionally been called words expressing strong feeling, but this is a hopelessly porous definition. Any word at all can express strong feeling. Let's say that interjections are certain recognized words or brief expressions that stand apart from other constructions in order to express strong feeling: *ah, damn, help, o, oh, ouch,* etc.

Note that an interjection isn't the same thing as an exclamation (p. 166). An exclamation often consists of or contains an interjection, but there's no necessary bond between the two. *O Henrietta Tittle, your hair is like peanut brittle* contains an interjection but it isn't an exclamation; *Drop dead!* is an exclamation but it contains no interjection. But words like *damn* and *help,* which have extended meanings, can be considered interjections only when they do occur in exclamations.

Articles

The indicators preceding certain nouns are sometimes regarded as belonging to a distinct part of speech, the article. Articles are divided into *definite* (*the*) and *indefinite* (*a, an*). *A* is used before consonant sounds, *an* before vowel sounds. When an initial *h* sound is distinctly pronounced, as in *historical,* most writers prefer to introduce it with *a: a historical inquiry,* not *an historical inquiry.*

PRIMARY SENTENCE ELEMENTS

The sentence has never been satisfactorily defined, but no literate person has difficulty recognizing one in a context of other sentences. The context can be decisive for a judgment as to whether expressions such as *Not a prayer* and *Certainly not mine* are to be considered sentences. A sentence is a complete expression. These expressions meet the test of completeness if, and only if, they are immediately preceded by other sentences such as *What are his chances?* and *Whose stereo will be thrown overboard?* Even *Hmm* and *What?* can qualify as sentences. But *He was going to the* wouldn't be a sentence in any circumstances. Why not? Because no imaginable context except *Let's hear a sentence fragment* would account for it. Even a very lengthy cluster of phrases and clauses would fail to qualify as a sentence if one of its main elements were *inexplicably* missing. A sentence, we might say, is a word or group of words that we understand to be complete, whether or not it contains the normal main ingredients of a sentence.

Those ingredients are a *subject* and a *verb*—and, if the verb is transitive or linking (see p. 144), an *object* or a *complement.*

Subject

The subject of a sentence is a nominal element (usually a noun, pronoun, infinitive, gerund, or noun clause) that governs the main verb. The following sentences show various nominal elements serving as subjects (s):

COMMON NOUN AS SUBJECT:
s
* *Exercise* is good for circulating whatever happens to be in your bloodstream.

PROPER NOUN AS SUBJECT:
s
* "I adore the way you nibble cheese," said *Mickey* to Minnie.

PRONOUN AS SUBJECT:
s
* Did *you* say your name was Helga R. Hughes?

INFINITIVE PHRASE AS SUBJECT:
s
* *To have been a great pitcher* is worth a few decades of bursitis.

GERUND AS SUBJECT:
s
* *Camping* is easier now that the freeway goes right through the wilderness sanctuary.

NOUN CLAUSE AS SUBJECT:

- *What you tell Martha* will become general knowledge.

A subject is often the first noun or pronoun in its sentence, but you can't count on this. Subjects may be delayed, for example, by *inversion* (subject follows object) and by *anticipatory constructions*.

INVERSION:

- A more attractive mouse *I* have never seen.

ANTICIPATORY CONSTRUCTION:

- It is regrettable *that fiscal responsibility means the closing of hospitals.*

(*It* is merely an anticipatory signal that the real subject will follow.)
   The only sure way to locate the subject of a sentence is to ascertain which is its main clause (see below), to find the verb in that clause, and then to ask who or what governs that verb. Who or what, in other words, did what was done or was in the state described by the verb and its complement? Thus, for the sentences above, you can find the subjects by asking:

- Who has never seen a more attractive mouse? *I.*
- What is regrettable? *That fiscal responsibility means the closing of hospitals.*

A *simple subject* is the single word or phrase that governs the verb. A *complete subject* is the simple subject plus all the words that modify it. Note that a complete subject can be extremely complex:

- Having gone for thirty years without any human contact, and with no means of sending a message to the outside world, was finally too much for the poor wretch's sanity.

(Here the complete subject consists of everything preceding the main verb *was*; the simple subject is the gerund *Having gone.* What was too much? *Having gone for . . . world*)
   A subject consisting of more than one main term is called a *compound subject:*

- *Nichols and May* were considerably funnier than Cheech and Chong are.

(In this example *Cheech and Chong* constitutes another compound subject—but it is the subject of a subordinate clause [p. 164], not the subject of the sentence.)

Verb

The term *verb* is used both for the part of speech (p. 140) and for the sentence element that conveys what a subject is or does. It typically, but not invariably, follows its subject:

          s   v
- *I have* no idea what you mean.
       s   v
- *They should be made* aware of the penalties for vandalism.
     v   s   v
- *Do you want* me to repeat the point?
        v   s
- How *dare you* speak to me like that!

A verb can consist of more than one word: *is trying, has been driven, will have been noticed.* You could also say that the verb in the second example above is *should be made aware,* on the assumption that *make aware* is a merged verb (p. 149).

Verbs generally agree in number (singular, plural) with their subjects.

The verb and its objects, complements, and modifiers are jointly considered the *predicate* of a sentence.

Direct Object

A direct object is a noun, pronoun, or nominal element that receives the action conveyed by a transitive verb:

                        D OBJ
1. Lefty aimed a vicious *uppercut* at Righty's chin.
         D OBJ
2. He chose *Agnes* as his lifetime sparring partner.
                           D OBJ
                           D OBJ
3. She didn't understand *why he gave her a* **mouthpiece** *for Christmas.*

The way to locate the direct object is to ask who or what receives the action of the verb:

1. Aimed what? *Uppercut.*
2. Chose whom? *Agnes.*
3. Didn't understand what? *why he gave her a mouthpiece for Christmas.* Gave what? *mouthpiece.*

Indirect Object

An indirect object is a noun or pronoun identifying the party receiving the action in verbs of asking, giving, telling, and receiving. Note that this is not the word identifying *what* is given or received. Confusion is spared by the fact that the indirect object always precedes the direct object when both are supplied. Note also that the indirect object is always equivalent to a prepositional phrase beginning with *to* or *for:*

>   I OBJ D OBJ
> • She baked *him* a *cake.*
>   OBJ PREP
> • She baked a cake for *him.*
>   I OBJ
> • How many times must I tell *you?*
>   OBJ PREP
> • How many times must I tell it to *you?*
>   D OBJ
> • Myrtle gave Winston an authentic George Harrison *mandala.*
>   OBJ PREP
> • Myrtle gave an authentic George Harrison mandala to *Winston.*

Complement

A complement is a noun or adjective that follows a linking verb (p. 144). Unlike a direct or indirect object, it specifies something about the *subject* of the sentence. Complements are either *predicate nouns* or *predicate adjectives:*

PREDICATE NOUN:
>   PRED N   PRED N
> • You may be a good *sculptor*, but that is an abominable *snowman.*

PREDICATE ADJECTIVE:
>   PRED ADJ
> • Your snowman is *abominable.*

SECONDARY SENTENCE ELEMENTS

The basic structural units of a sentence are those just reviewed: subject, verb, direct object, indirect object, complement. Very few sentences, however, consist only of these elements. The other elements are mostly *modifiers:* that is, they specify or qualify the main elements. Modifiers already treated above include adjectives (p. 155), adverbs (pp. 155–156), articles (p. 158), and prepositional phrases (p. 157). Other modifiers and minor sentence elements are mentioned here:

Appositives

An appositive is a noun or nominal element (and its modifiers) following another noun or nominal element and serving to identify it or provide further information about it:

APP   APP
- Henry *the tailor* married Rosie *the riveter.*

APP
- Phase Seven, *the deportation of the unemployed,* was quietly revoked before it could be put into effect.

Infinitives and Infinitive Phrases

An infinitive (p. 141) or an infinitive phrase (the infinitive plus its object and modifiers) sometimes functions as a main sentence element:

AS A SUBJECT:

INF PHRASE
- *To get out of Lodi* was his main desire.

AS A DIRECT OBJECT OR PART OF ONE:

INF PHRASE
- His mother wanted him *to be successful.*

(The infinitive phrase and its subject *him* constitute the direct object of *wanted.*)

AS A COMPLEMENT OR PART OF ONE:

INF PHRASE
- His father's secret dream was *to acquire a new Lamborghini.*

But infinitives and infinitive phrases can also be modifiers, as here:

INF PHRASE
- He went off *to think about it.*

(The infinitive phrase is adverbial, modifying *went off.*)

INF PHRASE
- He despaired of finding a car *to please her.*

(The infinitive phrase is adjectival, modifying *car.*)

(For the case of pronouns serving as subjects and objects of infinitives, see p. 187.)

Participles and Participial Phrases

A participial phrase consists of a participle (p. 140) and its object or complement and modifiers. Its function is always adjectival:

PART PHRASE
- *Having bought a Nehru jacket just when the fad was ending*, Sam was reluctant to get a caftan now.

(*Having bought* is a past participle; *Nehru jacket* is its object; and *when the fad was ending* is a subordinate clause modifying the participle. The whole construction modifies *Sam.*)

PART PHRASE
- Aged batters *lacking knee cartilage* are benefiting from the new pinch-hitting rule.

(The participial phrase modifies *batters.*)

Gerunds and Gerund Phrases

A gerund (pp. 150–151) and its modifiers can occupy any sentence function normally taken by a noun or pronoun. Thus gerunds and gerund phrases usually constitute main sentence elements. Sometimes, though, they can serve as appositives:

GER PHRASE
- Steve has discovered that his hobby, *sitting around in his undershirt*, demands that he keep plenty of cold beer in the refrigerator.

Absolute Phrases

An absolute phrase is one that modifies a whole sentence or clause:

ABS PHRASE
- *Considering the demand*, the price of waterpipes is still remarkably low.
ABS PHRASE
- *The Gauls having been defeated*, Caesar sat down to practice his declensions.

Some absolute phrases look precariously like dangling modifiers (p. 196), but we don't hear them that way. In the first example above, for instance, we accept *Considering the demand* as equivalent to a sentence adverb like *nevertheless* or *indeed*.

Subordinate Clauses

A subordinate (or dependent) clause, as the name implies, depends on a more important clause to complete its meaning. It has a subject and a predicate, but its function is either to modify part of another clause or to form one syntactic unit within another clause.

Some subordinate clauses are *adjectival:*

ADJ CLAUSE
- The day *when I see Tony Curtis* will be the happiest day of my life.

(The subordinate clause functions as an adjective modifying *day*.)
Others are *adverbial:*

ADV CLAUSE
- *Because you have never answered my letters,* Tab Hunter, I have started corresponding with Troy Donahue.

(The subordinate clause functions as an adverb modifying *have started.*)
And still others, called *noun clauses,* are syntactically equivalent to nouns:

N CLAUSE
- *That you are a major poet* is apparent from your headband, boots, and buckskin shirt.

(The subordinate clause is the subject of the main verb *is.*)
A subordinate clause introduced by a relative pronoun (p. 153) is called a *relative clause.* Its function is always adjectival:

REL CLAUSE
- Someone *who can make an entire poem out of zip codes* deserves to be taken seriously by the critics.

(The relative clause modifies *Someone.*)
In some relative clauses the relative pronoun is only implied:

REL CLAUSE
- You are the bard [*that*] *America has been waiting for.*

A *restrictive clause* is one that restricts the meaning of its antecedent by serving to identify it:

RESTR CLAUSE   RESTR CLAUSE
- The poem *that I like best* is the one *you copied from the index to the Sears catalog.*

(The first marked clause identifies *poem;* the second identifies *one.*)
A *nonrestrictive clause* adds new information about an antecedent that's already identified:

NONRESTR CLAUSE
- The poem, *which shows your creative powers at their summit,* does raise some delicate questions of copyright.

(The marked clause says something new about a known *poem.*)

The difference between restrictive and nonrestrictive clauses calls for differences in punctuation (pp. 276–277) and perhaps also in choice of a relative pronoun (pp. 184–185).

TYPES OF SENTENCES

Sentences can be classified both by *purpose* and by *structure.*

Purpose

declarative sentences   A declarative sentence makes a statement:

- Grammar gives her goosepimples.

questions   • Why do you ask so many questions?

commands   • Send our boys back to Vietnam, Mr. President!

(The subject *you* is usually left implicit.)

exclamations   • Alas!

miscellaneous   Some groups of words are technically sentence fragments but, like exclamations, are recognized in context to be sufficiently complete. These include brief answers to questions, passages rendering snatches of dialogue or mental activity, summations such as *So much for the population problem,* and introductions such as *And now for a closer look at the small intestine.*

Structure

simple sentences   A simple sentence contains only one independent clause and no subordinate clauses. It may, however, contain a compound subject or a compound predicate and any number of modifiers other than a subordinate clause:

- The chicken crossed the road.
- Seeing the sign announcing a half-price fire sale on "Win with Willkie" buttons, Sam leaped up and pulled the cord so as to get the bus driver to let him off at the next corner.

(Both sentences are simple. In the second, as in the first, there is only one independent clause, *Sam leaped up and pulled the cord*, and there are no subordinate clauses.)

compound sentences   A compound sentence contains at least two independent clauses and no subordinate clauses:

- I came, I saw, I conquered.
- Max ordered a sensible fudge sundae but Bessie, with characteristic daring and *joie de vivre*, chose a double peppermint split with a hint of mock crème de menthe added just before serving.

(Both sentences are compound; the first contains three independent clauses, the second two: *Max ordered a sensible fudge sundae* and *Bessie chose a double peppermint split.*)

The independent clauses in a compound sentence are known as *coordinate clauses*. They are usually but not always linked by co-ordinating conjunctions (p. 157). (For problems of punctuating the linkage between coordinate clauses, see p. 278.)

complex sentences   A complex sentence contains only one independent clause and at least one subordinate clause:

- I came, though I didn't conquer.
- In view of the fact that my advances apparently mean nothing to you, and because we cannot go on like this, and finally because, still loving you, I want the world to know what a splendid girl you are, I have decided to sell the story of our tragic courtship to *True Confessions*.

(The only independent clause is *I have decided . . . Confessions.*)

compound-complex sentences   A compound-complex sentence contains at least two independent clauses and at least one subordinate clause:

- I came and, though I didn't conquer, at least I saw.
- He wrote his autobiography and then, after he had had a few more piquant adventures, he decided to bring out a sequel to inform the world of his doings between ages nineteen and twenty-three.

(The independent clauses are *He wrote his autobiography* and *he decided . . . sequel.* The subordinate clause is *after he had had a few more piquant adventures.*)

EXERCISES

I. Read the following passage and then answer the questions below.

(1) The car stood in the middle of the yard, quite unattended, the stable-helps and other hangers-on being all at their dinner. (2) Toad walked slowly round it, inspecting, criticizing, musing deeply.

(3) "I wonder," he said to himself presently, "I wonder if this sort of car *starts* easily?"

(4) Next moment, hardly knowing how it came about, he found he had hold of the handle and was turning it. (5) As the familiar sound broke forth, the old passion seized on Toad and completely mastered him, body and soul. (6) As if in a dream he found himself, somehow, seated in the driver's seat; as if in a dream, he pulled the lever and swung the car round the yard and out through the archway; and, as if in a dream, all sense of right and wrong, all fear of obvious consequences, seemed temporarily suspended. (7) He increased his pace, and as the car devoured the street and leapt forth on the high road through the open country, he was only conscious that he was Toad once more, Toad at his best and highest, Toad the terror, the traffic-queller, the Lord of the lone trail, before whom all must give way or be smitten into nothingness and everlasting night. (8) He chanted as he flew, and the car responded with sonorous drone; the miles were eaten up under him as he sped he knew not whither, fulfilling his instincts, living his hour, reckless of what might come to him. [Kenneth Grahame, *The Wind in the Willows*, 1908]

1. List all the nouns in the above passage.
2. List all the verbs, adding (*tr*) or (*intr*) after each one to indicate whether it is being used transitively or intransitively.
3. Which of the verbs are linking verbs?
4. Indicate the tenses of all the verbs.
5. Which, if any, of the verbs are in the passive voice?
6. Are there any auxiliaries in the passage? If so, list them.
7. List all the infinitives. Indicate the complements or objects, if any, of the infinitives.
8. In two columns list all the participles and gerunds in the passage.
9. List all the pronouns in the passage.
10. List all the adjectives in the passage.
11. List all the adverbs, and indicate what word or words each adverb modifies.
12. List all the prepositional phrases, underlining the prepositions once and their objects twice.
13. In two columns list all the coordinating and subordinating conjunctions.

14. Copy all the independent clauses in the passage and mark their primary sentence elements: subject (*S*), verb (*V*), direct object (*D Obj*), indirect object (*I Obj*), predicate noun (*Pred N*), and predicate adjective (*Pred Adj*).
15. Repeat item 14 for all the subordinate clauses.
16. Are there any appositives in the passage? If so, list them.
17. Identify the relative clauses, if any, in your list of the subordinate clauses, and explain how you identified them as relative clauses.
18. For each of the eight numbered sentences, indicate whether the sentence is simple, compound, complex, or compound-complex in structure.

II. Identify and explain the uses of the subjunctive mood in the following passage:

> Coming, as it were, to see his situation clearly for the first time, the Colonel decided to notify everyone that no more dissension among the ranks would be tolerated. If he were to allow things to deteriorate further, he reasoned, there would be hell to pay. "Public opinion be damned!" he shouted, pounding his fist on the table lest anyone think him lily-livered. "I decree that every man in this unit get a crew cut, read nothing but the funny papers, and play Guy Lombardo records!"

III. List in separate columns the pronouns of different types (personal, relative, interrogative, reflexive, intensive, demonstrative, reciprocal, and indefinite) in the following passage:

> Arnold and Joanne had a warm, satisfying relationship based on each one's respect for the other's interests. Arnold prided himself on his tolerance. If two people loved each other, he thought, neither of them should be dominant. He knew what he liked, and what he liked was late-late movies. For herself, Joanne preferred talk shows. That is why they decided to buy "his" and "hers" sets in matching Philippine mahogany Colonial cabinets. Who could complain? Joanne herself never felt closer to Arnold than when they sat together in the den, she with her earphones and he with his.

IV. Briefly discuss the grammatical differences between the italicized words in the following pairs of sentences:

1. a. He charged *up* the field.
   b. He charged *up* the battery.
2. a. She wants *alimony*.
   b. She wants *alimony* to be her largest source of income.

3. a. *Standing in the middle of the road*, Fido blocked traffic for hours.
   b. *Standing in the middle of the road* was Fido's idea of exercise.
4. a. Philo *himself* believes in immortality.
   b. Philo believes *himself* to be immortal.

PROB-8 LEMS OF USAGE

FROM SPEAKING TO WRITING

Authorities on composition usually divide contemporary English into categories such as formal, general, informal, and colloquial (or slang), with the first three designated as "standard" and the last as "nonstandard." Our speech, they say, tends to draw on the general, informal, and colloquial levels, thus combining standard and nonstandard forms; but our writing should be purer, using mostly general but sometimes dipping into formal and informal English. The advice can be represented like this:

$$
\text{SPEAKING} \begin{cases} \text{formal} \\ \text{general} \\ \text{informal} \\ \text{colloquial} \end{cases} \left. \begin{array}{l} \\ \text{WRITING} \end{array} \right\}
$$

formal

general ⎱ WRITING

informal ⎰ Standard English

colloquial   Nonstandard English

This looks reasonable enough, and it does convey a sense of the levels on which most good writing is done. As an account of the way native speakers use the language, though, it's seriously defective. Who are the "we" that speak mostly standard English? Hillbillies? Prep-school graduates? Ghetto blacks? By pretending to forget that these groups speak separate dialects, the grammarian leaves you to suppose that they're all trying with different success to speak one dialect, standard English. All dialects other than standard have been relegated to a wastebasket called nonstandard. It's as if the only way to be articulate and rule-abiding were to adopt the speech habits of one linguistic group—the group, not surprisingly, containing nearly all the most powerful members of society.

When levels of usage are ranked in this covertly social order, some highly questionable ideas begin to emerge. Sociologists declare that ghetto English "is a basically non-logical mode of expressive behavior,"[1] and they devise kindly programs to make black children sound more like white sociologists. Amateur geneticists, seeing that these programs always fail, speculate about an inherited incapacity to use language properly. And, more to our purpose here, composition teachers announce that "Standard English is more expressive than nonstandard" and that you ought to write standard English because "the use of nonstandard expressions is usually taken as a sure sign of inferior social background."[2]

Such advice is well-intentioned and perhaps even prudent, given the persistence of racism and class prejudice. It might be even more prudent, however, to state the facts about language correctly. Linguists are unanimous in saying that every dialect is just as expressive and logical as all the others; to call one dialect "good English" is a political judgment, a reinforcing of the belief that one element in society is destined to rule. This doesn't seem to me to be the proper business of a grammarian.

Students who weren't raised speaking standard English already know that the supposed law, *"nonstandard English has no place in college writing,"*[3] can serve as an instrument of discrimination. Obliged to compose in an unfamiliar dialect, they sometimes feel that they're being asked to choose between their cultural identity and the demands of the educational system. Many who do conform produce an abstract, ornate, important-sounding style that's a negation of everything they feel. When this prose too is penalized, the nonstandard speaker may be ready to give up on composition and accept the idea that he's unteachable. Yet his "handicap" might turn out to be an advantage if only his instructors made some allowance for the reality of cultural difference. It's no accident that some of the richest modern stylists—Joseph Conrad, James Joyce, Vladimir Nabokov, Dylan Thomas, Ralph Ellison, James Baldwin, for example—have felt and reconciled the pressure of opposing traditions.

Why, then, is the present book devoted entirely to standard English, and how can I presume to talk about right and wrong ways of putting a sentence together? The answer is threefold:

1. All dialects, including standard English, do have rules that can be stated in the form of advice;
2. Standard English remains overwhelmingly the dialect used for public writing by speakers of English, regardless of their vernacular speech; and
3. It is the only dialect that arouses people's worry over whether they and others are using it correctly.

This and subsequent chapters are addressed to that worry. I anticipate, not that you will necessarily want to write standard English on all occasions, but that you may need some guidance when you do.

Even for the children of bank presidents and newscasters, writing standard English correctly is a taxing challenge. English possesses an enormous and growing lexicon of expressions, many of which are widely misunderstood among the educated people who use them. Unlike, say, French, which was kept fastidious for centuries by aristocratic purists, our language has always been rough-and-tumble, an amalgam of coinages and borrowings from every segment of society and from different parts of the world. Its grammar is so problematical on certain points that no one, not even the greatest writer or authority on usage, can make such a simple choice as "It is I" or "It is me" without wondering if he's wrong. As for the rules of spelling, they admit of so many exceptions that they can scarcely be called rules at all. Of all Western languages, English is probably the one whose literate native speakers experience the most difficulty in writing it. The possibilities for ambiguity in an English sentence are the delight of poets and the despair of essayists.

There are, to be sure, certain broad principles that can be stated briefly and dogmatically. The heart of this chapter, for instance, is contained in these do's and don'ts:

---

1. Make your subjects and verbs agree in number.
2. See that your pronouns are in the right case and form.
3. Make sure that your pronouns are clearly related to antecedents.
4. Don't confuse adjectives with adverbs.
5. Choose appropriate modifiers.
6. Watch out for misrelated and dangling modifiers.
7. Use possessives where meaning demands them.
8. Be consistent in using tenses.
9. Don't treat passive constructions as if they were active.

10. Watch for ambiguous and double negatives.
11. Give parallel structure to elements that are parallel in meaning.
12. Don't compare incomparable things.

Of course the difficulty comes in putting these rules to practical work. As soon as you do, you find that they have to be accompanied by specifications, examples, and idiomatic exceptions. Without these details the rules are just empty pieties.

The chapters that begin here will focus on difficulties of two sorts: common errors and finer questions that arise from disagreements among commentators on usage. On many points the grammatical purists and the liberals offer opposite advice, and by following either party you will offend the other. Instead of choosing sides myself, I will try to show you how opinion is weighted and how you can avoid making lesser-evil choices. Given the confused state of grammar on some matters, your best course is to reject both of the available expressions and to find a completely new way of making the same statement. In short, don't let yourself get trapped. Let the experts haggle over doubtful issues; you have other work to do as a writer, and you can do it most effectively by using constructions that sound like normal standard English to every ear. The ideal, after all, isn't to put yourself forward as a champion of frigid rightness, nor to flaunt your contempt for purism, but to allow people to concentrate on what you're saying.

Note that some typical problems of usage, such as the avoidance of run-on sentences and the unnecessary separation of main sentence elements, are treated in the chapter on punctuation (pp. 268–295). The meaning of basic grammatical terms is explained in Chapter Seven (pp. 138–167).

AGREEMENT OF SUBJECT AND VERB

In standard English, verbs are supposed to agree in number with their subjects. Everyone knows this, yet the rule is hard to apply when the number or identity of the subject is debatable. Compound subjects make for ambiguities; terms that look deceptively like subjects come between the subject and its verb; predicate nouns challenge the subject's control of the verb; inverted syntax makes for confusion; and so do subjects consisting of phrases or clauses. Even when the subject is plainly a certain word, that word may appear singular to some people and plural to others. Here are the problem areas:

Collective Nouns

A collective noun is a word that is singular in form but possibly plural in meaning, since it refers to a collection of individuals or items: *administration, army, audience, band, class, committee, crowd, faculty, family, fleet, government, public, team,* etc. In England such terms are regularly treated as plural: *Oxford are giving Cambridge the drubbing of their lives.* To an American, however, this sounds wrong. We tend to favor a singular verb if the group as a single whole is meant:

- The orchestra *is playing* better now that the conductor is sober.
- A strong, united faculty *is needed* to stand firm against the erosion of parking privileges.
- Priscilla objects to the middle class because, in her opinion, it *is* simply too middle-class.

Less often, we construe a collective noun to be plural because we are thinking of its separate members:

- The orchestra *have tuned* their instruments.

But such sentences always sound a bit awkward, and you would do better to rephrase: *The members of the orchestra have . . .*

Majority, minority, plurality, mass, and similar words can be either singular or plural, depending on what is being discussed, the totality (singular) or the items that make it up (plural). When you write *A minority of ten is too small,* you are thinking of *minority* as a single idea; when you write *A minority of dogs are terriers,* you are thinking of a sum of individual dogs. Thus:

TOTALITY (singular):
- The Democratic majority *is composed* of workers and shirkers.
- The mass of the two particles *was* difficult to measure.

SEPARATE ITEMS (plural):
- The majority of Democrats *are* staunchly *opposed* to local blackouts of the Game of the Week.
- The mass of men *lead* lives of quiet desperation.

Words like *group* and *body,* which don't denote a quantity of members, are less flexible in number than *majority,* etc. You should reserve them for singular uses: *the body is assembled.* In a sentence like *A large group of doctors agree with the Governor's criticism of Teddicare, group* is being misused for *number. Many doctors agree* would be even better on grounds of brevity.

Words like *part* and *portion* are customarily singular. Don't write *A portion of the audience were bored.*

The number of *number* needn't be bothersome if you keep in mind that *the number of* always takes the singular and *a number of* almost always takes the plural:

- The number of times Priscilla has prayed to be spared from vulgarity *is* beyond counting.
- A number of further prayers *are expected* in the next few days.

Though it's technically possible for a word to be both singular and plural within one sentence, such constructions always sound imperfect and should be avoided:

- Random House *has accepted* his manuscript, but they want him to make it a little dirtier.

(Here *Random House* is first a collective entity, then a number of editors.)

Quantities

When the subject of a clause is a plural quantity, don't instinctively choose a plural verb. As in the case of *majority*, etc., ask yourself whether the quantity is intended as a unit (singular) or a number of items (plural):

AS A UNIT (singular):
- Twenty-six miles *is* the length of the race.
- Richie says that thirteen dollars *is* the price of this authentic term paper.

AS A NUMBER OF ITEMS (plural):
- Those five glorious days in Newark *are* the ones she remembers best.
- Eleven identical papers *are* enough to arouse any teacher's suspicion.

When adding and multiplying, you may use either a singular or a plural verb:

- One and one *is* (*are*) two.
- Eleven times three *is* (*are*) thirty-three.

In multiplication, however, the singular is more common. When the multiplication is expressed without *times*, the plural is required:

- Eleven threes *are* thirty-three.

Use the singular for all subtraction:

- Sixty minus forty *is* twenty.
- Twenty from sixty *is* [*leaves*] forty.

Troublesome Terms

each   As a subject, *each* is always singular, even when followed by *of them:*

- Each of them *has* his own way of doing things.

But note that *each* often appears in apposition with a plural subject. In this role it means *apiece* and doesn't affect the number of the verb:

- They each *have* their own habits.

-ics   Words ending in *-ics* that refer to a body of knowledge (*dialectics, dynamics, mathematics,* etc.) are singular if the whole field or subject is meant:

- Priscilla's paper argues that ethics *is* nothing more than a branch of esthetics.

In more limited senses, where the practical application of the field is meant, these words govern plural verbs:

- Stanley's politics, by the time he left Berkeley, *were* so altered that he now suspected the masses of being an elitist clique.

it is   The verb in a relative clause following *it is* is governed in number by the antecedent noun or pronoun, not by *it:*

- It is his vices that *make* him so endearing.

(*Make* agrees with the plural *vices.*)

means   *Means* in the sense of *money* is always plural: *Her means were exhausted.* In other senses, however, it is flexible in number, and you can write what sounds best to you. Both verbs are correct in this sentence:

- Harry's means of operation *is* (*are*) to quote the customer an attractive price and then count the tires as options.

nobody, no one   Because these are invariably singular, they can be substituted for *none* when a singular meaning is intended:

- Nobody who *has heard* Stanley's proposal is . . .

none   Is it singular or plural? Experts disagree. Purists who tell you that *none* can never take a plural verb aren't describing normal usage.

The fact that *none* literally means *no one* (singular) isn't decisive; *agenda*, after all, means *things to be done*, yet it's invariably singular. What counts is the intended meaning in a given sentence. In most sentences either a singular or a plural verb would sound correct, and the choice should be made according to whether you want to emphasize the sense of *not a single one*. For example:

- None among us *is* likely to agree with Stanley's proposal to smash racism by blowing up Kentucky Fried Chicken.

(The writer's use of a singular verb highlights the insistence that *not one* supporter can be found.)

In the following sentence the plural verb gives *none* a less pointed sense:

- None of us *are* enthusiastic about Operation Fingerlicker.

Both of these sentences would still be grammatical if the verbs were reversed. But since some readers will always regard the plural as wrong, you should probably incline toward the singular in doubtful cases.

Relative clauses following *none* should match the number you've chosen for the main verb:

- None that have heard Stanley's proposal *are* willing to support it.

(*Are* is required by the plural main verb, *have heard*.)

one of those who   This formula should be followed by a plural verb. The verb is part of a relative clause (p. 165) beginning with *who* and is governed in number by the antecedent of *who*, which is always plural:

ANTE   V
- Harry is one of those *people* who *come* up to you with a leer, slap you on the back, and say, "Free the Indianapolis 500! Haw, haw, haw!"

You can't apply this rule unthinkingly, though. Once in a while the antecedent of *who* turns out to be *one*:

- Roberta is the only one of those feminists who *believes* that men, having been given a fair test of their ability to run the country, should now be deprived of the vote.

there is,
there are   These anticipatory constructions shouldn't be considered as a normal subject-and-verb. *There* indicates that the real subject will follow; the verb should be governed by that delayed subject. Thus, in the following sentences, *reason* and *reasons* are the subjects:

- There *is* every reason to think so.
- There *are* three possible reasons for this strange turn of events.

Sir Ernest Gowers observes, "It is true that Ophelia said 'There is pansies.' But she was not herself at the time."[4]

those kind of This phrase is widely considered to be a mistake in itself because of the clash between a plural modifier and a singular noun. Rather than try to decide whether the phrase should take a singular or a plural verb, you'd do better not to use it at all.

what When followed by a plural predicate, *what* makes for verb trouble. Consider:

- What Stanley wants *is* [*are?*] revolutions everywhere.

Some writers, thinking that *what* must always be singular, would consider *are* a mistake in this example. All the authorities agree, however, that *what* can be considered either singular or plural depending on the context. But what does the context call for here? On this point the authorities disagree among themselves. The result is that (a) you can choose either verb, and (b) you might be better advised to rephrase, since either choice will sound wrong to some readers. Try *Stanley wants . . .* or *What Stanley wants is world-wide revolution.*

Compound Subject

and When a subject is made up of coordinate items joined by *and*, the verb is nearly always plural:

- Harry says that December and January *are* good months for selling cars because of the tricky winter light.

There are a few exceptions, notably subjects that make up a single unit and subjects that identify a singular item in different ways. These subjects take a singular verb:

SINGLE UNIT:
- William and Mary *is wondering* why Roberta addressed her admissions application to "Mary College."

DIFFERENT WAYS OF IDENTIFYING A SINGULAR ITEM:
- A revolutionary chick and a girl who knows how to mend socks *is* what Stanley says he's looking for in an old lady.

But a writer who uses a singular verb with a compound subject usually does so by mistake. He has reached for a compound cliché without noticing its plural sense, or he has carelessly allowed the verb to be governed by the nearest portion of the subject.

or, nor When *or* or *nor* joins the parts of a compound subject, the verb should be governed only by the nearest part of the subject. But you shouldn't strain this rule by putting singular and plural parts together, as here:

- Neither Priscilla's old high-school *teachers* nor her *mother understands* a word she says on her vacations from Radcliffe.

(It would be better to take a few extra words and say *Priscilla's old high-school teachers don't understand . . . , and neither does her mother.*)

either . . . or; neither . . . nor Don't mix pronoun forms requiring completely different verb forms:

- Either you or I *am* lying.

One of us is lying says the same thing without agony.
    The temptation to treat disjunctive parts of a subject (*either x or y*) as if they were cumulative (*both x and y*) is especially strong where a cumulative *sense* is implied. Most grammarians would balk at the following sentences, but they represent a common speech habit:

- Neither of us *are* [*is*] completely innocent of that charge.
- She has offered two reasons, neither of which *impress*[*es*] me in the slightest.

(The writer means *Both of us are guilty* and *Both of her reasons fail to impress me.* Understandably, he has allowed the intervening phrases *of us* and *of which* to affect the number of his verbs. But having chosen in each case to use *neither* with a total of two items, the writer would have done better to keep to singular verbs.)
    It isn't true that you must have only two items in an *either . . . or* or a *neither . . . nor* construction. Remember, though, that no heaping-up of items justifies a plural verb unless the items themselves are plural. The singular verb is correct here:

- Neither war, nor the decline of the economy, nor racial tension, nor the pollution of the environment *prevents* politicians from boasting of their accomplishments.

Terms like *as well as, in addition to, together with,* and *plus* should be treated as prepositions, not as coordinating conjunctions linking the parts of a compound subject. The presence of these terms doesn't guarantee a plural verb. The following sentences are correct:

- The giant corporation, together with its various satellite companies, its major clients, and its suppliers, *is* so powerful and far-reaching that it constitutes a miniature economy in itself.
- Roberta, as well as the other sisters in her collective, *spends* her leisure time hurling darts at Hugh Hefner's picture.

Intervening Terms

Phrases inserted, however appropriately, between a subject and its verb can exert a powerful charm on the number of the verb. This attraction has to be resisted. You won't have any trouble recognizing that these sentences are faulty, but you might occasionally make similar mistakes through carelessness:

- Stipulations as to the precise width of this unit *has* [*have*] not been received.
- Harry says that the major cause of highway fatalities *are* [*is*] hippie-freak pedestrians.

Only the bracketed forms are acceptable.

Predicate Nouns

A verb should always be governed in number by its subject, never by a predicate noun. These sentences are wrong:

- Priscilla's salvation after a hard day of dealing with ordinary people *were* [*was*] her long-playing motets and liturgical chants.
- Several newly passed state laws *was* [*were*] the chief obstacle to Richie's success.

Try to avoid writing sentences whose subject and predicate noun differ in number; this will relieve your verbs of conflicting pressures.

Inverted Syntax

When a subject follows the verb it should govern, the verb may wrongly borrow its number from a preceding noun. This mistake occurs here:

- Immediately after the light rains of early November have dampened the woods *come* [*comes*] the time when Melody can be found gathering certain prized mushrooms.

(The subject here is *time*, and the verb should be *comes*; the writer has allowed a direct object, *woods*, to influence the number of the verb.)

Subjects Consisting of Phrases or Clauses

When a subject is a whole phrase or clause, it usually takes a singular verb, regardless of the plural items it may contain. These sentences are correct:

* That none of his customers wanted to buy a 1947 De Soto *was* a disagreeable surprise for Harry.
* Having the phone numbers of several bail bondsmen *is* useful in an emergency, Stanley found.

But there are apparent exceptions to the rule. Consider:

* Whatever measures you have taken *are* likely to fail.
* What are sovereign property rights to some people *are* nothing at all to Stanley.

(The verbs sound right here, and the best interpretation is that they're governed by *measures* and *rights*, not by whole clauses.)

Titles

Titles of books, articles, etc., are always construed as singular in American English:

* *Troilus and Cressida*, Biff learned, *is* a problem play, and his problem was how to get past the first page.

Organizations

Organizations with plural names govern plural verbs unless the names are abbreviated:

* The Marines *are* a familiar sight in Central America.
* The U.S.M.C. *makes* amphibious landings to preserve self-determination.

PRONOUN FORMS

Pronoun reference — the relation of pronouns to their antecedents — is a complex matter treated separately (see pp. 190–193). Other problems with pronouns have to do with the choice between one pronoun and another, the formation of possessives, and the choice between subjective, objective, and possessive case forms.

Choice of Pronoun

reflexives and intensives   Pronouns like *himself* and *themselves* are considered either reflexive or intensive, depending on whether they receive the action of the verb (reflexive: *I hurt myself*) or are used for emphasis (intensive: *I myself was hurt*). Intensive pronouns shouldn't be freely substituted for personal pronouns like *me*, *him*, and *them*. This advice applies especially to *myself*, which some people think is more discreet than *I* or *me*. Actually it's just a screen to cover the writer's uncertainty between choosing *I* or *me:*

- The other Fingerlickers and *myself* [*I*] will stop at nothing in our terrorism against Colonel Sanders.

that* versus *which   A clause that identifies an antecedent is called *restrictive* because it serves to limit the antecedent's meaning. Either *that* or *which* can be used to introduce such a clause:

- Melody's hang-loose attitude was the reason *that* [*which*] the store manager gave for firing her from the lingerie department.

(The clause beginning at *that* or *which* serves to identify the antecedent *reason.*)

A *nonrestrictive* clause is one that comments on an antecedent instead of identifying it. Nonrestrictive clauses can be introduced by *which* but never *that:*

- A more specific reason, *which* the manager didn't mention to Melody, was that she always asked the customers for spare change.

(*Which the manager didn't mention to Melody* is a nonrestrictive clause, since it doesn't serve to identify its antecedent *reason.* Note how the commas convey the nonrestrictive sense [see pp. 276–277]. The sentence would be incorrect if *which* were replaced by *that.*)

Some writers, recognizing that *which* and *that* aren't interchangeable in nonrestrictive clauses, prefer to use only *that* in restrictive clauses. In the first example above, they would regard *which* as a mistake. Although this distinction isn't strictly required for correctness, it has the advantage of always serving notice when a clause is going to be restrictive. No harm can come from holding yourself to this "rule": *that* for restrictive, *which* for nonrestrictive clauses.

When a relative pronoun is both restrictive and objective in case, it can be omitted for the sake of economy:

• This Studebaker is the car [*that*] Bobo stole from Harry's lot.

In general it's useful to omit the relative pronoun in sentences like this one. Note that the omission can neatly solve a *that/which* dilemma such as the one in the sentence about *Melody's hang-loose attitude* (p. 184).

whose versus of which Some grammarians say that *whose* can't be used for inanimate things, but most good writers intuitively know that this supposed rule can make for ungainly sentences:

• The earth, in the depths *of which* volcanic disturbances continually occur . . .

(This is not only awkward but ambiguous: *which* looks for a moment as if it modified *disturbances. In whose depths* is better on both counts.)

coordinate possessive pronouns Note that most of the personal pronouns (p. 152) have two possessive forms, one for use before nouns (*my* hat, *your* knee, *our* foolishness) and one to stand alone (the hat is *mine/yours/ours*). Coordinate pairs of the first type (*my and your hat, our and their knees*) make an awkward impression. It's preferable to use one possessive of each type: *my hat and yours, our knees and theirs*.

Formation of Possessives

possessives of personal and relative pronouns Personal and relative pronouns (p. 153) don't have apostrophes in their possessive form:

wrong	right
your's	yours
her's	hers
our's	ours
their's	theirs
who's	whose
it's	its

possessives of indefinite pronouns The *-'s* possessive form shouldn't be given to *all, any, both, each, few, many, most, none, several, some*, or *such*.

WRONG:
- Both's views were taken into account.

RIGHT:
- The views of both were taken into account.

Other indefinite pronouns can become possessive by adding -'s: *another, anybody, anyone, each one, everybody, everyone, nobody, no one, one, other, somebody, someone.* Thus, *no one's fault, somebody's joy,* etc.

Choice of Case

English has little use for case endings (pp. 151–152). We customarily rely on a word's position to tell us whether it's subjective (the *man* swallowed the acid) or objective (the acid swallowed the *man*). But most of the personal pronouns and the relative or interrogative *who* still change their form to indicate case. In conversation the cases are sometimes ignored: *Who* [not *whom*] *do you think I mean? It is me* [not *I*]. In writing, however, most people expect "good grammar" to prevail over informality.

Beware of automatically choosing the formal-sounding subjective case: *This is for we* [*us*] *to decide.* Of course you have to examine the syntax of each sentence to see which form is called for. In this example the pronoun is the subject of the infinitive *to decide,* and therefore it has to be *us* (see p. 187). Note that the object of the preposition *for* is the entire phrase *us to decide.*

objects of prepositions; As the names imply, the pronouns serving these
direct objects; indirect objects functions should be written in the objective case:

                I OBJ
- Stanley gave *her* a copy of his pamphlet on brotherhood, but Roberta
                OBJ PREP   D OBJ
  sent it back to *him* with a note saying that she saw *him* now for the patri-

  archal chauvinist that he was.

Mistakes sometimes occur when pronouns occur in pairs or are paired with nouns:

- Roberta appointed *she* and *I* [*her* and *me*] to a subcommittee to investigate why Suzie allowed her picture to appear in *Playboy.*

(*She* and *I* are direct objects. *Her and me* would be technically right, *us* preferable.)

• No one could ever explain to Melody and *she* [*her*] why they couldn't buy morning glory seeds with their food stamps.

(*She* should be *her* because it is the object of a preposition.)

pronoun complements   Whereas pronoun objects are in the objective case (the pronoun receives the action of the verb: *He hit her*), pronoun complements are in the subjective case (the pronoun identifies the subject: *It is she*). This, at least, is the accepted rule. But if *It is her* sounds ungrammatical, *It is she* sounds rigid and fastidious. The moral is to avoid pronoun complements wherever you can.

comparisons with *than*   When *than* is a conjunction, a following pronoun should be in the subjective case: *She was taller than he was.* When the verb is missing, most grammarians advise that the subjective pronoun be retained: *She was taller than he.* But this sounds forced. A wiser policy would be to restore the verb so as to remove all ambiguity. Note, however, that in some sentences both terms of comparison are objects and belong in the objective case: *Biff tackled him harder than me.*

but constructions   Like *than*, *but* can be considered either a preposition or a conjunction, with different effects on the pronoun following it. Experts quarrel over the correctness of sentences like this:

• All the sisters but *she* [*her*?] had finished their commando training.

Authority can be found for both versions — and therefore both versions can make for uneasiness. You would do well to circumvent the dilemma instead of trying to solve it: *Suzie was the only sister who hadn't finished her commando training.*

subjects of infinitives   These are always in the objective case:

S INF
• Biff bought a hypodermic needle after the coach gave *us* to understand that speed makes a winning team.

(You could also regard *us* as the indirect object of *gave*. Either way, the objective case is called for.)

objects of infinitives   These of course belong in the objective case, as every native speaker senses: *He wanted to catch her.* *Her* is the object of the infinitive *to catch*.

complements of infinitives A pronoun following the infinitive of a linking verb (p. 144) is considered a complement (p. 162) rather than an object. Nevertheless, it too should be placed in the objective case:

- In the self-criticism meeting Roberta told Suzie she was glad not to be *her.*

Many writers would regard this *her* as a blunder for *she*, but *her* is strictly correct. To avoid confusion, carefully note the difference between the complement of a *verb form* (subjective case) and the complement of an *infinitive* (objective case):

COMPLEMENT OF A VERB FORM:
- It is *she.*

COMPLEMENT OF AN INFINITIVE:
- He wanted it to be *her.*

(For the case of pronouns preceding a gerund, see pp. 198–199.)

pronouns followed by relative clauses The case of a personal pronoun shouldn't be affected by the case of a relative pronoun immediately following it. Look at this sentence:

- Philo believed that women tend to prefer *he* [*him*] who skips all the boring preliminaries.

(In this sentence *who skips all the boring preliminaries* is a relative clause. Relative clauses, you remember, always function adjectivally, and in this case the relative clause modifies the pronoun it follows. But the writer has allowed that pronoun to be seduced away from its own clause, *Philo believed that women tend to prefer him*, and to acquire the case of *who*. Since each clause should mind its own business and not covet the other's object, the pronoun has to be *him*. But *him who*, like all juxtapositions of pronouns in different cases, sounds awkward, and the writer should contrive a way around it. Try *Philo believed that women tend to prefer a man who . . .*)

pronouns followed by appositives When a pronoun is followed by a close appositive (appositives are defined on p. 163), many writers are inclined to put the pronoun in the subjective case:

- Parking is a problem for *we* [*us*] professors.

(This is an error. The pronoun here is the object of the preposition *for*, and it has to be in the objective case.)

The rule about appositive nouns is that they should have no effect on the case of pronouns. The pronoun's *own* function in the sentence determines its case. The following sentences are correctly formed:

S   V
- *We* Americans *are* connoisseurs of bubble gum.
  OBJ PREP
- Digestion is a problem for *us* Americans.
  I OBJ
- They gave *us* Americans a royal welcome.

Pronoun complements sound awkward with appositives. Try to avoid writing "correct" sentences like this:

- The people most affected by this regulation will be *we* students.

who versus whom   Strictly interpreted, the rules say that:

1. *Who* is mandatory for subjects, no matter how strongly they may resemble objects:

- Suzie had no doubt about *who* would be elected chairperson.
- Stanley, *who* they suppose is ignorant of their plans, is preparing a little surprise for them.

(Both sentences are correct, since in each case *who* is the subject of a clause: *who would be elected chairperson; who is ignorant of their plans.* But it would be easy to go astray and write *whom* in both sentences.)

2. *Whom* is mandatory for objects of prepositions, direct objects, indirect objects, subjects of infinitives, and objects of infinitives, regardless of where these forms occur in a sentence:

OBJ PREP
- To *whom* was it given?
  D OBJ
- You said you kissed *whom?*
  I OBJ
- *Whom* have you sent?
  S INF
- *Whom* did you order to be arrested?
  OBJ INF
- *Whom* in this drama do you want me to play?

So much for strict interpretation of the rules. But *should* they be strictly interpreted? Most of us feel uncomfortable using objective-case pronouns in sentence positions that "feel" subjective. In conversation we tend to say *Who did you see there?*, overlooking the fact that the pronoun is a direct object of the verb *see*. Many writers take the same liberty—but many readers resent it. Suit yourself, or perhaps your teacher, but try to keep the problem from arising in the first place. Instead of either *Who did you see there?* or *Whom did you see there?* you can write *Who was there?*, *Which people did you see there?*, etc.

PRONOUN REFERENCE

Some indefinite pronouns, such as *anybody* and *no one*, are regularly used without antecedents (words they stand for). Interrogative pronouns in noun clauses also lack antecedents; *who* doesn't refer to any prior word in *I asked who he was*. Otherwise, pronouns must have antecedents. Two problems are associated with this fact: the antecedent isn't always sufficiently identifiable, and the writer sometimes fails to make the pronoun agree with it in number or person.

Identification of the Antecedent

explicit antecedent   As a rule, the antecedent of a pronoun is a noun or nominal element (a word or set of words occupying the function of a noun) in the same sentence or in the preceding sentence. There are cases in which a personal pronoun is so clearly identified that it can be repeated in several successive sentences without repetition of the antecedent, but you should realize that your pronoun credit is quickly exhausted.

An antecedent ought to be explicitly there, even when the reader has a clear idea of what it is. The following sentences don't quite measure up:

- The French generals knew that they could put up little resistance to the German army. But war was inevitable, and *she* had to pay dearly for her unpreparedness.

(*France* isn't mentioned.)

Note that even a noun won't do as an antecedent if it stands in an attributive (adjectival) position:

- The *sherry* bottle was empty, but we were tired of drinking *it* anyway.

(Drinking the bottle? *Sherry* is adjectival.)

The justification for a pronoun is that it can refer without fuss to a previously established person, thing, or idea. As soon as the reader must pause, even for a moment, in order to identify the antecedent, your pronoun is causing more bother than it's saving. We have just considered some sentences from which the necessary antecedent is absent. Here now are sentences in which the antecedent appears, but too dimly to be recognized without effort:

- Biff thought it was a shame that Roberta had expelled Suzie from the Abzug Collective, but he certainly was glad *she* was seeking new companionship.

(Two nouns, *Roberta* and *Suzie*, could be the antecedent of *she*. Our acquaintance with Roberta suggests that the antecedent is *Suzie*, but the writer has put *Roberta* in more prominent contention; both *Roberta* and *she* are subjects of clauses.)

- For those with eyes to see *it* is obvious that Richie is headed for the top of his profession.

(*It* looks at first to be the direct object of *see*, but it's really an anticipatory signal of a delayed subject, the clause *that Richie is headed . . .* The problem can be solved by a comma after *see*.)

a whole statement as antecedent   There are exceptions to the rule that a pronoun must have an explicit antecedent. The demonstrative pronouns *this*, *that*, and *which* sometimes stand for whole preceding statements:

- Bobo heard an ecologist on television talking about the importance of the food chain. *That* was what gave him the idea of holding up the supermarket.

(*That* refers to the previous sentence in general.)

- Bobo insisted on getting Blue Chip Stamps in the amount of the robbery, and *this* proved to be his big mistake.

(*This* means Bobo's whole action.)

- As he was being handcuffed, Bobo complained bitterly about the poor service—*which* the clerk thought was rather poor sportsmanship.

(Here the writer wants *which* to mean everything from *Bobo* to *service*. But the sentence runs into a problem: *service* looks like a specific antecedent of *which*. If a demonstrative pronoun is to stand for a whole statement, you have to be on the lookout for nouns that might be mistaken for one-word antecedents. Note that even the first two examples aren't altogether free of ambiguity. What gave Bobo his idea—the importance of the food chain or the ecologist's televised remarks? And what proved to be Bobo's big mistake—his getting the stamps or his insistence on getting them? The safest policy is to keep to explicit antecedents.)

Agreement with the Antecedent

Pronouns should agree with their antecedents in number and person, but not necessarily in case. A main cause of error in pronoun reference has already been discussed (p. 188). To repeat, the case of a pronoun has to be judged by its syntactical function within its own clause, not by the syntactical function of its antecedent. Problems arise with both personal and relative pronouns.

personal
pronouns

Many speakers and some writers shift from a singular antecedent to a plural pronoun:

> ANT
> • Melody thought that a *person* could never be too careful about where
> PRO
> *they* hid their stash.

Such changes of number are so widespread that they might well be considered normal. They do have one great advantage: they get around the objectionable masculine common gender, *he hides his stash* (see p. 193). You should know, however, that most conscientious writers would regard *they hid their stash* as a simple blunder, not a protest against male-dominated grammar.

When an antecedent consists of two coordinate terms, the pronoun must be plural (*x and y . . . they*). When an antecedent consists of two disjunctive terms, both singular, the pronoun must be singular (*x or y . . . he, she, it; neither x nor y . . . he, she, it*). This at least is the grammarians' rule, which would require you, for example, to write *Neither Melody's parents nor Melody herself is prudish.* But this sounds extremely awkward. It's better to recast all sentences in which disjunctive terms differ in number: *Melody's parents aren't prudish, and neither is Melody herself; Melody is just as free of prudishness as her parents are;* etc.

***one* as an antecedent** *One* shouldn't be followed by a plural equivalent, as it is here:

> • One has to watch *their [one's]* manners and never open doors for Roberta.

(*One's* or *his* would be equally correct in place of *their*.)

When *one* clearly refers to a female, it can be followed by a feminine pronoun (*she, her*):

> • One expects her husband to be startled when *she* first mentions the renegotiation of the marriage contract.

In general, however, *one's* or *his* prevails wherever the *one* doesn't clearly refer to a female. This is a legitimate matter for complaint, but as yet no substitute form has been widely adopted. *His* is still regarded as "common gender," with the somewhat cumbersome *his or her* available for times when you want to indicate unmistakably that both sexes are intended.

relative pronouns The case problems raised by the relative pronouns *who, whose, that,* and *which* are confined to the choice between *who* and *whom,* already discussed (pp. 189–190). The rule, once again, is that a pronoun's case has to be decided according to its function within its own clause. Subtler difficulties occur in some sentences where a relative pronoun is asked to do either too much or too little syntactic work. Thus, in the two following sentences, the relative pronouns *who* and *that* are overburdened:

- Roberta is an efficient worker who, if you wanted to employ [*her*], would spare you an ugly lawsuit.

(The relative clause here is *who would spare you an ugly lawsuit,* but *who* is being illegitimately borrowed as the direct object of *employ.* The personal pronoun *her* has to be supplied after *employ* so that each clause will be complete in itself.)

- Cracking heads is the task that [*it*] will be Biff's destiny to fulfill.

(This is a teaser which may look acceptable. But *that* is being saddled with two incompatible jobs within its own clause: it's the subject of *will be* and the object of *to fulfill.* An *it* is needed after *that* to relieve *that* of its extra function as subject of the clause.)

Conversely, an extra personal pronoun sometimes sneaks into a relative clause that is already complete without it:

- Priscilla is someone that nobody could decide what to give *her* for Christmas.

(*Her* is competing with *that* as the object of the infinitive *to give.* The sentence would be improved, though not perfected, by deletion of *her.* Of course, the easiest solution is to write *Nobody could decide what to give Priscilla for Christmas.*)

MODIFIERS

A modifier is any word or set of words that defines or describes another word. The fundamental modifiers are *adjectives* and *adverbs;* other modifiers when analyzed always prove to be serving the function of either adjectives or adverbs. Elements that constitute modifiers include *appositives* (p. 163), some *infinitives* and *infinitive phrases* (p. 163), *participles* and *participial phrases* (pp. 163–164), *possessive nouns* and *pronouns* (pp. 151–152), *prepositional phrases* (p. 157), and most *subordinate clauses* (p. 164). Problems associated with possessives (pp. 197–199) and subordinate clauses (pp. 88–94) are treated elsewhere.

Wrong Choice of Modifier

The close resemblance of adjectives and adverbs (p. 156) is a source of potential trouble. Note that (a) some adjectives and adverbs are identical in form, and (b) it's important to have a sense of the difference between them. Otherwise you might compose sentences like this:

- She takes me *real serious* [*really seriously*] now that I've proved how *impressive* [*impressively*] I can play the kazoo.

All the italicized words are adjectives trying to pass for adverbs. The question should always be: What does the word modify? If it doesn't modify a noun or pronoun, it must be an adverb. But don't indiscriminately tack -*ly* onto an adjectival form every time you decide that it's functioning as an adverb. Some adverbs, like *bad* and *deep*, are appropriate in certain contexts where the -*ly* form would be wrong:

- *Deeply* [*deep*] down inside, Richie was feeling *badly* [*bad*] about selling Biff a paper on Tennessee Williams for Biff's course in the geology of Appalachia.

(To *feel badly* is to do an inferior job of feeling.)

Misrelated Modifiers

A *misrelated* modifier is one with a flawed relation to the term it modifies. Either the modified term is hard to identify, or the modifier unnecessarily interrupts another construction, or there's too much distance between the modifier and what it modifies.

squinting modifiers   Beware of sandwiching a modifier between two sentence elements that might compete to serve as the modified term. This becomes a *squinting* modifier—one that seems to be looking in two directions at once:

- How Harry silenced the transmission *completely* amazes me.

(Does *completely* modify *silence* or *amazes?* In saying the sentence aloud, a speaker would control the meaning by his use of pauses and stresses, as you can see if you speak each of the possible versions in turn. On the page, however, these signals are missing. A reader may *suspect* that the writer means either *silenced completely* or *completely amazes*, and with luck he may get the right interpretation. But a writer's business is to take the luck out of reading.)
    Again:

- Priscilla was *confident* on Tuesday she would receive a divine signal.

(Was she confident on Tuesday, or would she receive the signal on Tuesday? A timely *that*, placed either before or after *on Tuesday*, would make everything clear.)

split infinitives   Much nail-biting over adverbs can be traced to the taboo of the *split infinitive*—the most discussed, but by no means the most important, point of debate among commentators on usage. A split infinitive is one containing an adverb between *to* and the next verb form: *to thoroughly understand*. Most writers would now indulge in an occasional split infinitive, but only where every alternative position for the adverb would make for even more awkwardness:

- Harry always made it a point to *clearly* state that his cars carried a twenty-minute, thirty-mile guarantee.

(If the writer were in terror of splitting an infinitive he might have written *clearly to state* or *to state clearly*. But the trouble with these alternatives, especially the first, is that they would have called attention to the writer's discomfort. It's better to split and have done with it than to sound overfastidious.)
    Although opinion is divided about the importance of avoiding split infinitives, everyone agrees that adverbial constructions of more than one word make an ugly effect in the split-infinitive position: *I want to soberly and patiently analyze the problem*. Rephrase: *I want to analyze the problem soberly and patiently* or *I want to make a sober and patient analysis . . .*
    Like other taboos, the one against splitting an infinitive tends to spread irrationally. Some writers would consider *I have soberly and*

patiently analyzed the problem an example of a split infinitive, and they would labor to recast the sentence. Of course it contains no infinitive at all; the adverbs are right where they belong.

misplaced sentence elements Sentence elements such as participial phrases, prepositional phrases, infinitive phrases, appositives, and whole clauses are liable to faulty placement. By the time a writer has finished a lengthy phrase, he may have lost track of what it was supposed to modify. Thus:

- Head of the Fingerlickers from the start, *they* naturally looked to Stanley for ideological guidance.

(The sentence begins with an appositive, and we expect the modified term, *Stanley*, to come immediately after it. Instead we get the misleading *they* in the key position.)
    Again:

- Thinking how delighted Priscilla would be with his advances, *it* was impossible for Philo to know that she had decided to give up everything for Lent.

(The participial phrase, *Thinking . . . advances*, ought to be followed at once by *Philo*, but the modified term is buried in the middle of the sentence.)
    Further:

- Philo would remember how Priscilla struck him with her prayer book *for the rest of his life.*

(The two prepositional phrases *for the rest of his life* belong at the beginning. As it stands, the sentence implies that Priscilla kept whacking Philo until he died.)
    As these sentences show, the way to correct a misrelated modifier is to bring it close to the modified term, making sure that no one could misunderstand the relation between them.

Dangling Modifier

If the modified term is altogether absent, the modifier is called *dangling*. The following sentences illustrate the problem:

- *Trying vainly to kick a field goal,* Biff's foot flailed the air like a dangling modifier.

(The term immediately following an initial participial phrase should be the thing modified. A foot can't try, even vainly; the participle calls for *Biff* alone.)

* *Embracing the astonished Priscilla*, a rash erupted behind Philo's left knee.

(A rash can't embrace.)

* The coat is Suzie's, a *woman* who leaves things behind like a retreating army.

(A possessive form, *Suzie's*, can't be in apposition with a nonpossessive one, *woman*.)

* *To protest ecological imbalance*, ball bearings will replace Easter eggs this year.

(The infinitive phrase dangles; nobody is identified as the protester.)
Once you find a dangling modifier, you can either supply the modified term or try a completely new construction. Here, for instance, a subordinate clause helps out:

DANGLING MODIFIER:
* *Making a date with the dermatologist*, Philo's appointment book was no longer empty.

CORRECTION:
* Philo's appointment book was no longer empty when he had made . . .

Note that the rule against dangling modifiers doesn't apply to certain *absolute phrases* (p. 164) which modify entire statements rather than single terms:

* *Granted that Biff is very strong*, it is still hard to account for Suzie's bruised ribs.
* *Generally speaking*, Melody's memory is rather smoky.

(In these sentences *granted* and *speaking* aren't intended to modify any single word.)

POSSESSIVES

Formation of possessives is discussed earlier (p. 152, p. 185). Most people have no trouble seeing where possessives should be used, but problems arise over double possessives and subjects of gerunds.

Double Possessives

A possessive relation can be indicated either by *of* or -*'s*, but there are times when both indicators can be used together. Compare:

- He enjoyed the observation *of* Lindbergh.

(Was he watching Lindbergh fly or listening to him speak? The sentence is ambiguous.)

- He enjoyed the observation *of* Lindbergh*'s*.

(No ambiguity: one of Lindbergh's remarks is intended.)
  Thus the double possessive, regarded as archaic by some grammarians, can occasionally serve to make your meaning clear. What it does is to insist on the possessive sense of *of*, ruling out other possible relationships. Note that everyone uses double possessives with pronouns: *a phobia of hers, that nasty habit of his.* You can use them just as easily with nouns: *a bookkeeping trick of Richie's, that sawed-off shotgun of Bobo's.*

Subjects of Gerunds and Gerund Phrases

The rule is that the subject of a gerund (p. 151) goes in the possessive case:

                                              S GER GER

- Biff didn't know why everyone laughed at *his saying* he would like to be an astronaut and see all those steroids going by.

But the rule is hard to apply in many instances. For example, if the gerund's subject is separated from the gerund by other words, that subject goes in the objective case instead of the possessive:

                                 S GER   GER

- People were surprised at *him*, a veteran speaker on many campuses, *having* no ready reply when Stanley seized the microphone and called him an irrelevant murderer.

When the subject of a gerund is a plural noun or more than one noun, the possessive is sometimes omitted:

- There is an excellent prospect of the Fingerlickers and the Abzug Collective severing relations.

When the subject of a gerund is an abstract noun (p. 140), the possessive can usually be omitted:

• We cannot ignore the danger of catastrophe striking again.

Furthermore, there is the problem of distinguishing a gerund from a participle and of deciding whether or not the word preceding a gerund is a true modifier. These sentences show the range of possible correct sentences:

• I saw Stanley throwing tear gas at the National Guard.

(Here *throwing* is an ordinary participle and *throwing tear gas at the National Guard* is a participial phrase.)

• Stanley, throwing tear gas at the National Guard, was a sight to behold.

(Again we have a participial phrase, in this case modifying a subject instead of a direct object.)

• Stanley's throwing tear gas at the National Guard was a sight to behold.

(*Throwing* is now a gerund and *throwing tear gas at the National Guard* a gerund phrase, serving as the subject of the sentence. *Stanley* must take a possessive form here in order to serve its modifying function: the sight to behold was Stanley's throwing, not Stanley alone.)

• Stanley throwing tear gas at the National Guard was a sight to behold.

(This is the hard one. Some people might say that *throwing . . . Guard* is once again a participial phrase, modifying *Stanley*. But note that the sight to behold is the complete phrase, *Stanley . . . Guard*. By saying *Stanley* instead of *Stanley's*, the writer shifts our interest from the action of throwing to the picture of Stanley throwing.)

VERB TENSES

It's obvious that you shouldn't change tenses capriciously when you're still referring to the same time. Occasionally, however, you can find yourself wondering how one time should be expressed in relation to another.

Past Tense Related to Prior Action

If your main verb is in the past tense and you want to relate it to a prior action, you should use the past perfect:

PAST   PAST PERFECT
- Philo *said* that Priscilla *had made* some truly repugnant accusations and that

PAST PERFECT   PAST   PAST PERFECT
he *had replied* to her with rancor. Suzie *wanted* to know what *had happened*

PAST   PAST PERFECT
before that, but Philo just *remarked* that he *had* always *thought* college girls

PAST
liked pink teddy bears.

Conditions and Consequences

When you state a condition in one clause and its consequence in another, be sure that the verb in the clause stating the condition is in the right tense. A hypothetical condition in the present should be expressed by a *past* verb:

PAST
- If you *tried* baby talk with Priscilla, you would regret it for a long time.

A common mistake is to put both verbs in the present, repeating the auxiliary *would:*

PRESENT
- If you *would try* baby talk with Priscilla, you would regret it for a long time.

Similarly, the statement of a past hypothetical condition requires the past perfect tense:

PAST PERFECT
- If Philo *had consulted* Roberta, he wouldn't have made that error.

Don't write *If Philo would have consulted Roberta, . . .*
   Note that these rules apply only to unlikely or untrue conditions. Native speakers of English generally don't have trouble with tenses when the condition is a plausible one: *If Roberta was watching, she must have been amused; If this is your idea of courtship, I feel sorry for you.*
   (For use of the subjunctive in unlikely conditions, see p. 148.)

Narrative Present

Writers of fiction sometimes place a narrative in the present so as to heighten its immediacy:

- I *turn* around and there she *is*, big as life. I *ask* her what she thinks she's doing, using my sauna without permission.

Tenses in Discussion of Literature

When you discuss the action of a literary work, you should rely on the present and present progressive tenses, with the past progressive and future tenses kept available for prior and subsequent moments in the plot:

    PRESENT   PAST PROG
- Lear *finds* himself alone on the heath. He *has been abandoned* by two of his

                          PAST PROG   FUTURE
    daughters and he *has spurned* the third. Before long he *will recognize* his

                                      PRESENT PROG
    abject state, but for the moment he *is* still *expecting* his loyal subjects to

    obey him.

This convention does make for some awkwardness when a quoted passage itself contains verbs in the past tense:

            PRESENT
- Lawrence *describes* Cecilia as "a big dark-complexioned, pug-faced young

                      PAST   PRESENT
    woman who very rarely *spoke* . . ." When she *does speak*, however, her

           PRESENT
    words *are* sharp enough to kill her aunt Pauline.

The temptation is to shift your summary of the action into the past to match the tenses of the narrative (*did speak*), but this is generally regarded as improper.

Unnecessary Duplication of Future

Don't duplicate the future tense when it's only needed once:

                      FUTURE   FUTURE
- The likeliest outcome *will be* that Stanley *will become* a stockbroker.

(*The likeliest outcome is* would be better.)

Participles and Infinitives in Relation to Tenses

A participle or infinitive expressing the same time as the verb should take a present form, even if the verb isn't in the present tense:

WRONG:
       PAST PERFECT   PAST INF
- He *had expected to have remained* loyal to the party.

RIGHT:
                 PRESENT INF
- He had expected *to remain* loyal to the party.

WRONG:

FUTURE PERFECT   PAST PART
* By tomorrow Bobo's wife *will have finished having read The Godfather* to him.

RIGHT:

PRESENT PART
* By tomorrow Bobo's wife will have finished *reading . . .*

PASSIVE VOICE

In addition to the stylistic abuse of the passive (pp. 86–87), two grammatical problems arise in passive constructions: faulty reference and duplication of emphasis.

Passive verbs are sometimes used after participial phrases that require an explicit referent:

* *Anticipating every taste*, it *was decided* to advertise the car as "an oversexed, pulse-quickening respecter of environmental quality."

(Nobody is doing the anticipating here; the participle dangles. Try: *Anticipating every taste, they decided . . .*)

Don't refer to a passive construction as if it were active:

* Thursday is when the job *ought to be undertaken*; if you *do so*, you will surely have finished it by Saturday.

(The difficulty here is that *do so* requires an active antecedent such as *undertake the job*. Don't use pronouns like *so, such, this*, and *that* unless a grammatically equivalent antecedent stands in plain view.)

Double passive constructions—a passive verb followed by a passive infinitive (*to be loved*) or passive participle (*being loved, having been loved*)—tend to be awkward, and sometimes they make the recipient of an action look like the agent:

* This misfortune is hoped to be averted.

(A misfortune is not really being hoped. The writer had better say *We hope to avert . . .*)

NEGATIVES

To handle negative statements unambiguously sometimes calls for a delicate touch. It isn't always clear how much of the sentence is being negated, and sometimes a negative intrudes where an affirmation was meant. Here are the most common sources of trouble:

Double Negatives

Accepted for centuries as imparting some extra emphasis to denials, double negatives are now regarded as canceling them and forming roundabout affirmations: *I don't intend to tell you nothing* means *I intend to tell you something*. Certain phrases that are fairly common in speech are widely disapproved in writing:

negatives with *shouldn't wonder;* In a sentence like *I shouldn't wonder if Bobo didn't*
**   *wouldn't be surprised;* etc.** *kill Mario Puzo,* the negative sense is unnecessarily doubled and made questionable. *Didn't kill* should be *killed* or *were to kill.*

cannot help but Many writers consider this a double negative, since *not* and *but* are separate forms of denial. You can satisfy everyone by changing *cannot help but wonder* to *cannot help wondering.*

**   *can't hardly;*** Since a negative sense is already attached to *hardly* and *scarcely,*
**   *can't scarcely;* etc.** the verb should be left in positive form: *He can hardly wait to get his finger on the trigger.*

**   *doubt but what;*** Both *doubt* and *but* have a negative force; thus in combination
**   *no doubt but that*** they make a double negative. In every case where *doubt but what* or *no doubt but that* comes to mind, what you want is *doubt that:*

- I don't *doubt that* fleas and mosquitoes will one day inherit the earth.
- There is no *doubt that* this is so.

**   *not . . . not*** A double negative sometimes results when a clause or lengthy phrase intervenes between *not* and the clause to be negated. The writer tosses in an extra negative because he no longer feels guided by the first one:

- Melody didn't think that, just because the trip was a short one, she *shouldn't* [*should*] go without a guide.

(Note that negative prepositions like *without* or *unless* can add to the confusion in such sentences.)

Ambiguous Scope

**   *all . . . not;*** Does *all . . . not* mean *fewer than all,* or does it mean *none?* Consider:
**   *not all***

- *All* the tea in China is*n't* worth exporting.

(The sentence could mean either that *only some* of the tea is worth exporting or that *none* of it is.)

It's true that many writers don't seem to care about this problem; they use *all . . . not* even when *not all* would save them from ambiguity. But this is a point where you might do well to observe a neglected distinction. Reserve *not all* for "fewer than all," steer clear of *all . . . not*, and choose a plainly universal negative when that's what the sense demands:

- *Not all* the people in attendance agreed with him.

(Some of them did.)

- Among the people in attendance, *none* agreed with him.

(The sentence says what it means.)

not . . . because   Without an explanatory *but* clause to follow it, this construction is open to misinterpretation. Consider:

- I did *not* do it *because* I am indifferent to your advice.

(Was the action not done at all, or was it done for a reason other than indifference to the listener's advice? If the clauses were reversed, or if *it* were followed by a comma, the ambiguity would disappear.)

nothing more than; nothing less than   Consider these sentences:

- I like *nothing more than* oysters for dinner.
- I like *nothing less than* oysters for dinner.

(Both sentences are ambiguous. The first could mean *I prefer to eat nothing but oysters* or *Oysters are my favorite dish.* The second could mean *I like the fanciest dinner of all, namely oysters* or *Oysters are what I most despise.*)

If you use these formulas, make sure that your sentences contain other signals that will remove any ambiguity:

- Although I clearly asked for the seafood plate, *nothing more than* oysters was served.
- *Nothing less than* a dozen bluepoint oysters on the half shell will satisfy me on my birthday.

either, neither; or, nor This is largely a matter of parallelism (see next section), but there is also the problem of choosing the right terms to indicate a negation. Beware of using *either* where *neither* is required:

- Stanley wasn't prosecuted, and *either* [*neither*] was Roberta.

A comparable mistake is to follow *not either* with *nor* instead of *or:*

- They have not either built the freeway *nor* [*or*] explained the delay.

Finally, *neither* should always be followed by *nor*, not *or:*

- They have neither built the freeway *or* [*nor*] explained the delay.

PARALLELISM   *and, but, or – coordinating conjunctions*

One rule covers all instances of parallelism: when elements in a sentence are parallel in meaning, they should also be parallel in structure. This sounds easy enough, yet everyone stumbles over parallelism from time to time. Even the late Wilson Follett, in introducing his excellent book on usage, could write a sentence beginning like this:

- If, then, we assume that language is not only to be spoken and suffered but can also be used . . .[5]

Here is a classic faulty parallelism, and you ought to be able to see where the difficulty lies. *Not only* announces a parallel structure to come: *not only x but y*. Everything depends on the placement of that *not only*. Since it comes after the verb (*is not only*), then there shouldn't be another verb after the *but: can be* has wrongly invaded the parallelism. There are several possible corrections, but the best one would be to get those past participles, *spoken, suffered*, and *used*, into concise alignment:

- . . . language is to be not only spoken and suffered, but also used.

(*Not only* participle *and* participle, *but also* participle.)

The fewer words that have to be repeated within the parallelism to keep it in balance, the better. But wherever you choose to start a sequence, you should supply neither more nor less than what you've promised.

Yet good writers do disagree among themselves about how exact a parallelism need be. Most of them, for instance, would be happy enough with the following sentences, which seem to go against the rule:

- The wolf is not only overrated as a killer, he hasn't been reliably impli-cated in a single attack on a human being.

(This seems to violate the formula *The wolf is not only x, but also y.* Some writers would insist on putting the *Not only is* at the begin-ning of the sentence.)

- I am not only going to interrogate Clifford, but also Edith.

(We might prefer the strictly parallel *I am going to interrogate not only Clifford, but Edith as well.*)
You have some leeway in deciding whether to keep to a higher standard of precision than the one represented by these sentences, which are less obviously askew than Follett's. But you can't go wrong by being a strict constructionist as a writer, however tolerant you may be as a reader.
Of course the *not only . . . but* formula is involved in only a mi-nority of parallelisms. Most problems arise in connection with the following categories, which are treated elsewhere in the book: ele-ments in a series (pp. 271–272); compound subjects and verbs (pp. 180–181); comparisons (pp. 207–211) and equations (pp. 87–88).
In addition, the following faulty sentences indicate some typical problems:

- The Marquis de Sade was not an agreeable man, and neither are his novels.

(This sentence appears to say that Sade's novels are not an agree-able man. The noun *man* commits the second clause to the mention of a second man. What the writer wants is *The Marquis de Sade was not agreeable, . . .*)

- Harry hoped, neither as a citizen nor as a father, to see Dr. Spock elected President.

(The parallelism looks perfect in itself, but it's wrongly attached to the rest of the sentence. The commas set off a parenthetical aside, leaving the main statement *Harry hoped to see Dr. Spock elected President.* Harry would resent this implication. Try *Both as a father and as a citizen, Harry hoped for Dr. Spock's defeat.*)

- The painting reminded Harry of a moonscape and that his driveway needed repairing.

(It's awkward to put a prepositional phrase, *of a moonscape*, into parallelism with a clause, *that his driveway needed repairing*. Try *The painting reminded Harry of two things—a moonscape and his pitted driveway.*)

- She can, and indeed has been, winning every tournament.

(Auxiliaries like *can* and *should* must be completed by infinitive forms: *can win*. Present and past progressive verbs are formed with the participle: *has been winning*. You can't use a participle to complete a parallelism between an auxiliary and a progressive form. The sentence could read: *She can win, and indeed has been winning, . . .*)

- Roberta was sad rather than angry at Melody for hitchhiking in both directions at once.

(*At Melody* has a retroactive force affecting both parts of the parallelism *sad rather than angry;* thus we get the absurdity *Roberta was sad at Melody.*)

COMPARISONS

When one term in a sentence is compared with another, you must make sure that they're comparable and syntactically equivalent. This is largely but not entirely a matter of parallelism (previous section). Here are some further puzzles and pitfalls.

Missing Terms

At least two terms should be explicitly present if a comparison is to be made. This seems obvious, but it is blurred by the influence of advertising style: *Get 23 percent less emphysema!* It's true, to be sure, that some normal expressions contain incomplete comparisons: *I feel better today, It is best for you to leave, You have been most helpful,* etc. No one would regard these sentences as erroneous; either the rest of the comparison is clearly implied (*I feel better today than yesterday*) or the comparative word is being used merely as an intensifier (*most* = "very"). The problem sentences are those in which we wait for the second shoe to drop:

- Biff learned that it was *more* important for a pro quarterback to be able to shave in front of a TV crew without snickering.
- *Fewer* grapefruit-eaters are now wearing goggles.

These sentences goad us into asking *than what?* and *than when?* Even if we can easily supply answers, we've been put to unnecessary trouble.

Many writers object to the use of superlative adjectives for emphasis when no comparison is intended. The effect is gushy:

- Biff has had the *oddest* complexion since he started taking those shots.

Comparison of Absolutes

Words like *complete, equal, infinite, perfect,* and *unique* are sometimes called absolutes; that is, they are regarded as not lending themselves to qualification. If something isn't altogether unique, it isn't unique at all. But does this mean that such words should never be modified or compared? When you look at sentences one by one you find that matters aren't so simple. Thus the comparison of *perfect* sounds normal enough in this sentence:

- Our purpose in founding this institute in Zurich is to form a *more* perfect Jungian.

Or again:

- The inclusion of his early letters to Santa Claus makes this the *most* complete edition of Dickens ever published.

But compare:

- The sands of Lake Havasu City are *less* infinite than those of the Sahara.

(Here the dictionary meaning of *infinite* is being violated: the word can't be applied to any number or size smaller than the greatest. *Perfect* and *complete,* by contrast, have allowable secondary meanings of *excellent* and *thorough,* and this is why they can be used more flexibly.)

Comparative versus Superlative

When only two items are being compared, use the comparative form: *Bobo is the better marksman of the two.* If there are more than two items, use the superlative: *Of all the businessmen in town, Richie was the best at double bookkeeping.*

Fewer versus *Less*

Fewer refers to numbers of separate items: *fewer assassinations, fewer popovers. Less,* when used as an adjective, refers to bulk amounts: *less blood, less flour.* A common mistake is the use of *less* in place of *fewer: We play less commercials than KROK*. Remember that if the items can be separately counted, *fewer* is the right word.

Suspended Comparisons

A suspended comparison is one that is interrupted to suggest a different relationship:

• The population of Asbury Park is *as large as, if not larger than,* that of Port Jervis.

This is cumbersome but correct. Very often, however, a writer embarking on a suspended comparison loses track of the parallelism:

• The population of Asbury Park is *as large, if not larger than,* that of Port Jervis.

(A necessary *as* has been omitted after *large*, leaving the impossible *as large . . . that*.)

• The population of Asbury Park is *as large as, if not larger, than* that of Port Jervis.

(The words are right but the second comma is wrongly placed, leaving *as large as . . . than*.)

Perhaps you can see, not only that suspended comparisons frequently run into trouble, but that they're cumbersome even when correctly formed. It's always better to rephrase:

• The population of Asbury Park is as large as that of Port Jervis, if not larger.
• The population of Asbury Park is at least as large as that of Port Jervis.

Comparing the Incomparable

Beware of allowing your language to suggest that you're stating a relation between items that couldn't possibly be compared:

• Melody thought that the widsom of *The Prophet* was greater than the Bible.

(Wisdom is being compared to a book. The writer should say *than that of the Bible*, or *than the Bible's*.)

Like versus *As*

Only a purist could settle all choices between *like* and *as* without a qualm. The "rule" is fairly clear, but not very many native speakers observe it, and some essayists sacrifice it to their sense of idiom.

You'll have to decide this one for yourself. All I can do is explain what the issues are.

Strictly speaking, *as* is a conjunction introducing an adverbial clause and *like* is a preposition introducing a prepositional phrase:

- As *The Maine* goes, so goes the nation.
- Like General MacArthur, Melody was very fond of wading.

In the first sentence one verbal action is being compared to another; hence *as*. In the second, one nominal person is being compared to another; hence *like*. The rule, then, can be restated this way: *as* for actions or states, *like* for things, people, or ideas.

The trouble with the rule is that *like* is always more emphatic than *as*, regardless of syntax. Not many diners would say, or even write,

- This juicy steak smells *as* a steak ought to.

A person who could write such a sentence unflinchingly would probably kill his mother for dangling a participle or splitting an infinitive. The juicy steak would be wasted on him, too. To substitute *like* for *as* in this sentence, however, would be offensive to some people. The solution, as usual, is to finesse the problem with a different phrase. *The way* can stand in place of either *like* or *as* in this example and many others.

My own practice is to observe the distinction between *like* and *as* wherever it doesn't sound pompous or timid; the difference in syntactic function is real, and you can gain clarity by respecting it. But note that this entails thinking through each construction, not instinctively fleeing to *as* because it somehow sounds more "grammatical":

- *As* King Lear, Melody was always asking somebody to unbutton her.

Such a sentence proclaims that you're desperately afraid of sounding like the man on the street who says *like* whenever *as* is called for; here *as* is incorrect. The same effect is produced by the cowardly *as with:*

- *As with* many people today, Philo would be lost without his electric hair styler.

(The writer means *like*, he is entitled to say *like*, and by not saying it he merely reveals a bewildered wish to follow "good grammar.")

As with does, of course, have legitimate uses when it isn't a euphemism for *like:*

- With Melody today, *as with* Priscilla yesterday, Philo imitated a suave man of the world.

The necessity to think through each sentence is accentuated by the versatility of *as*, which can be used with an implied subject and verb, as [it is] in this very clause. *As* can also be a preposition:

• He cherished her *as* his most deductible possession.

The moral is that, once having reached a decision whether to keep to the grammarians' distinction or to follow popular speech, you still have difficult choices to make. Don't trust yourself to arrive at correctness simply by running away from *like*.

Compared to versus Compared with

To compare one thing *to* another is to affirm its likeness to that second thing:

• Bobo's voice has been compared *to* that of a wounded elephant.

To compare one thing *with* another is simply to make the act of comparison:

• Comparing Priscilla *with* Helen of Troy, Philo estimated that her face might launch two junks and a surplus kayak.

By comparing one thing *with* another you can determine whether or not the first should be compared *to* the second.

Other

This word is sometimes necessary to indicate that two compared items belong to the same class:

• Philo was a more impulsive lover than the *other* suitors.

But when the two terms belong to different classes, *other* is out of place. In the following sentence, for example, *other* undermines the main statement:

• The President is a truth-loving man, unlike the *other* liars in office today.

More . . . Rather Than; Prefer(able) . . . Than

These formulas are regarded as errors:

* Stanley said that the dean was *more* like a Gestapo officer, *rather than* a liberal administrator.

(Correct to *more like a Gestapo officer than . . .*)

* Priscilla *preferred* staying home *than* exposing herself to microbes and viruses at the party.

(Correct to *preferred staying home to exposing . . .*)
    In short, *more* requires *than*, and *prefer* or *preferable* requires *to*.

EXERCISES

I. Choose the correct verb form in each sentence:

1. It is their own secret vices that (allows, allow) people to tolerate the vices of others.
2. Mathematics (is, are) not Biff's favorite subject.
3. Neither of them (remembers, remember) who ran for President against Harry Truman.
4. My ambitions are boundless, but my means (is, are) limited.
5. Above the wealthiest section of Rio (stands, stand) some of the world's most miserable slums.
6. Baseball, along with all the other televised sports, (strikes, strike) her as perfectly meaningless.
7. There (is, are) four candidates in this election.
8. A number of people (dislikes, dislike) mushroom pizza.
9. Each of them (is, are) equally certain of being right.
10. Any idea for improving this company's profits (is, are) welcome.
11. He is one of those revolutionaries who (learn, learns) everything from books.
12. The number of people who dislike mushroom pizza (is, are) very small.

II. Choose the correct pronoun form in each sentence:

1. Philo sought (she, her) (who, whom) fate had chosen to be his partner.
2. The revival of big-band jazz is a mystery for you and (I, me) to solve.
3. Biff, (who, whom) everyone thinks is fearless, is really a hypochondriac.
4. The responsibility for your impending starvation is entirely (your's, yours).
5. I know (who, whom) I want to play the leading role in *Strait Is the Watergate*.
6. He expected the winning contestant in the Miss Emeryville Pageant to be (she, her).
7. (It's, Its) a shame that white-collar crime usually goes unpunished.
8. It is nearly impossible for (we, us) Americans to reduce our consumption of candy.

III. Explain any errors you find in these sentences:

1. The Russians are people who, although it is hard to get to know, become extremely warm and generous on longer acquaintance.
2. People seem to think that pornography is America's greatest social problem, which is why real crimes like burglary and rape continue to flourish.
3. If your goldfish won't eat its food, feed it to the canary.
4. Although she was worried at first, it diminished after a while.
5. This is an animal that almost anybody would want to have it for a pet.
6. Someone who turns in their friend to the police isn't going to be very popular.
7. His father always told him what to do, but sometimes he wasn't sufficiently familiar with the facts.
8. I want to drum some statistics into your heads which are concrete.
9. Bobo really meant it when he yelled "Kill the umpire," but he couldn't recall it at the inquest.
10. When Biff tries not to think about his shoulder separation, it makes him tingle all over.

IV. Which of the following sentences need correction? Make any necessary changes.

1. I shouldn't wonder if it didn't rain next Tuesday.
2. He being there came as a shock to his admirers.
3. Strictly speaking, the rules forbid any visits at this hour.
4. They wanted the capital of Italy to be moved from Turin to Rome, and they did so.
5. In order to get through the dense jungle, a native guide is necessary.
6. If he would have stayed ten minutes longer, he would have learned exactly what he wanted to know.
7. Although she wrote with feverish speed, Priscilla was hardly pressed to finish the exam.
8. She had always wanted to have become a guide to the Kodak Picture Spots at Disneyland.
9. Philo was not at all sure that, given Priscilla's hostility, he shouldn't pay any more attention to her.
10. His coach, awkward as he was, thought he detected some athletic promise in the eight-foot teenager.
11. Harry can't hardly wait for the Edsel to be declared a national monument.
12. By turns fascinated and appalled, Desdemona listened to Othello's wild tales of adventure.
13. A kite is flying highly above the city, but the citizens, deep absorbed in their work, don't see it.
14. Thinking how to avoid any extra effort in course work, his eye was inevitably attracted to the advertisement for Bill's term-paper service.
15. The complaints of passengers are earnestly hoped to be reduced by this new service.
16. Before going to bed, the false teeth should be removed for maximum comfort.

17. I will always remember the image of you conducting the orchestra with a pool cue.
18. To honestly and comprehensively state my opinion would take several hours.
19. She repented of her sins in the intimacy of the confessional.
20. The King wanted to, as it were, have his blackbird pie and eat it too.
21. In *Man and Superman* Jack Tanner tried his best to escape the clutches of Ann Whitefield.

V. Indicate how any errors in these sentences could be corrected:

1. This isn't a good excuse for your absence, and neither was the reason you gave for being late on Friday.
2. Neither Iraq or Kuwait is going to sell oil to us at bargain rates.
3. They expect, neither this summer nor next fall, to have an opening for a left-handed acupuncturist.
4. She has no intention of going because so little would be accomplished.
5. She knew not only why she had been singled out for praise, but she also knew what would happen next.
6. Melody didn't care for politics, and either did Bill.

VI. Correct any errors in these sentences:

1. The chemical structure of smog is entirely different from cigarette smoke.
2. Of the two players, Robertson is unquestionably the better.
3. As many other people, Bobo resented any government interference in his business affairs.
4. My strontium-powered engine will be adopted by General Motors when they realize that it delivers more power.
5. A nine-to-five job may be unpleasant, but it is more preferable to being on welfare.
6. She is more totally exhausted now than she has ever been before.
7. There are as few as, if not fewer, split-level Elizabethan houses being constructed now than ever before.
8. Less lilacs than ever are now growing by the dooryard.

NOTES

1. Carl Bereiter, quoted in William Labov, "Academic Ignorance and Black Intelligence," *Atlantic*, June 1972, p. 60.

2. Both statements are by James M. McCrimmon, *Writing with a Purpose*, 4th ed. (Boston: Houghton Mifflin, 1967), pp. 170–171.

3. McCrimmon, p. 171; italics in original.

4. Sir Ernest Gowers, *The Complete Plain Words* (1954; rpt. Baltimore: Penguin, 1962), p. 186.

5. Wilson Follett, *Modern American Usage: A Guide* (New York: Hill & Wang, 1966), p. 22.

AN 9 INDEX OF USAGE

It's time now to put aside general principles and get to particulars, looking at the language phrase by phrase to define what's considered "good usage." You may know perfectly well that a verb should agree in number with its subject, but suppose you aren't sure whether the word in question—*research*, let's say, or *critique* or *author*—should be used as a verb in the first place. No rule provides the answer; in fact, today's answer may be obsolete a decade from now. You have to know how educated writers are construing the word and whether there's a consensus about it among students of usage. Again, it's fine to know that jargon, euphemisms, and slang should be avoided in standard essay prose, but how can you tell that a given word falls into one of these categories? Our speech is full of expressions that look wrong on paper, not because they're ungrammatical, but simply because they offend the taste of people whose judgments are influential.

Even where contemporary practice seems to be leaving the experts behind—for instance, in the widespread use of *data* in the singular, or of *disinterested* to mean *uninterested*, or of *hopefully* to mean *it is hoped*—you still have to contend with conservative opinion. I know several tolerant, humane people who think that one *hopefully* is proof of a writer's incompetence. If you want to reach such readers as well as those who don't take usage so solemnly, you should try to circumvent the booby-trapped phrases. And beyond disputed points there are many more expressions that every informed reader considers substandard. The Index that follows consists mostly of advice that isn't controversial among people who care about accuracy and economy.

Where an expression does involve controversy, the Index doesn't automatically side with the purists. It recognizes that there's such a thing as straining too hard to sound correct. On *different from* versus *different than*, for example, it suggests that you ought to prefer the "improper" *than* if your only alternative is an awkward, windy construction. And it points out that *shall* in the first person—the strictly correct form, according to some people—makes a rigid, ceremonious effect that you may not want.

Although my own taste has necessarily colored this Index, it is largely a summary of other commentators' views. I have consulted Theodore M. Bernstein, *The Careful Writer;* Margaret M. Bryant, *Current American Usage;* Bergen and Cornelia Evans, *A Dictionary of Contemporary American Usage;* Rudolf Flesch, *The ABC of Style;* Wilson Follett et al., *Modern American Usage;* H. W. Fowler, *A Dictionary of Modern English Usage;* Sir Ernest Gowers, *The Complete Plain Words;* Alexander M. Witherspoon, *Common Errors in English;* numerous handbooks of composition; and most extensively, Roy H. Copperud, *American Usage: The Consensus.* Because Copperud's is the only book that systematically compares the opinions of recognized authorities, I recommend it to you for more extensive guidance than my own Index provides.

For the sake of convenience, the Index assumes that you're trying to write ordinary standard English. (See pp. 172–174 for exceptions.) Most of the disapproved expressions are simply labeled *colloq.* (colloquial) without further explanation, but for many expressions you will also find references to the types of jargon (bureaucratese, journalese, psychologese, sociologese) they exemplify (see p. 68). My intention isn't to analyze problems at length, but to show you succinctly what present-day writers consider acceptable and to note disagreements among the authorities.

I recommend that you read through this Index once, marking the entries that look helpful to you, and then review those items later. After that, the Index can serve as a reference guide to be consulted when you come across new problems.

The following abbreviations appear in the Index:

adj.	adjective
adv.	adverb
ambig.	ambiguous, susceptible of misinterpretation
ant.	antonym, a word with a meaning opposite to that of another given word
cf.	compare
colloq.	colloquial, to be avoided in standard essay prose
conj.	conjunction
e.g.	for example
i.e.	that is
inf.	infinitive
intrans.	intransitive, the verb takes no object
n.	noun
obj.	object (direct unless otherwise stated)
p.p.	past participle
part.	participle (present)
plu.	plural
prep.	preposition
pro.	pronoun
sing.	singular
subj.	subject
syn.	synonymous, having the same meaning
trans.	transitive, the verb takes an object
v.	verb

a, an Use *a* before words beginning with consonants or pronounced with initial consonants: *a usual day.* Use *an* before vowels: *an orange.* Words with initial pronounced *h*'s can be preceded by either *a* or *an*, but *an* sounds affected to many readers and often causes an unnecessary change in pronunciation of the next word. Write *a humble man*, not *an humble man.* Unpronounced *h* words take *an: an hour.*

Watch out for an extra *a* or *an* where it isn't justified, as in *What kind of a man is that?* In this sentence the *a* is wrong because *man* refers to men in general, not to the individual.

above (n., adj.) Pedantic or legalistic in phrases like *in view of the above* and *the above reasons.* Wherever possible substitute *therefore, for these reasons*, etc.

abrogate, arrogate Often confused. To *abrogate* is to *nullify: Congress abrogated the treaty.* To *arrogate* is to *appropriate to oneself unjustly: He arrogated all the privileges of a dictator.*

absolute, absolutely Too frequently used as meaningless intensifiers: *He is absolutely the greatest poet I have ever read.* The effect is insincere. Save *absolute* to mean *utter, unrestricted: an absolute monarch.* When you're tempted to write *I am absolutely certain*, ask yourself whether *I am certain* doesn't sound more confident.

absolve, acquit Close in meaning, but *acquit* implies that a formal trial is involved. Note that these verbs are followed by different prepositions: *absolve from guilt, acquit of murder.* Though frequently seen, *absolve of* is a mistake.

accent, accentuate Close in meaning, but should be kept distinct. Where the sense is *pronounce emphatically*, use *accent: He accented the third syllable.* Accentuate can then be kept for *emphasize* more generally: *In his letter of resignation he accentuated the company's failings.*

accused, suspected When these are used as adjs., the nouns following them sound more decisive than they should: *the accused burglar, the suspected arsonist.* The reader thinks of a burglar who has been accused, an arsonist who has come under suspicion. If you simply mean *the suspect* without any imputation of guilt, beware of these constructions.

acoustics The discipline is sing.: *Acoustics is my favorite branch of study.* But as the quality of sound in a hall the word is plu.: *The acoustics were acceptable.*

acquiesce Followed by *in*, not *to: They acquiesced in his decision.*

A.D. Should precede the date: *A.D. 1185.* Note that it's redundant to write *in the year A.D. 1185*, since A.D. already says "in the year of our Lord."

ad A bit slangy for *advertisement.*

adapt, adopt To *adapt* something is to *change* it *for a purpose: He adapted the Constitution to his own ends.* To *adopt* something is to *take control or possession* of it: *He adopted the Constitution as his code of ethics.*

addicted Shouldn't be used as a syn. of *devoted*, as in *She is addicted to charitable works.* That sentence is meaningful only as a sarcastic criticism.

admit, confess Save the latter for serious charges. A suspect *admits* that he's the hunted man, but may not be willing to *confess* having committed the crime.

adversary, opponent The words are close, but the first implies some hostility: *Her cynical behavior made adversaries out of her opponents.*

adverse, averse *Adverse* means *antagonistic, unfavorable.* It always takes *to: Conditions were adverse to her undertaking.*

Averse means *disinclined, opposed.* In American English it usually takes *to*, not *from: She was averse to his proposal.*

advise Save this v. for *give advice*, instead of extending it journalistically to mean *say, declare*. In *The press secretary advised that the conference would be delayed*, the first v. should be changed to *said* or *announced*.

affect, effect (v., n.) As a v. to *affect* is to *influence: This affected the whole subsequent course of events*. To *effect* is to *bring about: He effected a stunning reversal*.

As a n. *affect* is a technical word for *feeling: The patient was flooded with affect during her anxiety attacks*. *Effect* is *result: The effect of the treatment was negligible*.

again, back Don't use these words redundantly after *re*-prefixed words that already contain the sense of *again* or *back: rebound, reconsider, refer, regain, reply, resume, revert*, etc.

aggravate, aggravating Some readers object to these words in the sense of *annoy, annoying: I had an aggravating day today*. Strictly speaking, you can only *aggravate* a condition that's already disagreeable; the v. means to *make worse*. Don't write *You really aggravate me*.

aggression Beware of using this abstract term as a plu. sum of feelings: *get rid of my aggressions*. This is pop-psychologese. Keep *aggression* sing., and ask yourself whether you don't mean *hostility* or *ill will* anyway.

ago Redundant in the company of *since: It is three years ago since it happened*. Delete *ago*.

ahold There's no such word in standard English.

ain't Colloq. for *aren't* or *isn't*.

all, all of Use the second only when real items or proportions are involved: *not all of the skillets were sold; all of them are on hand*. *All* deserves preference in all other circumstances: *all her enthusiasm vanished; he was a hermit all his life*.

all that Colloq. in sentences like *I didn't like her all that much*. All *what* much?

allege Not a syn. of *profess;* it should always carry an implication of complaint. Don't write *McKeon is alleged to be a poet*, even if you think he isn't one.

In the active voice, *allege* takes a *that* clause or a direct obj. In the passive it takes an inf. The following sentences are correct:

- The prosecutor alleged her guilt.
- He alleged that her alibi was a fabrication.
- She was alleged to be a terrorist.

allude, refer To *allude* is to *refer glancingly*, without specifically naming the thing in mind: *Eliot alludes to Wagner by borrowing some phrases from* Tristan und Isolde.

To *refer* is to *direct the reader's attention specifically: Eliot refers to* Tristan und Isolde *in his notes to* The Waste Land, *thus making his allusion intelligible to readers who may not have remembered the opera*.

allusion, illusion, delusion The first is a *glancing reference: an allusion to Shakespeare*. An *illusion* is a *deceptive impression: the illusion of reality in laser photography*. A *delusion* is a *mistaken belief*, usually with pathological implications: *the delusion of thinking he was Napoleon*.

almost Shouldn't be combined with comparative words like *better, worse, slower*, and *more meaningful*. *Almost* expresses one degree and the comparative adj. or adv. expresses a different one. *He is almost more learned than I am* should be *He is almost as learned as I am*.

alone Can be ambig. when sandwiched between a subj. and a v.: *One man alone can accomplish this feat*. Does the writer mean that only one man is capable of doing it, or that two men aren't required?

along the lines of   See *in terms of.*

along with, in addition to, together with, with etc. Phrases containing these preps. don't influence the number of the v. (see pp. 187–188). This is correct: *Phil, along with his many friends and hangers-on, has made a great nuisance of himself.*

already, all ready   Not syns. *They were already there, and they were all ready to do their best.*

also   Weak as a conj.: *He had ten fingers, two ears, also two feet.* Some authorities also object to *also* as a sentence adv. meaning *besides: He turned blue; also, his heart rate suddenly jumped.*

alternately, alternatively   Something done *alternately* is done *by turns: Teams come to bat alternately in baseball.*
 Something done *alternatively* is done by choosing one action *instead of* another: *You could, alternatively, decide not to go at all.*

altogether, all together *Altogether* means *entirely: She is altogether convinced. All together* means *everyone assembled: They were all together at the reunion.*

alumnus, -i, -a, -ae   An *alumnus* is always a male graduate, and an *alumna* is always female. The graduates of coeducational schools and colleges are collectively known (however unfairly) as *alumni. Alumnae* are the graduates of all-female institutions.
 The discriminatory implications of *alumni*—why should the masculine form have precedence?—make *graduates* an attractive syn.

a.m., p.m.   Shouldn't be used as nouns: *at six in the a.m.* And they shouldn't be accompanied by *o'clock,* which is already implied.

ambiguous, equivocal An *ambiguous* statement has a double meaning, whether or not the writer intended it: *The Vehicle Code is ambiguous about safe speeds.* An *equivocal* statement is one that *deliberately* hovers between two meanings: *Stop being equivocal and tell me what you really think.*

ambivalence, ambivalent; hesitancy, hesitant   The first two words are psychologese, except where they have the exact clinical meaning of *simultaneous harboring of powerful negative and positive feelings,* with the negative feelings usually repressed. *Ambivalence* and *ambivalent* often express nothing more than *hesitancy* and *hesitant,* or perhaps *indecision* and *indecisive* or *unsure. Marie felt ambivalent about turning down the radio.* No; this cheapens the word.

among, between *Among* is appropriate when there are at least three separable items: *among his friends, among all who were there.*
 Between can be used for any plu. number of items, though some purists think it should be reserved for two items (also see *between*). The real difference is that *among* is vaguer and more collective than *between,* which draws attention to each of the items:

- They hoped to find one good man *among* the fifty applicants.
- The mediator saw a basis for agreement *between* the radical parties.

amoral, immoral   Not syns. An *amoral* act stands outside the categories of moral judgment. Logic and actuarial statistics, for example, are *amoral,* i.e., unaffected by moral considerations. *Immoral* means *violating moral principles: His destruction of the files was thoroughly immoral* [not *amoral*]. (Also see *ethics.*)

amount, number   If the items are countable, *number* is right: *a small number of crabs.* Reserve *amount* for total quantities that aren't being considered as units: *the* *amount of the debt, a large amount of trash*. The common error here is to use *amount* for *number*, as in *the amount of people in the hall was extraordinary*.

ample, enough   Very nearly syns., but some careful writers reserve *ample* for *more than enough: The food at the banquet seemed ample at first, but there was barely enough to go around*.

amplify   Takes an obj. without the intervention of *on: Why don't you amplify your statement?*

analog, analogue   Both spellings are possible, but *analog* is now standard as an adj. in *analog computer*, whereas *analogue* is still the preferred n.

analyzation   Always a mistake for *analysis*.

and yet   Can always be revised to *yet*.

angry at, angry with   You're angry *at* a situation or thing, but angry *with* a person: *I am not angry with you, but I am angry at the loss of precious time from your interference*.

another   Purists say this means *one more* and is thus wrong in *Another thirteen people arrived*. No one else seems to agree, but if you want to be scrupulous you can always write *thirteen more*.

ante-, anti-   The first prefix means *before*, the second *against: ante-bellum, antedate; anti-Darwinian, antifascist*.

any and all   Always redundant. Choose one of the terms and discard the other.

anybody, any body; nobody, no body; somebody, some body   The single words are indefinite pros.: *Anybody can plainly see . . .* The others are separate words: *Flour gives some body to a sauce*.

any more, anymore   Only the first is standard English. Don't write *They just don't make disposable diapers the way they used to anymore*.

any place, anyplace   Authorities disagree as to whether the second is too informal. You're better off using *any place*.

anyway, any way, anyways   *Anyway* is an adv.: *There's no hope, anyway*. Don't confuse this with the two words *any way: I haven't found any way to do it. Anyways* is always colloq.

anywheres   Always colloq. *Anywhere* is the correct form.

appraise, apprise   Very different in meaning. To *appraise* is to *make an estimate of the value of: He appraised the property of the deceased*. To *apprise* is to *notify: He apprised me of his intentions*.

appreciate   Many authorities rage against this as a syn. of *be grateful for*, but usage has passed them by. *I appreciate your frankness* is now perfectly acceptable. The purists, who needn't be humored in this instance, would say that *appreciate* can only mean *increase in value*.

apprehend, comprehend   When you *catch the meaning of* something, you *apprehend* it: *I think I apprehend what you're driving at*.

When you *understand thoroughly*, you *comprehend: After years of study I still don't comprehend transformational grammar*.

apropos   Written as one word (cf. French *à propos*) and followed by *of*, not *to: apropos of our previous discussion*.

apt, liable, likely   These words are very close in meaning, but some people like to reserve *liable* for *undesirable* possibilities: *liable to be misunderstood. Liable* means *exposed*, whereas *likely* means *probable* or *probably: He was liable to prosecution, but not likely to be prosecuted*.

As for *apt*, its most precise use comes when habitual disposition is intended: *Miss Fuller's cow is apt to kick over the pail*.

arbitrator, mediator An *arbitrator* has a binding power to reach a decision. A *mediator* comes between contending parties to see whether they can agree, but he has no power over them.

area See *field*.

argue, quarrel They can be syns., but *argue* has a special meaning of *make a case*, and this meaning has no overtones of quarrelsomeness.

aroma Should be applied only to agreeable smells, not to disagreeable ones as in *the aroma of Snuffy's feet.*

around As a syn. of *about*, *around* is considered all right by some authorities and condemned by others. To stay on the safe side, write *about five months.*

as (conj., prep.) Stay away from conj. *as* in the sense of *because*. It's grammatical but sometimes ambig.: *As I said it, she obeyed.* Does *as* here mean *while* or *because?*

Don't use *as* to mean *whether* or *that: I can't say as I do.*

In sentences like *Janet is not as tall as Mary*, some writers would consider the first *as* a mistake for *so*. The "rule" is that *so* must be used if the comparison contains *not*. But the *not as . . . as* formula is widely accepted and can be considered correct.

Avoid unnecessary use of prep. *as*. The following are improved by the deletion of *as:*

* She was considered [as] the best in her class.
* He was voted [as] the most likely to succeed.
* They were named [as] co-chairpersons.

as, like See pp. 209–211.

as, such as Not syns. Don't write *Santa's bag contained many toys, as ray guns, cluster bombs, and torture kits. Such as* would be appropriate.

as far as . . . is concerned If you're going to use this formula at all, it must be completed. Don't write *As far as money, I have no complaints.*

as follows Always sing., no matter how many items are to be listed: *I received twelve gifts, as follows: one turtle dove, two French hens . . .*

as good as Colloq. when used for *practically: He as good as promised me.*

as how Should never be written for *that: She told me as how she didn't love my horse any more.*

as if, as though Equally proper. When they introduce a clause stating a condition contrary to fact, the v. ought to be subjunctive: *As if she weren't already busy enough, . . .*

as of, as of now Regarded as colloq.: *I sail as of the fifth; I have no worries as of now.* It's better to write *I sail on the fifth; I have no worries now* [or *at the moment*].

as regards Pompous for *about* or *concerning.*

as such Often says nothing. It should be deleted, for instance, from *The planets as such have no effect on people's destiny.* But *as such* is meaningful in sentences like *A physicist as such shouldn't be considered an authority on ethics.*

as well as Doesn't affect the number of the v. (see pp. 187–188): *John, as well as his many aunts and uncles, was present at the reunion.*

The construction is often involved in faulty parallelism (see pp. 205–207).

aspect A much overworked term. Literally, an *aspect* is a *view from a particular vantage*. Moving around the object, you see different *aspects* of it. As a cliché, though, *aspect* has lost any sense of this physical basis and become a syn. of *con-*

sideration: the following eight aspects; the problem has many aspects.

Aspect may be impossible to do without, but you should try to use it with at least a shadow of concreteness: *When the issue is regarded from a Marxian perspective it shows a wholly new aspect.*

assume, presume; assumption, presumption To *assume* is more tentative and hypothetical than to *presume*. You can make an *assumption* simply for the sake of argument, but your *presumptions* are your axioms.

assure, ensure, insure To *assure* is to *promise, give assurance: I assure you that I mean well. Ensure* and *insure* can be considered variant spellings of the same word, meaning *make certain*. Because *insure* has become associated with the selling of insurance policies, though, many writers prefer to use only *ensure* to mean *make certain: He ensured his family's security by insuring his life for $50,000.*

Don't adopt the journalistic habit of using *assure* without an object: *The economy, he assured, will continue to expand.*

at the same time that Wordy for *while.*

at this juncture, at this point in time, at this moment in time Should usually be *now*. Note that a *juncture* is a *point of convergence*, not simply a *time*. And there is no imaginable reason why a *moment* should have to be clarified as a *moment in time.*

at variance Followed by *with*, not *from: at variance with his ideals.*

attend, tend Where they differ, *attend* means *pay heed to*, and *tend* means *care for, look after.*

attorney Commonly regarded as a syn. of *lawyer*. But technically, an *attorney* is someone who has been empowered to transact business for someone else; an *attorney* may or may not be a *lawyer*, someone who has been admitted to the bar.

augment, supplement To *augment* something is to *add more of the same;* to *supplement* it is to *add from a different source*. A teacher may *augment* his salary by teaching summer school at the same institution, but if he "moonlights" in a second job he is *supplementing* his salary with further income.

author (v.) Journalese: *He authored his third novel last year.* Say *wrote* instead, and keep *author* as a n.

average, mean, median An *average* is reached by dividing the sum of quantities by the number of items. Four neckties priced at $3, $5, $7, and $9 have an *average* price of $6 ($24 divided by 4).

A *mean* is a *midpoint*. The *mean* between 10 and 20 is 15. (If there are only two figures, the mean and average are the same.)

A *median* is a *point having an equal number of items above and below it*. If the *median* income of American families is $10,000, the same number of people have incomes smaller and larger than $10,000.

Some writers object to *average* as a syn. of *ordinary: He's just an average person.*

avocation, vocation An *avocation* is a *hobby;* a *vocation* is a *regular employment* or *calling*.

awake, wake, waken The choice between these verbs is difficult. I recommend *awake* to mean *become awake; wake* in the transitive sense of *wake* [somebody else] *up;* and *waken* in passive uses: *I was wakened at six.*

award, reward (n.) An *award* is always the result of an official decision, but a *reward* can be official or not: *His reward for diligent exercise was a long and vigorous life.*

awful(ly), dreadful(ly), terrible (-bly), etc. Avoid as syns. of *very;* see pp. 72–73.

awhile, a while *Awhile* is an adv.: *I worked awhile. While* is a n. in *a while ago*. The adv. is wrongly substituted for the n. in *awhile ago* and *I worked for awhile.*

background Overused as a syn. of *origin, reason, credentials*. In constructions like *Give me some background on this*, it's outright bureaucratese. Try to use the word sparingly, and if possible with retention of some of its concrete pictorial meaning in contrast to *foreground*.

bad Don't use as an adv. meaning *badly* or *severely: It hurt so bad I wanted to cry.*

badly Can be used to mean *very much*, but only in negative senses: *His paper was badly lacking in content.* In positive senses it's colloq.: *He wanted badly to be invited.*

bail, bale (v.) To *bail* is to *remove water: He bailed out the leaking boat.* To *bale* is to *tie in a bundle: He baled the hay.* When a pilot ejects himself from a crippled plane, he *bails out*. One also *bails out* a person awaiting trial.

barbaric, barbarous Something *barbaric* is *uncivilized in style: a barbaric habit of tickling people's armpits. Barbarous* means *cruel, savage: They executed the villagers in a barbarous manner.*

barely For problems with negatives, see p. 203.

basically, essentially, ultimately These advs. all have legitimate uses, but all are overworked as vague means of emphasis. Delete them from sentences like *Basically, he supports the Tigers; This is essentially what I mean; Ultimately, we have to begin somewhere.*

basis, on the basis of The terms are overworked and often redundant: *She admired it on the basis of clarity* should be *She admired its clarity. I decided to do it on the basis that there was no alternative* should be *I decided to do it because . . .*

bass, base Spelled differently but pronounced alike, except when *bass* refers to a fish. *Bass* (or *deep-toned*) notes sound *base* (or *ignoble*) to some listeners.

before . . . first A common redundancy: *Before he departed, he first brushed his teeth. First* should be dropped.

beg the question Doesn't mean *evade the issue*. It means *treat an open issue as if it were already settled* — for example, by using "loaded" terminology. See pp. 53–56.

being (part.) Often used redundantly: *The city is divided into three districts, with the poorest being isolated from the others by the freeway.* Either *with* or *being* should be dropped. *Being* is usually a sign of wishy-washy sentence construction; it's a makeshift for appending afterthoughts instead of writing an integrated, dramatically weighted sentence. Even in other positions, *being* sometimes has an air of pedantry: *This being so, it was concluded . . .*

being as, being that Colloq. for *because, since.*

bemused Doesn't mean *amused*, but *bewildered.*

beside, besides *Beside* means *at the side of; besides* means *in addition to. Besides her father and the groom, no one stood beside Susanna at the altar.*

better (adj.) Colloq. as a syn. of *well*, as in *She was all better on Tuesday.*

As a syn. of *more, better* is disapproved by some writers: *Better than half of the members were present.* You should probably stay away from *better* in this sense.

between Can be used for more than two items [see *among*], but does require at least two. This is violated, for example, in *Hamlet's conflict is between his own mind* and in *The poems were written between 1956–58*. In the second sentence *1956–58* is one item, a period of time. The sentence should read *The poems were written between 1956 and 1958.*

Between always requires a following *and*, not *or*. Don't write *The choice is between anarchy or civilization.*

between each, between every Because *between* implies at least two items, it shouldn't be joined to sing. adjs. like *each* and *every: He took a rest between each* *inning*. Try *after every inning* or *He rested between innings.*

between you and I Always wrong for *between you and me.* The prep. *between* requires an objective pro.

bi- A treacherously ambig. prefix. It always means *twice;* but what is being doubled, e.g., in *biweekly?* If the weeks are doubled, *biweekly* means *every two weeks;* if the times are doubled, *biweekly* means *twice a week.* There's no way of deciding which sense a writer intends. Consequently, you'd do better to find another phrase: *every other week, twice a week.*

bid (v.) Journalese when used for *try: He bids to become the best man in his field.*

billion A *billion (1000 million)* in American English is the same as a *milliard* in England. The English word *billion* means, not *1000 million,* but *a million million.*

blame on Some readers regard *blame on* as a mistake: *He blamed it on Paul.* Although this may be too fastidious, you can satisfy everyone by writing *He blamed Paul for it.*

bloc, block A *bloc* is an *alliance of states or interests;* in all other meanings the right word is *block.* Don't write *the Communist block.*

blond, blonde As a n., *blond* designates a male and *blonde* a female. As an adj., *blond* predominates for both sexes: *a blond beauty.* But *blonde* is seen so frequently as a feminine adj. that it can't be considered incorrect.

boast Journalese for *possess* or *take pride in: She boasts four handsome sons.*

boost, hike (n.) Journalese in the sense of *increase: a pay boost.*

bored Followed by *with* or *by,* not *of.* Don't write *He was bored of skiing.*

born, borne The first has to do with birth, the second with carrying. But note that childbearing is itself a form of carrying: *She had borne six children. Born* should be used only in the passive sense: *I was born twenty years ago.*

both Beware of redundant phrases such as *both alike, both agree, both together: Both alike were upset.* Try *Both were upset* or *Both of them were upset.*

When two items are connected by *both,* the companion word is *and,* not *as well as: Both Ralph and* [not *as well as*] *Linda were upset.*

breakdown Standard English in the sense of *collapse.* But it's bureaucratese in the sense of *itemization* or *analysis: a breakdown of the statistics.* Wilson Follett issued the classic warning about the possible ambiguity of *breakdown* and its derivatives; his example was *This was a report on the population of the U.S. broken down by age and sex.*

bring, carry, fetch, take You *bring* something from one place to a nearer one. You *carry* something in any direction. You *fetch* something by going from one place to another and bringing the thing back. And you *take* something from a nearer place to a farther one.

broad, wide Almost syns., but a careful writer might be interested in the fine difference. *Wide* refers to the distance separating the borders: *a wide berth, a wide canyon to cross, a wide misunderstanding. Broad* refers to the amplitude of the thing itself, not to the emptiness between its sides: *a broad highway, a broad trailer, a broad hint.*

broke (adj.) Colloq. in the sense of *penniless.*

bunch, crowd (n.) A *bunch* is a dense collection of *things;* a *crowd* refers to *people* or *animals.* The film *The Wild Bunch* should have been about grapes.

burglar, robber, thief A *burglar* breaks and enters in order to steal. A *robber* takes money from people by threatening or harming them in person. A *thief* is someone who steals, usually without the victim's knowledge. A dishonest bank teller, for example, may be a *thief* without being either a *burglar* or a *robber*.

but The case of a pro. following *but*, as in *All but she [her?] had left*, is hard to determine. See p. 187 for discussion.

but however, but nevertheless, but yet Redundant. The redundancy isn't lessened by putting some space between the *but* and the adv., as in *But Tom, having better things to do that day, nevertheless refused to come along*.

but that, but what These are clumsy equivalents of *that* in clauses following an expression of doubt: *I don't doubt but that you intend to remain loyal*. Negative expressions of doubt are sometimes threatened with ambiguity, but the irrelevant *but* only adds to the confusion.

calculate See *figure*.

calculated See *designed*.

can, may When asking for permission, should you write *Can I leave?* or *May I leave?* Time is on the side of *can*, but purists continue to protest. Both forms are currently acceptable, but *may* has a more polite air than *can*. Suit yourself, according to the formality or informality of the context.

can but, cannot but, cannot help but These formulas are stilted and possibly ambig. You can use *cannot help* with a part., though: *She couldn't help giggling at the funeral*.

can not, cannot Unless you want to emphasize the *not, cannot* should always be preferred over *can not*.

canine (n.) Pompous for *dog*.

canvas, canvass The material is *canvas*. *Canvass* is a v. meaning *solicit*.

carat, caret A *carat* is a unit of weight in gemstones; a *caret* (∧) is a mark of insertion in a text.

case, instance Involved in numerous circumlocutions. *Who was to blame in the case of the Olympic massacre?*, for example, should be *Who was to blame for the Olympic massacre?* The preferred wording is concise and direct.

cast, caste *Cast* means, among other things, *type* or *tendency: I wouldn't trust a person of that cast*. *Caste* means *hereditary class: the untouchable caste*.

catalog, catalogue Both spellings are possible, but *catalog* is now more common.

Catholic, catholic When capitalized, *Catholic* refers to the *Catholic Church* or *faith*, with *Roman* usually understood. Uncapitalized, *catholic* means *universal* or *wide-ranging: She has catholic interests*.

cause, reason Not syns. A *cause* is what produces an effect: *The earthquake was the cause of the tidal wave*. A *reason* is someone's *professed motive or justification: He cited a conflict of interest as his reason for not accepting the post*.

cause is due to Redundant. A cause *is* something that must be directly specified.

celebrant, celebrator A *celebrant* officiates in a religious rite; a *celebrator* participates or rejoices, irrespective of ceremony.

censor, censure A *censor* is an official who judges whether a publication or performance will be allowed. *Censure* is *vehement criticism*.

center around Open to two objections. Since a center is a point, not a circle, *center around* looks self-contradictory. *Center on* or *center upon* appears more logical.

All these expressions, however, are usually circumlocutions. *The problem centers around a shortage of funds* should be simply *The problem is a shortage of funds.*

ceremonious, ceremonial *Ceremonious* means *ostentatious* or *formally polite: a ceremonious manner. Ceremonial* as an adj. means *pertaining to a ceremony: a ceremonial invocation.*

character Found in many redundancies and circumlocutions. *He was of a studious character* should be *He was studious* unless you have a special reason for highlighting his *character*, i.e., his total set of qualities. *The character of this play is such that I feel deeply moved by it* should be *This play moves me deeply.*

childish, childlike Both mean *like a child*, but *childish* is usually scornful: *Why are you acting in this childish way? Childlike* emphasizes the better aspects of childhood: *a childlike innocence.*

chronic Means *constant* or *recurrent*, not *severe*. A *chronic disease* may in fact be mild.

class (v.) Should always be *classify*. Don't write *He classed the documents under three headings.*

classic, classical These terms overlap in some senses, but you should use *classic* when you mean *extremely typical or important* without any reference to tradition. When you mean only tradition, use *classical: classical Japanese theater.* Don't write *Max got a classical case of dysentery.*

climactic, climatic *Climactic* means *pertaining to climaxes, decisive: a climactic encounter. Climatic* means *pertaining to climate: climatic conditions.*

close proximity Always redundant, since *proximity* contains the idea of nearness.

coed (n.) Why should there be a second-class word to describe female students? You can write that a college is *coeducational*, but *coed* is journalese. Note also that the word is technically misused when applied to students in an all-female college.

collaboration, collusion Both imply partnership, but whereas a *collaboration* can be directed toward any end, a *collusion* is always conspiratorial, involving both secrecy and an unethical purpose.

collective (adj.) Often used absurdly, as in *Our collective noses will stop running when spring arrives.* Instead of adding some meaning, the word merely highlights the writer's difficulty in reconciling sing. and plu. ideas.

collision A *collision* should always involve at least two *moving* objects. A car doesn't *collide with* a parking meter; it *crashes into* it.

commence Almost always pompous for *begin, start.*

communication Pompous for *letter, note,* or *memorandum.*

compare, contrast *Compare* means either *make a comparison* or *liken*. To compare something *with* something else is to make a comparison between them; the comparison may show either a resemblance or a difference. To compare something *to* something else is to assert a likeness between them. (Also see p. 211.)

To *contrast* is to emphasize differences: *He contrasted the gentle Athenians with the warlike Spartans.* As a v., *contrast* should always be followed by *with.*

compendium Widely misunderstood. A *compendium* is a *brief, abridged treatment* of a subject, not an *exhaustive* or *voluminous* treatment.

comprise, compose, constitute *Comprise* means *embrace, include: The curriculum comprises every field of knowledge. Compose* and *constitute* mean *make up: All those fields together compose* [or *constitute*] *the curriculum.* The most common mistake is to use *comprise* as if it meant *compose: The parts comprise the whole. Is comprised of,* though frequently seen, is always wrong: *The whole is comprised of the parts.* Try *The whole comprises the parts* or *The parts compose the whole.*

concept, conception, idea The broadest of these terms is *idea*, and it should be the preferred term unless you're quite sure you mean *concept* or *conception*. A *concept* is an abstract notion meant to characterize a class of particulars: *the concept of civil rights.* A *conception* is a particular idea, often carrying a sense of fallibility: *She had an odd conception of my motives.* Note that *idea* would have been suitable even in these examples.

concern (v.) Sometimes used fuzzily, as in *The problem concerns how to win the election.* By changing the verb to *is* you can express the true relation between the subj. and complement.

conclave Journalese for *convention* or *assembly.* A *conclave* is properly a *secret or private meeting.*

concur in, concur with You concur *in* an *action* or *decision: He concurred in her seeking a career.* But you concur *with* a *person* when you agree with him: *He concurred with her in her decision.*

connive May be gaining acceptance in the sense of *conspire,* but many authorities consider this a mistake. Save *connive* for the sense of *deliberately avoid noticing* (something objectionable): *He connived at his campaign manager's illegal activities.*

conscious, aware Almost syns., but you can observe a difference. A person is *conscious* of his own feelings or perceptions, but *aware* of events or circumstances.

-conscious See *-wise.*

consensus Don't use this n. unless you mean something very close to unanimity.

And beware of the redundancy *consensus of opinion. Consensus* says exactly that.

consider as When *consider* means *regard,* it shouldn't be followed by *as: He considered me [as] his friend.* The error is common because *regard* does take *as.*

considerable Colloq. in the sense of *many* (items): *Considerable dignitaries were there.*

consist of, consist in Something *consists of* its components: *The decathlon consists of ten events. Consist in* means *exist in* or *inhere in: Discretion consists largely in knowing when to remain silent.*

contact (v.) Purists object to it as a syn. of *get in touch with,* but the objection is weak by now. Still, the word is a bit sloppy when used to cover *write, call, notify, send a telegram to,* etc. It has a slightly bureaucratic flavor.

contagious, infectious Not syns. *Contagious* means *communicable by personal contact; infectious* means *communicable by organisms* (e.g., germs), whether they're transmitted by contact or not.

contemn Not an alternate spelling of *condemn,* but a distinct v. meaning *treat with scorn.* A judge may *condemn* a defendant to life imprisonment but merely *contemn* him for his lack of regard for his victims. The two words are very close when *condemn* is used to mean *express disapproval of; contemn* is appropriate only if the disapproval is accompanied by open scorn.

contemplate Use only when a serious act is being considered. *I contemplated taking a bath* has a facetious air.

contemptible, contemptuous Altogether distinct. *Contemptible* means *deserving contempt; contemptuous* means *feeling or showing contempt.*

continual, continuous Used interchangeably by many writers, but they shouldn't be. *Continual* means *recurring at inter-*

vals; continuous means *uninterrupted.*

contributing factor See *factor.*

convince, persuade Often treated as syns., but you can preserve a valuable distinction by keeping *convince* for *win agreement* and *persuade* for *move to action.* If I *convince* you that I'm right, I may *persuade* you to do what I recommend.

Observing this distinction, you'll have to avoid writing *convince to,* as in *I convinced him to come.*

cope Somewhat colloq. when used without *with* and its obj.: *He just couldn't cope.*

corporal, corporeal Both mean *pertaining to the body,* but in different senses. *Corporal* has a physical meaning, as in *corporal punishment. Corporeal* is the right word when a contrast with *spiritual* is involved: *He turned his mind away from corporeal things.* In short, *corporal* for the body itself, *corporeal* for the idea of the bodily.

correspond to, correspond with *Correspond to* means *match; correspond with* means *exchange letters with.*

council, counsel, consul A *council* is a governing or advisory board: *the city council. Counsel* means *advice* or *attorney: The defendant's counsel gave him counsel.* A *consul* is a foreign-service officer stationed abroad: *the British consul.*

couple, pair *Couple* refers to two things that are united; it's colloq. when nothing more than *two* is intended, as in *I have a couple of questions to ask you.* When you do use *a couple of,* be sure not to drop the *of,* as in *a couple reasons.*

Pair refers to two things that are inseparably used together: *a pair of skis. The Joneses are a couple, but they aren't much of a pair.*

Pairs tends to prevail over *pair* in the plu.: *three pairs of shoes.*

Verbs governed by *couple* and *pair* are generally plu., although a sing. v. might be

appropriate in rare cases: *A couple becomes a trio when the first child is born.*

cowardly Means *displaying cowardice.* The word is abused in sentences like *It was a cowardly deed to have stabbed the shopkeeper.* Running away from a shopkeeper may be cowardly, but stabbing him isn't.

credible, incredible; credulous, incredulous *Credible* and *incredible* mean *believable* and *unbelievable. Credulous* refers to a gullible state of mind or habitual disposition; a credulous person is too easily convinced. *Incredulous* means *withholding belief, skeptical. His incredible claims left me incredulous.*

crescendo A *crescendo* is a gradual increase in force, loudness, or volume. It's widely misused in the sense of *climax.*

criteria Always plu.: *these criteria.* The sing. is *criterion.*

critique (v.) Should be *criticize* or *write a critique of. He critiqued the proposal* is bureaucratese.

crucial Often used wrongly to mean *important.* Something is *crucial* only if it presents a decisive, momentous choice. Think of *important, critical,* and *crucial* as representing increasing degrees of urgency, and use *crucial* only when the milder terms won't do.

cute Colloq. for *pretty* or *clever: a cute idea.*

data Opinion is divided over the number of *data.* You would do well to keep *data* plu.: *these data,* not *this data.* The sing., rarely seen, is *datum; fact* or *figure* would sound more natural.

debut Widely condemned as a v.: *She debuted on Thursday.* Stay with *made her debut.*

decimate Strictly means to *reduce by one-tenth,* but it's widely used to mean *almost totally destroy.* Most authorities would now consider this acceptable. However, you shouldn't remind a reader of your departure from the original meaning by using such phrases as *decimate three-quarters of the army.*

decline comment, refuse comment Space-saving journalese, as in *The Senator declined comment.* The objection is that *comment*, being an inf. rather than a n., ought to be preceded by *to: declined to comment.*

deduce, deduct Both form the same n., *deduction*, but *deduce* means *derive* or *infer* and *deduct* means *take away* or *detract.*

defect, deficiency A *defect* is a *fault* or *imperfection;* a *deficiency* is an *incompleteness.* If someone is *deficient*, it's in relation to certain standards: *his spelling was deficient.* A *defect* is a more permanent flaw: *His main defect is his stubbornness.*

definite, definitely; definitive, definitively Often confused. *Definite* means *clearly defined* or *exact* or *positive: There were definite limits to her patience. Definitive* means *final* or *conclusive: a definitive edition.*

Too often *definite* and *definitely* convey nothing at all, as in *I definitely believe that . . .* and *This house has a definite advantage for a buyer like you.* This uncalled-for reinforcement of *believe* and *advantage* arouses suspicion that the writer is insincere.

delighted at, delighted in, delighted with You are delighted *at* an *idea* or *with* an *object: She was delighted at the thought of freedom, and she was delighted with her new outfit.* You delight *in* an *activity: He delighted in sailing.*

denotation, connotation A word's specific meaning is its *denotation.* Its *connotations* are its secondary meanings or overtones.

depend Don't omit *on* or *upon*, as in *It depends whether the rain stops in time.* And don't use *it depends* without specifying a reason: *It all depends* is incomplete.

dependant, dependent *Dependent* is the more common spelling for both the n. and the adj., but *dependant* can be used for the n. The only outright mistake is to use *dependant* as the adj., as in *They were dependant on my support.*

deprecate, depreciate To *deprecate* is to *express disapproval of;* to *depreciate* is to *lessen the value of. I deprecated the President's depreciation of the dollar.*

desert, dessert The former is the barren place where you have mirages of the latter.

designed, calculated Misused in passive constructions where no designing agent is envisioned: *The long summer days are designed to expose your skin to too much sunlight.* It's doubtful that this is what the Creator had in mind. Again, don't write *This medicine is perfectly calculated to turn you into an addict.*

desirable, desirous Something worth having is *desirable;* to hanker after it is to be *desirous* of getting it.

desperation, despair Not syns. *Desperation* means *readiness to take extreme measures because of despair or urgency: He showed his desperation by leaping from the train. Despair* is a state of *hopelessness: He fell into despair and confessed everything to the police.*

device, devise In common uses the first is always a n., the second a v. You *devise devices.*

diagnose Should be applied to the disease, not the patient. Not *The doctor diagnosed Richard as diabetic*, but *The doctor diagnosed diabetes as Richard's disease.* Even this sounds less than perfect, perhaps because *diagnose* is a somewhat artificial v. derived from *diagnosis.* Use the n. wherever you can.

dialectal, dialectical *Dialectal* means *pertaining to dialect: a dialectal pronunciation. Dialectical* means *pertaining to dialectic* (logical argumentation) *or to dialectics* (Hegelian reasoning).

dialogue Means *conversation* (among any number of characters) *in a literary work*. In its extended meaning of *exchange of ideas*, it has become a bureaucratic cliché: *Let's get some dialogue going with the ghetto.*

dichotomy Overworked for *split* or *difference.*

differ from, differ with To differ *from* someone is to *be different* from him; to differ *with* him is to *express disagreement.*

different Often used unnecessarily, as in *I have five different reasons for refusing to comply.* If they weren't different they'd be one reason.

different from, different than *Different from* is always "good grammar," but sometimes it sounds awkward, as in *Things are different now from the way they were a year ago.* This is just a long detour around *Things are different now than a year ago.* Although some grammarians consider *different than* an error every time it appears, their opinion isn't shared by most educated speakers and writers. My advice is to prefer *different from* in most circumstances but to resort to *different than* when it makes a saving of words: *John is different from Bill,* but *The results were different than I anticipated.*

dilemma, difficulty, predicament Some writers use them interchangeably, but this is wrong. A *difficulty* is a *specific obstacle* to be overcome. A *predicament* is a *difficult situation* from which a safe exit may or may not be possible. A *dilemma* is *a situation in which all the possible choices are seriously unattractive.* If you say that someone *faced the dilemma of what to wear for dinner,* you're cheapening the word.

discern, distinguish, discriminate To *discern* is to *recognize* or *make out* something; it carries no implication of contrast. To *distinguish* is to *see or state a contrast* between one thing and another; and to *discriminate* is to *make active use of the power to distingish. Discriminate,* when not used in the sense of *show prejudice,* belongs to the realm of taste and judgment.

discover, invent You *discover* what's already there, waiting to be noticed; you *invent* something new.

discreet, discrete The first means *prudent* or *judiciously reticent,* the second *separate. She was discreet about revealing the three discrete meanings of the hieroglyph.*

disinterested, uninterested Both can mean *not interested,* but you would do well to reserve *uninterested* for this use. Then you can keep *disinterested* for its unique meaning of *impartial: What we need here is a disinterested judge.*

dissemble, disassemble To *dissemble* is to *give a false appearance to* or to *feign.* To *disassemble* is to *take apart. The mechanic was dissembling when he said he had disassembled the engine.*

dissociate, disassociate Mean the same thing. The first is usually preferred.

distinctive, distinguished Something *distinctive* is *different, readily identified: a distinctive cauliflower ear. Distinguished* means *eminent* or *having an air of importance: a distinguished statesman.*

divert Shouldn't be used intransitively, as in *The pilot diverted to Algeria.*

don't Colloq. when used with the third person sing.: *he don't care; don't she ever take a bath?*

doubt (v.) Can be followed by *if, whether,* or *that.* But don't try *but that;* it can leave the reader wondering whether you do or don't question the statement that follows.

doubtless(ly) *Doubtless* is already an adv.; the *-ly* is excessive.

drastic Once meant *violent*, and still retains a sense of harshness and sacrifice. Don't write *a drastic improvement*.

dream (n., v.) Now a cliché for *hope, plan: She has a dream of living in Hawaii; She dreams of living there.*

dubious, doubtful An outcome or a statement may be *dubious;* the person who calls it into question is *doubtful*. The distinction is useful, though not observed by all good writers.

due to Criticized by some authorities when it's used in the sense of *owing to* or *because of: Due to his absence, the team lost the game.* The objection is that *due to* is being given an illegitimate adverbial role. No one would object to *due to* in *The loss was due to his absence.* Popular usage accepts both sentences, but you should be aware that opinion is divided.

due to the fact that Wordy for *because, since.*

duo, trio, quartet, etc. Imply a formal connection. It's wrong to say *a trio of jaywalkers were arrested yesterday*, unless perhaps the three had locked arms in solidarity against traffic laws.

during the course of Can always be *during.*

each For the number of *each*, see p. 178.

each and every Redundant for *each* or *every.*

each other, one another Form the possessive by adding *'s*. The next n. must be plu.: *George and Marsha admired each other's belts.* But an exception is made for abstract nouns that don't easily accept plu. forms: *one another's bravery.*
Some purists say that *each other* can

only apply to two persons, but this superstition can be disregarded.

economic, economical *Economical* always means *thrifty* or *avoiding waste: an economical use of words. Economic* can bear the same meaning, but it usually means *pertaining to economics or finances: Keynes's economic theory.*

educator Pompous if all you mean is *teacher*. A real *educator* (John Dewey, A. S. Neill) should have ideas about education that reach many people beyond his classrooms. Many teachers resent being called *educators* because the term is frequently used to characterize school officials who never teach at all.

effect See *affect.*

efficacy, efficiency *Efficacy* is *effectiveness: the efficacy of a medicine. Efficiency* is *the achieving of results relative to the time and effort expended: The workers' efficiency was low.*
The adjs. *efficacious* and *efficient* follow the same distinction: *efficacious* means *effective*, and *efficient* means *performing with little or no waste.*

e.g., i.e. Often confused. *E.g.* means *for example;* it can only be used when you're *not* citing all the items you have in mind. *I.e.* means *that is;* it can only be used when you're giving the *equivalent* of the preceding term. Except in footnotes and parenthetical references, use the written-out equivalents *for example* and *that is.* Don't write *I am utterly faithful to my loved one, i.e., Marsha, who has many charms, e.g., her nose.*

egoism, egotism Not syns. *Egoism* is a philosophical position emphasizing the central importance of the self; it can also mean an attention to one's own interests. *Egotism* is what's popularly called "conceit." It's an unwarranted puffing-up of one's self-estimation. A widespread error is the use of *egoism* or *egoist* in this derogatory sense.

elemental, elementary *Elemental* means *pertaining to the elements, basic* or *primitive*, as in *an elemental struggle to survive. Elementary* means *simple* or *introductory: an elementary explanation.*

elicit, illicit Sometimes confused. *Elicit* is a v. meaning *draw forth: His performance elicited applause. Illicit* is an adj. meaning *unlawful: illicit entry.*

emigrate, immigrate Describe the same action, but from different vantages. The action is travel from one's native country to another where one hopes to reside. In *emigrating*, one *leaves* the first country; in *immigrating*, one *arrives* at the second country. If an Englishman moves to Mexico, he is *emigrating* from the standpoint of England and *immigrating* from the standpoint of Mexico.

emote Acceptable only as a derogatory term characterizing bad acting. Don't use it to mean *show emotion.*

endeavor Usually pompous for *try.*

enhance Doesn't mean *increase*, as in *I want to enhance my bank account.* It means *increase the value or attractiveness of*, as in *He enhanced his good reputation by making further sacrifices.* In order to be enhanced, something should already be valued to some degree. Note that it's the quality, not the person, that gets enhanced. Don't write *She was enhanced by receiving favorable reviews.*

enjoin This v. is subject to ambiguity. To *enjoin upon* or *enjoin to* is to *urge with a certain moral sternness: He enjoined me to keep the secret forever.* To *enjoin from* is to *forbid: The judge enjoined them from resuming the picket line.*

enormity Doesn't mean *vastness* or *enormousness;* it means *atrocious wickedness.* Don't write *the enormity of his feet.*

enthuse Widely condemned, even though it looks like a plausible substitute for *show enthusiasm.* Don't write *He enthused over the performance.*

epic (adj.) Cheap when applied to forward passes, talkathons, press conferences, etc. If you take the exploits of Hercules or Aeneas as your standard of what's *epic*, you'll give this adj. a needed rest.

epoch, era Now nearly syns., but *era* expresses a longer period. An *epoch* was originally the beginning phase of an *era.* Don't, in any case, use *epoch-making* to mean *novel* or *record-breaking.* An epoch-making event is properly one that inaugurates a new era in history.

equally as Always redundant. Wherever you feel inclined to write *equally as*, you'll find that either *equally* or *as* will do: *It was [equally] as far to Denver as to Colorado City.*

eruption, irruption An *eruption* is a breaking out; an *irruption* is a breaking in. *The submarine captain no longer feared the eruption of war; he was preoccupied with the irruption of water into the damaged chamber.*

escalate An inaccurate cliché when the meaning is simply *increase*, as in *The price of meat has escalated.* Used properly, *escalate* means *increase in magnitude by calculated stages.* Military leaders *escalate* hostilities when they deliberately intensify their actions to a certain degree, ''raising the ante'' in order to force the enemy to match the intensification or give in.

escape (v.) When used with a direct obj., it should mean *elude*, as in *They escaped punishment. They escaped the jail* is wrong.

especial(ly), special(ly) *Especial* and *special* are sometimes interchangeable in the sense of *distinct*, but *especial* is losing out. *Especially*, however, deserves to be kept separate from *specially. Especially* means *outstandingly: an especially important point; all these things, especially the last. Specially* means *for a particular pur-*

pose, specifically: *This racket was special-ly chosen by the champion.*

Watch out for meaningless uses of *spe-cial: There are two special reasons why I came here.* This just means *there are two reasons*, not *two of the reasons are special ones.*

-ess Feminine suffixes are under attack in the age of the chairperson. Steer away from needless *-ess* forms such as *poetess* and *ancestress.* But certain standard forms such as *hostess, stewardess,* and *waitress* seem to be surviving, for what-ever reason. All you can do is listen for the existing consensus and follow it.

Words like *Jewess* and *Negress* are con-sidered especially offensive.

et al. Means *and other people*, not *and other things.* It belongs in footnotes and parenthetical references, not in your main text.

etc. Means *and other things,* and shouldn't be extended to mean *and other people. Et al.* is available for that purpose.

Keep all such abbreviations out of your main text. (See p. 43 for another abuse of *etc.*)

ethics, morals; ethical, moral *Ethics* re-fers to a *system of principles guiding con-duct;* it may be either a philosopher's system (*the ethics of Aristotle*) or the standards accepted by an individual (*Gracie's ethics*). *Morals* are *specific habits*, the successful or unsuccessful practice of ethics: *He had the highest ethics, but his morals were a different matter. Ethics* always has a theoretical flavor; it suggests *ideas* of morality. Some-one who has *poor ethics* is one who fol-lows a lax code of fairness; one who has *poor morals* may or may not share so-ciety's ethical standards, but his behavior (usually sexual) is loose.

Ethical and *moral* are closer in meaning than *ethics* and *morals* are, but they retain some of the difference. A person is *ethical*

or *unethical* according to the specific code of ethics pertaining to his activity: *unethi-cal business practices. Moral* and *immoral* refer to broader standards: *He lived an immoral life.*

(Also see *amoral.*)

euphemism, euphuism A *euphemism* is a *fancy word used in place of an ordinary one; euphuism* is a *certain affected literary style using much alliteration.*

ever so often, every so often *Ever so often* is a gushy way of saying *frequently: She sees her psychiatrist ever so often! Every so often* means *now and then.* The danger is that *ever so often* will crowd out *every so often*, as in *Ever so often he likes to go to the zoo.*

everyday, every day *Everyday* is an adj. meaning *normal, habitual: an everyday practice.* Don't use *everyday* where the two words *every day* are called for: *They did it every day.*

everyone, every one *Everyone* means *everybody.* It shouldn't be put in place of *every one*, as here: *Everyone of your argu-ments is false.*

(For the number of pros. like *everyone* and *everybody*, see pp. 178–179.)

everywheres Always colloq. *Everywhere* is the correct form.

evince Doesn't mean *evoke*, but *show;* and *show* is usually preferable on grounds of simplicity.

exact Don't use *exact* as an adv.: *the exact same symptoms.* Write *exactly the same.*

exceed, excel To *exceed* is to *go beyond a fixed limit: she exceeded the bounds of decency.* To *excel* is to *perform very well: She excelled at tennis.*

exceeding(ly), excessive(ly) *Exceeding* means *very much; excessive* means *too much.* It's no criticism to call someone *exceedingly rich.*

except Shouldn't be used as a conj., as in *She told him to leave, except he didn't want to.*

exception that proves the rule A long history of misunderstanding surrounds this formula, which is almost impossible to use in a clear fashion. Besides, it's a cliché. Do without it.

exceptional, exceptionable, unexceptionable *Exceptional* means *extraordinary: an exceptional feat. Exceptionable* means *liable to objection: Your ideas may be right, but your language is exceptionable. Unexceptionable* thus means *not liable to objection: An unexceptionable performance* isn't a mediocre one, but one against which no complaint can be made.

excess (adj.) Sometimes redundant, as in *excess waste, excess verbiage.* The same holds for *excessive spendthrift, excessively murderous,* etc.

excuse, forgive, pardon You *excuse* small faults; you *forgive* a debt or injury; you *pardon* someone who is already under sentence for having committed a serious offense.

executer, executor The first is *one who carries out a planned act;* the second is the *legal administrator of an estate.*

ex-felon The term is a contradiction because, rightly or wrongly, the law regards a convicted felon as a felon for life. Try *ex-convict.*

exist Often meaningless, as in *Among all the problems that exist today. Among all current problems* says the same thing with no leakage of energy.

exodus Should be reserved for the *departure of masses,* not of individuals.

expect Mildly colloq. in the sense of *suppose, believe: I expect I won't be able to get there.*

expensive Because *expensive* already means *high-priced,* you shouldn't combine it with *price* or *prices: The price was expensive.* That's like writing *The heat was hot.* The item being sold is what's *expensive.*

express When followed by a reflexive pro., *express* takes *as:* not *He expressed himself amazed* but *He expressed himself as amazed.* Of course *He expressed amazement* would be better yet.

extended Proper when something has been *prolonged (an extended engagement),* but improper when all you mean is *long: They didn't meet again for an extended period.*

fabulous For this and similar words of exaggerated astonishment or praise, see pp. 72–73.

facet Suffers from excessive metaphorical use without any memory of the literal sense. A facet is one of the surfaces of a gem; thus it comes into view as the gem is turned. A sentence containing *facet* should retain some idea of this shift in perspective: *An unexpected facet of the problem appears when we adopt the Indians' point of view.* The danger is that *facet* will become a syn. of *part: The problem has four facets.*

fact, fact that Can't be used with untrue statements, as in *The fact that the moon is inhabited was vigorously denied by the astronomer.* Once *fact* is used, the statement is presumed to be true; a *true fact* is redundant.

The fact that can often be deleted for economy: *I appreciate the fact that you are helping me* should be *I appreciate your help.*

factor A *factor* is a *contributing element helping to produce a given result.* All too often it's misused to mean *item* or *point: I want to emphasize four factors in this lecture.* Another sign of the word's recent abuse is the redundancy *contributing factor.* If a factor isn't already contributing, it isn't a factor.

fail Use only in the context of an attempt. Don't write *Nixon failed to agree with Mc-Govern.* Was Nixon trying?

fallacy Like other logical terms (p. 000), *fallacy* is often used too loosely. A *fallacy* is a *formal error of reasoning* or a *conclusion arrived at by faulty means.* It can be extended to mean a *misleading statement*, but it shouldn't be used to cover a statement that is simply *wrong.* Words like *error, mistake*, and *lie* are often more precise.

famous, notable, noted, notorious *Famous* means *possessing fame* in a wide sense, whether positive or negative. *Notable* and *noted* mean *reputed* (for some specific reason that's usually flattering); but *noted* is widely condemned as journalese. *Notorious* means *famous in a negative, discreditable sense: a notorious criminal; a notorious liar.*

fantastic Means *fanciful, imaginary.* Don't use it as an all-purpose term of enthusiasm: *I had a fantastic time at the party.* (Also see p. 75.)

farther, further *Farther* usually refers to distance, but *further* is often used in all possible senses. Many careful writers, however, restrict *further* to its abstract meaning: *I would like to make one further remark.* This has the advantage of leaving *farther* free to cover all occasions when physical distance is involved.

Farthest, furthest are the superlatives (not *fartherest, furtherest*).

fascist Refers to a particular political philosophy characterized by nationalism, dictatorship, and close ties between government and the dominant corporations. *Fascist* is not a loose syn. of *authoritarian.* When you say *The dean is a fascist*, the odds on your being right are very poor.

fatal, fateful Sometimes confused. Something *fatal* leads to death; something *fateful* is *momentous*, whether or not the outcome is *fatal.*

favor (v.) Colloq. as a syn. of *resemble: He favors his brother Donald.*

faze, phase *Faze* means *daunt* and is seen only in negative contexts: *It didn't faze me. Phase* is a n. meaning *stage* or a v. meaning *schedule* or *synchronize.*

feature (v.) To *feature* is to *give prominence to: This circus featured the world's greatest sword-swallower.* Don't use it in the milder sense of *possess* or *contain*, as in *The English department features a wide range of courses.*

feel bad, feel badly See pp. 72–73.

feel good, feel well To *feel good* is to have an exhilarating sense of being in good health or spirits. To *feel well* is simply to be free from feeling sick. *She feels well today, but she doesn't feel good about her husband's disappearance.*

feline (n.) Pompous for *cat.*

fellow Colloq. for *person.*

few, little *Few* refers to things or persons that can be counted; *little* refers to things that can be measured or estimated, but not itemized. *Few people were on hand, and there was little enthusiasm for the speaker.*

(For the comparatives *fewer* and *less*, see p. 194 and *fewer*.)

fewer, less, lesser, least *Fewer* refers to numbers, *less* to amounts: *fewer members, less revenue. Lesser* is an adj. meaning *minor* or *inferior: The lesser emissaries were excluded from the summit meeting. Least* is the superlative of *little;* as an adj. it should only be used when more than two items are involved.

Fewer in number is a redundancy.

field *The field of* is often superfluous, as in *He majored in the field of astronomy.* Write *He majored in astronomy.* The same goes for *subject* and, worst of all, *area.*

fight against, fight with *Fight against* is always clear, but *fight with* can be ambig. *He fought with Joe Louis on Guadalcanal.*

Did they fight side by side in the war or against each other in the ring? Make sure that the context shows which meaning you intend.

figure, calculate   These verbs are colloq. for *think, suppose,* or *believe: I figure she will be here by the fifteenth.*

final   Often redundant, as in *final conclusion, final result, final outcome.* (See pp. 70–72 for similar redundancies.)

finalize   Bureaucratese for *complete.*

financial, fiscal, monetary, pecuniary   *Financial* refers to money matters, especially large ones. *Fiscal* has to do with public revenue.
   Monetary refers to the policies of issuing and regulating money. *Pecuniary* refers only to the money affairs of individuals.

firm, corporation   A *firm* is a collection of individuals working in formal partnership; a *corporation* is a legal entity apart from the individuals composing it.

first, firstly; second, secondly, etc. See p. 338.

first and foremost   A cliché.

fiscal   See *financial.*

fix (v., n.)   Some people think that *fix* is colloq. as a v. meaning *repair,* but the objection doesn't carry much force. As a n. meaning *predicament,* however, *fix* is colloq.

flaunt, flout   Widely confused. To *flaunt* is to *display arrogantly: They flaunted their superior wisdom.* To *flout* is to *defy contemptuously: They flouted every rule of proper behavior.*

fled, flew   *Fled* is the p.p. of *flee; flew* is the p.p. of *fly.*

flounder, founder   Keep distinct. To *flounder* is to *thrash about;* to *founder* is to *fill with water and sink.* A policy may be said, metaphorically, either to *flounder* or

to *founder,* but the criticism is sharper in the second instance.

flowed, flown   *Flowed* is the p.p. of *flow; flown* is the p.p. of *fly.*

flunk   Colloq. for *fail: She failed* [not *flunked*] *the course.*

for   It's all right to begin a sentence with a conj., but *for* is tricky. Often it can be taken as either a conj. or a prep., as in *For many days passed uneventfully.* The first three words look at first like a prepositional phrase. Don't begin a sentence with *for* unless the next word makes clear what part of speech *for* is.

for free   Should be *free.*

for the purpose of   Usually wordy. *He came to the city for the purpose of getting rich* should be *He came to the city to get rich.*

for the simple reason that   Should be *because.*

for . . . to   Colloq. in sentences like *She wants for me to grow a beard.* Try *She wants me to . . .*

forbid   *Forbid* takes *to* and an inf.: *I forbid you to go.* A common mistake is to use *from* and a part. instead: *I forbid you from going.* The mistake seems to derive from a confusion of *forbid* with *prevent* (see *prevent*).

forestall   Tricky because, though it properly means *prevent, exclude,* it's often taken to mean *delay, postpone.*

former, latter   These terms should be used only when there are two items and when the reader will have no difficulty identifying them; you shouldn't use them after intricate constructions. Note that each item can be plu.: *The admirals and generals flatly disagreed; the latter prevailed.*
   When *former* means *ex-,* don't combine it with *ex- (a former ex-nun)* or use it with a past v. *(She was a former nun)* if the person is still alive.

formulate Usually pompous for *form.* Save *formulate* for the sense of *state systematically: He formulated a new theory of solar storms.* In *I formulated my plans for the summer*, the v. should be *formed.*

fort, forte A *fort* is a *fortified place;* a *forte* is a (metaphorical) *strong point* or *special skill.*

fortuitous Doesn't mean *fortunate*, as some writers imagine, but *by chance*, irrespective of advantage or disadvantage. *It was fortuitous that they should both be in Saigon at the same time.* This indicates nothing about whether the coincidence was a lucky one.

framework Fast becoming a bureaucratic cliché, as in *Consider this problem in the framework of factor analysis.* A *framework* is properly a *skeletal structure designed to support or enclose something.* Thus, metaphorically, you could say that a person's religious beliefs provide the framework for his day-to-day behavior. Compare this with the abstract and meaningless use in the first example.

free, freely *Free* is both an adj. and an adv., meaning, among other things, *without cost.* People who suspect that *free* can't be an adv. are inclined to use *freely* in its place: *I give it to you freely.* But this is ambig.: *freely* means *liberally, unreservedly.* Don't be afraid to write *I give it to you free* if you mean *without charging you.* If you mean *unreservedly*, write *I freely give it to you.*

free gift, free pass *Gift* and *pass* already contain the idea of *free.*

frightened, afraid You're *frightened by* an immediate cause for alarm; you're *afraid of* a more persisting danger. The erroneous *frightened of* jumbles the two senses.

-ful, -fuls Some writers pride themselves on the exquisite precision of *handsful, shovelsful*, but contemporary usage favors *handfuls, shovelfuls*, etc.

fulsome Doesn't mean *abundant;* it means *offensively insincere.*

fun Colloq. as an adj.: *a fun affair.*

function (v., n.) Overused as a v. meaning *work, operate: I function best in the morning.* The term always has a mechanical air about it; a body *functions* but a person doesn't, unless he conceives of himself as a machine.

As a n., *function* is often pretentious for *event* or *occasion.* Use it only when the event has a certain importance and formality: *a diplomatic function. Function* also has a precise mathematical sense which is sometimes pretentiously extended: *My character is a function of my upbringing.* Try *result.*

funny Mildly colloq. for *odd: That's a funny mistake for a mathematician to have made.* Substitute *odd, strange*, or *peculiar.*

gambit A *gambit* isn't any old ploy; it's an *opening move* (originally in chess) *that sacrifices something to gain an advantage.*

gamble, gambol The first means to *bet*, the second to *frolic.*

gap A cliché in phrases like *communications gap, credibility gap.*

gay Now so common for *homosexual* that you must watch out for ambiguity when you mean to use the word differently.

gender Reserve for grammar, not sex. Don't write *He went to Sweden to have his gender changed.* And genders are always *masculine* and *feminine*, never *male* and *female.*

general public Redundant for *public.*

genial, congenial *Genial* means *jovial; congenial* means *kindred, compatible.*

get The p.p. is either *got* or *gotten.* In American English *gotten* is more widely seen, but the choice is open. In some contexts, though, the two forms have different meanings: if *Frank has got money*, he possesses it; if he *has gotten money,* he has obtained it in the not very distant past.

Some phrases containing *get* are colloq.:

- This running really gets to me in the lungs.
- The smell of that sewer gets me.
- She got him fired after he broke off their engagement.
- You get on my nerves.

gift Don't use *gift* as a v.: *He gifted me with his company.*

got to Colloq. for *have to, has to.* Don't write *She got to leave now.*

gourmet, gourmand A *gourmet* is a *connoisseur of fine food;* a *gourmand is a glutton.* Don't confuse them, and don't weaken the sense of *gourmet* to include anybody who enjoys a square meal: *Millions of gourmets love chiliburgers.* Try *people* or *diners.*

graduate (v.) Some writers still believe that *graduate* has to be put in the passive: *He was graduated from Haverford.* By now, however, this is a ridiculous genteelism. Write *He graduated from Haverford.* Note that *He graduated Haverford* would be wrong.

graffiti Construed as plu.: *These graffiti are obscene.* The sing. is *graffito.*

grisly, grizzly *Grisly* means *gruesome; grizzly* means *gray* or *grizzled. The killing of the grizzly bear was a grisly thing.*

had better Don't shorten *had better* to *better,* as in *You better pay attention.*

hale, hail (v.) To *hale* is to *haul: He was haled before the judge.* To *hail* is to *greet, acclaim,* or *signal: The judge hailed a taxi; He was hailed for his fairness.*

half a Don't precede *half a* with a redundant *a,* as in *He was there for a half an hour.*

hanged, hung Criminals aren't *hanged*

very often now, but grammarians still insist on this p.p. While the distinction lasts, you should observe it: *hanged* is for executions, *hung* for all other uses of *hang.*

hangup Colloq. for *inhibition, problem, reservation, perversion.* All these terms can be used precisely; *hangup* can't, because it calls up all of them at once.

hard, hardly Both of these can be advs. Fear of using *hard* in its legitimate adverbial sense sometimes leads to ambig.: *I was hardly pressed for time.* This could mean either *I was rushed* or *I had plenty of time,* with a presumption for the latter. Hyphenation can be helpful: *I was hard-pressed for time.*

(For the use of *hardly* in negatives, see p. 203.)

hardly . . . than An error for *hardly . . . when.* Don't write *Hardly had she finished composing the letter than the telephone rang.*

has reference to Rarely preferable to *means.*

head up (v.) Colloq. for *head, direct,* as in *She headed up the string quartet.*

healthful, healthy *Healthful* means *bestowing health; healthy* means *possessing health, in good health. A healthful apple may keep you healthy.*

hear, listen You *hear* anything that comes to your notice as an auditory sensation; you *listen* by focusing your auditory attention. *Listen* is the more active word: *He listened, but heard nothing.*

heartily, wholeheartedly *Heartily* means *cordially; wholeheartedly* means *without reservation.*

hesitancy, hesitation Close in meaning, but you can keep *hesitancy* for the *feeling* of reluctance to proceed, and *hesitation* for the *act* of hesitating. *I understood her hesitancy, but her hesitation proved inconvenient for the rest of us.*

high, highly Remember that *high* can be an adv. as well as an adj. and is preferable in such phrases as *he jumped high; a high-flying pilot*. An antique vase may be *highly prized* and therefore *high-priced* at an auction.

historic, historical *Historic* means *history-making, figuring in history: Marx's carbuncles may have had historic importance. Historical* means *pertaining to history: There is a historical controversy about Marx's carbuncles* (that is, historians quarrel about their significance).

For use of *a* or *an* before *historic* or *historical*, see *a, an*.

hitherto Means *until now*. It is thus inappropriate in the sense of *previously*, as in *Hitherto she had been sad, but now she was happy*. The point of reference for *hitherto* must be the present.

hoi polloi A snobbish term meaning *the ordinary people*. Some writers, however, seem to think it means *the high and mighty*. Among the reasons for not using it is the fact that *hoi* already means *the. The hoi polloi* thus contains a redundancy.

hold one's peace Means *remain silent*. Those who spell it *hold one's piece* are in for some snickers.

home, house The distinction between these is fading, but it's still useful. A *home* is a *house* that's been made into somebody's dwelling. Don't mimic the advertising jargon, *Baronial all-electric homes while they last*.

hopefully Many people resent the use of *hopefully* to mean *it is hoped;* they remember that until recently it meant only *in a hopeful manner*. A majority of readers do accept the new meaning, but you should keep the others in mind.

host Journalese as a v.: *She hosted fourteen guests*.

how Do not use in place of *that: I told her how I wouldn't stand for her sarcasm any*

more. Note that this abuse of *how* can easily lead to ambiguity; we read *how* in its ordinary sense of *in what manner*.

how ever, however Distinct terms. *How ever are you going to tie that knot? You, however, know more about it than I do*. The same distinction applies to *what ever* and *whatever*.

(For sentence position and punctuation of *however*, see pp. 92, 274–275. Also see *but however*.)

human history Redundant for *history*.

humanism, humanity, humaneness, humanitarianism *Humanism* is a doctrine emphasizing the central importance of mankind; *humanity* is human kind or the possession of *humaneness*, that is, sympathy and compassion; *humanitarianism* is a deliberate devotion to charitable public causes.

To call someone a *humanist* is to say nothing about his character; it means either that he's an advocate of the philosophy of humanism or that he's a student of the humanities, the "liberal arts."

hurt (v.) Should be trans. Cf. the journalese, *The Forty-Niners are really hurting this season*. Hurting a season? The intrans. *hurt* is, admittedly, gaining ground, but it still sounds colloq. in an essay.

identify, relate These verbs are increasingly used in a reflexive sense without reflexive pros.: *I identify [myself] with John Wayne; He can't relate [himself] to the Army point of view*. To include the reflexives sounds stuffy, but to exclude them sounds pop-psychological. Look for alternatives: *feel an identity with, accept*, etc.

i.e. Means *that is;* see *e.g.*

if and when, when and if Clichés. Usually you can do without one of the paired words.

if not Dangerously ambig., as in *There were good reasons, if not excellent ones, for taking that step*. A reader has no way of knowing whether this means that the reasons decidedly weren't excellent or that they may have been excellent after all.

if . . . then   When an *if* clause is followed by a main clause, there's no need for *then* in the main clause. Cf. *If I were to stay home, then she would go*. The *then* merely reflects a lack of confidence that *if* has done its work.

if worst comes to worst   This is the right phrasing, not *if worse comes to worst*. But *if worst comes to worst* is a cliché all the same.

ignorant, stupid   Often confused. To be *ignorant* of something is not to know it: *Newton was ignorant of relativity*. An *ignorant* person is one who has been taught very little. A *stupid* person is mentally unable to learn: *The main cause of his ignorance was his stupidity*.

imaginary, imaginative *Imaginary*, meaning *unreal* or *imagined*, is sometimes wrongly displaced by *imaginative*, which means *showing imagination: I reject your idea as totally imaginative*. Substitute *imaginary*.

immanence, imminence, eminence *Immanence* means *indwelling*, usually with a religious sense: *the immanence of the universal spirit* (i.e., its presence in the world). *Imminence* is *nearness in the future: no one was aware of the imminence of the earthquake. Eminence* is *prominence, distinction: He had earned his eminence by decades of service*.

immortal   Public-relations jargon for *memorable*. Not being mortal in the first place, artistic works can't become *immortal*. Neither can touchdowns, melodies, and political speeches. As for artists themselves, it's a laughable piece of human vanity, and a cliché, to call them immortal.

immunity, impunity *Immunity* is *exemption*, and so is *impunity*. When you use *immunity*, however, you have to specify what the immunity is from: *immunity from cholera, immunity from prosecution. Impunity* always has the narrower meaning of *exemption from punishment*, and it always occurs alone: *He did it with impunity*.

impinge, infringe *Impinge*, which is widely misused to mean *affect*, really means *strike* or *dash*. When one thing metaphorically *impinges* on another, the second should be seriously jolted: *They impinged on our freedom by moving in with us*.

Infringe, sometimes confused with *impinge*, means *violate* or *transgress;* its usual obj. is a right or principle. *They infringed the rules of the game*. Used intransitively, *infringe* usually takes *on* or *upon: They infringed on our rights. Impinge* is never trans.

implement (v.)   Bureaucratese if all you mean is *apply* or *carry out*, as in *He implemented his intentions*. Properly used, *implement* means *put into effect according to a plan or procedure: They implemented the reorganization in three stages*.

implicate, involve   Can be very close in meaning. But *implicate* carries a special sense of responsibility for something bad. To be *implicated* in a crime is to be under suspicion of guilt: *His fingerprints implicated him as a member of the ring; his wife, who knew nothing of the plot, was horrified to learn that she too had been involved*.

implicit, explicit, tacit *Implicit* can cause ambiguity, for it means both *implied* (left unstated) and *not giving cause for investigation*. In the sentence *My trust in her was implicit*, both interpretations are possible. Was the trust beyond question, or was it left unstated? Wariness is advised whenever you feel like using *implicit* to mean *unshakable* or *profoundly clear*.

Explicit is the ant. of *implicit* in one of its senses: *In his will he spelled out the explicit provisions that had previously been left implicit. Tacit* is close to *implicit* but means *silent, unspoken;* its reference is not to expression in general but to speech.

imply, infer Widely confused, with *infer* often used where only *imply* would be right. To *imply* is properly to *leave* an implication; to *infer* is to *take* one. *She implied that she was still loyal to him, but he inferred otherwise from her embarrassed manner.*

important Acceptable in an adverbial sense, as in *More important, he announced that he was entering the ministry. Important* has an advantage over *importantly* in such a sentence; it runs no risk of being considered a modifier of *announced.*

in, into, in to It's pedantic to insist that *into* must be preferred with all verbs of motion. Follow your own sense of idiom: *Go jump in the lake!*

In to is distinct from *into: we went into Cleveland; we went in to do some shopping.* The chief danger is that *into* will be used where *in to* is required, as in *The guilty sorcerer's apprentice confessed his crime and turned himself into the sorcerer for punishment.*

Also watch out for the hip-jargon use of *into* in sentences like *I'm into ceramics.*

in a very real sense Pointless verbiage. Your statements are presumed to have a very real sense already; this cliché can only stir up suspicion that they don't.

in all probability, in all likelihood Always wordy for *probably.*

in case Can usually be improved to *if: If* [not *in case*] *you don't like this model, we will refund your money. In case* should be saved for *in the event: This sprinkler is provided in case of fire.*

in connection with See *in terms of.*

in excess of Invariably wordy for *over* or *more than.*

in his own right Wordy if all you mean is *himself* or *also: Biff, a linebacker in his own right . . .* Try *Biff, himself a linebacker . . .*

in number, in length, in size, in volume, in area, etc. Can almost always be deleted with profit: *The plot was two acres* [*in area*].

in re An error for *re*, meaning *concerning. In re* probably comes from a mistaken analogy with *in regard to* or *in reference to. Re* is the full Latin word for *about;* it thus takes no period. Its use should be restricted to memoranda—where, I admit, *in re* is very often seen.

in spite of (despite) the fact that Can always be *although* or *though*, either of which is preferable on grounds of brevity.

in terms of, along the lines of, in connection with These vague bureaucratic phrases are subject to the same abuse as *regarding, in regard to*, etc. When your sentence says *In terms of prowess, Tarzan was unconquerable*, see how much you can lop off. *Tarzan was unconquerable* says the same thing with fewer than half the words. Similarly, *He was pursuing his studies along the lines of sociology* should be simply *He was studying sociology.*

in the affirmative, in the negative Pompous for *yes* and *no.*

in the event that Means, and should always be, *if.*

in the form of Usually excess baggage, as in *His Christmas present arrived in the form of a teddy bear.* Would the present have changed its form in any circumstances? Save the phrase for sentences like *The witch appeared in the form of his aunt Grace.*

in the neighborhood of Tiresome when it simply means *about. There were in the neighborhood of 80,000 people on hand.* Note how the two extra preps. help to throttle the sentence.

in the worst way Colloq. for *extremely.* Besides, it can be ambig.: *She loves him in the worst way.* Should she find a better way?

in this day and age A wordy cliché for *now*.

in view of the fact that Wordy for *because, since*, or *considering that*.

inaugurate A very formal v.; shouldn't be used where *start, begin*, or *open* would do.

incidence, incident, instance Sometimes confused. *Incidence* means *rate of occurrence: the incidence of crime.* An *incident* is *one occurrence.* Thus it's wrong to write *An incidence of murder happened yesterday.*

Note also that *incident* has become journalese for *serious disorder*, as in *The students heckled the speaker, but there were no incidents.* Every reported event, however peaceful, is an incident.

An *instance* is an *example*, something instanced. *In the instance of*, like *in the case of*, is almost always unnecessary and cumbersome. And *often* is preferable to *in many instances.*

include Shouldn't be used loosely to mean *are*, as in *The Marx brothers include Groucho, Harpo, Chico, and Zeppo.* Only when at least one member is unnamed, as in *The Marx brothers include Chico and Zeppo*, should you write *include.* Note also that *include* is wrong after a limitation has already been indicated: *A few of my reasons for saying this include . . .*

incredibly Overused as a vague intensifier: *an incredibly believable alibi.*

index The plu. can be *indexes* or *indices*, but *indexes* is more common when the meaning is *alphabetical listings.*

indicate Overused in the sense of *say.* *Give indication of* is still worse.

indict, indite Pronounced alike, but *indict* means *charge* and *indite* is a poetical archaism for *write.*

individual (n.) Often pompous for *person: He was a kind-hearted individual.* When you use *individual* as a n., keep in mind its sense as an adj.: *personal, not general. Our laws respect the individual* illustrates the n. in its correct use; the individual is implicitly contrasted with the collectivity.

inept, inapt, unapt *Inept* means *incompetent, clumsy; inapt* and *unapt* mean *inappropriate. It is inapt to make the ambassador sit through an inept performance.*

inevitable, inevitably Don't use these words unless you really mean *unavoidable, unavoidably.* The mere fact that something has happened doesn't mean that it was *inevitable. Inevitably, Hamlet succeeds in killing Claudius.* Really? The whole play casts doubt on this *inevitably.*

infect, infest Sometimes confused. *Infect* means *contaminate with germs: She infected the other patients. Infest* means *overrun in great numbers: Thousands of rabbits infested the farmland.*

infringe See *impinge.*

infuse, imbue Can describe the same action, but from different vantages. You *infuse* something *into* someone: *He infused courage into the troops.* You *imbue* somebody *with* something: *He imbued them with courage.* Thus *He infused them with courage* is a mistake.

ingenious, ingenuous *Ingenious* means *clever, brilliantly resourceful; ingenuous* means *naïve.*

input, output Both (especially *input*) are brutally overworked clichés. Restrict them to their mechanical sense (*the computer handles input*), and abandon such bureaucratese as *Let's get more input into our thinking.*

inside of Can always be *inside;* and some people regard *inside of* as ungrammatical. For metaphorical uses, *within* is preferable, anyway: *within twenty minutes.*

insofar as, inasmuch as Legalistic; can usually be simplified to *because, since*, or *for.* If you use them at all, do so precisely: *She did approve of the report insofar as it* *dealt with rent control, but she couldn't accept its conclusions about sewage rates.*

insupportable, unsupportable Not syns. *Insupportable* means *unbearable: Your screeching voice is insupportable. Unsupportable* means *not capable of being supported: an unsupportable cantilever; a program that's idealistic but unsupportable on budgetary grounds.*

intense, intensive Very close in meaning, but *intensive* ought to be saved for contexts in which a given space or time is being crowded with activity: *intensive cultivation of the land; intensive therapy. Intense* is the more general term, meaning *in high degree, extreme.* There's a tendency to use *intensive* where nothing more than *intense* is meant.

internecine Now means *mutually destructive within a group.* The old meaning of *destructive* alone is widely regarded as wrong; both mutuality and common membership should be involved. The Koreans had an *internecine* war, but the Americans and North Koreans did not.

interpersonal Usually redundant and always chilling in effect: *Our interpersonal rapport was outstanding.* The word is meaningful in sociological discourse but in other contexts is sociologese.

intrigue Widely accepted (over protest) in the sense of *fascinate*, but frequent use of it leads to a stale effect. *Intriguing* is a bit gushy as an adj., too.

invincible Means *unconquerable: an invincible champion.* Don't extend the word to mean *extreme* or *stubborn*, as in *an invincible fool, invincible arrogance.*

invite (n.) Colloq. for *invitation.*

invited guest Redundant for *guest*, unless you mean to draw a contrast with party-crashers.

involve See *implicate.*

involved Stale in the sense of *socially concerned: I admire Hannah because she's so involved.* Since *involve* means *envelop, wrap in*, it's important to supply an obj.

irony, ironic, ironical Only use when there's a significant contradiction between a statement and its real import, or between an expectation and a result. It's *ironic* if a plane crashes into the home of the director of the Civil Aeronautics Board, but not if a person tries unsuccessfully to get rich; there's got to be a twist.

Ironic and *ironical* are nearly interchangeable, but some writers prefer to save *ironic* for circumstances and *ironical* for attitudes: *an ironic fate* but *an ironical mind.*

(Also see *sarcasm.*)

irregardless A mistake for *regardless, irrespective*, or *nevertheless.*

is Do not use in Madison Avenue style, as in *The Snuggo Company is people.* Of course you wouldn't write that, but in a sentimental moment you might try *Marriage is forever*—or, more realistically, *Divorce is forever.* Here an adv. is trying to pass for a predicate adj.

issue with Should be *issue: She was issued a locker.*

it is, there is, there are These are useful phrases for deferring a subj., but don't let them become habitual. They interpose a cushion of words between you and your statement. When you've written *It is the Air Force that keeps America strong* or *There are three reasons that prevent me from agreeing with you*, see if the anticipatory formulas are adding anything to your meaning. The chances are that you'd be better off writing *The Air Force keeps . . .* and *Three reasons prevent . . .*

its, it's See p. 306.

-ize In American spelling, *-ize* almost always prevails over *-ise.*

New verbs made from nouns plus *-ize* continually appear, and some of them will eventually be accepted as standard. This has already happened to *editorialize, hospitalize,* and *socialize,* for example. Others, like *finalize* and *randomize,* are used widely in certain quarters but are regarded as jargon elsewhere. Stay away from them in essay prose, and don't invent *-izes* of your own.

join together   Can always be *join,* since things are never joined apart.

judicial, judicious   *Judicial* means *pertaining to courts of law; judicious* means *showing sound judgment.*

just exactly   Redundant, as in *This is just exactly what I meant to say.* Delete one word or the other.

kidnap   Open to objection as a n. Stay with *kidnapping.*

kind, sort   These overworked words, when used at all, should take the sing.: *this kind of man, this sort of woman.* There's nothing ungrammatical about *those kinds* and *those sorts* if different kinds and sorts are intended: *I don't like any of those kinds of argument.* But such constructions are almost always clumsy and redundant. Why not *those arguments,* or *such arguments?* This advice is reinforced by the embarrassment over the number of the ensuing object: *kinds of argument* or *kinds of arguments?* The first is preferable but both make for uneasiness.

Sort of and *kind of* are awkward in the sense of *somewhat,* and they often appear in the unnecessary form *sort of a, kind of a: He was an odd sort of a king.* Don't use *sort* and *kind* unless your sentence needs them to make sense. If *He was an odd king* will do, there's no reason to drag in *sort* or *kind.* A legitimate example is *This kind of bike has only been on the market for three months.*

knack   Should take *of,* not *for: He had a knack of finding studies that seemed to support his prejudices.*

lack, need, want   A *lack* is a *shortage* or *absence;* a *need* is the *condition arising from a lack;* and a *want,* in the pertinent sense, is a *lack of necessary things and an awareness of that lack:*

- There was a lack of power reserves.
- The people had a need for emergency shipments of food.
- The people felt the want of bread and rice.

lack for   Should be *lack: Oregon doesn't lack rain.*

large   Can be an adv., as in *loom large.* Don't "improve" the phrase to *loom largely.*

large part, large portion, large share, large number of   These formulas are often wordy for *many* or *much: a large number of people; a large share of the explanation.* Try *many people, much of the explanation.* The same holds for other adjs. of size or amount: *a small number of deer* should be *few deer.*

latest, last   *Latest* means *most recent,* but *last* means *final.* Thus *the latest message* is the one received most recently, but not necessarily the final one.

laudable, laudatory   *Laudable* means *praiseworthy: a laudable feat. Laudatory* means *bestowing praise: a laudatory citation.*

lb., lbs.   Refer to weight, not money. The British *pound sterling* (£) can be typed with a hyphen through an upper-case L.

lead, led   The past and p.p. of the v. *lead,* meaning *direct* or *head,* are *led,* not *lead.*

leading question   Doesn't mean *embarrassing* or *insinuating question,* but a *question that leads to its own answer.* A leading question can be altogether friendly if, for example, it's addressed to a defense witness by a defense attorney.

leave, let Have different senses in phrases like *leave him alone* and *let him alone*. The first means *get out of his presence;* the second means *don't bother him* (even if you remain in his presence). *Leave* means *depart; let* means *allow*.

legal, legitimate The first is more technical, having to do with what the law allows. *Legitimate* is a broader term meaning *in accord with established principles*. Someone might say that the Vietnam war *may not have been legal, but it was legitimate under the circumstances;* i.e., a correct principle overruled treaty commitments and the letter of the Constitution.

legible, readable *Legible* means *written or printed clearly; readable* means *affording pleasure when read*. The most *legible* writing isn't always the most *readable*.

lend, loan Some writers prefer to keep *lend* as a v. and *loan* as a n.; but *loan* can also be a v. *Loan* as a v. is most often seen in past forms: *I loaned it to her*.

lengthy Not an exact syn. of *long;* it also carries an implication of *too long*. Thus a *lengthy discourse* is one that strains the patience of its hearers.

let's Do not follow by a pro., as it already contains *us*. *Let's us sit down and talk about it* is redundant.
Don't lets and *lets don't* are colloq.

level (v., n.) As a v., *level* is often unnecessary. *He leveled an accusation* has nothing to recommend it over *He accused*. In the sense of *be candid, level* is colloq.: *She leveled with me*.
Level as a n. is overworked in the colorless, indefinable sense illustrated by *at the public level; on the wholesale level*. The n. is inappropriate unless a real hierarchy, a ranking of elements, is involved, as in *He was a competent amateur, but when he turned professional he found himself beyond his level*.

lie, lay If nothing more than repose is intended, the intrans. *lie* is the right word: *lie down*. The trans. *lay* means, among other things, *set: lay it here*. Avoid unintentional sexual humor: *Why don't we lay here a while?*
The past forms of these verbs are troublesome. All the following sentences are correct:

- I lay down. [present is *lie*]
- I laid down my cards. [present is *lay*]
- I have lain in bed all day. [present is *lie*]
- I have laid down my cards. [present is *lay*]

lightning, lightening *Lightning* consists of *flashes of light in a storm; lightening* is the p.p. of the v. *lighten*.

like, as See pp. 209–211.

likely Weak as an unmodified adv.: *She likely had no idea what she was saying*. Some readers would also object to *very likely, she had . . .* Try *probably* or even *in all likelihood*.

likewise An adv., not a conj. You can write *Likewise, Myrtle failed the test*, but not *Jan failed the test, likewise Myrtle*.

line Avoid *line* as a catch-all term: *in this line of endeavor; along the lines of my previous remark*. Find a more succinct equivalent.

literally Means *precisely as stated, without a figurative sense*. If you write *I literally died laughing*, you must be composing from beyond the grave. Many writers wrongly use *literally* to mean *definitely* or *almost* or even its opposite, *figuratively*.

live, alive Both can be adjs., but only *live* should precede a n. You can write *He was really alive*, but don't write *He is an alive man at a party*. The right term here would be *lively*.

loath, loathe *Loath* is an adj. meaning *reluctant; loathe* is a v. meaning *despise, abhor.*

lonely, lonesome Cousin words, but *lonesome* is more restricted in meaning. A place or a person can be *lonely;* if it's a place, the meaning is *isolated. Lonesome* refers only to a lonely state of mind, and emphasizes the sadness of being solitary.

look (v.) When it means *appear*, it takes an adj.: *You look revolting tonight.* When it means *glance, gaze*, etc., it takes an adv.: *He looked longingly at her.* The danger is that an adv. will be used where only an adj. is proper: *She looks well* [i.e., *good*] *in that dress.*

lot, lots Some people find *a lot* and *lots* colloq. in the sense of *a great many* or *a great deal: a lot of reasons, lots of reasons.* In an adverbial sense these phrases are also questionable: *I admire him a lot, she pleases me lots.* The prudent thing is to let the purists have their way and write *many, much*, etc.

Never join the two words *a lot* into the single nonword *alot*.

loud Can be an adv. as well as an adj. *He played loud* is just as "good English" as *He played loudly.*

luxuriant, luxurious *Luxuriant* means *profuse of growth; luxurious* means *lavish, showing luxury.* A weed can be *luxuriant*, a coat can be *luxurious*, but the two adjs. can't be reversed.

mad, angry *Mad* means *insane*, but many writers also use it as a syn. of *angry: She was mad at me.* If you use *mad* in this sense, you can expect complaints from purists.

magnitude Often pompous for *size.* (Also see *on the order of magnitude of.*)

majority, plurality *Majority* is often used pretentiously where *most* is all that's meant. Don't use *majority* unless you have in mind a contrast with *minority.* And make sure that the majority consists of individual members. You can write *the majority of the group* but not *the majority of the time.*

A *majority* is *more than 50 percent;* a *plurality* is the *number of votes* (for example, 42 percent) *received by the leader among three or more candidates.*

many, much *Many* refers to quantity, *much* to amount: *Many problems make for much difficulty.* Don't reverse these senses and write, e.g., *There were too much people in the line.*

marginal Widely misued for *small. Marginal* means *near the lower limits, at the threshold;* the word should only be used for degrees that barely qualify or barely fail. A test score is *marginal* if it just manages to pass, and *marginally failing* if it almost passes. Don't say *His talents were marginal* if you mean *He had very little talent.*

(Also see *optimum.*)

marginalia Plu.: *these marginalia.* For the sing. you had better use *marginal note.*

massive Stale for *large, extensive: a massive crusade against littering; massive cleanup efforts.* Give this bit of political jargon a vacation, and use the word only in its literal sense of *bulky: a massive landslide.*

masterful, masterly Meanings overlap but should be kept distinct. *Masterful* means *domineering* or *commanding: a masterful leader. Masterly* means *expert, displaying mastery: a masterly rendition of the concerto.*

material, materiel *Material* is substance; *materiel* is arms or equipment. The adj. is always *material* (meaning *consisting of matter*).

may, might In hypothetical or past conditions, the auxiliary should be *might*, not *may: If I had known this, I might* [not *may*] *have acted differently. If you could see her* *now, you might* [not *may*] *not believe your eyes.*

Many writers use *might* for simple conditions, as in *I might come and visit you tomorrow.* Strictly speaking, *might* should be *may* here.

means (n.)   For the number of *means*, see p. 178.

media   Always construe as plu. Don't give in to a sloppy fashion and write *The media is to blame.* The correct sing. is *medium.*

mental attitude   Almost always redundant for *attitude. Mental* would be meaningful only if a contrast, e.g., with *spiritual*, were implied.

mental telepathy   Redundant for *telepathy.*

mentality   Means *mental capacity* or *endowment*, not *attitude* or *morale.* You can write *His mentality was retarded*, but don't write *The staff had a good mentality toward the new rules.*

methodology   A *methodology* is a *system or theory of methods*, not a *single method.* Academic inflation has tended to drive out *method*, which is the right word in nearly every case.

mighty   Colloq. as an adv. meaning *extremely: a mighty big job.*

militate, mitigate   Often confused. To *militate* is to *have an adverse effect;* it's followed by *against*, as in *His poor eyesight militated against his chances of becoming a pilot.*

Mitigate means to *reduce an unpleasant effect;* it takes a direct obj., as in *The doctor's cheerful manner mitigated the bad news.*

-minded   See -*wise.*

monetary   See *financial.*

moot   A difficult word to use clearly, because it can mean either *open to debate* or *of no practical value or meaning.* Thus *The question is moot* is an ambig. sentence. Find a clearer way of making the statement.

more preferable   A common redundancy for *preferable.*

more . . . rather than   See pp. 211–212.

more than one   Used with both sing. and plu. verbs, but authorities favor sing.: *More than one reason appears . . .*

most   Colloq. as an adv. meaning *almost: We were most dead by the time we got there.*

motive, motivation, reason   A *motive* is a psychological cause for a specific action: *the motive for the crime; my motive in leaving. Motivation* is a more general term, referring either to the whole topic of motives or to the state of being motivated: *I am interested in human motivation; his motivation was weak.* A common error is use of the general word *motivation* where the specific sense of *motive* is intended: *I never learned his motivation for running away.* The plu. *motivations* is always awkward.

Reasons are consciously recognized: *He offered this as his reason for hiding. Motives* and *motivation* can operate unconsciously and be quite different from the *reasons* put forward in self-justification.

much less   Use only in negative contexts, as in *He hasn't even appeared, much less begun his work.* Watch out for positive senses: *Skiing is difficult, much less surfing.*

muchly   Always wrong for *much.*

must   As a n., *must* has become acceptable to most readers: *Conservation is a must.* But it's still disapproved as an adj.: *This is a must game for us.*

mutual, common   Grammarians generally insist that *mutual* can only mean *reciprocal*, as in *They had a mutual affection. Common*, they say, should be used when two parties share something with regard to a third party or thing: *They had a common interest in boating.* The distinction is often ignored, especially in the phrase *a mutual friend;* but it's worth observing.

Note that *mutual* is often unnecessary: a *mutual agreement* is simply an *agreement.*

naïve, naïveté These are the preferred spellings for words that also appear frequently as *naive* and *naivety.*

nature The word is often unnecessary: *Books of this nature offend me.* Try *Such books . . .*

nauseous, nauseated *Nauseous* means *causing nausea. Nauseated* means *experiencing nausea.* A substance can be *nauseous* but not *nauseated* or *nauseating;* a person can be *nauseated* but not *nauseous*—unless other people throw up when they look at him. The distinction should be maintained, though it often isn't.

near future; not too distant future Wordy in sentences like *I hope to see you again in the not too distant future.* Try *soon* or *before long.*

needless to say If you find this phrase in a draft, ask yourself: *If it's needless to say, why am I saying it?* At times *needless to say* can be rhetorically useful, but don't overwork it.

no sooner . . . than The right formula. *No sooner . . . that* and *No sooner . . . when* are mistakes, as in *No sooner had I left when my typewriter was stolen.*

nohow Authorities maintain that *nohow* has a standard sense of *in no way: I could nohow determine her motives.* But *nohow* is so often misused in colloq. double negatives (*I can't understand her, nohow*) that the "correct" sense will also appear wrong to many readers. You should forget about *nohow* altogether.

noisome Doesn't mean *noisy,* but *disgusting, offensive, bad-smelling.*

none Can take either a sing. or a plu. v.; see pp. 178–179.

none the less, nonetheless *None the less* means *not any the less* and requires an adj.: *She was none the less unhappy after her good fortune. Nonetheless* is a sentence adv. meaning *nevertheless: Nonetheless, she was unhappy.*

not about to Colloq. and ambig.: *She was not about to disguise her age.* This could mean *she was not on the verge of disguising her age* or *she had no intention . . .*

not all, all . . . not See pp. 203–204 for the choice between these phrases.

not so much . . . as The right formula. Avoid *not so much . . . but* and *not so much . . . but rather. She was not so much selfish, but rather impulsive* illustrates the mistake. *She was not so much selfish as impulsive* is better.

not too, not that Colloq. when used to mean *not very: I'm not too sure about that; He's not that interested in sailing.*

not un- *I am not unaware of your kindness* does have a different sense than *I am aware of your kindness;* it implies greater diffidence and a sense of (perhaps grudging) obligation. The *not un-* formula can thus be used where it really conveys something beyond a straight affirmation. But beware of resorting to it simply for its air of importance: *He died young, a not unnatural outcome of his dissolute behavior.* Double negatives are sometimes unclear, and *not un-* usually sounds pompous as well.

nothing like, nowhere near These shouldn't be used in place of *not nearly,* as in *I am nothing like* [or *nowhere near*] *as spry as I used to be.*

notorious See *famous.*

now As an adj., *now* is hip jargon: *Brautigan is a now writer.* Keep *now* an adv. in your writing.

nowheres   Should always be *nowhere*.

number   See p. 177 for the choice between sing. and plu. interpretations of *number*.

Don't write *The number was fewer*. If the items were fewer, then the number of items was *smaller* or *lower*.

numerous   Properly an adj., not a pro. meaning *a number of*. Don't write *Numerous of his debts remain unpaid*.

obliged, obligated   Close but not syns. To be *obligated* is to be *bound morally or legally*: *I am obligated to serve as an officer after finishing ROTC*. *Obliged* has a less technical sense, and it implies a *feeling* of obligation: *I am obliged to you for your favors*.

oblivious   Strictly interpreted, *oblivious* means *forgetful*, not just *unaware*. The distinction is disappearing, however. When used in the sense of *forgetful*, *oblivious* should always be followed by *of*: *He was oblivious of his duties*. If you use the extended sense of *unaware*, either *of* or *to* is acceptable: *She was oblivious to [of] the danger*.

observance, observation   Keep distinct. An *observance* is a *formal keeping of a custom: the observance of Yom Kippur*. It shouldn't be used interchangeably with *observation*, meaning *watching*.

obviate   Means *make unnecessary*, not *remove*. If *difficulties were obviated*, they were never faced at all.

occur, take place   *Take place* is the narrower term; it should be used only with *scheduled* events. Don't write *The storm took place last Wednesday*.

-odd   Redundant with *about, some*, or *approximately: some eighty-odd immigrants*. When you do use *-odd*, be sure to retain the hyphen so as to prevent ambiguity. Don't write *Thirty odd friends of mine came to the party*.

of between, of from   Avoid pairing preps.: *an estimate of between thirty and forty-five people*. Try *an estimate of thirty to forty-five people*.

off of   Should always be *off* instead: *She got off the train*, not *She got off of the train*.

offhand   Preferable to *offhanded* and *offhandedly*, as both adj. and adv.

oftentimes   Should always be *often*.

O.K.   Colloq. in writing. The spelling *O.K.* is more common than *o.k., okay*, etc.

old adage   Should always be *adage*, since an *adage* is precisely an *old saying*.

old-fashioned   The correct form, not *old-fashion*.

on, upon, up on   *On* and *upon* are interchangeable in most uses, but you should save *upon* for deliberately formal effects: *She swore upon her word of honor . . .* Note that *up on* is different in meaning from *upon: He climbed up on the ledge*.

on account of   Never preferable to *because of*.

on the one hand . . . on the other hand   Once you've written *on the one hand*, you've committed yourself to dropping the second shoe, *on the other hand*. But *on the other hand* can be used alone when you want to introduce a qualification; it doesn't always have to be preceded by *on the one hand*.

on the order of   Change to *about* or *approximately* when estimates of quantity are involved.

on the order of magnitude of   Almost always a mistake for *about* or *approximately*. An *order of magnitude* is a range from some number x to $10x$. Leave this phrase to the mathematicians.

on the part of   Usually wordy for *by* or *among: Strong objections were voiced on the part of welfare mothers*. Substitute *by*.

one (pro.) *One* is useful in truly impersonal statements like *One doesn't often see a Packard these days.* But don't use *one* to cover up your subjectivity, as in *One notices that Mailer's novels always end clumsily.* And don't switch from *one* to *you*, as here: *One doesn't have any choice; you get searched or you can't board the plane.*

(Also see *we*.)

one of the few . . . if not the only This formula can be troublesome, as in *She is one of the few, if not the only, person who . . .* Should it be *person* or *people*? Both are wrong, because neither of them can reconcile the plu. and sing. modifiers *few* and *only*. You can try to correct the sentence by writing *She is one of the few people, if not the only person, who . . . ,* but this still leaves the awkward problem of whether the following v. should be sing. or plu. It's better to recast: *Few if any people are as . . . as she is.*

one of those who Takes a plu. v. See p. 179.

one or more Should be construed as plu.: *One or more cars were manufactured every hour.*

optimism, optimistic; pessimism, pessimistic An *optimist* is someone with a general tendency to expect favorable outcomes. To be *optimistic* is therefore to be temperamentally or philosophically disposed toward hopefulness. Don't misuse these terms to cover *specific* predictions, as in *I am optimistic about tomorrow's weather.* The same caution applies to *pessimism* and *pessimistic*.

optimum, optimal; minimum, minimal These don't mean *most* and *least*, but *the most* [or *least*] *possible, given the circumstances.* Don't use these words unless you are relating an outcome to a set of implicit or explicit conditions: *The general achieved optimum results with his badly equipped troops.* (Also see *marginal*.)

Before a n., *optimum* and *minimum* can

serve as adjs.: *minimum damage.* But for predicate adjs. you should choose the plainly adjectival *optimal* and *minimal: The damage was minimal. Optimal* and *minimal* can also precede a n.

orate Shouldn't be used unless you intend a pejorative meaning: *He orated for hours and hours.* Today the term implies a tedious windiness.

ordinance, ordnance An *ordinance* is a *decree; ordnance* is *weaponry*, especially cannons.

organic A cliché. You would do well to save it for its literal meaning of *pertaining to living organisms*, and forget about *organic form, an organically related idea*, etc.

orient, orientate *Orient*, in the sense of *familiarize*, tends to prevail over *orientate* in American English.

-oriented See *-wise*.

other than Generally condemned as an adv. meaning *except, except for*, or *otherwise than*. Don't write *I can't behave other than I've been doing. Other than that* makes an especially clumsy adv.: *Other than that, I can follow your reasoning.* Substitute *otherwise*.

other times Shouldn't be construed as a complete adv., as in *Other times she felt depressed. At other times* is what you want.

otherwise Keep as an adv. and do not extend to supplant the adj. *other*. In *He loved old buildings, Victorian and otherwise*, the adj. *Victorian* is being forced into parallelism with an adv. If *other* sounds odd, recast the sentence.

ought Always followed by *to* and never preceded by *had*. Thus this sentence contains two errors: *She hadn't ought go there in such bad weather. She oughtn't to have gone* is correct, though *She shouldn't have gone* sounds more natural.

ourself Should always be *ourselves.*

outside of Should be simply *outside.* In metaphorical uses (*Outside of these reasons*) it should be replaced by *except for.*

overall (adj.) Sounds precariously like the sing. of *overalls.* You'd do better to choose a syn.: *total, comprehensive, general, complete.* Note also that in some sentences the word conveys nothing at all: *The overall outcome was that the Dodgers won.* Look for opportunities to delete.

owing to the fact that Wordy for *because, since.*

pack (v.) Colloq. in sentences like *He packs a heavy punch; The engine packs 325 horsepower.*

parricide, patricide *Parricide* is the *murder of parents* without regard to their sex; *patricide* is the *murder of fathers* only. Hamlet rejects the idea of *parricide* against his mother. Oedipus, who kills his father, has committed both *parricide* and *patricide.*

part, portion A *part* is a *fraction of a whole;* a *portion* is a *part allotted to some person or use.* Thus you shouldn't write *A large portion of the sea is contaminated.*

part from, part with To *part from* is to *take leave from* or *go away from: She parted from her poodle,* i.e., she bade her poodle farewell. To *part with* is to *give up: She parted with her poodle,* i.e., she got rid of the dog.

partial, partially Can be ambig., since they mean either *incomplete(ly)* or *biased, in a biased manner.* A *partial survey* could be a survey that lacks completeness or one that lacks objectivity. Make sure that you let your reader see which sense you intend. Where *partially* means *incompletely,* it can be replaced by *partly.*

particular Serves no purpose in phrases like *no particular purpose.*

party (n., v.) Has a legalistic sense when it's a n. meaning *person.* Don't use it this way unless you want the person to be conceived abstractly as a litigant, defendant, or other formal participant in an action or relationship. In *Four parties refused to go,* the n. should be changed to *people.*

Party as a v. is colloq.: *We partied all night.*

past history, past experience, past record, etc. The presumption is that *history, experience,* and *record* already refer to the past. Thus *past* can and should be dropped.

patronize Can be ambig. between *sponsor, be a customer of,* and *condescend to.* Make sure that the context eliminates doubt.

peer Means *equal,* not *superior.* Members of the House of Peers are supposedly one another's equals.

per Sounds excessively technical where *a* or *an* would do: *twice per month, fifty miles per hour.* As per is bureaucratese for *in accordance with: as per your letter of the fifteenth.* Don't use *per* to mean *by,* as in *She sent it per first-class mail.*

percent, percentage Both *percent* (sometimes written *per cent*) and *percentage* mean *rate per hundred. Percent* should be used with numbers (whether written-out or numerals): *twenty percent. Percentage* appears without numbers: *a high percentage.*

Don't use either *percent* or *percentage* where you simply mean *part.* And don't assume that a percentage is always small, as in *Only a percentage of them agreed.* A *percentage* could be any portion less than 100 percent.

persecute, prosecute To *persecute* is to *single out for mistreatment;* to *prosecute* is to *bring to trial.*

personal, personally Often meaningless, as in *my personal preference* and *personally, I would say . . .* Since you are obviously the person making the statement, the extra word is just a little piece of false modesty. Use *personal* only as an ant. of *impersonal* or *general*.

personnel   Has a bureaucratic aura and shouldn't be used indiscriminately for *people*. Some authorities object to *personnel* in conjunction with numbers: *250 personnel*. In this phrase *employees* would be better. Keep *personnel* for more abstract uses: *No American personnel remained except 50,000 civilian advisers.*

persons, people   Some authorities insist that you can't use *people* with numbers, as in *forty people*. But this contradicts normal current usage. The real distinction to observe is that *persons* makes us think of the individual members who go to make up the *people*. Thus, *three persons were arrested at the rock concert attended by 80,000 people.*

peruse   Means *read with care;* it shouldn't be used for *read* in general, still less for *scan*.

pessimism, pessimistic   See *optimism*.

phenomenon   The only correct sing. form. Don't write *This phenomena*. The most common plu. is *phenomena*.

philosophy   Widely misused to mean *belief, idea, practice: Here is my philosophy about refunds*. A *philosophy* is a *whole system of doctrine: Kant's philosophy; the philosophy of pragmatism*. The plu. *philosophies* sounds especially ridiculous in sentences like *I have come to this college to develop and extend my philosophies.*

place   Some readers consider words like *any place, no place*, and *some place* to be colloq. It's safer to write *anywhere, nowhere, somewhere. Go places* is colloq. in the sense of *make progress: Now we're really going places.*

plan   The v. is followed by *to*, not *on: He plans to run*, not *He plans on running*. Note that *plan* implies a future action, so that it's never necessary to write *plan ahead* or *future plans*.

plenty   As an adj., *plenty* must be followed by *of*. Don't write *She has plenty reasons for her opinion.*

plus (adv.)   Do not use in place of *besides* or *moreover: I was late for the test; plus, I was feeling ill.*

point of view   See *standpoint*.

poorly   Colloq. in the sense of *ill* or *sick: I feel poorly*. Of course *poorly* is acceptable in the more common meaning: *She performed poorly.*

popular   Implies favor with a large number of people. Don't use it when only a few people are meant: *The hermit was popular with his three visitors; That idea isn't very popular with me.*

pore, pour (v.)   Don't confuse these words, as in *He poured over the document*. To *read attentively* is to *pore*.

position (v.)   Used as a v., *position* raises objections; some readers think it can only be a n. In *He positioned himself*, substitute *placed*.

possess   Too formal when all you mean is *have* or *own*. Save *possess* for contexts that call for a ceremonious or legal air: *The squatter established his right to possess the property.*

possible, feasible   The first adj. is broader than the second. Anything that can happen, such as an earthquake, is *possible*, but only projects or intentions can be *feasible*. It is both *possible* and *feasible* to get a Ph.D. degree in five years; *A cyclone in Arkansas is only possible.*

possible, possibly   Don't use *possible* as an adv.: *a possible missing airliner*. Substitute *possibly*.

Watch for redundancy in phrases like *can possibly, may possibly*, and *possible likelihood*. These should be *can, may*, and *likelihood* alone.

practicable, practical *Practicable* means *capable of being done; practical* means *worth doing on grounds of usefulness,* or *having to do with real conditions.* Thus it is *practicable* to send a million fruit flies to Mars, but the idea lacks *practical* appeal.

precede See *proceed.*

precipitous, precipitate (adj.) *Precipitous* means *steep: a precipitous ascent. Precipitate* means *unduly hasty: a precipitate attack.*

preclude Always takes the thing being prevented as a direct obj. Don't write *This law precludes children from working.* That would imply that the children themselves were being prevented. Try *This law precludes child labor.*

predominate, predominant You would do well to keep these separate: the v. is *predominate,* the adj. *predominant.* So many people use *predominate* as an adj. (*the predominate tendency*) that some authorities have given up the struggle; but most good writers haven't.

prefer Followed by *to,* not *than.* Don't write *She preferred running for office than sitting at home.*

preferable Like *prefer, preferable* takes *to,* not *than.* Note also that it shouldn't be combined with comparative words, as in *That alternative was more preferable.* The sense of *more* is already contained in *preferable.*

prejudice Not always bias *against;* it can also be bias *for: She was prejudiced in favor of all radical measures.*
Note that the adj. is *prejudiced,* not *prejudice.* Don't write *She was prejudice.*

prescribe, proscribe To *prescribe* is to *designate;* to *proscribe* is to *forbid.* Pharmacists are *proscribed* from *prescribing* medicine.

present (adj.) Redundant in *the present incumbent,* cumbersome in *at the present*

time (try *now*), and stuffy in *the present writer (I).*

pressure Hasn't gained full acceptance as a v.: *He pressured us to agree.* Try *pressed.*

presumptive, presumptuous *Presumptive,* meaning *based on inference,* shouldn't replace *presumptuous,* meaning *unwarrantably bold.* In *She couldn't bear his presumptive manner,* the adj. should be *presumptuous.*

pretty Mildly colloq. for *rather: He was pretty fond of camping. Pretty nearly* should be *almost;* cf. *He was pretty nearly exhausted.*

prevent, prohibit To *prevent* is to *keep from happening;* to *prohibit* is to *forbid.*
Both verbs take *from* and a gerund: *She prevented him from going; I was prohibited from smoking.* It's a mistake to write *I was prohibited to smoke.* (Also see *forbid.*)

preventive, preventative These are syns. both as adjs. and as nouns. *Preventive* is usually preferred on grounds of brevity.

previous to, prior to Never better than *before.*

proceed, precede To *proceed* is to *go forward;* to *precede* is to *go ahead of.* The *king preceded his courtiers as they proceeded toward the castle*
Proceed is pompous if all you mean is *go: He proceeded to the supermarket.* Use *proceed* only in the sense of a continued action.

prophecy, prophesy *Prophecy* is a n.: *I make this prophecy. Prophesy* is a v.: *I prophesy this outcome.*

proportion Often involved in wordy formulas: *the greater proportion* for *most, in greater proportion* for *many.*
Some authorities object to *proportions,* a mathematical term of *relationship,* when all that's meant is *dimensions* or *size.*

proposition (n., v.) Inaccurate as a syn. of *project, undertaking,* etc. A *proposition* is an *offer of terms,* a *statement of plan,* or, in logic, a *statement affirming or denying something.*

As a v., *proposition* is colloq. for *propose sexual relations.* You'll be sorry if you try to make it mean *propose* in the wider sense.

provided, providing Syns., but *provided* is more common: *He agreed to sign the contract, provided that all his demands were met.* But *provided* (or *providing*) is often an unnecessary euphemism for *if.* Use it only in formal contexts.

pseudo-, quasi- Both mean *false* or *seeming,* but *pseudo-* is somewhat more biting as a term of denigration. Beware of tacking *pseudo-* onto miscellaneous words simply to show disapproval of a party or attitude: *pseudo-liberal, pseudo-intellectual.* The prefix is only appropriate where a *false* pretension is involved.

purchase (v.) Stuffy if all you mean is *buy. Purchase* calls attention to the exchange of money (or effort, or work) for the object gained: *He purchased his security at the price of his happiness.*

question as to whether, question of whether Can usually be shortened to *whether.*

quick Makes an awkward adv. *She went quick* should be *She went quickly.*

quiet, quieten The v. should always be *quiet* in American English.

quote (n.) Widely used to mean *quotation,* as is *quotes* for *quotation marks.* But this sounds colloq. to many readers, and you'd be safer using the longer forms in your writing.

rabid *Rabid* means *having rabies* or, metaphorically, *irrationally extreme, raging.* Too many writers use it as a general term of abuse: *She is a rabid socialist if you ask me.* If you aren't willing to call your opponents mad dogs, don't call them *rabid.*

raise, rise (v., n.) As a v. *raise* is trans.: *raise the roof. Rise* is intrans.: *rise and shave.* Don't use these terms interchangeably.

As a n. many people continue to think that *raise* in a *raise in pay* is "bad English." In America, however, the phrase is standard, and a *rise in pay* is a fussy genteelism.

raison d'être Means *reason for being, reason for existence: The raison d'être of prostitution is sexual hypocrisy.* It's grossly clumsy to use *raison d'être* when all you mean is *reason: That is my raison d'être for being here today.*

rarely ever Redundant for *rarely.*

rather, somewhat, slightly Don't combine these terms of qualification with strong adjs. like *tremendous* and *astounding.*

rather than This formula gets involved in difficulties of parallelism: *She wanted to ride rather than walking. Walking* should be *walk,* since it's equivalent to the inf. *ride.* Again: *Rather than risking a new war, the President decided to compromise. Risking* should be *risk.*

ravage, ravish *Ravage* means *destroy; ravish* means *rape, abduct,* or *fill with strong emotion.* Don't write *She was ravaged by the concert.*

real Colloq. as an adv., as in *I am real interested in finishing this book.*

really Overused as an intensifier: *I really mean what I say.* The sentence carries more force when *really* is deleted.

reason is because The idea of *because* is already contained in *reason;* the phrase is therefore redundant. Even though many good writers fall into it, you would do well to avoid it. Write *the reason is that.*

rebut, refute Widely confused. To *rebut* is to *oppose* in formal argument; to *refute* is to *disprove.* The most common mistake is to use *refute* as if it were *rebut: George refuted the point, but he was mistaken.*

Save *refute* for instances in which the point has been definitively exposed as wrong.

reckon   Colloq. for *suppose, think: I reckon I'll come.*

reconciled to, reconciled with   *Reconciled to* means *resigned to: she became reconciled to the necessity for a change. Reconciled with* means *restored* or *harmonized* after a dispute: *she became reconciled with her estranged husband.*

record (n.)   Can be preceded by *intercollegiate, American*, etc., but shouldn't be combined with *new* or *all-time*. The meaning of *record* already contains such adjs.

recur, recurrence; reoccur, reoccurrence   The differences are only of spelling, not of meaning. In American English *recur* and *recurrence* are more common.

redolent   Follow by *of*, not *with*.

regarding, in regard to, with regard to, with respect to, relating to, relative to   These are flourishing elements of bureaucratese. *On, about*, and *concerning* are almost always preferable. See also *in terms of.*
    Note that *regards* is wrong in *in regards to;* keep to the sing. if you must use the phrase.

regretful, regrettable   To be *regretful* is to *feel regret;* to be *regrettable* is to *cause regret.* An *accident* may be *regrettable* but it's never *regretful.*

regular   Colloq. for *real* or *genuine*, as in *a regular clown.*

relation, relationship   Overlap in meaning, and many writers use *relationship* for all possible senses. *Relation*, however, is correct and preferable when an abstract connection is meant: *the relation of wages to prices.* Save *relationship* for connections of mutuality: *his relationship with Susie; the President's relationship with the press.*

relatively, comparatively   Don't use these words without showing what the relation or comparison is *to: comparatively few cars are Buicks.* Compared to what standard of reference?

relevant   Perhaps the most soiled word of recent times. It is a term of relationship meaning *pertinent*, and it's meaningless without a following n.: *relevant to my interests.* But recently it's been used in an absolute sense: *You just aren't relevant; I want a course that's relevant.* Many readers are justly offended by this, and not only on stylistic grounds. If you don't specify what something is relevant *to*, you're implying that *your* interests ought to be everybody's.

repel(led), repellent; repulse(d), repulsive   Both *repel* and *repulse* can mean *drive back* in a physical sense, but only *repel* is correct when aversion is meant: *Modern art repels me*, not *Modern art repulses me.*
    As adjs., however, both *repellent* and *repulsive* can be used to indicate aversion. *Repulsive* is the stronger of the two words. The idea of spending all day at work may be *repellent* to you, and so you go home early; the idea of peanut butter soup may be *repulsive* to you, and so you experience a moment of real disgust.

replace   See *substitute.*

requisite, requirement   A *requisite* is something needed, whether or not the need has been voiced; a *requirement* is something for which a demand has been expressed.

research   Very widely accepted as a v.: *She researches her dissertation.* But a significant number of writers consider this ugly and would take the trouble to write *She does research on . . .*

respective(ly)   Use only where absolutely needed for clarity. In *The teams returned to their respective dugouts* the word *respective* is superfluous. Would anyone have imagined that both teams returned to *each other's* dugouts? *Respective* is almost always unnecessary. *Respectively* does have a function in sentences like this: *The Smiths and Joneses bought stocks and savings bonds, respectively*. Even so, you should remember that *respectively* makes the reader stop and puzzle out the division.

rest, remainder, residue, balance   *Balance* and *remainder* are almost syns., but some writers prefer to use *balance* only for money matters. *Rest, remainder,* and *residue* all refer to leftovers, but in slightly different contexts. *Rest* is the most general term. *Remainder* implies an act of subtraction and refers to countable things. *Residue* implies an act of removal or destruction, and refers to a bulk. Thus:

- The rest of my time is free.
- The first days of his vacation had to be spent in house repair, but the remainder were free.
- She found a residue of crystals in the bottom of the test tube.
- You can make a deposit now and pay the balance next month.

reticent   Doesn't mean *reluctant*, as in *They were reticent to comply*. It means *disposed to be silent*, as in *Reticent people sometimes become talkative after a few drinks*.

reverend, reverent (adj.)   *Reverend* means *worthy of reverence; reverent* means *feeling or showing reverence*.

revolution, revolt, rebellion   A *revolution* is the *complete overthrow* of a government—or, metaphorically, a *sweeping change*, as in *the modernist revolution in taste*. If all you mean is *armed resistance*, the right word is *rebellion: the rebellion at Wounded Knee*. If you mean simply *protest*, write *revolt: a taxpayers' revolt*. Save *revolution* for a rebellion that spreads and succeeds. The word is being debased in all senses: *the revolution in waterbed construction; the revolution at P.S. 121*.

rob, steal   *Rob* takes as its obj. the person or institution robbed; *steal* takes as its obj. the thing stolen: *He robbed the store, stealing eight television sets*. Don't write *He robbed eight television sets*.

same, the same   Don't use these as pros.: *He raced for the train and caught same*.

sanction, sanctions   Very different in meaning. The sing. *sanction* means *permission: sanction to go*. The plu. *sanctions* means *penalties: The U.N. voted sanctions against Rhodesia*.

saving, savings   A *saving* is a *sum saved* by a given action: *The budget cut resulted in a saving of $50,000. Savings* are *funds set aside: He had to draw upon his savings*. Don't confuse the two by writing, e.g., *This discount provides a savings of $80*.

scarce, scarcely   *Scarce* makes an ugly adv., as in *I had scarce finished speaking when . . .* The genuine adv. *scarcely* should be substituted. Note that *scarcely* should be followed by *when*, not *than*.

Watch for double negatives (see p. 203) with *scarcely: He didn't scarcely mind; She didn't do scarcely enough*. These are substandard expressions.

scarify   Doesn't mean *frighten*, but *scratch* or *wound*.

scenario   Overworked in the loose metaphorical sense of *plan* or *expected outcome: The President's scenario calls for a leveling-off of prices*. The Pentagon's use of the word to mean a *set of predicted mutual responses by hostile powers* is at least closer to the original sense of *dramatic outline* or *screenplay*. Even this use, however, is by now a borderline cliché.

scene   Colloq. in several recent senses: *the drug scene; making the scene*, etc. Try to stay near the literal sense of the locale of a specific action: *the scene of the crime; a scene of havoc*.

seasonal, seasonable *Seasonal* means *pertaining to seasons: Rainfall comes in seasonal concentration here. Seasonable* means *at the right time: The market crash made him realize that his decision to sell had been seasonable.*

seldom ever Should be *seldom.*

sensibility, sensitivity, sensitiveness *Sensibility* is *capacity for discriminated feeling: a poet of extremely keen sensibility. Sensitivity* and *sensitiveness* can both mean *acute susceptibility to impressions.* When an *object* or *instrument* is the thing registering those impressions, however, *sensitivity* is the right word; only people have *sensitiveness.*

sensible of, sensitive to The first means *mindful of: I am sensible of your favor.* The second means *acutely susceptible to: I am sensitive to extreme heat.*

sensual, sensuous Widely confused. *Sensual* means *carnal, voluptuous,* or *having to do with sex: a sensual thrill. Sensuous* means *pertaining to the senses, showing a general receptivity of the senses: The baby was delighted by sensuous impressions.*

shall, will Except in questions (*Shall I come?*), *shall* has been falling into disuse. Some grammarians still hold to the original conjugation of *to be* in the future indicative:

I shall
you will
he, she, it will

we shall
you will
they will

Today, however, most writers use *will* for all these forms. You can still use *shall* in the first person, but this makes for a somewhat formal effect.

When the *shall-will* distinction was more widely observed, the way to express em-phatic resolution or insistence in the future tense was to reverse the conjugation:

I will
you shall
he, she, it shall

we will
you shall
they shall

This too is still possible, but the *shall* forms may sound pretentious. It's better to get emphasis from surrounding words, punctuation, or underlining: *You will pay the rent!*

shape (n.) Colloq. for *condition: in good shape.*

-ship Plu. words like *leaders, readers, members* shouldn't be replaced by *leadership, readership, membership. The membership disapproved* should be *The members disapproved.* Save the *-ship* forms for abstract uses: *The membership dropped again last year; We train young men in leadership.*

should, would Like *shall* and *will* (see *shall*), *should* and *would* used to be differentiated by person as conditional forms of *to be:*

I should
you would
he, she, it would

we should
you would
they would

But in contemporary American English *I should* and *we should* sound stuffy as forms of *to be.* In the sense of *ought to,* however, *should* is required in all persons: *I should come, but I've decided not to.*

In formal prose *should* is sometimes used to express a condition, with *would* as its consequence: *If you should come tomorrow, you would find me at home.* But it sounds more natural to use the present tense of the main v. for likely conditions (*If you come tomorrow, you will . . .*) and the past tense of the main v. for more doubtful conditions (*If you came tomorrow, you would . . .*). For conditions already unfulfilled, you want the past perfect (*If you had come yesterday, you would have . . .*). It's a mistake to write *If you should have come*; if you want more formality, try *Had you come . . .* (Also see pp. 146–149.)

show (v.) Colloq. for *appear: Nobody showed. Showed up* is better but still questionable. Try reserving *show* for trans. uses.

The p.p. of *show* can be either *showed* or *shown*, but *showed* sounds like an error to many readers. You'd better write *shown* every time: *I have shown it.* The past tense is always *showed: I showed it.*

similar Means *resembling*, not *same.* Thus it's wrong to write *Ted died in 1964, and Alice suffered a similar fate two years later.* The writer doesn't mean to assert any difference between one death and the other, but *similar* implies both likeness and unlikeness.

Don't use *similar to* as an adv. meaning *like: This steak smells similar to one I had last Tuesday.* Substitute *like.*

since Pay no attention to those who tell you that *since* can't be used in place of *because.* But note that a problem of ambiguity sometimes arises. In *Since she went away he does all the housework*, for example, both the temporal and causal meanings are possible. Has he been doing the housework *ever since* she left, or *because* she left? Don't use *since* unless it's free of ambiguity.

sit, set With few exceptions, *sit* is intrans.: *She sat. Set* is usually trans.: *She set the table.* You can of course write *The judge sat the jury* and *The sun set*, but don't write *I set there sleeping* or *I want to sit these weary bones to rest.*

situation, position These words, useful in their place, tend to get inflated in bu-

reaucratic prose, especially when urged on by the catchall connectives *regarding, with respect to*, etc. (see *regarding*). *With respect to our position regarding the perilous situation* should be *About the danger.*

slow Remember that *slow* is a perfectly acceptable adv. as well as an adj. (see p. 156).

so, so that Don't use *so* as a vague intensifier: *She was so egotistical!* The *so* demands a following *that* clause: *She was so egotistical that no one could work with her for more than a week.*

So is overworked as a coordinating conj. The problem is that it often appears where subordination is called for by the meaning: *He didn't have anything else to do, so he went to the movies.* This is grammatical but weak. Try *Having nothing else to do, . . .* Then there's clearly one main idea in one main clause.

So, often followed by *that*, can also be a subordinating conj.: *I confessed so that my burden of guilt would be removed.* Here *so that* has its proper meaning of *in order that.* When preceded by words like *enough* and *sufficient*, however, *so that* is clumsy. Thus in *She has earned enough money so that she can go to Mexico next year, so that she can* should be replaced by *to.* Similarly, in *It is sufficiently sunny so that I can get a tan*, you should change *so that I can* to *for me to.*

someone, some one *Someone* means *somebody. Some one* refers to an unspecified person or thing, followed by an *of* phrase to make the meaning clear: *Some one of his friends must have lent him some money.*

something Do not use as an adv. meaning *somewhat*, as in *He is something under six feet tall.* Note also that *something* can be ambig.: *She smells something like a dead fish.* And *She smells something awful* is both ambig. and colloq.

sometime, sometimes, some time *Sometime* means *at an unspecified time.*

Sometimes means *now and then*. *Some time* means *a span of time*, as in *It has been some time now since the last snowfall*. The chief danger of confusion is between *sometime* and *some time*.

somewheres Should be *somewhere*.

sort See *kind*.

Soviet Union, Russia The government or state is the *Soviet Union*, founded in 1917; the country has been *Russia* all along. Don't refer to Russians as *Soviets*, as in newspaper style; this would be like calling Americans *Uniteds*.

special(ly) See *especial(ly)*.

specie, species Unrelated in meaning. *Specie*, always sing., means *coined money*. A *species* (the plu. is also *species*) is a *class of similar individuals*.

stall for time Redundant for *stall*.

standpoint, viewpoint, point of view, perspective, angle These terms can be used metaphorically, but they can also become clichés, as in *He considered the consumer angle* or *She likes it from an ecology standpoint*. The problem is that none of the literal meaning of *standpoint* or *angle* survives in these examples. When you use such a word, try to carry through its consequences: *Regarded from the standpoint of ecology, the project looks very different; The chairmanship gave him the perspective needed to see both sides of the debate*. In short, your sentences should show an awareness that a particular point of view alters the way the viewed object is *perceived*.

stanza, verse A *stanza* is a group of poetic lines forming a division of the poem. Some writers use *verse* in the same sense, but *verse* also means *one poetic line* (as well as *metrical composition* in general). It's best, therefore, to use only *stanza* when you mean a group of lines.

state (v.) Don't use *state* indiscriminately for *say*. To *state* is to *make a declaration*; its connotation is formal or official.

stimulus, stimulant, stimulation A *stimulus* is an *incitement* or *incentive: He was motivated by the stimulus of greed*. A *stimulant* is something that causes arousal: *Coffee is a stimulant. Stimulation* is the *effect of a stimulus or stimulant: Mrs. Jones found stimulation in quiz programs*.

stop (v.) Colloq. for *stay: She stopped in Oklahoma City for a week*.

straight, straightened; strait, straitened *Straight* means *not bent*, and *straightened* means *made straight*. *Strait* means *narrow*, and *straitened* means *confined*:

- The straight path leads to the strait gate.
- Finding himself in straitened circumstances, he went crazy and was put in a strait jacket.

As a n., *strait* means a *narrow passage of water between two large bodies of water*. It's sometimes plu., but not so often as some writers think. For example, it's the *Strait* [not *Straits*] *of Magellan. Straits* can also mean a position of difficulty: *She was in desperate straits*.

strata Should be kept plu., with the sing. *stratum*. The plu. *stratums* is sometimes seen, but *strata* is much more common: *These social strata . . .*

structure (v.) Overused as a syn. of *order, arrange, construct,* one of which is always preferable: *Give me a moment to arrange* [not *structure*] *my thoughts*.

stultifying To *stultify* is to *make foolish*; something *stultifying* makes a foolish impression. The word is widely misused to mean *suffocating* or *stuffy: The atmosphere at the Club is too stultifying for a liberal like Ralph*.

subconscious Smacks of popularized psychology. The right adj. is *unconscious;*

the unconscious mind; unconscious compulsion.

subject (n.) See *field*.

substitute, replace *Substitute* takes as its obj. the new item that is supplanting the old one: *She substituted margarine for butter. Replace* takes as its obj. the item being abandoned: *She replaced the butter with margarine.* Note that these sentences are describing the same act.

such, no such Be sparing with *such* as an intensive unaccompanied by a *that* clause: *I had such a good time.*

When it precedes a relative clause, *such* is followed by *as*, not *that: He took such belongings as he could save from the fire.*

The formula *no such* shouldn't be followed by *a*, as in *There is no such a thing as a unicorn.*

suppose Beware of writing *suppose* where *supposed* is necessary: *We are suppose to finish early.*

sure Frowned upon as an adv.: *She sure likes muffins.* But *surely* would sound like a genteelism in this sentence. Try *really.*

sympathy for, sympathy with, sympathize with To feel *sympathy for* someone is to *experience compassion: She has sympathy for the people of Bangladesh. Sympathy with* is a *feeling of kinship or identity: Her sympathy with Jane Fonda made her a radical.* To *sympathize with*, however, is once again to *experience compassion: She sympathized with the poor.*

synchronize Contains the idea of *time* and shouldn't be used when the harmonizing is nontemporal: *The newlyweds synchronized their peculiarities.* No doubt they synchronized their watches and their bedtimes, but they must have *reconciled* their peculiarities.

tactics, strategy *Tactics* are *immediate moves*; a *strategy* is the *total plan* for victory. Both of these military terms are widely used in a metaphorical sense, but *strategy* has tended to usurp *tactics: My strategy today is to scan the want ads.* You should save *strategy* for contexts in which various *tactics* are integrated into a general scheme.

target Overworked in the sense of *goal*, and its literal sense is sometimes disastrously forgotten: *Our efforts have enabled us to go high above the target.* That's very far from the bull's-eye.

teen-age, teen-ager These are acceptable terms, but they became acceptable too recently to be made retroactive to before, say, 1940. Don't write *Mozart was an unusual teen-ager* or *Romeo and Juliet had a teen-age romance.*

temblor Journalese for *earthquake.* Some writers mistakenly spell it *tremblor.*

temerity, timorousness Sometimes confused. *Temerity* is *reckless boldness; timorousness* is *fearfulness.*

terrify, terrorize Overlap in meaning, but you can observe a difference. To *terrify* is to *fill with terror*, whether intentionally or not: *Snails terrify me.* To *terrorize* is to *intimidate brutally.* Terrorism is always intentional, and it doesn't always work: *They terrorized the population with raids on civilians, but there were no thoughts of surrender among the sufferers.* Don't use *terrorize* where *frighten* would do, as in *The President is trying to terrorize us with these statistics.*

than For the case of pros. following *than*, see p. 187.

that, which For omission of *that* in restrictive clauses (*He is the clown* [*that*] *I saw*), see pp. 184–185. (For the choice between *that* and *which*, see p. 184.)

Beware of using *that* as a demonstrative adj. without indicating a basis of reference: *He doesn't have that much to say.* How much is *that much?* The author usually neglects to tell us.

Beware too of an unnecessary doubling of *that: She told him that, after all they had been through together, that she certainly intended to keep his diamond ring as a memento.* The second *that* should be omitted.

theirselves Always a mistake for *themselves.*

there is, there are See *it is.*

therefor, therefore Different in meaning. *Therefor* means *for that* and tends to appear in highly formal or legal contexts: *My client did commit the crime, but his motive therefor has not been established. Therefore* is the familiar word meaning *thus: Therefore Socrates is mortal.*

they, he For the choice between *they* and *he* in sentences involving words like *no one* and *nobody,* see pp. 178–179.

those kind See *kind.*

though, although Ignore the authorities who tell you that *though* is colloq. for *although.* In all the sentence positions where you'd be tempted to use *though,* it's standard. The choice between the two forms is a matter of taste.

It's colloq. to shorten *though* to *tho.*

throes *Violent spasms,* often ending in death. The word is excessively diluted in sentences like *I am in the throes of two midterms and a paper.*

thusly Always a mistake for *thus.*

till, until, til, 'til, 'till *Till* and *until* are interchangeable; suit yourself. The other forms, *til, 'til,* and *'till,* are all inappropriate in prose.

to all intents and purposes Tiresome for *in effect, practically.*

to the contrary notwithstanding A stuffy formula, as in *Agnew to the contrary notwithstanding, we must question all our institutions.* Some writers would "correct" this sentence by deleting *notwithstanding,* but this is questionable syntax. Find a completely different way of making the

statement: *Despite what Agnew says, we must question all our institutions.*

together Resist the trend that makes *together* an adj.: *Wally is really a together person.*

too Don't use *too* as a syn. of *very: I'm not too happy today.*

totally Means *entirely, wholly.* It is especially appropriate when the idea of a total sum or amount is involved: *His savings were totally exhausted.* The word is abused when it simply means *very,* as in *We had a totally marvelous experience.*

toward, towards Interchangeable, but *toward* is somewhat more common in American English. Choose whichever form you please, but don't mix it with the other.

transcendent, transcendental *Transcendent* means *supreme, surpassing,* with or without mystical connotation. *Transcendental* means *beyond ordinary experience, supernatural,* and thus it overlaps somewhat with *transcendent.* But the correct term is always *transcendent* if your meaning isn't religious or philosophical: *He won the race with one transcendent burst of energy.*

transpire Means both *become known* and *happen;* but in the second sense it's regarded as an error by some authorities, and in both senses it has a pretentious ring.

treat, treat of, treat with To *treat* is to *deal with* or *take up: She treats him harshly.* To *treat of* is to *take as a subject of discourse: This book treats of the Indian wars.* To *treat with* is to *negotiate with: Treating with Kissinger isn't easy.*

trek A *trek* is a *mass migration,* with an implication of hardship. Don't use it for ordinary movements, especially by individuals: *my trek to the dentist's office; she trekked over to see Madge.*

truculent Formerly meant *savage, barbarously fierce,* but the secondary meanings of *stubbornly defiant, sulky* have now become predominant.

turbid, turgid   Many writers wrongly treat these as syns. *Turbid* means *unclear, murky, stirred-up: a turbid stream. Turgid* means *swollen, inflated*, and thus also *bombastic*. A piece of writing could be criticized as either *turbid* or *turgid*, but the two complaints would be quite different.

type   Colloq. in place of *type of: You are a headstrong type girl.* In technical contexts *type* is sometimes acceptable as part of a hyphenated compound: *a rotary-type engine.* But in all contexts *type* can usually be omitted with profit: *a headstrong girl, a rotary engine.*

unbend, unbending   Look like a single v. and part., but they have opposite meanings. To *unbend* is to *relax*; to be *unbending* is to be *incapable of relaxing or compromising.*

unbound, unbounded   Shouldn't be confused. *Unbound* means *not tied: The pages were unbound. Unbounded* means *limitless: He had unbounded ambitions.*

under way   The right form, not *under weigh* or *underway: The project finally got under way.*

underneath of   Should always be *underneath.*

underwater, under water   Keep distinct. *Underwater* is an adj. or adv.: *an underwater adventure; he stayed underwater for fifteen minutes. Under water* is a prepositional phrase: *Place the boiled eggs under water.*

undue, unduly   Often redundant, as in *Undue haste isn't called for* or *You shouldn't worry unduly.* Both statements are absurd truisms which might become meaningful if the offending word were dropped.

unique   For use of comparatives with *unique,* see p. 208.

unknown, unidentified, undisclosed   Something *unknown* is not known at all. Something *unidentified* (e.g., a mutilated corpse) has an identity that hasn't been determined yet. Something *undisclosed* may or may not be fully known, but it hasn't yet been revealed to the curious.

up till, up until, up to   In each case the *up* can be profitably omitted.

upcoming   Widely regarded as colloq. for *forthcoming, approaching.*

usage, use   Widely confused. Save *usage* for contexts implying *convention* or *custom: English usage; the usages of our sect.* Don't write *He discouraged the usage of cocaine* or *Excessive usage of the car results in high repair bills.* Substitute *use* in both sentences.

use, utilize; use, utilization   *Utilize* and *utilization* are almost always bureaucratese for *use.* To *utilize* is to *put to use* or to *turn a profit on,* and it sounds least phony when coupled with an abstraction: *to utilize resources.* Because *utilize* and *utilization* have a depersonalizing effect, they sound especially odd when applied to people. *The underutilization of women,* for example, was coined to give a name to sex discrimination in jobs, but it makes the writer or speaker sound exploitative.

use of   Look for opportunities to condense sentences containing *use of: By his use of symbolism Ibsen establishes himself as a modern playwright.* Try *Ibsen's symbolism establishes him . . .*

use to   Can sound awkward in past negative constructions: *Didn't she use to take the bus? He didn't use to be such a bore.* These sentences aren't ungrammatical, but some readers would object to them.

In an affirmative past construction, make sure you write *used* and not *use: I used to go there.*

valued, valuable, invaluable Something *valued* is *esteemed*, whether or not it has a price: *a valued friend*. Something *valuable* is *of great value*, usually monetary: *a valuable vase*. *Invaluable* means *above value, priceless*: *He offered me a million dollars for it, but I couldn't part with such an invaluable treasure*.

various of An awkward replacement for *several, some, certain*: *Various of my friends are alienated*.

venal, venial, venereal *Venal* means *open to bribery*; *venial* means *minor, able to be forgiven*; *venereal* means *pertaining to sexual urges, acts, or diseases*. *The venal official was not committing a venial offense when he acquired the venereal infection*.

verbal, oral *Verbal* means *in words*, whether or not the words are spoken. *Oral* means *by mouth*. You can foster clarity by choosing *oral* over *verbal* when you mean *spoken*.

verbiage Means *wordiness*, an overabundance of words. Some writers mistakenly use it to mean *use of words* in general: *His voice was low but his verbiage was excellent*. Try *rhetoric* or *command of language*.

veritable Almost always meaningless, as in *Trixie was a veritable Pavlova of the roller derby*. Its proper meaning is *genuine* or *true*, either of which is less starchy-sounding.

very *Very* shouldn't be used before a p.p. unless the p.p. is to all intents an adj. Thus you can write *very pleased* because *pleased* strikes the reader not as the p.p. of *please* but as an adj. in its own right; but you shouldn't write *I was very affected by the performance*. Here *affected* is clearly the p.p. of *affect*, and it has to be preceded by *much* or *greatly*.

Very is overworked as an insincere intensifier; see pp. 72–73.

viable A cliché for *workable*, as in *viable alternative*. The word deserves a rest after overuse by planners, politicians, and commentators.

vital statistics Facts concerning births, deaths, marriages, and divorces. Don't extend the term to cover any figures that seem important to you, as in *Her vital statistics were 36-24-36*.

volatile Doesn't mean *inflammable, highly combustible*. It means *evaporating quickly*. Metaphorically, *volatile* can be extended to mean *changeable* or *explosive*: *a volatile personality*.

vow As both n. and v., *vow* is journalese for *promise*: *The Mayor vowed to look into the matter*. A *vow* is a solemn promise, usually undertaken in a ceremony: *The new judge vowed to uphold the Constitution*.

wait on Colloq. for *wait for*: *She was waiting on the train*.

want (v.) Colloq. in several phrases: *want for* (*She wants for me to go away*), *want that* (*She wants that I go away*), *want in* and *want out* (*Muggsy got scared and said he wanted out*). The first two examples should be *She wants me to go away*.

wave, waive, waver, waiver The motion is *wave*: *He waved farewell*. To *waive* is to *relinquish*: *He waived his right to counsel*. To *waver* is to *flutter*. Watch out for confusing the v. *waver* with the n. *waiver*, a *relinquishing*.

way, ways Don't use *ways* in the sense of *distance*: *It was only a short ways*. The correct form is *way*.

we Like *one*, *we* can be a dodge, a hiding of the individual writer in an imaginary crowd. When you mean *I* you should write *I*. But *we* and *I* can sometimes be usefully played off against each other by an essayist who wants to argue a point: *I maintain that . . . Thus we have to agree with Riesman when he concludes . . .* Here the

I properly identifies the writer as an individual putting forth a claim, and the *we* properly incorporates the writer and his readers into a group of the converted. The conversion may not have occurred at all, but the writer is at least permitted to hope that it has. (Also see *one*.)

wean To *wean* is to *deprive after accustomed privilege: He was weaned from the breast; She was weaned from her lazy habits*. Don't use *wean* as a syn. of *rear, bring up: I am honest today because I was weaned to respect the truth.*

well- For hyphenation of compound adjs. beginning with *well-*, see p. 312.

what ever, whatever The interrogative form should be, but often isn't, *what ever: What ever do you mean?* Although *whatever* is by now so common in this position that it is scarcely an error at all, some readers will consider it such.

Whatever, the pro. meaning *anything that*, shouldn't be followed by a redundant *that*, as in *You can do whatever that pleases you.*

(Also see *however*.)

when, where Often involved in false predication: *A war is when opposing countries resort to violence; Massage is where you lie on a table and . . .* When should only be matched with times; *where*, with places. Often a correction can be found in alteration of the v.: *A war occurs when . . .*

where . . . at A colloq. redundancy, as in *I don't know where you're at.*

while Like *since, while* can be used in a nontemporal sense: *While some might disagree, I feel strongly that . . .* But also like *since*, the word can be ambig. between *although* and *during: While the King played with boats in the bathtub, the Queen plotted an invasion of France.* Some authorities recommend that you use *while* only in the temporal sense. But even this won't spare you the trouble of check-ing for ambiguity, for your readers may not have noticed that you never employ the second meaning.

who, whom For the choice between these forms, see pp. 189–190.

whose, of which For the choice between these forms, see p. 185.

will See *shall*.

-wise Acceptable when it means *in the manner of*, as in *clockwise* and *lengthwise* and when it means *having wisdom: penny-wise and pound-foolish; a ring-wise boxer.* But most authorities protest coinage by adding *-wise* in the sense of *with respect to: taxwise, agriculturewise, conflict resolutionwise.* These terms do save space, but the feeling against them is strong. Look for concise alternatives: not *the situation taxwise* but *the tax situation;* not *America's superiority agriculturewise* but *America's superiority in agriculture.*

with Often used sloppily: *With all the turmoil in the world today, you would think that people would do anything for peace.* The sentence is grammatical but slack. The writer hasn't taken the necessary pains to work out the relation between the two parts of his statement. Better: *You would think that people today, finding the world in turmoil, would do anything for peace.* Another weak example: *As with everything in her life, Mary failed to complete the project.* What does the opening phrase modify? We have to wait too long to extract any information from it.

without Shouldn't be used for *unless: Without she comes with me, I won't go.*

Without hardly and *without scarcely* are colloq., as in *She passed by without scarcely nodding at me.* Try *She passed by, scarcely nodding at me.*

would like for Colloq. in sentences like *They would like for me to go away.* The remedy is *want*.

IV

MECHANICS

PUNC-TUATION 10

Punctuation, in the eyes of some students, amounts to a dreary question-and-answer game. The question is *Where does the comma go?* The answer is always the same: *Not where you put it in your last paper.* Understandably, the students come to regard an interest in punctuation as mere fussiness, or at best as something to be faked for the duration of a writing course. And they despair of ever getting that comma in the right place.

Like other widespread grievances, this one is rooted in fact. Choices of punctuation are usually settled by appeal to a mechanical set of rules, yet the rules can't resolve many of the sentence-by-sentence dilemmas a writer must face. In observing one rule you may sometimes be violating another. More frequently, you'll find yourself getting contradictory advice not from two rules, but from a rule and your sense of emphasis. If you "punctuate for meaning" you get one result; if you "punctuate for correctness" you get a different one. It's little wonder that some people develop a fatalistic idea that they can't win.

Perhaps this explains why teachers of composition find themselves reading sentences whose punctuation amounts to a kind of stuttering:

• And so we see that, the idea of universal education is noble but, how many lives are in fact, ruined by it?

This is an actual sentence from a paper. There's nothing wrong with the writer's mind, but evidently he's been stunned by comma-consciousness. Punctuation, he thinks, is something that teachers would like to see from time to time, and so he supplies it at random intervals. The commas are little valentines expressing good intentions. *You want commas? I send you these commas.* The writer doesn't notice that they destroy his sentence, for he doesn't think of the sentence as a communication, a transcribed statement that might have been spoken aloud. He's trying to write "English" instead.

One thing that all the uncertainty and difficulty go to prove is that punctuation is *not* entirely a matter of boring routine. It's also a matter of precise expression and style. The rules count, but only as guidelines, not taboos; it's your job to adjust them to what you want to say and to the effect you hope to make. One writer, by using commas only where they're absolutely necessary, presents himself as someone who cuts through formalities and wastes no time. Another, by using commas more often, tells his reader that he cares about fine distinctions and complex relationships. The first writer may never use semicolons at all; the second may have one or two in every paragraph. Again, prose that is riddled with dashes suggests a certain haste and excitability in the writer. Each mark of punctuation says something about the person who habitually uses it, and two essays that are equally "correct" in avoiding outright errors may be punctuated in very different ways.

The trick, then, is neither to ignore the rules nor to treat them as immutable laws, but to use them with common sense, personal taste, and a concern to avoid ambiguities. In most cases you can punctuate by sound—that is, by reading your sentence aloud and hearing where the pauses occur. A punctuation mark is comparable to a musical notation. It tells the reader to slow down here, interrupt himself there, or make a full stop elsewhere. If you think of that mark as a way of orchestrating your thoughts for a reader, you'll see that punctuation has a creative as well as a mechanical side.

Along with the rules, I will offer reminders of the leeway you sometimes have in applying them. Where all authorities agree, I'll simply report the consensus; but elsewhere I'll try to indicate the range of your freedom.

PERIOD   •

End of Sentence

A period normally indicates the end of a complete sentence—that is, one containing at least a subject and a verb. Deliberate sentence fragments can also be stopped with periods:

- Indeed.
- So much for his claim of innocence.

Difficulties arise only when a fragment isn't truly independent of a neighboring sentence, as in these bad examples:

- Let me introduce Sergeant Pepper's Band. A most remarkable group.
- He found himself unable to proceed to Vancouver. Having forgotten his raincoat.

(In both cases the material after the period should have formed part of the original sentence.)

Indirect Questions

An indirect question requires a period, not a question mark:

WRONG:
- He asked me whether I could go?

RIGHT:
- He asked me whether I could go.

Abbreviations

Abbreviations such as *Mr., Dr., Jr.,* and *N.Y.* require periods, but some common abbreviations and acronyms (p. 334) often appear without periods: *UAW, CORE, DDT,* etc.

(For the periods that make up the marks of omission called ellipses, see pp. 288–290.)

COMMA

Because commas almost always indicate natural pauses, the reading-aloud test can often tell you whether and where a comma should be inserted. But sometimes an apparent pause has to go unmarked, and sometimes it has to be marked by a period or semicolon instead. Here are the typical situations in which problems arise:

Joining Independent Clauses

Independent clauses are customarily joined by a comma and a co-ordinating conjunction (*and, but, for, or, nor, yet*):

* George was lonely at first, but after a while he came to like having the whole house to himself.

But when the first independent clause is short, the comma can usually be omitted:

* He ate constantly but he still couldn't get enough food to fill his cravings.

The comma can also be omitted to show that one independent clause logically belongs with another one:

* George's reliance on prepared foods was total, for Susan had left him and she had taken her cookbooks with her.

(The omission of a comma after *him* helps to show that everything from *for Susan* to the end of the sentence constitutes a single explanation of the first clause.)

The common error of a *run-on sentence* (or *comma splice*) occurs when independent clauses are joined by a comma without a conjunction:

* George's health was much improved, his diet was now rich in preservatives.

(Without a conjunction such as *for* or *since*, the two clauses become separate sentences wrongly fastened together.)

In rare cases an apparent run-on sentence can be rhetorically effective:

* He saw the frozen tamale pie, he yearned for it, he stuffed it eagerly into the shopping cart.

(The absence of conjunctions emphasizes the rapidity and compulsiveness of the activities described.)

Series of Words, Phrases, or Clauses

The rule is that words, phrases, or clauses in series are to be separated by commas. But there's a legitimate difference of opinion about the application of the rule. Traditionally, all terms in a series have been marked off by commas: *a, b, c, and d*. Many writers and editors now prefer to omit the last comma: *a, b, c and d*. Which formula should you follow? The answer is that you can follow either of them, provided you do so with consistency. But the older practice, it seems to me, does more justice to the actual equivalence of the terms in the series, and it avoids an occasional ambiguity. Consider:

• Her favorite comedians were Chaplin, Keaton and Abbott and Costello.

(A comma after *Keaton* would indicate more clearly that Abbott and Costello are a team.)

• The returning knight had countless tales to tell of adventure, conquest of hideous monsters and helpless damsels in distress.

(Did he conquer the damsels as well as the monsters? A comma after *monsters* would remove any ambiguity.)

Terms that aren't truly coordinate shouldn't be separated by commas. In *good old Charlie Brown*, for example, *good* and *old* aren't distinct adjectives, each modifying *Charlie Brown*. They function as a single adjective, a stock phrase. A comma after *good* would change the phrase to mean that Charlie is virtuous and aged.

Similarly, two adjectives shouldn't be separated by a comma if the second adjective serves to identify the entire object modified by the first:

• George fixed himself a delicious American dinner of Gatorade and Chun King Chop Suey.

(What is delicious is an *American dinner*. Since *delicious* and *American* don't form a coordinate series, they shouldn't be separated by a comma.)

• George fixed himself a delicious, nutritious American dinner of . . .

(Here *delicious* and *nutritious* do form a coordinate series. Both words modify *American dinner*, and the comma helps to make this clear.)

When you're in doubt as to whether several terms amount to a coordinate series, try shifting the position of the terms. If the meaning remains much the same (*nutritious, delicious American dinner*), you have a coordinate series; if the meaning changes (*old good Charlie Brown*), you don't.

If all the members of a series are connected by conjunctions, commas aren't needed:

• From listening to Rupert you might gather that the universe consisted entirely of Mustangs and Mavericks and Camaros.

Adverbial Clauses and Modifying Phrases

These are usually set off by commas if they precede the main clause:

ADVERBIAL CLAUSES:
* *After Susan left*, George spent a few evenings reading Dr. Lincoln Dollar's helpful book of advice, *The Aerobic Kama Sutra.*

MODIFYING PHRASES:
* *In order to prove that he wasn't narrow-minded*, Rupert decided to buy a trail bike and a snowmobile.

But when the clause or phrase is short and its grammatical distinctness from what follows is clear, the comma is often omitted:

* *When Susan came back* she found George sitting in the lotus posture and eating a Ho-Ho.
* *For Mother's Day* Rupert took his mother to Altamont Speedway to see the Demolition Derby.

Wherever the omission of the comma might cause ambiguity, you should leave it in:

* If you can't stand the college, try the university.
* Although Susan begged, George said that she could go live with Julia Child for all he cared.

(The commas prevent us from momentarily reading *the college try* and *Susan begged George.*)

Your voice will tell you whether to supply a comma when an adverbial clause or modifying phrase *follows* a main clause. If a reading of the sentence indicates no break, leave the comma out:

* Try the university if you can't stand the college.
* An apple a day was all Betsy allowed herself until the diet was completed.

In the following sentences a comma is demanded by the natural break after the main clause:

* It is time for me to leave now, unless you would like to summarize my shortcomings once more.
* Rupert preferred a Volkswagen bus to Betsy, all things considered.

Parenthetical Elements

A parenthetical element is a word or group of words that interrupts the main flow of a sentence. It is usually set off by commas:

- *Moreover*, nothing can be done about it.
- Reindeer droppings on the roof, *to be sure*, count as strong evidence for Santa's existence.

(*Moreover* and *to be sure* are parenthetical; note that they interrupt the main syntax of their sentences.)

In general, reading a sentence aloud is the surest test of whether a parenthetical element should be set off by commas. Where your voice pauses, commas are required:

- Congress, of course, has no intention of closing tax loopholes.

Compare:

- Of course Congress has no intention of closing tax loopholes.

(Both sentences are correctly punctuated.)

sentence modifiers Conjunctive adverbs (p. 158) that link a whole statement to a previous one are called *sentence adverbs: also, however, furthermore,* etc. These words are usually isolated by commas:

- Millionaires, *furthermore*, have ways of impeding new legislation.

(Here *furthermore* modifies the whole statement, linking it to a preceding sentence.)

Other words, not normally considered conjunctive adverbs, can also serve as sentence modifiers, and so can longer phrases. Thus, in the sentence above, *furthermore* can be replaced by *unfortunately, regrettably, to be sure, as it seems,* etc. In each case the modifier has to be set off by commas. Note that the modifier doesn't attach itself to the verb, as in *Millionaires certainly have ways . . . ;* instead it "floats," qualifying the entire statement. The commas ensure this effect.

Some sentence adverbs can serve as normal adverbs as well. As sentence adverbs they are parenthetical and should be set off by commas, but as normal adverbs they shouldn't cause an interruption:

AS SENTENCE ADVERB:
- *Also*, we ought to consider the effect of lobbying.

AS NORMAL ADVERB:
- We *also* ought to consider the effect of lobbying.

Listen for the pause and you'll always sense the difference.

Note that the presence of a sentence adverb between two inde-

pendent clauses doesn't rescue them from being a run-on sentence
(p. 271):

* Rupert liked driving his snowmobile up the ski slope on Sunday afternoons, *however*, some other people seemed to resent his fun.

(The comma after *afternoons* must be changed to a semicolon or
period.)

sealing off Parenthetical elements that don't occur at the beginning or end of
parenthetical a sentence must be sealed off on both sides if they're punctuated
elements at all. One of the most frequent errors of punctuation is the leaking
of a parenthetical element into a sentence at one end or the other:

* General Custer *however*, had a foolproof scheme of his own.
* General Custer, *however* had a foolproof scheme of his own.

(Both sentences need an extra comma to enclose *however*.)

optional Sometimes you'll find that a parenthetical word or phrase could be
commas interpreted as either requiring or not requiring commas, depending on the particular way you want it to be heard. Thus, all these
sentences are allowable:

* You *too* can be slim and desirable without giving up chocolate éclairs.
* You, *too*, can be slim . . .
* Betsy *of course* was willing to try anything.
* Betsy, *of course*, was willing . . .

(The commas impart a certain formality, and in the last sentence
they help to associate *of course* with *Betsy* instead of with the verb.
Without the comma *of course* is given less importance and pointed-
ness.)

initial Don't mistake initial conjunctions for parenthetical elements that
conjunctions should be set off by commas. These sentences illustrate a widespread
but unacceptable practice:

* *But*, I didn't say you *were* a hotbed of social rest.
* *And*, do I have to apologize every day?

Remember that conjunctions belong with the clauses or phrases
they introduce. An initial conjunction shouldn't be separated from
its clause unless a truly parenthetical element intervenes, as here:

* But, *thought George*, there seems to be no way of making myself believed.

Even when a conjunction is followed by a parenthetical element, you can often treat both conjunction and parenthetical element as a single unit and punctuate accordingly:

- *But without hesitating for a moment*, Betsy enrolled in the autohypnosis course.

(This may look like a violation of the rule that parenthetical elements must be sealed off at both ends or neither end. In cases like this, however, the natural sound of the sentence should prevail. *But without hesitating for a moment* feels like one phrase and can be punctuated as such.)

names in direct address Names in direct address are parenthetical and require commas:

- You, *George*, have been chosen by the computer to be Betsy's mate.

appositives Terms in apposition (see p. 163) usually require commas:

- The computer, *an antique Univac*, was badly in need of repair.

Sometimes, however, a term in apposition is really more important than the term preceding it. By omitting commas you can bring this out. Compare:

- The union leader *John L. Lewis* was not amused by the headline "*Lewis Drops Union Suit.*"
- The union leader, *John L. Lewis*, was not amused . . .

(In the first sentence we read *John L. Lewis* as the real subject of the verb *was amused;* in the second sentence the subject is clearly *leader.* Note too that different meanings are involved. *The union leader John L. Lewis* identifies Lewis as *a* union leader among many others; *The union leader, John L. Lewis*, identifies Lewis as the leader of one particular union, previously named. So, too, a comma after *headline* would make a slight difference in effect, shifting some attention from "*Lewis Drops Union Suit*" to *headline* itself.)

restrictive versus nonrestrictive modifiers Nonrestrictive modifiers (see p. 165) are parenthetical and should be set off by commas:

- Transcendental Weight-watching, *which had recently become George's newest spiritual discipline*, sounded like a promising idea to Betsy.

Compare the lack of commas when the modifier is restrictive:

• The spiritual discipline *that George had recently adopted* was called Transcendental Weight-watching.

Separation of Main Sentence Elements

Commas should *not* intervene between main sentence elements such as subject and verb, verb and direct object, verb and complement. These sentences show violations of the rule:

• Betsy, found it difficult at first to chant through the dinner hour.

(Comma wrongly separates the subject *Betsy* from the verb *found*.)

• George's main worry was, that the vulgar materialist Susan would come back again and try to retard his development.

(Comma wrongly separates the linking verb *was* from its complement *that . . . development*.)

• George and Betsy agreed that modern man had neglected, the important inner values.

(Comma wrongly separates the verb *had neglected* from its direct object *values*.)

The rule becomes harder to apply when it conflicts with natural pauses. Consider these sentences:

• That Susan, skiing away her troubles at Squaw Valley, had been badly injured by a hit-and-run snowmobile, came as an ugly shock to George.

(The comma after *snowmobile* sounds right, but it separates the subject *That Susan had been badly injured by a hit-and-run snowmobile* from the verb *came*. The sentence is more coherent without that last comma.)

• A delightful drive through the Holland Tunnel, an exquisite hour on the Pulaski Skyway, and a whiff of the fragrant North Jersey marshlands, were Gertie's idea of a fine outing.

(The comma after *marshlands* would sound right to many speakers of the sentence, but it shouldn't be there. Everything preceding *marshlands* constitutes the subject of *were*, and the comma disguises this relationship.)

• The phobias which, during the first months at boarding school, had given Wellington Wellington's parents and teachers so much worry were now abating.

(Is the sentence correctly punctuated? Yes. A comma after *worry* would separate the subject *The phobias which had given Wellington Wellington's parents and teachers so much worry* from the verb *were abating*. Note that the presence of a parenthetical phrase *within* a continuing subject shouldn't affect the punctuation at the *end* of the subject.)

* Home, with its many servants, its elegant stables, and its tutors in French and fencing was now almost forgotten as Wellington began learning how to be a dormitory bully.

(Is the sentence correctly punctuated? No. In this case the parenthetical element *with its . . . fencing* comes *after* the complete subject *Home*. A comma is needed after *fencing* to close off the parenthetical element.)

Note that you can sometimes put a comma after an object that might otherwise be temporarily mistaken for a subject:

* What most Americans call democracy, the Wellingtons considered mobocracy.
* That Walt Whitman is nothing less than a cosmos, few readers would accept without question.

(The commas are useful as a means of marking off the noun clauses that constitute direct objects of *considered* and *would accept*.)

Separation of Compound Elements

In general, commas between compound elements weaken the effect of relationship and should therefore be avoided:

* It didn't matter to Biff whether the pitch he missed had been a curve that made him swing early or a fastball.

(*A curve* and *a fastball* are compound elements—that is, they are syntactically equivalent parts of a single direct object. A comma after *early* would have deceived us into thinking that the direct object ends at that point.)

* Sterno, which has been called a killer drug by some people, and a modest depressant by others, remains largely untested in the laboratory.

(Here a comma wrongly separates compound elements. The linking verb *has been called* is followed by a double complement, *a killer drug* and *a modest depressant*. The comma after *people* makes us think we are through with the complement at that point. Deletion of the comma would bring the two parts of the complement into proper alignment, as you can clearly see if the words are replaced by symbols: *Sterno, which has been called x and y, remains . . .*)

Comparisons and Statements of Preference

When two terms are being compared, or when preference is expressed for one term over another, try to keep commas from intervening between them. These sentences are faulty:

- She felt more wistful and nostalgic, than resentful.

(Schematically reduced, the sentence says *She felt more x than y.* The comma should be dropped.)

- Mrs. Wellington preferred the mathematical elegance and understatement of Bach, to the orotund phrasing of Berlioz.

(*She preferred x to y;* the comma should go.)

Quotations

To decide whether a quotation should be enclosed in commas, disregard the quotation marks and think of the quoted matter as an ordinary part of the sentence. A quotation that fits readily into the syntax of a clause or phrase needn't be set off by commas:

- Macbeth expresses the depth of his despair when he describes life as "a tale told by an idiot."

(A comma after *as* would wrongly separate a preposition from its object.)
    But a quotation that doesn't form part of a phrase or clause in the rest of the sentence should be introduced by either a comma or a colon:

- When asked what he thought of Western civilization, Gandhi smiled and replied, "I think it would be a very good idea."

(A colon after *replied* would be equally correct.)

Conventional Uses

Commas occur routinely in certain contexts:

numbers of more than four digits Commas should separate every three digits of a number consisting of more than four digits: *109,368,452*. In four-digit numbers the comma is optional: *6083* and *6,083* are both correct.

No commas separate the digits of years (*2001*), telephone numbers, zip codes, serial numbers, and other figures meant to identify an item or place. Such figures are sometimes divided into segments by hyphens.

dates A comma should separate the day of the month and the year if the month is given first: *July 6, 1934*. If the day is given first, no punctuation is necessary: *6 July 1934*.

A comma is optional between a month and a year: *July 1934* and *July, 1934* are both correct.

addresses New York, New York
7713 Radnor Road, Bethesda, Md. 20034
Department of Economics, Simon Fraser University, Burnaby 2, B.C., Canada

titles and degrees following names Herbert Moroni, Ph.D.
Adlai Stevenson, III

(But *Adlai Stevenson III* would also be acceptable.)

Avoidance of Ambiguity

The need to be clear is more important than any technical rule about where commas should be included or omitted. If you use common sense about avoiding double meanings, you won't come up with sentences like these:

• I argue with Burke that institutions shouldn't be quickly dismantled.

(Is the author in agreement or disagreement with Burke? He probably means *I argue, with Burke, that* . . .)

• No one died because the earthquake occurred after the town had been evacuated.

(But did someone die for some other reason? We can't tell. With a comma after *died* the sentence is no longer ambiguous.)

(For the appropriateness of commas before and after parentheses, see pp. 286–287.)

QUESTION MARK

Direct Questions

Question marks follow direct questions wherever they occur in a sentence:

- Can a camel pass through the eye of a needle?
- I know that many strange things are possible, but can a camel really pass through the eye of a needle?
- It was just fifteen years ago today—remember?—that the camel got stuck in the eye of the needle.
- "Can a needle," asked the surrealist film director when he met the Arab veterinary surgeon, "pass through the eye of a camel?"

Indirect Questions

These take periods, not question marks:

- He asked me how it was possible for such a young man to have such senile ideas.

Conventional Questions

In business letters, certain routine questions are sometimes followed by a period instead of a question mark:

- Would you kindly reply at your earliest convenience.

But a question mark would be equally correct and would sound less like a command.

Indications of Doubt

A question mark within parentheses expresses doubt:

- Saint Thomas Aquinas, 1225(?)—1274

Some writers use such question marks as a form of sarcasm:

- The Senator was surely joking (?) when he said he would like to lob one into the Kremlin men's room.

You should use this device sparingly or not at all.

Questions Within Questions

When a sentence asking a question also *contains* a question at the end, one question mark will serve the purpose:

- Who was it who asked me, "When are you going to tell us about syllogisms?"

EXCLAMATION POINT

Exclamation points should be used sparingly to punctuate outbursts or statements requiring extraordinary emphasis:

- "My geodesic dome! My organic greenhouse! My Tolkien collection! When will I ever see them again?"
- Standing in the bread line, he had a moment of revelation. So *this* was what his economics professor had meant by structural unemployment!

Frequent use of exclamation points dulls their effect. Be especially slow to use sarcastic exclamation points in parentheses:

- The General told them on Monday that the battle had to be completely won (!) by Wednesday afternoon.

SEMICOLON

To Join Independent Statements

The main function of the semicolon is to link two independent statements that would be complete sentences if they stood alone. The semicolon tells a reader that the two statements are closely related:

- Mark got a remarkably good buy on a used snowmobile; the former owner had to leave town immediately and didn't want to quibble about the price.

(The second statement amplifies the first.)

Be sure that you do have complete statements on both sides of the semicolon. Don't write *Mark got a remarkably good buy on a used snowmobile; the owner being in a hurry to leave town.*

Some people—the same ones who think you should never begin a sentence with a coordinating conjunction—would say that it's poor usage to put a coordinating conjunction after a semicolon. In their opinion this sentence would be faulty:

- A good French restaurant is hard to find; and by the time you've found it, so have a thousand other hungry snobs.

There isn't in fact any current rule of style or usage to prevent you from adopting such constructions if they fit your meaning.

Beware, though, of employing semicolons too frequently. Some writers overuse them as a way of covering up inadequacies of logic and consecutiveness. In a first draft the semicolon often serves as a stepping stone from one complete thought to the next; it helps you to believe that things hang together. In revision you can see that many of your linked statements ought to stand alone.

In Series

When items in a series *contain* commas, it's advisable to *separate* them not with commas but with semicolons:

- Wellington first decided that he couldn't bear to live without his mother, who wrote to him every day; then that he might be able to stand his loneliness until Thanksgiving vacation; and finally that if she continued to pester him with mail and telegrams, he would have to get himself a lawyer and seek an injunction.

(The semicolons help to show where each of the three items ends; otherwise the commas would be too confusing. Note that the items in a series punctuated by semicolons don't have to constitute independent clauses.)

COLON

To Introduce a Statement or Figure

A colon marks a formal introduction:

- Mark only disliked one thing about Susan: she was always dropping little hints about the joys of parenthood.

A colon implies a symmetry or equivalence between items on either side. Something is to be presented: here it is. If you don't mean to insist on the equivalence, you may want a semicolon rather than a colon. A semicolon announces development of, or relationship to, what has just been stated; a colon delivers the thing itself in different terms.

But in many cases there's only a stylistic choice, not a grammatical one, between a colon and a semicolon. Consider:

- The teacher found himself in a delicate situation: Wellington clearly deserved to fail the course, but his father happened to be chairman of the school's trustees.

(A semicolon would have been perfectly all right, but the colon was chosen to indicate that the indefinite first statement was going to be clarified.)

Colons are normally used to introduce figures:

- The results of the poll were surprising: 7 percent in favor, 11 percent opposed, 82 percent no opinion.

To Introduce a Quotation

A quotation that can be suitably introduced by a comma (p. 279) can also be introduced by a colon. The difference is that the colon makes for a more formal pause, a greater separation between your own prose and the quotation:

- Wellington delivered an ultimatum: "I won't come home for Thanksgiving unless you promise to stop that barbaric fox hunting."

As usual, you should choose the punctuation by disregarding the quotation marks and thinking of the whole sentence as your own. If no punctuation is called for *without* the quotation marks, none is called for *with* them:

- Wellington's postcard said that "the fellows and I are spending Christmas in Jamaica this year."

(Some writers would put a comma after *that*, but this would separate a conjunction from the clause it introduces.)

- The Mayor at the freeway opening urged the assembled dignitaries to "Reason not the need."

(This is correct. A colon placed after *to* would wrongly interrupt an infinitive, *to reason*.)

(For the use of a capital letter in the first word following a colon, see p. 327.)

DASH ▬

A dash, typed as two unspaced hyphens wedged between the words it separates, signifies an abrupt break in thought. If the main sentence doesn't resume after the break, only one dash is used:

- The Senator stood ready to remedy any grievances — for a price.

If the main sentence resumes, a second dash is needed:

- The Senator stood ready — for a price — to remedy . . .

Don't allow a comma to substitute for the second dash, as many careless writers do. And be sure that your sentence would make complete sense if the portion within dashes were omitted. Sentences like this are all too common:

- Although Betsy took up massage — somebody told her it would increase her human potential — but she soon discovered that she was too ticklish.

(The material between dashes has caused the writer to forget that he has already written *Although*. The *but* has to be deleted.)

A dash can serve as a less formal equivalent to a colon:

- At least Betsy had accumulated some souvenirs — a black eye from Encounter, bruised ribs from Rolfing, and a whiplash from Aikido.

Dashes can be used to mark the beginning and end of a series which might otherwise get confused with the rest of the sentence:

- Mark's outstanding virtues — his Porsche, his bank account, and his wine cellar — appealed to Susan after her years of frugal life with George.

Very rarely, a dash can be used to segregate the *first* part of a sentence from the rest:

- A preacher who says he "must" wear a black veil forever but can't say why, who allows the veil to prevent his marriage from ever taking place, and who frightens and amuses his parishioners instead of comforting them — such a man can hardly be intended to represent Hawthorne's idea of the model Christian.

(The dash here says in effect that *preacher* won't be the subject of the main verb after all. Everything preceding the dash becomes appositive to the real subject *man*.)

Dashes are also used to mark the interruption of a sentence in dialogue:

"Run, Jane, run!" yelled Dick. "I see the principal and he's coming toward us with—"
"It's too late, Dick, it's too late! The curriculum enrichment consultants have blocked the gate and—"
"Oh, Jane, oh, Jane, whatever will become of us?"

Dashes shouldn't be combined with other punctuation marks. A comma and a dash together are redundant; a period and a dash are contradictory.

As a stylistic matter you should be frugal with dashes, or you'll make a scatterbrained impression.

PARENTHESES

Parentheses mark a gentler interruption than dashes do. The material enclosed is parenthetical in both cases, but parentheses have the effect of *subordinating* it, so that the reader saves most of his attention for the rest of the sentence. They can be used either to set off incidental information such as numbers, dates, and references or to signal a digression from the main thought:

- Your furniture will be repossessed in thirty (30) days.
- The article appears in *Commentary*, 52 (December 1971), 67–74.
- Julia Moore (revered in her lifetime as "the Sweet Singer of Michigan") offered the memorable observation that "Literary is a work very difficult to do."

Like dashes, parentheses should be regarded as a stylistic luxury. If your prose is full of them, you will annoy your reader and lead him to believe that you're temperamentally unsuited to straightforward assertion:

- The "King of Swing" (I use quotation marks because in my judgment this was a misnomer from the first) thought he had to have a concert (?) in Carnegie Hall (where else?) before he could be accepted by the mass public.

To read a sentence like this is comparable to being poked in the ribs several times by a drunken jokester.

No mark of punctuation should ever *precede* a parenthesis, but you can supply punctuation *after* the closing of the parenthesis if necessary. The rule is that the parenthesis shouldn't affect the punctuation of the main statement. If the main statement calls for a comma but a parenthesis intervenes, the comma is delivered at the end of the parenthesis:

- After she had tried Primal Jogging and I'm-O.K.-You're-Not-O.K. (she still hadn't met any interesting men), Betsy resolved to become a Hatha Backpacker. ·

Similarly, if no comma would have been required without the parenthetical material, none is required with it:

- The phantom trail biker of the Sierra (imagine her surprise) turned out to be none other than her old date Rupert.

When a parenthetical statement is placed between complete sentences, it too should be punctuated as a complete sentence. The end-punctuation comes within the parenthesis, not after it:

- Rupert told her all about the hit-and-run snowmobile incident. (She had gained his confidence by constantly praising his trail bike.) And Betsy agreed that Rupert would have to remain a fugitive from justice.

Try to avoid situations in which parenthetical material occurs *within* parenthetical material, but if you can't, use brackets for the inner set. The problem arises most often in footnotes:

[8]It may be difficult to imagine why anyone would want to challenge the idea of insanity. (See, however, D. L. Rosenham, "On Being Sane in Insane Places," *Science*, 179 [19 Jan. 1973], 250–258.)

The date would normally have gone into parentheses, but brackets are useful because they distinguish this material from the larger parenthesis.)

BRACKETS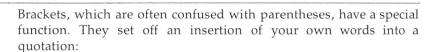

Brackets, which are often confused with parentheses, have a special function. They set off an insertion of your own words into a quotation:

- "My personal idols," said the forty-four-year-old defendant, "are Jerry [Rubin] and Abbie [Hoffman]."

Note that parentheses in place of brackets would imply a

parenthetical remark *by the speaker*, not by the writer. Brackets are necessary to indicate that the quotation is being interrupted.

The bracketed, italicized word *sic* (Latin 'thus') is used to signal that a peculiarity occurs in the original and therefore isn't an error of your own. A misspelling, for instance, could be marked this way:

- "Beachcombbing [*sic*] no longer appeals to me," Wellington wired. "Send money."

But don't abuse this device to get a cheap advantage over an opponent:

- The Republican nominee, who describes himself as a "statesman" [*sic*], wouldn't know that World War Three had started if they didn't print it on the sports page.

If your typewriter doesn't have keys for brackets, you can improvise in one of several ways:

1. type slashes (/) and complete the sides with underlinings (_);
2. type the slashes and add the sides later by hand; or
3. leave blank spaces and do the brackets entirely by hand.

ELLIPSES

Material Omitted from Quotations

The ellipsis mark, consisting of three spaced periods, is chiefly used to signify that something has been omitted from a quotation:

- President Clearance declared that he had "nothing . . . to hide," and that "secrecy in University affairs is . . . contrary to all my principles."

If an ellipsis occurs within a sentence, type three spaced periods preceded and followed by a space, as in the example above. If the ellipsis occurs just after the end of a sentence, retain the end-punctuation of the sentence and then add the ellipsis:

- Clearance was lavish in his praise for the University: "Everything is fine. . . . We're tooled up to turn out a real classy product."

If the ellipsis occurs before the end of a sentence and the quotation then resumes with the beginning of a new sentence, the end-punctuation of the first sentence is discarded. Just provide the usual three spaced periods followed by two spaces before the new sentence begins:

• "I resent the implication that nerve gas is being developed on this campus . . . Besides, every safety precaution has been taken."

If you are omitting a whole line or more of verse, or a whole paragraph or more of prose, mark the ellipsis by a complete line of spaced periods:

What have U done fer yr poets O Amerika?
I'm sitting here waiting fer a call from the Nash
Ional Endowment fer the Arts and Humanities.
Is it arty to keep me waiting Amerika?
Is this yr crummy idea of a humanity?
. . . .
How much longer must I borrow & steal?
O Amerika I hold U responsible fer this hole in the seat of my Levis!

Some writers think they must introduce a quotation with an ellipsis mark if the quotation is less than a complete sentence. But so long as the reader can see that the passage is fragmentary, no ellipsis is needed:

• Is the poet referring to his high vocation when he writes that he is "waiting for a call"?

When you do use ellipses in quoting, make sure that you don't distort the author's meaning by your omission. Selective quotation is sometimes as unfair as misquotation (pp. 43–45).

Dialogue

Ellipses sometimes occur in dialogue to indicate incomplete or interrupted statements or thoughts:

• "You may be right," she said pleadingly, "but I don't really see why you can't . . ."
"Oh, stop your infernal whining, will you?"

Weak Use of Ellipses

Some writers abuse ellipses as a semi-apologetic way of getting from one topic to another. In the following example the ellipses don't indicate omitted material, but simply a trailing-off of thought:

- I could go on and on about yogurt's properties as an aphrodisiac. . . . However, we have to get back to the question of its curative properties.

And some writers use ellipses as all-purpose punctuation marks, for example to punctuate the items of a series:

- Yogurt improves your morale . . . releases your inhibitions . . . postpones death . . .

Avoid all such mannerisms.

APOSTROPHE

Apostrophes are used chiefly in the formation of possessives (pp. 151–152), certain plurals (p. 309), and contractions (*won't, didn't, havin' fun,* etc.). The apostrophe also marks the omission of one or more digits of a number: *the winter of '65.* In dates expressing a span of time, however, the apostrophe is usually dropped: *1847–63.* And when page numbers are shortened, the apostrophe is never used: *pp. 207–91.* (But it's better policy to write the full number: *pp. 207– 291.*)

In addition, apostrophes are used to form the past participles of certain verbs derived from nouns:

- Frazier was K.O.'d in the second round.
- Young parents these days are so Spock'd and Gesell'd that they hardly trust their own feelings about how a child should be raised.

HYPHEN

A hyphen, typed without spaces before and after, sets off certain prefixes, separates the parts of certain compound words, connects the parts of compound modifiers and the words in certain compound phrases, and indicates that an uncompleted word at the end of a line will be completed at the beginning of the next line. Problems of hyphenation are considered under spelling (see pp. 309–313).

QUOTATION MARKS

Quotation marks, which are usually double (" ") in American English, set off direct speech in dialogue, quoted material, certain titles, definitions and translations, and words given certain special emphases. (Single quotation marks are normal in British usage.)

Dialogue

Direct speech in dialogue is usually rendered within quotation marks:

• "But Rupert, darling, what would we do with a Hatchback Hornet up here where there aren't any roads?"

Quoted Material

When you are quoting material other than dialogue, you have to be aware that there are two ways of doing so. *Short* quotations—prose passages of less than about a hundred words or verse passages of a line or two—should be placed within quotation marks and integrated into your main text. *Longer* quotations should be *indented* so that they stand apart from your text; they are *not* enclosed in quotation marks.

A verse passage of two lines could be quoted in either of the standard ways:

• The poet tells us, "Ain't got my food stamps yet this month, & wonder if/ Maybe this is fascism at last."
• The poet tells us:
  Ain't got my food stamps yet this month, & wonder if
  Maybe this is fascism at last.

(The slash or virgule in the first version indicates a line ending. It's necessary only in verse quotations.)

When you do indent a quotation, reproduce it exactly, including any quotation marks it may already contain. But when you run a quotation into your own text and put it within quotation marks, any quotation marks already in the passage must become *single:*

• "The concluding lines of Wratto's 'Ode to Amerika,'" observes Pieper in *The Defenestrated Imagination*, "rest on an ingenious paradox."

In general, quotations-within-quotations require single marks. In the rare case in which a third set of marks must be boxed in, they become double (" ' " " ' "):

- Orwell's friend Richard Rees informs us that "when Socialists told him that under Socialism there would be no such feeling of being at the mercy of unpredictable and irresponsible powers, he remarked: 'I notice people always say *"under* Socialism." They look forward to being on top—with all the others underneath, being told what is good for them.' "[1]

Certain Titles

The titles of essays, poems, articles, stories, chapters, and other units smaller than a whole volume are indicated by quotation marks:

- Joyce's story, "The Dead"
- Keats's poem, "To Autumn"
- " 'Tango': The Hottest Movie," *Newsweek*, 12 February 1973, pp. 54–58.

Except in newspapers, where italics are generally not used, you should italicize (underline) the titles of whole volumes, without using quotation marks (see pp. 331–332). If a poem occupies a whole volume, it should be italicized: *Paradise Lost, The Prelude, Paterson.* Names of newspapers, magazines, and journals are also italicized rather than placed in quotation marks:

- Biff felt sure that marijuana would soon be legalized when he spotted an article in the *Reader's Digest* called "I Owe My Life to L-Dopa."

Definitions and Translations

When a word or phrase is cited in italics and defined or translated, the definition or translation should be put within quotation marks:

- *Benevolent*, which means "desiring to do good to others," should be kept distinct from *beneficent*, which means "doing good to others."
- The German term for "a little" is *ein wenig.*

When a foreign word is immediately followed by a translation, you can put the translation in single quotation marks without intervening punctuation:

- *ein wenig* 'a little'
- They call the Fiat 500 *Topolino* 'Little Mouse.'

Special Emphasis

Quotation marks call attention to the words they enclose. Some writers use them in place of italics to indicate that a word is being treated *as* a word, not as the thing it stands for:

- One doesn't hear the term "civil rights" quite so frequently these days.

It may be necessary now and then to put a word within quotation marks to show that you don't share a certain attitude:

- Nero's solution to "the Christian problem" also helped to cut the monthly budget for lion food.

But like several other devices (sarcastic capitals, derisive exclamation points and question marks, and bracketed *sic*'s), such quotation marks can become a bad habit. Some writers, for example, use them to slander anything they can't understand:

- Proust's "novel" consists of nothing but endless, tedious reminiscences narrated in a tone of pure snobbery.

Try to do without free rides; let your argumentation make its own case.

Quotation Marks Combined with Other Punctuation

In British usage quotation marks generally go inside other punctuation, but American usage is more complicated. You have to know the following conventions:

1. *Commas* and *periods* should be placed *inside* the closing quotation marks in all circumstances. You don't have to consider whether the comma or period is part of the quotation, or whether the quotation is short or long. Just put the comma or period inside the closing quotation marks in every case:

- Quoth the Raven, "Nevermore."
- "Nevermore," quoth the Raven.

2. *Colons* and *semicolons* are just as rigidly placed as commas and periods. They always go *outside* the closing quotation marks:

- "Nevermore": that's what the daffy bird said.
- Once again the bird said "Nevermore"; and I said, "Why do you always have to take such a negative attitude?"

3. *Question marks, exclamation points*, and *dashes* go *either inside or outside* the closing quotation marks, depending on their function. If they are punctuating the quoted material itself, they go *inside:*

- "Why is it," Stanley asked, "that the market collapses just when I've swallowed my politics and bought into aerospace and mutual funds?"

The same marks go *outside* the closing quotation marks if they aren't part of the quotation:

• Do you think the Raven could be taught to say "I'll think it over and let you know in the morning"?

4. When the quotation must end with a question mark or exclamation point and your own sentence calls for a period at that point, the period vanishes:

• Grandpa used to listen to Walter Cronkite every evening and constantly scream, "Horsefeathers!"

5. Otherwise, the end-punctuation of the quotation makes way for your own punctuation. If the quoted passage, for example, ends with a period but your own sentence doesn't stop there, you should drop the period and substitute your own punctuation, if any:

• "I wonder why they don't impeach newscasters," said Grandpa.

(The quoted passage would normally end with a period, but the main sentence calls for a comma at that point.)

6. In general, a closing quotation mark can be accompanied by only one other mark of punctuation. But exception can be made for the rare case in which extra punctuation rescues a sentence from ungrammaticality:

• When the Dow-Jones Index fell through 600—the market analysts had the nerve to call it a "technical adjustment"!—Stanley decided to become a revolutionary again.

(The quotation marks, exclamation point, and dash after *adjustment* each serve a necessary function.)

7. When a quotation is accompanied by a footnote number, the footnote number should come *after* all other punctuation except a dash that may resume your own part of the sentence:

• Burgess finds "no substance to these charges."[2]
• Burgess finds "no substance to these charges"[2]—and I emphatically agree with him.

8. When a quotation is integrated into your text (without indentation) and is followed by a parenthetical citation (pp. 369–370), the parenthesis should come *after* the final quotation marks but *before* a comma or period—even if the comma or period occurs in the quoted passage:

- Dr. Dollar says, "No modern home should be without a queen-sized trampoline" (*Aerobic Kama Sutra*, p. 217).

9. But if the quotation ends with a question mark or an exclamation point, you should include it before the closing quotation marks and add your own punctuation after the parenthesis:

- "Should we in the education industry," Clearance asked, "allow ourselves to lag behind in the vital areas of packaging and promotion?" (*Times* interview, p. 18, col. 2).

10. When, finally, a quotation is indented and set apart from your text, the parenthetical citation follows *all* punctuation and is customarily given either in a footnote or on a separate line:

- I'm just sittin here washing telvision
  washin telvsn
  wshn t.v.
  (yeah!)
  wshn *teee veeee.*

  ("Ode to Amerika," ll. 13–17)

(Fuller advice about citation is given in Chapter Fourteen.)

EXERCISES

I. Most of the following sentences contain errors of punctuation. Correct errors wherever you find them, leaving the phrasing as it is. Make corrections only where the given mark is a *distinct violation* of rules stated in this chapter.

1. Animals, vegetables, and minerals, all get involved in the exciting game of "Twenty Questions."
2. Henry James was fond of Italy, in fact he wrote a whole book about its civilized pleasures.
3. September 1939 was a bad time to be in Europe.
4. Did it ever occur to you that the rule that a captain should be the last person to desert his ship originated in the days when ships tended to capsize but remain afloat and that the captain might therefore be the safest person of all?
5. But without a broad-brimmed hat or an umbrella, no one can go out in this tropical sun.
6. Airline passengers seem to prefer a safe trip with armed guards, to an unsafe trip without them.
7. They won't lower the taxes, merely because ordinary people complain.
8. Did you know that, the first baseball game played under electric lights occurred in 1883?

9. Whether the earthquake was caused by fault slippage, or by excessive drilling, couldn't be determined.

10. The nutrition expert expressed some doubts about a generation of American children raised on, "Crazy Cow, Baron Von Redberry, Sir Grapefellow, Count Chocula, and Franken-Berry."

11. A good reason for moving to San Antonio, is that it's the cleanest city in the United States.

12. Every person, no matter how incompetent he may be at everything else is the world's greatest expert at deciphering his own handwriting.

13. Aunt Sophia was disoriented by the family reunion. Never having played frisbee with thirty-five people before.

14. Nothing significant occurred on 4 August, 1904.

15. What Shaw called the most licentious of institutions, other people call holy matrimony.

16. He wondered if I would like to shoot the rapids with his novelist friend?

17. Statisticians, who are slavishly admired by some people, and criticized as frivolous by others, have discovered that the taste for dill pickles declines after age sixty-five.

18. Most Americans it seems, suffer from aching feet.

19. The reason why, after more than seventy-five years, the origin of the Spanish-American war remains unexplained, is unclear to me.

20. A man likes to enjoy a cigar after a large and gratifying meal but he doesn't enjoy watching a woman do the same.

21. Housewives agree that soyburgers are the best, low-cost, high-protein food to serve these days.

22. A porcupine has approximately 30,000 quills for your information.

23. And, I certainly don't see why Jane Fonda should be invited to address our American Legion chapter.

24. For some mysterious reason the U.S. Department of Labor defines a "mature" woman as one between 45 and 64 years of age.

25. A torsion bar would be useful in my opinion if you are planning to turn any corners in your Corvair.

26. On Wednesday they received an unpleasant surprise, for when they tried to go through customs at Bangor they discovered that they hadn't landed in the capital of Thailand at all.

27. As the press had expected, the President announced on Friday that the price of steak, not gold, would henceforth define the value of the dollar.

28. Betty Crocker, who receives more proposals of marriage every year than any other American woman, doesn't exist.

29. In a house work is more tedious than in an office.

30. The one mystery, that I can't explain, is why Luci and Desi had to call it quits.

31. You Gertie are a woman of taste and sensitivity.

32. Of course I know exactly what you mean.

II. Correct any errors of punctuation, leaving the phrasing as it is:

1. "Reggie (Jackson) and Sal (Bando) hit the long ball for us," said Catfish.
2. "How can you explain," she asked, "why 80,000 people in Victorian London were prostitutes"?
3. "We want a "G" rating for this movie," said the director, "so I'd like you to stab her only in the throat and stomach."
4. Is it true that the witness said, "I refuse to answer on the grounds that my answer might tend to incinerate me?"
5. He spent his vacation at Redwood National Park . . . and had a good time fishing . . . hiking . . . and watching the clear-cut logging . . .
6. In her opinion my proposal was "absurd"; and there the matter was dropped.
7. The banker assured the judge that his trip to Switzerland with the missing $2,000,000 resulted from "an unfortunate. . . . oversight."
8. Signora Faggiani tried to explain that her slowness was due to an *infarto* 'heart attack.'
9. This matter is thoroughly discussed on pages 312–'19.
10. "They'll never stand for this." said Sitting Bull.
11. The poet tells us a good deal about his life when he writes, "Counted up Fri. and saw I still got/Four lids and two caps,/One lovin' spoonful,/Three buttons from Southatheborder,/Some coke but no Pepsi,/And a bottle of reds./O Amerika, we can still be friends fer a few more weeks."
12. Why did Ted Lewis always ask, "Is everybody happy?"
13. The councilman called the plan "moronic".
14. A penny saved is a penny earned; but rich people, I've noticed, tend to put their pennies into shrewd investments.
15. She wanted her psychiatrist to tell her whether it was possible to get seasick in Iowa?
16. Since he hoped to become a dog trainer when his football career was over, Biff was especially eager to read the article in "National Geographic" called *Sikkim*.
17. The planning commissioner said that in his judgment the new skyscraper had: "all the earmarks of an eyesore."
18. I am not sure—will you correct me if I'm wrong—that porpoises are more intelligent than raccoons?
19. The delay in applying smog-control regulations, the impounding of funds for water purification, the veto of a bill to help rural communities build their own sewer facilities—these were a few of the signs that "ecology" was losing its political magic.
20. Special sunglasses have now been devised for skiers, who suffer acutely from glare; for people who want to wear only one pair of glasses in sun and shade; and for others who, for whatever reason, don't want their fellow citizens to catch sight of their eyes.
21. It is simply untrue,—and nothing you say will convince me—that trees make wind by waggling their branches.
22. The robber only asked for two things: her money and her life.
23. Although some researchers continue to blame LSD use for damage to chromosomes, others (knowing that people who take LSD tend to con-

sume other drugs as well), are now focusing their suspicions on marijuana.

III. Correct the errors of punctuation in this passage:

On 23 July, 1909 Jack London came home to California, after two years in the South Seas. His health finances and writing career were in deep trouble. London told San Francisco newspaper reporters that he was, "unutterably weary" and had, "come home for a good rest". Settled in his Sonoma County ranch he began to rebuild himself, and his career. "Of course, I may be going to pieces as you suggest" he wrote an anxious admirer but I'm living so damned happily that I don't mind if I do go to pieces[1]". Characteristically London was fooling himself. He cared deeply about going to pieces, — about the downhill slide to alcohol, fat and an idle pencil. He threw himself, into the therapy of ranching, a therapy that, in time became an orgy, and finally a dance of death. Through construction of an identity, as a great California rancher, London hoped to stave off chaos: instead, he invoked a nightmare. The Sonoma chapter of Jack London's life, his last chapter dramatized a modality of California madness.[2]

IV. Except for hyphens, all punctuation has been removed from the following paragraph by James Thurber. Supply what you consider to be the necessary marks.

One time my mother went to the Chittenden Hotel to call on a woman mental healer who was lecturing in Columbus on the subject of Harmonious Vibrations She wanted to find out if it was possible to get harmonious vibrations into a dog He's a large tan-colored Airedale Mother explained The woman said she had never treated a dog but she advised my mother to hold the thought that he did not bite and would not bite Mother was holding the thought the very next morning when Muggs got the iceman but she blamed that slip-up on the iceman If you didnt think he would bite you he wouldn't Mother told him He stomped out of the house in a terrible jangle of vibrations[3]

NOTES

1. Richard Rees, *George Orwell: Fugitive from the Camp of Victory* (London: Secker and Warburg, 1961), p. 153.
2. Kevin Starr, *Americans and the California Dream: 1850–1915* (New York: Oxford Univ. Press, 1973), p. 210. The punctuation has been jumbled.
3. James Thurber, "The Dog That Bit People," *Thurber's Dogs: A Collection of the Master's Dogs, Written and Drawn, Real and Imaginary* (New York: Touchstone, 1955), p. 81. Punctuation has been omitted.

SPELLING
11

There doesn't seem to be much correlation between good spelling and a knack for composition. Everyone has trouble spelling at least a few words, and some people, who may be excellent writers in other ways, misspell with creative abandon. F. Scott Fitzgerald, for instance, could hardly scribble a line of his evocative prose without botching a word or two. It didn't matter: his editor Maxwell Perkins fixed things up. You, however, probably won't be so lucky. Your misspellings will count against you, distracting readers from your arguments and making a general impression of sloppiness. If your spelling is weak, you have to set about the job of improving it.

Even though some people have an easier time with spelling than others, you mustn't think of yourself as doomed to spelling badly. If you cultivate the habit of always looking up doubtful spellings and keeping a list of the words that fooled you, you can gradually narrow the area of difficulty. Even if you haven't finally mastered a word, you can recognize it as an item from your list and look it up again before using it. Test yourself periodically against the list, and adopt any tricks you can think of to memorize correct spellings.

Some words can be spelled correctly in more than one way. In general you can assume that the first spelling offered by your dictionary is the one to use. Avoid Anglicisms (*centre, cheque, civilise, connexion, favour, labour, mould, programme*, etc.) and archaisms (*draught, mediaeval, encyclopaedia*, etc.) unless they occur in titles or names: *The Encyclopaedia Britannica*.

SOME RULES OF SPELLING

Since modern English derives from many languages, no rule can tell you with certainty how a given word is spelled. The best course by far is to tackle your errors one by one. As you list them, though, you may notice family resemblances among some of them: failure to double letters, extra -*e*'s in participial forms (*writeing*), confusion between -*ie* and -*ei*, etc. When you find such a pattern, you should memorize the principle you've been violating and try to apply it self-consciously until it becomes second nature. Below are some of the most common principles. For now, just check the examples under each rule and see if they typify your own mistakes; there's no need to memorize the reason for something you're already doing right.

Most of the uncertainties about whether words have single or double letters (*withold? withhhold?*) pertain to words consisting of a *root* plus a *prefix* or *suffix*. The root is the base: *hold*. A prefix consists of one or more letters that can be attached before the root to make a new word: *with*.

PREFIX + ROOT = NEW WORD
with + hold = withhold

A suffix is one or more syllables appended after a root:

ROOT   +SUFFIX =   NEW WORD
sincere + ly   =   sincerely
fool   + ish =   foolish
contagious + ness = contagiousness

Note that a word can have both a prefix and a suffix:

PREFIX + ROOT + SUFFIX = NEW WORD
pre + fix + es = prefixes

Single Versus Double Letters

1. When the last letter of a prefix is the same as the first letter of a root (*ad + dress*), retain both letters:

```
col + league  = colleague
con + note    = connote
dis + similar = dissimilar
mis + speak   = misspeak
re + enlist   = reenlist
un + noticed  = unnoticed
```

2. If a word ends in a single accented vowel and consonant (*man*), it usually doubles the final consonant when a suffix beginning with a vowel is added:

```
fit + ing     = fitting
man + ish     = mannish
regret + ing  = regretting
```

But when the suffix begins with a consonant, the doubling usually doesn't occur:

```
fit + ful     = fitful
man + like    = manlike
regret + ful  = regretful
```

3. Words of more than one syllable, if their accent falls strongly on a syllable before the last one, don't double a final consonant before a vowel suffix:

```
bigot + ed    = bigoted
despot + ic   = despotic
quarrel + ed  = quarreled
rivet + ed    = riveted
```

But even a minor accent on the final syllable can call for a double consonant:

```
handicap + ed = handicapped
outfit + ed   = outfitted
sandbag + ed  = sandbagged
```

You can see the point of the rule if you try pronouncing the words without the double consonant: *handicaped*, etc.

4. When *-ly* is added to words ending in *-l*, the *-l* is retained:

```
brutal + ly       = brutally
cynical + ly      = cynically
hypothetical + ly = hypothetically
```

5. Words ending in *-n* retain the *-n* before *-ness:*

clean + ness = cleanness
even + ness = evenness
open + ness = openness
plain + ness = plainness

6. The correct suffix is -*ful*, not -*full:*

artful
beautiful
rightful
wonderful

Change of Final -e, -ie, and -y

1. Except for words ending in -*ce* or -*ge*, most words that end in a silent -*e* drop the -*e* when adding a vowel suffix:

berate + ed = berated
give + ing = giving
note + able = notable
stare + ing = staring

In most words ending in -*ce* or -*ge* the -*e* is retained:

courage + ous = courageous
peace + able = peaceable
singe + ing   = singeing

Exceptions: *age + ing = aging; forage + ing = foraging; rouge + ing = rouging,* etc.

2. Most words ending in one or more consonants plus a silent -*e* (*haste, late*) retain the -*e* when adding a suffix beginning with a consonant:

waste + ful = wasteful
shame + less = shameless
vile + ly   = vilely

In American English, however, when -*dg* precedes the final silent -*e*, the -*e* is usually dropped before the suffix -*ment:*

abridge + ment   = abridgment
acknowledge + ment = acknowledgment
judge + ment   = judgment

3. Most verbs ending in -*ie* change the -*ie* to -*y* when taking -*ing:*

die + ing = dying
lie + ing = lying
tie + ing = tying

4. When one or more consonants precedes a final -*y* (*beauty, fly*) and further letters are added, the -*y* usually becomes -*i*:

beauty + ful   = beautiful
crazy + ness   = craziness
fly + er   = flier
prettify + ed   = prettified
rectify + cation = rectification

But note that *busyness* retains the -*y* so as to remain distinct from *business*.

5. When the first added letter is -*i*, a final -*y* is retained:

fly + ing   = flying
rectify + ing = rectifying

-c Versus -ck

Most words ending in -*c* add -*k* when an additional syllable beginning with -*e*, -*i*, or -*y* is added:

bivouac + ed = bivouacked
mimic + ed   = mimicked
picnic + ed = picnicked
traffic + ed = trafficked

Note how the -*k* in each case prevents a mispronunciation.

-ie Versus -ei

Remember the old jingle:

I before E
Except after C
Or when sounded as A
As in *neighbor* and *weigh*.

Thus:

I BEFORE E:
• achieve, believe, chief, field, fiend, niece, piece, shield, thief, wield, yield

EXCEPT AFTER C:
• ceiling, conceive, perceive, receive

OR WHEN SOUNDED AS A:
• freight, inveigh, obeisance, reign, sleigh, veil, weight

But note these exceptions among others: *either, financier, foreign, heifer, height, leisure, seize, weird.* The rule, then, can only jog your memory of a correct spelling; it can't tell you for certain whether a given word contains *-ie* or *-ei.*

FORMATION OF POSSESSIVES

Singular Nouns

Most, but not all, authorities say that singular nouns are always made possessive by the addition of *-'s,* whether or not the noun ends in an *s* sound:

a day's work
Camus's novels
Keats's verse

But some authorities and many good writers feel strongly that pronunciation, not an inflexible rule, should govern the forming of possessives. Their method is simply to listen for the extra *-s;* if they don't hear it, they don't write it. Thus, for them, the possessive of *Dickens* would be *Dickens',* not *Dickens's.* This seems entirely proper to me, but you will find some teachers and grammarians unalterably opposed to it. Odd as it seems, the truth is that no completely satisfactory advice can be offered about forming the possessive of nouns ending with an *-s* sound.

Everyone, however, does admit a few conventional exceptions to the *-'s* rule. Where an *-'s* would make a triple sibilant, the apostrophe alone can be used: *Demosthenes', Moses', Ulysses', Xerxes'.* (What these exceptions really prove is that people *do* recognize, however inconsistently, that spelling should reflect pronunciation.) And certain formulas also violate the *-'s* rule: *for conscience' sake, for goodness' sake, for Jesus' sake.* Some writers even omit the apostrophe in these phrases.

Of course, singular nouns can also be made possessive by a preceding *of: the work of a day, the novels of Camus, the verse of Keats.* Be careful not to add an apostrophe in such cases. (For "double possessives" in which *of* and an apostrophe *are* combined, see p. 198.)

Plural Nouns

Plural nouns normally become possessive either by a preceding *of* (*the views of Americans*) or by the addition of an apostrophe alone:

the Americans' views
several days' work

But plural nouns that do not end in -s become possessive in the same way that singular nouns do:

the children's room
those deer's habitat
three mice's tails
the alumni's representative

(When such a plural possessive sounds awkward, change it to the *of* form: *the tails of three mice.*)

Plural Possessives of Time

There is a growing tendency to drop the apostrophe in plural possessives of time: *two years parole, a six weeks holiday.* For the present, however, it might be wise to write *two years' parole, a six weeks' holiday.* The apostrophes serve a function in showing that the real nouns in these phrases are *parole* and *holiday.*

Compound Possessives

In compound possessives, only the final name takes the possessive form:

Bradley, Beatty, and Long's anthology
Laurel and Hardy's comedies

But note that this applies only when the possession is truly collective. Compare:

• Bradley's, Beatty's, and Long's efforts were pooled in the task of compiling and editing the book.

(The possessive forms are correct here because three separate *efforts* are being discussed.)

Possessives in Titles

In some titles the expected possessive form is lacking: *The Authors Guild, The Merchants Bank, Finnegans Wake.* Don't "improve" such titles by adding an apostrophe.

Possessives of Pronouns

Pronouns that are already possessive in meaning take no apostrophe: *his, hers, its, ours, yours, theirs, whose.* Note especially the treacherous *it's*, which is the correct form for the contraction of *it is* but a blunder for the possessive *its*.

Some indefinite pronouns form the possessive in the same manner as nouns: *another's, nobody's, one's, somebody's*, etc. But some other indefinite pronouns can only be made possessive in the *of* form: *of each, of all*, etc. (See pp. 185–186 for a full list.)

Awkward Possessives

Certain problems of spelling possessives can't be satisfactorily resolved at all. For example, how should you form the possessive of a noun that's followed by a parenthesis? Is it *Mrs. Jones (née Davis)'s coat, Mrs. Jones's (née Davis) coat*, or what? All possible versions are awkward, except possibly *the coat of Mrs. Jones (née Davis)*.

Again, don't try to form the possessive of a word followed by quotation marks: *"The Dead"'s symbolism*. Resort to the *of* form: *the symbolism of "The Dead."*

And finally, watch out for unnatural separation of the *-'s* from the word it refers to. You can write *someone else's problem* or *the Queen of Sheba's tuba*, but you shouldn't write *the house on the corner's roof*. In that phrase the *-'s* is just too far away from the word that "possesses" it, *house*. Once again, a timely recourse to *of* can rescue you: *the roof of the house on the corner*.

FORMATION OF PLURALS

Regular and Irregular Plurals

Most nouns become plural by the addition of *-s* or (if the plural form is pronounced with an extra syllable) *-es: hats, dishes*. Some nouns don't follow either pattern:

a. *-en plurals:* children, oxen
b. *Unchanged plurals:* deer, fish, mink, series, sheep, swine
c. *Vowel-changing plurals:* feet, geese, lice, men, mice, teeth, women

Nouns Ending in a Vowel plus -y

These usually form the plural by adding *-s: bays, boys, keys, trays*. Nouns ending in a consonant plus *-y* usually form the plural by changing *-y* to *-i* and adding *-es: berries, constabularies, emergencies, companies*.

But names ending in *-y* become plural by adding *-s: Bundys, Connallys, Kennedys, Rubys*. A few names of places do change *-y* to *-ies: Alleghenies, Rockies*.

Nouns Ending in -o

Nouns ending in a vowel plus -o become plural by adding -s: *patios, studios*. Most nouns ending in a consonant plus -o become plural by adding -es: *potatoes, vetoes*. But some words flout the rule (*solos, pianos, tyros, sopranos*), and some others have alternative plurals: *cargos, cargoes; zeros, zeroes*. Where your dictionary lists two forms, adopt the first.

Compound Nouns

Most compound nouns, whether or not they are hyphenated (see pp. 311–312), form the plural by adding -s to the final word: *cross-examinations, fire fighters, head starts*. But when the first word is the most significant one, it takes the plural form: *mothers-in-law, men-of-war, secretaries-general, senators-elect*.

Nouns Ending in *-ful*

These become plural by adding -s to the end: *cupfuls, shovelfuls, spoonfuls*.

Nouns with Foreign Plural Forms

A number of words taken from foreign languages, especially from Greek and Latin, retain their foreign plural forms. Some have also acquired English plural forms, and thus have two plural spellings. The rule for deciding which plural to use is: look it up! Even so, the dictionary can't settle your doubts in all cases. It won't tell you, for example, that the plural of *appendix* is *appendixes* if you're referring to the organ, but either *appendixes* or *appendices* if you mean supplementary sections at the end of books. Similarly, alphabetical guides are always *indexes*, but abstract indicators such as the rate of unemployment are sometimes *indices*. A bug has *antennae* but television sets are usually said to have *antennas*. *Formulas* for peace or integration, but either *formulas* or *formulae* for chemistry. *Mediums* who chat with the departed sometimes make guest appearances on the *media*. You have to trust your sense of idiom in making such choices. A guide to usage (see p. 62) can also settle some difficult cases.

When in doubt, you should lean toward the English plural. It's likely to sound less pretentious, and it won't risk an embarrassing mistake. Thus you can always write *apparatuses*, but if you want to get fancy and write *apparati* you will regret it. There's no such form; the Latin plural is *apparatus*. The same caution applies to *afflatus, conspectus, hiatus, impetus, nexus, prospectus,* and *status. Cactuses, curriculums, maximums, minimums, radiuses, sanatoriums, sanitariums,* and *syllabuses* are acceptable for all purposes. But we do still speak of social *strata*, spinal *vertebrae*, *data* (the singular should be *datum*), *criteria* (the singular must be *criterion*), and *phenomena* (the singular must be *phenomenon*). A few words that look plural are in fact singular; *kudos*, for example, is singular and shouldn't be used in a plural sense at all.

Greek and Latin derivatives ending in *-is* do show a high consistency. They regularly change *-is* to *-es: analyses, crises, parentheses, theses.*

Letters and Figures

Letters and figures usually become plural by the addition of *-'s:*

* Hester was rapidly losing whatever fondness she might once have felt for capital *A*'s.
* Now that the postal rates have gone up again, do you think we can expect a closeout sale on *8*'s?

Some writers omit the apostrophe and give the plurals simply as *As*, *8s*. But this can make for confusion. Does *ls*, for example, constitute the plural of 1 (*ones*) or the letters *ls*? It's better to use *-'s.*

Words Considered *as* Words

Whole words can be given the plural form *-'s* if you're trying to indicate that they *are* words:

* I hired you as my yes man, but in this memorandum of yours I find four *no*'s.

(Note how the italicizing of the isolated word, but not of the *-'s*, helps to make the writer's meaning clear.)

HYPHENATION

Only your dictionary can tell you whether, and at what point, many terms should be hyphenated. However, the following survey of problems offers some general guidelines:

Word Division at the End of a Line

In a manuscript or typescript, where right-hand margins are uneven, the problem of hyphenation can be dodged. Just end each line with the last word that you can *complete*. Your reader will never know or care whether you are someone who finds it hard to divide words at the right junctures. But if you find that you must divide a word, do so only at one of the syllable breaks as marked in a dictionary. (Some dic·tion·ar·ies divide syllables with dots; some dic tion ar ies with spaces.)

Observe these further conventions:

1. Never divide a one-syllable word, even if you might manage to pronounce it as two syllables (*rhythm, schism*).
2. Don't leave one letter stranded at the end of a line (o-ver, i-dea), and don't leave a solitary letter for the beginning of the next line (Ontari-o, seed-y).
3. If a word is already hyphenated, divide it only at the fixed hyphen. Avoid *self-con-scious, ex-Pre-mier.*
4. You can anticipate what the dictionary will say about word division by remembering that:
   a. Double consonants are usually separated: *ar-rogant, inef-fable.*
   b. But when the double consonants come just before a suffix, the division falls *after* the double consonants: *stall-ing, kiss-able.*
   c. When a word has *acquired* a double consonant in adding a suffix, the second consonant belongs to the suffix: *bet-ting, fad-dish.*

Prefixes

Hyphens are used to separate certain prefixes from the root words to which they are attached:

1. Words beginning with *all-*, *ex-*, and *self-*, when these are prefixes, are hyphenated after the prefix:

all-powerful
ex-minister
self-motivated

(Note that in *selfhood, selfish, selfless,* and *selfsame* the accented syllable *self* isn't a true prefix, and no hyphen is called for.)

2. Prefixes before a name are always hyphenated:

anti-Spock
pro-McCord
un-American

3. Prefixes ending with a vowel sometimes take a hyphen if they are followed by a vowel, especially if the two vowels are the same:

anti-intellectual
co-op
semi-invalid

The hyphen prevents ambiguity and mispronunciation.

But prefixed terms that are very common are less likely to be mis-construed, and many double vowels remain unhyphenated:

cooperate
coordinate
preempt
reeducate

You will find good dictionaries in some disagreement with each other about such words. Some dictionaries prefer hyphens in most double-vowel situations; some have all but abolished the conven-tion; and some recommend a dieresis mark over the second vowel to show that it's separately pronounced: *reëducate*. In contemporary prose, however, you won't come across many instances of the dieresis.

4. Certain words are sometimes hyphenated because they would otherwise look identical to very different words:

* If you don't *re-sort* the laundry I'll have to resort to buying new under-wear at the resort.
* Mystic Mandala Village, an authentic *re-creation* of a hippie commune, is being advertised as a future center of recreation.
* Having run in the Olympics, she had a *run-in* with the Rules Committee about pep pills.

5. When a modifier occurs with two alternative prefixes, the first prefix often stands alone with a hyphen:

* There was quite a difference between *pre-* and postwar prices.
* *Pro-* and antifascist students battled openly in the streets of Rome.

(Note that the first prefix takes a hyphen even if it wouldn't have one when joined to the root word.)

Compound Nouns

Many compound nouns (nouns formed from more than one word) are hyphenated: *bull's-eye, city-state, poet-philosopher, point-blank, secretary-treasurer,* etc. Many others, however, are written as sepa-rate words (*fire fighter, head start, ice cream, oil spill,* etc.) or as single unhyphenated words (*committeeman, earring, milkmaid, scofflaw, scoutmaster, underwriter,* etc.). As compound terms become familiar with long use, they tend to drop their hyphens. The dictionary can guide you in individual cases of doubt—though dictionaries them-selves will differ somewhat over various words.

Among the compound nouns that are hyphenated, many contain prepositions: *good-for-nothing, jack-in-the-box, man-of-war, mother-of-pearl, son-in-law*, etc. The hyphenation shows that the prepositional phrase is part of the thing named, not part of the rest of the sentence. Compare:

- She had a *son-in-law*.
- She had a daughter in medicine and a *son in law*.

Compound Modifiers

A compound modifier is usually hyphenated if it *precedes* the modified term:

a *well-trained* philosopher
an *out-of-work* barber

The hyphens are useful because they shift attention to the real noun: not a *well*, but a *philosopher*.

But no ambiguity is likely when a compound modifier *follows* the modified term, and in this position the hyphen usually disappears:

- The philosopher was *well trained*.
- A barber *out of work* is bound to resent people who cut their own hair.

If a modifier is hyphenated in the dictionary, of course, it remains hyphenated in all positions:

- She was an *even-tempered* instructor.
- She was *even-tempered*.

When a compound modifier contains an adverb in the *-ly* form, it doesn't have to be hyphenated in any position. The adverb, clearly identifiable *as* an adverb, does the hyphen's work of signaling that the real noun comes later:

a barely suppressed gasp
an openly polygamous chieftain
the hypocritically worded note of protest

Adverbs lacking the *-ly* form are another matter: *the fast-developing crisis, a deep-boring bit*, etc.

Compound Numbers

Numbers twenty-one to ninety-nine, when written out, are hyphenated, even when they form part of a larger number:

- Her waist was a perfect *forty-eight*.
- Two hundred *seventy-five* years ago there was an Indian burial mound on the site of this beautiful Texaco station.

(Note that *and* isn't a recognized part of any whole number. Strictly speaking, *two hundred and seventy-five years ago* would be incorrect.)

Fractions are hyphenated when they're used as modifiers, otherwise not:

AS MODIFIER:
- The jug of Thunderbird was *seven-eighths* empty at the end of the party.

(*Seven-eighths* modifies *empty*.)

NOT AS MODIFIER:
- *Seven eighths* of all adults have experimented with such dangerous drugs as nicotine, caffeine, and alcohol.

(The fraction serves as the subject of the verb *have experimented*.)

But many people ignore this rule, and by now it's debatable whether the commoner fractions such as *two thirds* and *one quarter* ever need to be hyphenated.

Don't add an extra hyphen to compound fractions such as these:

three seventy-thirds
twenty-one forty-sevenths

(Hyphens after *three* and *twenty-one* would blur the distinction between the numerator and the denominator in each case.)

Connection of Numbers

Hyphens are used to connect numbers expressing a range:

pages 136-198
the period September 11-October 4

(In such cases the hyphen means *between*. It's therefore redundant to write *the period between September 11-October 4*.)

COMMONLY MISSPELLED WORDS

The following list, according to my own and other teachers' records, contains many of the words most frequently misspelled by college students. Take some time to scan it. If you never misspell any of these words, you're a remarkably good speller. Any spellings that do look unfamiliar to you should be added to your own list and reviewed from time to time.

abdomen	allude (*refer*), *see* elude
abdominal	allusion (*reference*), *see* illusion
abridgment	ally (*associate*), *see* alley
absence	almost
absorption	already
academy	altar (*of a church*)
accelerate	alter (*change*)
accept (*take*), *see* except	altogether
access (*availability*), *see* excess	always
accessible	analysis, analyses (plural)
accident, accidentally	analytic
accommodate	analyze
accompaniment	angel (*spirit*)
accomplish	angle (*geometry*)
accoutrements	anonymous, anonymity
accumulate	apiece
accustom, accustomed	apparatus
achieve, achievement	apparent
acknowledgment	appreciate, appreciation
acquire	apprise (*inform*)
acquit, acquitted	apprize (*appraise*)
acreage	appropriate
across	approximate
actual, actually	aquatic
acumen	arctic
address	argue, arguing
adjacent	argument
adolescence, adolescent	arithmetic
advice (noun)	arraign
advise (verb)	article
affect (verb, *influence*), *see* effect	ascent (*climb*), *see* assent
aggravate, aggravated	ascetic
aggress, aggressive, aggression	assassin, assassination
aghast	assent (*agreement*), *see* ascent
aging	assistant, assistance
alcohol	athletic, athletics
all right	attendance
allege	auger (*tool*)
alley (*passage*), *see* ally	augur (*predict*)

auxiliary
badminton
bachelor
balloon
barbiturate
bare (*naked*), *see* bear
beachhead
bear (*carry*), *see* bare
beautiful
beggar
beginner, beginning
belief, believe
beneficent
beneficial
benefit, benefited, benefiting
besiege
biased
bigoted
biscuit
bivouac, bivouacked
born (*brought into being*)
borne (*carried*)
boundary
bourgeois, bourgeoisie
breadth (*width*)
breath (*noun*)
breathe (*verb*)
bridal (*of a bride*)
bridle (*horse*)
Britain
bulletin
bullion
buoy
buoyant
bureau
bureaucracy, bureaucratic
burglar
bus
business (*job*)
busyness (*being busy*)
cacophony
cafeteria
calendar
Calvary (*Golgotha*), *see* cavalry
camellia
camouflage
cannon (*gun*)
canon (*law*)
cantaloupe
canvas (*fabric*)

canvass (*solicit*)
capital (*city*)
capitol (*state house*)
careful
carriage
casserole
cataract
category
caucus
cavalry (*mounted soldiers*), *see* Calvary
ceiling
cemetery
censor (*forbid publication*)
censure (*criticize*)
census
certain
chagrined
champagne
change, changeable
characteristic
chassis
chastise
chauffeur
chief
chimneys
choose (*select*), chose (past tense)
chord (*tones*), *see* cord
cigarette
cinnamon
cite (*mention*), *see* sight, site
climactic (*of a climax*)
climatic (*of a climate*)
coarse (*rough*), *see* course
cocoa
coconut
colander
collaborate
colloquium
colonel
colossal
column
commit, commitment
committee
competent
competition
complementary (*matching*), *see* complimentary
complexion

complimentary (*flattering*), *see*
  complementary
concede
conceive, conceivable
concomitant
condemn
conferred
confidant (*recipient of secrets*)
confidante (*female confidant*)
confident (*assured*)
congratulate
connoisseur
conqueror
conscience
conscientious
conscious
consensus
consistent, consistency
consul (*official*), *see* council, counsel
consummate
contractual
control, controlled, controlling
controversy
coolly
cord (*rope*), *see* chord
corduroy
corollary
correlate
corroborate
council (*body of advisers*), *see* consul
counsel (*advice, adviser*), *see* consul
counterfeit
course (*direction*), *see* coarse
courtesy, courteous
criticism
criticize
crotchety
curiosity
currant (*raisin*)
current (*flow, present*)
cylinder
dahlia
dais
dealt
debatable
debater
decathlon
deceive
defendant
defense
definite, definitely

delirium
democracy
dependent
derelict
descendant (*offspring*)
descendent (*going down*)
descent (*lowering*), *see* dissent
desiccate
desirable
despair
desperate, desperation
destroy
develop, development
die, dying (*expiring*), *see* dye
dilapidated
dilemma
diminution
diphtheria
diphthong
disappear
disappoint
disastrous
discernible
disciple
discipline
disease
dispensable
dissent (*disagreement*), *see* descent
dissipate
divide
divine
doctor
dominant
drunkenness
dual (*double*)
duel (*fight*)
duly
dwarfs
dye, dyeing (*coloring*), *see* die
ebullient
echoes
eclectic
ecstasy
effect (verb, *accomplish;* noun,
  result), *see* affect
efficient
eighth
elicit (*draw forth*), *see* illicit
eliminate
elude (*evade*), *see* allude
emanate

embarrass, embarrassed,
  embarrassing

embodiment

emigrant (*one who leaves*), *see*
  immigrant

eminent (*famous*), *see* immanent,
  imminent

enemy

enthusiasm, enthusiastic

envelop (verb)

envelope (noun)

environment

equip, equipped, equipment

equivalent

especially

espresso

evenness

everybody

evidently

exaggerate

exceed

excellent, excellence

except (*omit, omitting*), *see* accept

excerpt

excess (*too much*), *see* access

excise

excruciating

exercise

exhaust

exhilarate

existence

exorbitant

expel

expense

experiment

explanation

explicit, explicitly

extraordinary

faint (*lose consciousness*), *see* feint

fallacy

familiar

fascinate

fascist

faze (*daunt*), *see* phase

February

feint (*pretend to attack*), *see* faint

fiend

fiery

finagle

finally

financier

fluorescent

fluoride, fluorine

forbear (*refrain*)

forebear (*ancestor*)

forebode

forehead

foreign

foresee, foreseeable

foreword (*preface*), *see* forward

forfeit

forgo

forth (*ahead*)

forward (*ahead*), *see* foreword

fourth (*4th*)

fracas

friend

fuchsia

fulfill

fulsome

fundamental

futilely

Gandhi

gases

gauge

genealogy

germane

Ghanaian

ghost

glamour, glamorous

goddess

government

governor

graffito, graffiti

grammar, grammatically

greenness

grievance, grievous

gruesome

guarantee

guard

guerrilla

guidance

gypsy

handkerchief

hangar (*for airplanes*)

hanger (*for coats*)

hara-kiri

harangue

harass

hear (*listen*), *see* here

height

helicopter

hemorrhage

here (*this place*), *see* hear

heroes

hindrance

hippopotamus, hippopotamuses

hoping

human

humane

humor, humorous, humorist

hundred

hygiene

hypocrisy

hypocrite

ice cream

iced tea

idiosyncrasy

ignorance, ignorant

illicit (*unlawful*), *see* elicit

illusion (*deception*), *see* allusion

imagery

imaginary, imagination

immanent (*indwelling*), *see* eminent, imminent

immediate

immigrant (*one who arrives*), *see* emigrant

imminent (*impending*), *see* eminent, immanent

impel

implicit, implicitly

impresario

inadvertent

inasmuch as

inchoate

incidentally

incredible

independent, independence

indestructible

indispensable

infinitely

inflammable

inflammatory

influential

innuendo

inoculate

insistence, insistent

insofar as

intellectual

intelligence, intelligent

interference, interfered, interfering

interpretation

interrupt

intramural

intransigeance, intransigent

inveigh

inveigle

involve

iridescent

irrefutable, irrefutably

irrelevant

irreparable, irreparably

irreplaceable, irreplaceably

irresistible, irresistibly

its (*belonging to it*)

it's (*it is*)

jeopardy

judgment

knowledge, knowledgeable

labor, laborer

laboratory

labyrinth

laid

lama (*priest*), *see* llama

languor

larynx

lavender

lead (noun, *metal;* verb, *conduct*)

led (past tense of verb *lead*)

legitimate

leisure

length

lessen (*reduce*)

lesson (*teaching*)

liaison

library

license

lightening (participle)

lightning (noun)

likelihood

lily, lilies

lineage

llama (*pack animal*), *see* lama

loath (*reluctant*)

loathe (*despise*)

loathsome

loneliness

loose (*slack*)

lose (*mislay*)

lying

magnificence, magnificent

maintenance
maneuver
mantel (*shelf*)
mantle (*cloak*)
manual
marriage
marshal (verb and noun), marshaled, marshaling
marshmallow
material (*pertaining to matter*)
materiel (*supplies*)
mattress
meant
medical
medicine
medieval
mediocre
Mediterranean
melancholy
memento
merchandise
metaphor
millennium
millionaire
mimic, mimicked
miner (*digger*), *see* minor
miniature
minor (*lesser*), *see* miner
minute
mischief, mischievous
missal (*prayer book*)
missile (*projectile*)
misspell, misspelled
moral (*ethical*)
morale (*confidence*)
moratorium
mortgage
mucus (noun), mucous (adjective)
muscle (*of the body*)
mussel (*mollusk*)
naphtha
naval (*nautical*)
navel (*bellybutton*)
necessary
nerve-racking
nickel
niece
ninety
noncommittal
noticeable, noticing

obtrusive
occasion
occur, occurred, occurring
occurrence
omission
omit, omitted, omitting
ophthalmologist
opossum
opportunity
oppose
optimist
oscillate
overrun
paid
pain (*agony*), *see* pane
pair (*set of two*), *see* pare
pajamas
pane (*glass*), *see* pain
paraffin
parallel, paralleled
paralysis
paralyze
pare (*peel*), *see* pair
parliament
particular
partner
passed (*went by*)
past (*previous*)
pastime
patent
pavilion
peace (*tranquillity*), *see* piece
peaceable
peal (*ring*)
peel (*strip*)
pejorative
perceive
perennial
perfectible, perfectibility
perform, performance
permanent
permissible
personal (*individual*)
personnel (*employees*)
perspiration
persuade
pharmaceutical
phase (*period*), *see* faze
Philippines
phony

phosphorus
phraseology
physical
physician
physiology
piece (*part*), *see* peace
pigeon
pirouette
plain (*level land; clear*)
plane (noun, *level;* verb, *smooth*)
playwright
pleasant
pleasurable
poignant
poison, poisonous
politician
pomegranate
pore (*scrutinize; small opening*), *see*
  pour
portentous
possess, possession
pour (*spill*), *see* pore
practically
practice
prairie
pray (*implore*), *see* prey
precede
precinct
predominant
prefer, preferred, preferring
preference
prejudice
prescribe
pretense
pretension
prevalent
prey (*victim*), *see* pray
principal (adjective, noun, *chief*)
principle (noun, *rule*)
privilege
probably
procedure
proceed
professor
pronunciation
propaganda
propagate
prophecy (*prediction*)
prophesy (*to predict*)
prostate (*gland*)

prostrate (*prone*)
psychiatry
psychoanalysis
psychology
psychopathology
psychosomatic
pumpkin
pursue, pursuit
putrefy
quay
queue
quizzes
rack (*framework*), *see* wrack
rain (*precipitation*), *see* reign, rein
raise (*lift*), *see* raze
rarefied
rarity
raze (*destroy*), *see* raise
realize
really
recede
receipt
receive
recipe
recognizable
recommend
refer, referred, referring
regretted, regretting
reign (*sway*), *see* rain, rein
rein (*restrain*), *see* rain
relieve
remembrance
reminisce
rendezvous
repellent
repentance
repetition
resemblance
resilience, resilient, resiliency
resistance
restaurant
restaurateur
rhetoric
rheumatism
rhinoceros
rhyme
rhythm
ridiculous
rigmarole
roommate

sacrifice
sacrilegious
said
sandwich
sapphire
satellite
satire (*ridicule*)
satyr (*woodland deity*)
schedule
secretary
seize
sense
sentence
separate
sergeant
severely
shepherd
sheriff
shriek
siege
sieve
sight (*vision*), *see* cite, site
significance
silhouette
similar
simultaneous
site (*locale*), *see* cite, sight
skeptic, skepticism
skiing, skis
smooth
smorgasbord
soliloquy
sophomore
source
sovereign, sovereignty
specimen
sponsor
staccato
stationary (*still*)
stationery (*paper*)
steely
straight (*not bent*)
strait (*narrow*)
strength
strictly
stupefy
substantial
subterranean
subtlety
succeed, success

succinct
succumb
suffrage
superintendent
supersede
suppose
suppress
surprise
syllable
symbol
symmetry
sympathize
synonym, synonymous
tariff
technique
temperament
temperature
tendency
testament
than
their
then
there
therefore
thinness
thorough
threshold
through
to, *see* too, two
tobacco
too, *see* to, two
track (*path*)
tract (*area*)
traffic, trafficked, trafficking
tragedy
tranquil, tranquillity
transcendent, transcendental
transferred, transferring
tries, tried
truly
turkeys
two, *see* to, too
tyranny, tyrannically
ukulele
unanimous
unmistakable, unmistakably
unnecessary
unshakable
unwieldy
vacillate

vacuum	were (past of *to be*)
valuable	we're (*we are*)
vegetable	where (*what place*)
vengeance	whether (*if*), *see* weather
venomous	whither (*where to*), *see* wither
vice (*immorality*), *see* vise	whole
vilify, vilification	wield
village	wintry
villain	wither (*dry out*), *see* whither
violoncello	withhold
viscount	woeful
vise (*holder*), *see* vice	worldly, unworldly
waive (*relinquish*), *see* wave	worshiped, worshiping
warring	wrack (*ruin*), *see* rack
wave (*movement*), *see* waive	wreak (*inflict*)
weather (*state of the atmosphere*), *see* whether	wreck (*ruin*)
Wednesday	your (*belonging to you*)
weird	you're (*you are*)

EXERCISES

I. Spell each new word that is made with the indicated roots, prefixes, and suffixes:

1. un + natural
2. mis + state
3. clan + ish
4. bet + ing
5. hit + ing
6. cat + like
7. wit + less
8. erotic + ally
9. pivot + ing
10. cat + ing
11. final + ly
12. moral + ly
13. wan + ness
14. wrath + ful
15. live + ing
16. compose + ition
17. debate + able
18. late + ly
19. fudge + ing
20. outlie + ing
21. try + ing
22. pacify + er
23. ply + able

If you find that you misspelled any of these words, find the pertinent rule and memorize it.

II. Spell the following words, inserting *ie* or *ei* in each case:

1. p__rce
2. conc__t
3. sl__gh
4. h__r
5. s__ge
6. y__ld
7. s__ve
8. c__ling
9. n__ce
10. f__nd

Review the rules on pp. 304–305 if you missed any of these spellings.

III. **Give the alternative possessive form for each of the following:**

    1. of the victor
    2. of the bystanders
    3. for the sake of goodness
    4. of a Pisces
    5. of the children
    6. of the louse
    7. a journey of four days
    8. the wives of the Yankee pitchers
    9. the partnership of John, Paul, George, and Ringo
   10. the fault of somebody

Review the rules on pp. 305–307 if you made any mistakes.

IV. **Give the plural forms of the following words:**

1. ox	6. woman	11. wrong turn
2. ax	7. alloy	12. chairman-elect
3. datum	8. ferry	13. forkful
4. radio	9. Murphy	14. phenomenon
5. wish	10. tomato	15. psychoanalysis

If you made any errors, see if they are covered on pp. 307–309.

V. **If it were necessary to hyphenate these words at the end of a line, where would breaks be appropriate?**

    1. overripe
    2. ex-Republican
    3. passionate
    4. butted
    5. penning

Check the rules on pp. 309–310 if you made any mistakes.

VI. **Correct any errors of hyphenation you find in the following:**

1. selfsufficient	8. an ill schooled student
2. antiAmerican	9. The doctor was poorly prepared.
3. semi-incapacitated	10. Teachers are under-paid.
4. redesign	11. a bad looking thunderhead
5. pre and postinflationary	12. a finely-tuned violin
6. suicide leap	13. sixty-five days
7. father-in-law	14. a hundred-thirty-one times

15. a three sixteenths opening   17. forty-three eighty-ninths
16. four-elevenths of those people   18. a delay of between 8–10 hours

Check the rules on pp. 310–313 if you made any mistakes.

VII. Find and correct any misspellings in this passage:

In order to accomodate the widespread public desire for a crack-down on vise, the Police Department last year finaly undertook a vigorous program to supress some of the more noticable violations. One result was announced today by Cheif Paola, who reported the arrest of Clem Foster, seventy two year old café owner, alledged to have payed real money to pinball winners on his premisses. It was Fosters bad fortune to be placed under survaillance by Officer John Beck, himself recently aquitted of agravated assault in connection with his under cover impersonation of a Hells Angle.

Beck's asignment was to frequent Foster's Friendly Oasis in plane clothes, remaining on the look out for illegal occurences. The roll was an easy one for the immaginative and enthousiastic Beck, a life long pinball athalete, to assume. Before many months had past, Beck suceeded in inviegling Foster into giveing him a nickle for each free game on the "Hubba Hubba Hula Girl" machine — where upon Officer Beck removed his camoflage and effected the necesary arrest. Released on $5,000 bale, Foster now awaits trial, while Officer Beck is believed to have allready asumed a new disguise to protect the citizens of his precint.

OTHER 12 CON-VENTIONS

CAPITALS

---

1. The first letter of every sentence or sentence fragment should be capitalized:

- *Are* you a Pisces? *Certainly* not! *Too* bad.

Sentences within sentences customarily begin with capitals:

- Max asked Bessie, "*Why* don't we skip the tourist spots and just hang around American Express today?"
- I wondered, How am I ever going to finish this book?

But once in a while, words that might be construed as sentence openers are left uncapitalized:

• Max was curious. Who had invented that awful French coffee? *when? and* why?

(By leaving *when* and *and* in lower case, the writer emphasizes that Max was asking a three-part question, not three distinct questions. Capitals would have been equally correct and more usual.)
   Note that indirect questions aren't capitalized:

• I wondered *how* I was ever going to finish that book.

2. Sentences contained within parentheses should begin with capitals only if they stand between complete sentences:

CAPITALIZED:
• Max and Bessie had a fine time in Moscow. (*They* especially liked shopping for used blue jeans and drinking Pepsi with Herb and Gladys.) But in Bulgaria Max missed the whole World Series because no one would lend him a short-wave radio.

UNCAPITALIZED:
• Dr. Dollar's bestseller, *Be Fat and Forget It* (*the* publisher decided on the title after a brainstorming session with his advertising staff), has freed millions of Americans from needless anxiety.

3. Many writers capitalize the first letter of a complete independent statement following a colon:

• Dr. Dollar faced this dilemma: *Should* he or shouldn't he appear on television and let people see that he only weighed 113 pounds?

(But *should* is also acceptable, and some commentators on usage would regard *Should* as incorrect.)

4. The first word of a quoted remark should be capitalized only if it introduces a complete sentence, or a fragment that functions as a complete sentence:

CAPITALIZED:
• Bessie told Max, "*There's* nothing like a good American cup of freeze-dried coffee."

UNCAPITALIZED:
• Bessie told Max that she didn't care what it tasted like, "*if* only they would make it hot."

Of course scholarly accuracy in quoting requires that capitals — as well as punctuation, spelling, and emphasis — appear as they do in the passage you are quoting from:

- Ben Jonson believed that *"Memory of all the powers of the mind, is the most delicate and fraile; it is the first of our faculties that Age invades."*

(Neither *Memory* nor *Age* would ordinarily be capitalized in the positions they occupy here, but the writer wants to reproduce Jonson's text exactly.)

- What Shelley considered immortal was "Thought/Alone, and its quick elements . . ."

(The capitals are found in Shelley's poem. Poetic quotations should always be rendered just as they appear, regardless of the sentences they are blended into.)

5. In citing titles in English, you should capitalize the opening letter of the first word, the last word, and other important words. If articles, conjunctions, and prepositions don't occur in the first or last positions, they are usually left in the lower case. But prepositions of more than five letters (*through*, for instance) are usually capitalized:

- *Dr. Dollar Raps with the Newborn*
- *Eternal Youthfulness Through Organ Transplants*

The same rules hold for subtitles in English. Note also that the first letter of a subtitle is uniformly capitalized:

- *Working Within the System: A Guide to Sewer Repair*

6. Names of people, places, and organizations are capitalized:

- Helen Gahagan Douglas
- Jerry Voorhis
- Whittier, California
- Hughes Tool Company
- Committee for the Re-election of the President

7. Specific events, movements, and periods are often known by capitalized names:

- the Bronze Age
- the Civil War
- the War Between the States
- the Romantic poets
- the Depression

8. Most adjectives derived from names are capitalized:

- Shakespearean
- American
- Maoist
- the French language

9. Days, months, and holidays are capitalized, but seasons usually aren't:

- next Tuesday
- May, 1975
- Christmas
- Columbus Day
- next winter

10. A rank or title is capitalized when joined to a name or when it stands for a specific person, but it is often left uncapitalized in other circumstances:

CAPITALIZED:
- *Captain* Howard Levy

UNCAPITALIZED:
- The *captain* was court-martialed for refusing to train Green Berets.

Note, however, that some high offices are uniformly capitalized: *the Queen of England, the President, Secretary of Defense, Chief Justice of the United States.* (There's no such office as *Chief Justice of the Supreme Court.*)

11. Organized groups and nationalities require capitals, but looser groupings don't:

CAPITALIZED:
- Christian
- Hungarian
- Republican
- Women for Peace

UNCAPITALIZED:
- the upper class
- the underprivileged
- the peace movement

12. Abbreviations after a name are usually capitalized: *M.A., Ph.D., M.D., Esq., U.S.N. (Ret.).* There is no consensus, however, as to whether *Jr., Sr., a.m.,* and *p.m.* require capitals.

13. Geographic directions are left uncapitalized, but specific places take capitals. When faced with a word like *northwest,* think

whether it refers in this case to a compass point (*northwest of here*) or to a fixed place or route (*Northwest Territories, Northwest Passage*).

CAPITALIZED:
* Southeast Asia
* the winning of the West

UNCAPITALIZED:
* southeast of Tucson
* go west until you meet the oily surf

14. Specific institutions are capitalized, and so are their formal subdivisions:

* Museum of Modern Art
* University of Chicago
* the Department of Business Administration
* Holy Names High School

Subsequent, shortened references to the institution or department are sometimes left uncapitalized:

* She retired from the *university* last year.

(But *University* would also be correct here.)
  Note that articles, brief prepositions, and conjunctions are left in the lower case, as they are in titles of publications.

15. Institutions meant in a general sense aren't capitalized:

* a strife-torn *museum*
* Every *university* is threatened by anarchy.
* His *department* fired him because the students were too fond of him.
* He dropped out of *high school* to give all his time to chess.

16. Sacred names are conventionally capitalized, whether or not the writer is a believer:

* the Old Testament
* the Bible
* God
* the Lord
* He, Him, His [pronouns of the Judeo-Christian deity]
* the Virgin Mary
* the Koran
* the Upanishads

17. Specific courses of study are capitalized, but general branches of learning aren't:

CAPITALIZED:
- Physics 1A
- Social Welfare 203

UNCAPITALIZED:
- He never learned the rudiments of *physics.*
- Her training in *social welfare* didn't prepare her for this.

18. Family relations should be capitalized only when they stand for a name or are part of a name:

CAPITALIZED:
- Everyone has seen posters of *Uncle Sam.*

UNCAPITALIZED:
- My *uncle Sam* was never the same man after the Dodgers moved to Los Angeles.

19. Sometimes a word has quite different meanings in its capitalized forms:

- The Pope is a *Catholic.* [He belongs to the Church.]
- Marjoe has *catholic* tastes. [His tastes are wide-ranging.]
- He became a *Democrat* after the President declared a national day of prayer for the Redskins. [He joined the party.]
- Tocqueville saw every American farmer as a *democrat.* [He believed that they all supported the idea of equality.]

ITALICS

Ordinary typeface is known as *roman*, and the thin, slightly slanted typeface that stands apart from it is called *italic* — as in *these words.* In manuscript or typescript, underlining is the equivalent of italic type. The conventional symbols *rom* and *ital*, when used in correction of a manuscript or typescript, mean respectively "do not underline" and "underline."

Italics are used for certain titles, foreign words, scientific names, names of ships, words considered *as* words, and words bearing a special rhetorical emphasis.

1. Titles of books, plays, films, newspapers, magazines, journals, and other works that form complete publications are usually italicized:

- *Esquire*
- *A Clockwork Orange*
- *Rosencrantz and Guildenstern Are Dead*
- the Philadelphia *Inquirer*
- *Paradise Lost*

Note that:

a. In the names of newspapers, the *place* of publication is usually left in roman type.
b. A single poem, if it happens to occupy a whole volume, is named in italics; if it is only part of the volume it is named in roman type, within quotation marks. This applies to the titles of chapters, essays, and short stories as well.
c. A work that was first published in a magazine may later be expanded into a whole book; or, if the book is itself a collection, it may bear the title of the story, article, or poem. Remember that when you print the title in italics (i.e., underline it on your typewriter) you are always referring to the complete volume, not to the item that gave the volume its title.
d. Newspapers and magazines have their own conventions for identifying titles. Some publications use italics sparingly or not at all. If you *know* that your writing will be printed by a given magazine or newspaper, follow its own rules. Student papers, scholarship, and writing that may be submitted to various publications should observe the rules given here.

2. Foreign words that have not yet been adopted as routine English expressions should be italicized:

- Dr. Dollar's *Weltanschauung* was a mixture of Dale Carnegie and Clifford Irving.
- After four bestsellers he was assured of *la dolce vita*.

But compare the following borrowed words, which are familiar enough to be printed in roman:

ad hoc	de facto
bourgeois	genre
cliché	junta
debutante	

Consult your dictionary for doubtful cases. Use foreign terms sparingly; they often sound affected.

3. Latin abbreviations are often italicized, but the tendency is now to leave them in roman. There's no need to italicize the following, for example:

c.f.	i.e.
e.g.	q.v.
et al.	viz.
f., ff.	vs.

(See pp. 335–336 for the meanings of these and other abbreviations.)

4. When translating foreign words, it's customary to put the foreign term in italics and the English one in quotation marks:

• The Italian term for "the book" is *il libro;* in French it is *le livre.*

(See also p. 292 for the use of single quotation marks in translation.)

5. Technical scientific names should be italicized:

• Don't mess around with the threadtailed stonefly (*Nemoura venosa*).

6. Names of ships are italicized: *Queen Elizabeth, Cristoforo Colombo.*

7. Words considered *as* words are often italicized:

• Bessie couldn't think of the Spanish word for *indigestion.*

Quotation marks serve this function equally well.

8. Italics can be used to impart emphasis to a word or group of words, but this device, if used too frequently, becomes a form of shouting. Try to resort to emphatic italics only when clarity demands them.

ABBREVIATIONS

In the main body of an essay you should avoid many abbreviations that would be perfectly acceptable in footnotes or in catalogs, bibliographies, business letters, recipes, and addresses. Of course some abbreviations are universal (*M.D.,* *a.m.*), but in more doubtful cases you should write out the word or phrase.

Abbreviations can look especially awkward when they stand alone:

- There were two famous Jameses, Henry and *Wm.*
- As the collection plate was being passed, the *Rev.* described how misers are everlastingly chained to the burning lake.

Here are some things that are customarily *not* abbreviated in essay prose, except in parenthetical citations that take the place of footnotes:

a. Titles: *the Reverend, the Honorable, Senator, President, General.*
b. Given names: *George, Richard, Martha.*
c. Months, days of the week, and holidays: *October, Monday, Christmas.*
d. Localities, cities, counties, states, and countries: *Point Reyes National Seashore, Philadelphia, Westchester, Alabama, Bangladesh.*
e. *Street, Lane, Avenue, Boulevard,* etc.
f. Courses of instruction: *Botany, Physical Education.*
g. Words preceding a figure: *number, page, chapter, volume.*
h. Units of measurement: *inches, meters, pounds, hours, pints.*

Exceptions: it's customary to use abbreviated units of measurement if they're preceded by figures (*986 m.p.h.*, but not *I want to know how many m.p.h.*); and certain places are commonly known by their abbreviated names (*U.S., D.C.*).

Some other abbreviations are considered standard for any type of writing:

a. *Mr., Mrs., Dr., Messrs., Mme., Mlle., St.,* etc., when used before names. Some publications now refer to all women as *Ms.*, and this abbreviation has rapidly gained favor as a means of avoiding designation of marital status.
b. *Jr., Sr., Esq., M.D., D.D., D.D.S., M.A., Ph. D., LL.D.,* etc., when used after names.
c. Abbreviations of, and acronyms for, organizations that are widely known by the shorter name: *CIA, FBI, ROTC, CARE, NATO, UNESCO,* etc. Note that very familiar designations such as these are usually written without periods between the letters.
d. *B.C., A.D., a.m., p.m.* These abbreviations should never be used apart from numbers (*in the p.m.*). *B.C.* always follows the year, but *A.D.* usually precedes it: *252 B.C.*, but *A.D. 147.*

Beware of redundancy in titles. You can write *Dr. Lincoln Dollar* or *Lincoln Dollar, M.D.*, but don't write *Dr. Lincoln Dollar, M.D.*, or *Mr. John Doe, Esq.* In American English *Esq.* is an affectation, anyway.

Abbreviations of complex technical terms, or of terms that will be used many times in one essay, can spare monotony. *ACTH* is better in every way than *adrenocorticotropic hormone*, provided it's been sufficiently identified. It's customary to give one full reference before relying only on the abbreviation:

- The best investment Dr. Dollar ever made was in Holiday International Tours (HIT). The corporate philosophy of HIT agreed with his own views in several respects.
- The Southeast Asia Treaty Organization (SEATO), formed for the mutual defense of national sovereignty, includes among its members Great Britain, France, and the United States. The circumstances under which SEATO came into being tell a good deal about its philosophy.

Here is a list of common abbreviations and their meanings. In general you should reserve the abbreviated forms for footnotes:

abbreviation	meaning
anon.	anonymous
b.	born
bibliog.	bibliography
©	Copyright
ca. or c.	about (with dates only)
cf.	compare (not *see*)
ch., chs.	chapter(s)
d.	died
diss.	dissertation
ed., eds.	editor(s), edition(s), edited by
e.g.	for example (not *that is*)
esp.	especially
et al.	and others (people only)
etc.	and so forth (not interchangeable with *et al.*)
f., ff.	and the following (page or pages)
ibid.	the same (title as the one mentioned in the previous note)
i.e.	that is (not *for example*)
introd.	introduction
l., ll.	line(s)
loc. cit.	in the place cited (in the same passage mentioned in a recent note)
MS, MSS	manuscript(s)
n., fn.	note, footnote
N.B.	mark well, take notice
n.d.	no date (in a book's imprint)
no., nos.	number(s)
op. cit.	in the work cited (in a recent note; but the page number here is different; cf. *loc. cit.*)
p., pp.	page(s)
pl., pls.	plate(s)
pref.	preface

abbreviation	meaning
pt., pts.	part(s)
q.v.	see elsewhere in this text (literally *which see*)
rev.	revised, revision; review, reviewed by (beware of ambiguity between meanings; if necessary, write out instead of abbreviating)
sc.	scene
sec., secs.; sect., sects.	section(s)
ser.	series
st., sts.	stanza(s)
trans.	translator, translation, translated by
viz.	namely
vol., vols.	volume(s)
vs.	verse, versus

Note that *passim*, meaning *throughout*, and *sic*, meaning *thus*, are full Latin words and are not followed by a period. (For the use and abuse of *sic*, see p. 288.)

When the letters of abbreviations are separated by periods (*M.D.*), no space should be left between the letters and the periods. The one exception is the initials of a name (*F. H. Bradley*).

NUMBERS

No universally applicable rules govern the choice between written-out numbers (*sixty-seven*) and figures (*67*). In scientific and technical writing, figures are generally preferred; newspapers customarily use figures for all numbers higher than ten; and in nontechnical books and journals, the usual rule is that figures are to be used only for numbers that can't be expressed in one or two words or a brief phrase. For your own essays, this last rule is the best one to follow. Thus you can write *forty-three pounds of lard*, but not *seventy-one dollars and twenty-eight cents ($71.28)*. There may be *eighteen counties* and *sixty-eight precincts* involved in an election, but the winning candidate's tally shouldn't be given as *two hundred ten thousand three hundred ninety-seven votes (210,397 votes)*.

Note, however, that a mixture of figures and written-out numbers can be confusing if they all refer to quantities of the same thing. If *any* figures are necessary in such circumstances, *all* the numbers should be expressed in figures:

- The initial orbit was 39–125 miles from the surface of the earth.
- The astronauts' heart rates varied between 55 and 120.
- It was later discovered that they had hidden between 25 and 347 trinkets in the capsule for later sale as souvenirs.

A number beginning a sentence should always be written out. But if the number is a long one, find a way of recasting the sentence so that the number comes later; then it can be stated as a figure.

Figures are regularly used for the following:

a. Apartment numbers, street numbers, and zip codes: *Apt. 17C, 544 Lowell Ave., Palo Alto, Ca. 94301.*
b. Tables of statistics.
c. Numbers containing decimals: *7.456, $6.58, 52.1 percent.*
d. Dates (except for extremely formal communications such as wedding announcements): *October 5, 1974; 5 October 1974; October 5th.*
e. Hours, when they precede a.m. or p.m.: *8 a.m., 12 p.m., 2:47 p.m.* Whole hours, unmodified by minutes, are usually written out before *o'clock, noon,* and *midnight: eight o'clock, twelve noon.* Don't write *twelve-thirty o'clock.*
f. Page numbers: *page 76, p. 76, pages 76–78, pp. 76–78.* All these forms are correct, but the abbreviated ones should be saved for footnotes and parenthetical references.
g. Volumes, books (e.g., of the Bible), acts, scenes, and lines. (See p. 370.)

Figures can be made plural by the addition of either *-s* or *-'s,* but the latter form is more common: *two 7's, many 10's.* Note that no apostrophe is used when the number is written out: *many tens.*

In general, the only reason for using Roman numerals (*XI, LVIII*) is that together with Arabic numerals (*11, 58*) they can distinguish one set of numbers from another. (See p. 370 for typical situations.) Lower-case Roman numerals are also used to indicate page numbers preceding the main text of a book (*Preface, p. xi*).

The following list will remind you how Roman numerals are formed:

1	I	10	X	50	L	200	CC
2	II	11	XI	60	LX	400	CD
3	III	15	XV	70	LXX	499	CDXCIX
4	IV	19	XIX	80	LXXX	500	D
5	V	20	XX	90	XC	900	CM
6	VI	21	XXI	99	XCIX	999	CMXCIX
7	VII	29	XXIX	100	C	1000	M
8	VIII	30	XXX	110	CX	1500	MD
9	IX	40	XL	199	CXCIX	3000	MMM

Numbers like *one, two,* and *three* (1, 2, and 3) are called cardinal numbers; numbers like *first, second,* and *third* (1st, 2nd, and 3rd) are called ordinal numbers. The choice between the cardinal and ordinal systems is usually a simple one, but differences between written and spoken usage do arise. You say *Louis the Fourteenth* but should write *Louis XIV;* you say *July seventh, 1962* but should write *July 7, 1962* or *7 July 1962.* When the year is omitted, however, you should write the date as an ordinal number: *July 7th* or, preferably, *July seventh.*

Note finally that ordinal numbers can serve as adverbs without the addition of *-ly:*

• Let me say, first, that . . . Second, . . .

The *-ly* forms aren't incorrect, but they're unnecessary. The only plainly wrong choice would be a mixture of forms: *Firstly, . . . Second, . . .*

EXERCISES

I. **Correct any errors of capitalization:**

1. Our most musical president was Harry Truman, who, after reading a review of one of his Daughter Margaret's concerts, threatened to beat up the critic.
2. Each year the Pelicans fly south to build their nests near the outfall pipe.
3. Realizing that her marriage was in trouble, Rose went straight to the lingerie department and asked if she could try on a Freudian slip.
4. She wondered Whether it was really necessary for the management to frisk people who lingered near the meat counter.
5. Stanley believed that the People, guided by himself and a few trusted friends, knew more about their true interests than any politician did.
6. Above the Sun and Moon (So the natives believed) lay a god who had been suffering from heartburn for a thousand years.
7. Harry was always hoping they would turn world war two into a movie.
8. It was in home economics 145 that she learned the difference between a pancake and a waffle.
9. For Christmas Rose gave her Mother doctor Dollar's latest volume, *Wit And Wisdom For The Terminal Patient.*
10. Bobo's idea of summer fun was to drain a trout stream so that there would be plenty of fish for the whole gang.
11. If you really want to learn Economics, make sure that you take your courses at a college with a large endowment.
12. She thought she had mailed the letter Last Tuesday.

13. Many sunday-school students have thanked the lord that the New Testament isn't any longer than it is.

II. Correct any errors in the use of italics, abbreviations, and numbers:

1. Most drunk drivers would find it difficult to count backward from 135 to twenty-one by threes.
2. He had only one reason for not wanting to ride—e.g., he was afraid of horses.
3. 40 dollars will buy an adequate dinner for 1 at that restaurant.
4. Four six'es are twenty-four.
5. The attack was planned for precisely 7:42 o'clock.
6. "Gone with the Wind" was the film that introduced profane language to the Hollywood screen.
7. Alimony was never an issue for the ex-wives of king Henry the VIIIth.
8. *The Falmouth Enterprise* is a typical small-town newspaper.
9. You can still get a sporty sedan, fully equiped with roll bars, seat belts, impact-absorbing bumpers, and collision insurance, for three thousand eight hundred forty-four dollars.
10. Melody thought that *A Midsummer Night's Dream* was the most realistic play she had ever seen.
11. She made an appointment with Dr. Calvin Gold, D.D.S.
12. The Titanic at its launching was the world's largest, and soon thereafter the world's wettest, ocean liner.
13. Over the loudspeaker came an urgent and repeated request for a dr.
14. Criminals are treated leniently in Rome if they committed their offenses during the scirocco, the hot, dry wind that supposedly makes people behave irrationally.

III. The following paragraph contains errors in the use or absence of capitals, italics, abbreviations, and numbers. Find the errors and correct them:

Dennis Barlow is the Hero of "the Loved One," a novel by the British author Evelyn Waugh. Dennis works for a Los Angeles Pet Mortuary called *the Happier Hunting Ground.* On the Anniversary of each dog's death he mails a card assuring the bereaved owner that the animal "Is thinking of you in heaven today and wagging his tail." The novel acquires a Romantic interest when Dennis meets *Aimée* Thanatogenos, a cosmetician at whispering glades memorial park. Whispering glades (Founded by a Doctor Wilbur Kenworthy, known as the Dreamer) is a lavish cemetery exploiting various *clichés* of western civilization: The Poetry of Homer and Burns, Rodin's sculpture, tiny scottish churches, the Lake Isle of Innisfree, *etc.* At 1st *Aimée* thinks that Dennis is l'essence of everything that is meant by the term cultivated, but later she discovers that all his Love Poems have been plagiarized from the Oxford Book of English Verse. Yet she cannot bring herself to marry her other suitor, Mister Joyboy, and in despair she kills herself in Mister Joyboy's laboratory, where she had once hoped to study Embalming. As a favor to his ex-rival, Dennis secretly cremates the body at the Pet Mortuary. Every Spring thereafter, Mister Joyboy will receive a memorial card: "your little *Aimée* is wagging her tail in heaven tonight, thinking of you."

THE RESEARCH PAPER

USING 13 THE LI- BRARY

GETTING ACQUAINTED

Few people feel altogether at home in a library, with its several systems of classification, its various catalogs and special rooms, its rules and privileges, its imposing tiers of stacks and their busy-looking habitués. It's hard to believe that this labyrinth is there for your convenience and enlightenment. Beyond the worry that you won't be able to track down what others have written about your topic lies another worry that the sources *will* turn up and anticipate or demolish what you were going to say. Half-deliberately, then, many people imagine that the library is impenetrable. Rather than risk unpleasant surprises, they stay home and put an excessive reliance on the few sources that happen to come to their notice.

This attitude is self-defeating. Although there's such a thing as irrational perfectionism (p. 26), there's no such thing as being too well-informed to write. The more you read, the more developed your thoughts will be; and the reading will provide you with rhetorical opportunities to support your case or to contrast it with others. The embarrassment of having to revise one of your ideas is very slight compared to the embarrassment of learning, too late, that you've written an ambitious paper in ignorance of important, easily accessible sources.

There's no need to master the whole library at once. Most libraries offer free tours and explanatory pamphlets, and there are people on hand at any time — most notably the reference librarian — whose business is to make knowledge available to you. (In fact, a reference librarian will often locate, not only a book or journal, but the one fact you're looking for.) By involving yourself in a specific research project and asking for help whenever you're confused, you can become familiar with certain aspects of the library while leaving others for later.

In essence the library is a vast information-retrieval system. As with a computer, the knack of using it successfully consists in knowing the right questions to present it with. Rummaging through the stacks without any questions at all would be as senseless as fishing blindly in the computer's memory bank. You have to know at least some of the overlapping ways in which sources can be found, and you have to keep narrowing your search as you get a clearer and clearer idea of the way your project is developing.

As you do more research, you'll gradually develop a better sense of the difference between a promising lead and a blind alley. The majority of available books on any topic, you'll find, have already been superseded by others; the more recent the work, the more eager you should be to lay hands on it. This is doubly true because an up-to-date work may contain a selective bibliography — a list of key books and articles for further reference — that can save you many hours of scrounging and many mistakes of judgment. An experienced researcher doesn't have to run through *all* the types of information-seeking described in the following pages; he finds a few key works as early as he can and then allows those works to guide his further moves. The writer of the sample paper on pp. 379–395, for example, consulted his library's card catalog and then an index of book reviews to discover four recent and important studies of W. C. Fields, which led him to his thesis.

LIBRARY RESOURCES

These are the main tools for acquiring information and learning which works on a given subject are important:

The Card Catalog

The card catalog is an alphabetical index of the library's printed holdings, usually including books, periodicals, pamphlets, and items on microfilm (but excluding manuscripts, phonograph records, and tapes). Most libraries use the dictionary form of catalog, in which items are cross-indexed (that is, listed under more than one heading) by author, subject, and title. Thus, one way of beginning to find the relevant materials for your project is to go directly to the subject heading in the card catalog: Flood Control, Magic, etc. In many libraries the author and title cards are kept in one catalog and the subject cards in another.

The most important piece of information on a card is the *call number* in the upper left corner, for this is the key to the book's location in the stacks. Whether you enter the stacks yourself or merely submit a call slip, this number is your way of obtaining the book. Small libraries sometimes have their own systems of numbering, but large ones follow either the *Dewey Decimal System* or the *Library of Congress System* of classification. In the Dewey Decimal System, the first three digits of the call number will be a figure from 1 to 999, grouped as follows:

000 General Works	400 Language	700 The Arts
100 Philosophy	500 Pure Sciences	800 Literature
200 Religion	600 Technology	900 History
300 Social Sciences		

In the Library of Congress System, the call number begins with a key letter:

A	General Works
B	Philosophy—Religion
C	Auxiliary Sciences of History
D	History and Topography (except America)
E–F	American History
G	Geography—Anthropology
H	Social Sciences
J	Political Science
K	Law
L	Education
M	Music
N	Fine Arts
P	Language and Literature
Q	Science
R	Medicine
S	Agriculture—Plant and Animal Industry
T	Technology
U	Military Science
V	Naval Science
Z	Bibliography and Library Science

If you have "stack privileges" and are familiar with your library's code of classification, you can go directly to the shelves and quickly check a large number of volumes. Examine their indexes and introductions to see if they deal with the problem you have in mind. Remember, though, that the more important books are likely to be in circulation, and that you won't even learn of their existence if browsing is your only method of research.

The card catalog itself provides several kinds of useful information. Here, for example, is a representative card from a library using the Library of Congress System:

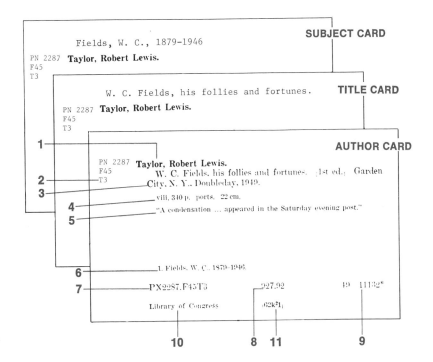

1. Author's name.
2. Call number indicating where in the library this book is shelved.
3. Title of book, number of edition, place of publication, publisher's name, and year of publication.
4. Format of book: "viii, 340 p." means that there are eight preliminary pages which are numbered in Roman numerals and are followed by 340 pages numbered in Arabic numerals; "ports." indicates that the book contains portraits; "22 cm." reveals the size of the book in centimeters.
5. Cataloger's note supplying information unique to the contents of this book.
6. Lists the subject heading under which the book is classified (see subject card above).
7. Library of Congress call number for the book.
8. Dewey Decimal System call number for the book.
9. Order number used by libraries when ordering the catalog card for this book.
10. Signifies that a copy of this book can be found in the Library of Congress.
11. Printer's key for this card.

Note that by glancing at the card you can learn which publishing house issued the book, which edition your library possesses, how recent it is, its length, and whether it contains special materials such as a bibliography. All these facts could help you decide whether you want to look at the book itself.

Once in a while you may come across a reference to an apparently indispensable book that isn't listed in your library's catalog. As there are some sixty thousand new volumes published each year in English alone, you can see that no library but the Library of Congress itself could acquire more than a minority of them. You can get essential information about the book's author, title, publisher, and date from the *National Union Catalog*, which reproduces the Library of Congress Catalog and includes titles from other libraries as well. If you can't visit a library that has the book, you can probably borrow it through *interlibrary loan* arrangement. The same holds for journals as well. By consulting the *Union List of Serials in Libraries of the United States and Canada* you can discover which libraries own sets of hard-to-find journals.

Indexes

Indexes, in the bibliographic sense of the term, are periodically issued lists of publications (usually articles). Of all indexes, the most useful for general purposes is the *Reader's Guide to Periodical Literature*, which gives references for articles in about 135 magazines. A typical column of the *Reader's Guide* looks like this:

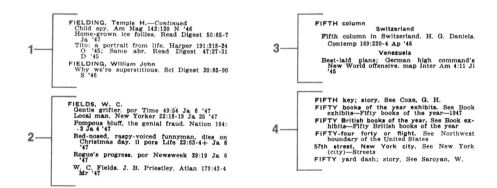

Here you see:

1. *Entries by authors.* The first entry under *Fielding, Temple,* for instance, is an article called "Child Spy" published in *The American Magazine,* volume 142, November 1946, page 120.
2. *Entries about a person.*
3. *Entries about subjects.*
4. *Cross-indexing* (references to entries elsewhere in the index) *by subject and title.*

Another central resource is *Book Review Digest,* which locates reviews of current books and summarizes the consensus, if any, about each book's merit. You can use the *Digest* to discover which books, among several you might want to use, are considered most reliable, and if you want to read a full review you can look it up. Here is a typical entry:

TAYLOR, ROBERT LEWIS. W. C. Fields; his follies and fortunes. 340p pl $3.50 Doubleday

B or 92 Fields, William Claude

A life of W. C. Fields which shows that his private life was as eccentric as that of any comic character he portrayed on stage and screen.

Atlantic 184:86 O '49 240w

Booklist 46:81 N 1 '49

Reviewed by Herman Kogan
Chicago Sun O 18 '49 600w

Reviewed by Horace Reynolds
Christian Science Monitor p15 N 10 '49 420w

Cleveland Open Shelf p22 D '49

"Taylor doesn't soft-pedal but neither does he mud-sling, and his account of his subject's life has a distinct love and understanding of such a difficult figure, and makes the most of the wry, biting humor that was part of Fields' life. Not as well written, perhaps, as the Gene Fowler books, but of a definite interest to all theater and moving picture fans."
+ — Kirkus 17:417 Ag 1 '49 160w

"Highly recommended." George Freedley
+ Library J 74:1605 O 15 '49 70w

"Mr. Robert Lewis Taylor has done a fine job. His book is more than a biography, more than a character study: it is also a cross-section of the entertainment world during the last half-century. Evidently, there is here a work of loving devotion: it abounds in reminiscences, in details, in anecdotes which could only have been garnered by patient inquiry and research. What is perhaps even rarer, it succeeds in giving a really vital impression of the exceptional personality which it commemorates." Iris Barry
+ N Y Herald Tribune Wkly Bk R pl O 2 '49 1250w

"Robert Lewis Taylor has written a hilarious history of the fabulous comedian, written it with understanding, sympathy and a gay respect for the scandalous facts involved." Richard Maney
+ N Y Times p4 O 2 '49 900w

"Mr. Taylor has tried to keep his account coherent while never neglecting the laughs, and he has undoubtedly done as good a job as can be done."
+ New Yorker 25:107 O 8 '49 200w

"His memory is so beloved of his fans that they would no more brook an author who treats him clumsily than Tiffany's would entrust its diamond-cutting to a blacksmith. Taylor, fortunately, is a skilled literary lapidary. The gems of Fields' comical exploits are neatly cut and polished in his hands. There are flaws, nonetheless. One is inherent in the original material. That is to say, in Fields' own exaggerations of fact and in the misty memories of his friends, enemies and relatives. . . . If the book lacks accuracy, however, it never lacks entertainment, and we heartily commend it to anyone the least bit interested in reading of one of the most fabulous figures who ever lived." Luther Nichols
+ San Francisco Chronicle p26 O 16 '49 1400w

"Mr. Taylor has written a careful, detailed and exhaustive chronicle of the great man and his work, leaving little out and going about his task with zeal and determination. In addition, he had the valuable aid of the notes and advice of Gene Fowler, an old and understanding friend of the eminent comic." Richard Watts
+ Sat R of Lit 32:26 O 22 '49 800w

Time 54:108 O 17 '49 600w

If your project deals with recent public events or issues, the first place to look for facts is in the *New York Times Index,* which can lead you to news items and articles of commentary in that newspaper.

When a research problem takes you into a narrow area, you may need an index geared to that specialty. The index in turn will lead you to journals devoted entirely to the field you're working in, and some of these journals contain annual bibliographies. Thus an index, even if it doesn't contain exactly the items you want, will usually put you on their trail.

Here are some commonly used indexes and the periods they cover:

Applied Science and Technology Index (1913 – date)
Art Index (1929 – date)
Bibliographic Index (1938 – date)
Biography Index (1947 – date)
Book Review Digest (1905 – date)
Book Review Index (1965 – date)
Dramatic Index (1909 – 1949)
Education Index (1929 – date)
Index to the Times [London] (1906 – date)
Monthly Catalog of United States Government Publications (1895 – date)
Music Index (1949 – date)
New York Times Index (1913 – date)
Poole's Index to Periodical Literature (1802 – 1907)
Public Affairs Information Service (1915 – date)
Reader's Guide to Periodical Literature (1900 – date)
Social Sciences and Humanities Index (1907 – date)

Booksellers' Bibliographies

If you know an author's name but not the title of his book; if you have the title but don't know the author; if you want to see whether new books on a certain topic appeared in a certain year; if you want to know whether a book is still in print, or has appeared in a paperback edition; then you should consult one of the following:

Books in Print (1948 – date)
Cumulative Book Index (1898 – date)
Paperbound Books in Print (1955 – date)
Subject Guide to Books in Print (1957 – date)

Guides to Reference Works

Reference works — that is, books that survey a field and tell you how to find materials within that field — are now so numerous that you may need to consult an even more general book that lists reference works and explains their scope:

Mary Neill Barton and Marion V. Bell, *Reference Books: A Brief Guide*, 7th ed. (1970)

The Bibliographic Index (1937 – date)

Saul Galin and Peter Spielberg, *Reference Books: How to Select and Use Them* (1969)

Jean Kay Gates, *Guide to the Use of Books and Libraries*, 2nd ed. (1969)

Louis Shores, *Basic Reference Sources: An Introduction to Materials and Methods* (1954)

Raymond H. Shove et al., *The Use of Books and Libraries*, 10th ed. (1963)

Constance M. Winchell, *Guide to Reference Books*, 8th ed. (1967)

A World Bibliography of Bibliographies, 4th ed., 5 vols. (1965 – 1966)

Of these works, the most widely used is Constance Winchell's *Guide to Reference Books*. By going to this volume and looking up your field of interest, you can quickly see which are the important reference works and what their scope is. This is also an excellent way of finding indexes and bibliographies that are even more specialized than the ones listed in the present chapter.

General Encyclopedias

An up-to-date edition of a general encyclopedia can provide initial orientation to a field or problem and a limited amount of bibliographic guidance. See especially:

Chambers's Encyclopaedia, 15 vols.
Collier's Encyclopedia, 24 vols.
Columbia Encyclopedia, 1 vol.
Encyclopaedia Britannica, 24 vols.
Encyclopedia Americana, 30 vols.

Special Encyclopedias, Reference Works, Handbooks, and General Histories

If you want to locate more facts about a field than you could find in a general encyclopedia article, you can consult a work that surveys the field or a significant portion of it. Such books are helpful both for locating a technical or historical fact and for acquiring a sense of the whole field before working on narrow problems.

The following titles are arranged by field:

art   Mary W. Chamberlain, *Guide to Art Reference Books* (1959)

Encyclopedia of World Art, 15 vols. (1959 –   )

Larousse Encyclopedia of Byzantine and Medieval Art (1963)

Larousse Encyclopedia of Modern Art (1965)

Larousse Encyclopedia of Prehistoric and Ancient Art, rev. ed. (1966)

Bernard S. Myers, ed., *Encyclopedia of Painting* (1955)

——, ed., *McGraw-Hill Dictionary of Art* (1969)

The Praeger Picture Encyclopedia of Art (1958)

business and economics

Douglas Greenwald, *The McGraw-Hill Dictionary of Modern Economics* (1965)

Byrne J. Horton et al., *Dictionary of Modern Economics* (1948)

Marian Manley, *Business Information: How to Find and Use It* (1955)

G. G. Munn, *Encyclopedia of Banking and Finance*, 6th ed. (1962)

Harold S. Sloan and Arnold J. Zurcher, *A Dictionary of Economics*, 5th ed. (1970)

drama

Blanche M. Baker, *Theatre and Allied Arts: A Guide to Books Dealing with the History, Criticism, and Technic of the Drama and Theatre and Related Arts and Crafts* (1952)

Estelle A. Fidell and D. M. Peake, eds., *Play Index* (1949–1967)

Alfred Harbage, *Annals of English Drama, 975–1700*, rev. S. Schoenbaum (1964)

Phyllis Hartnoll, *The Oxford Companion to the Theatre*, 3rd ed. (1967)

education

Carter Alexander and A. J. Burke, *How to Locate Educational Information and Data*, 4th ed. (1958)

Encyclopedia of Educational Research, 3rd ed. (1960)

International Yearbook of Education (1948–date)

UNESCO, *World Survey of Education* (1955–date)

folklore and mythology

Sir James G. Frazer, *The Golden Bough: A Study in Magic and Religion*, 12 vols. (1907–1915; suppl. 1936, 1955)

Funk and Wagnalls Standard Dictionary of Folklore, Mythology and Legend, 2 vols. (1949–1950)

Louis H. Gray, ed., *The Mythology of All Races* (1916–1932; rpt. 1964)

Larousse Encyclopedia of Mythology, rev. ed. (1968)

Larousse World Mythology (1965)

history

James Truslow Adams, ed., *Dictionary of American History*, 2nd ed., 6 vols. (1942–1963)

Henry P. Beers, *Bibliographies in American History* (1942)

The Cambridge Ancient History, 3rd ed. (1970–1971)

The Cambridge Medieval History, 8 vols. (1911–1936)

The Cambridge Modern History, 14 vols. (1902–1926)

Oscar Handlin et al., eds., *Harvard Guide to American History* (1954)

William L. Langer, *An Encyclopedia of World History*, 5th ed. (1972)

Richard B. Morris, *Encyclopedia of American History*, rev. ed. (1970)

literature   Richard D. Altick and Andrew Wright, *Selective Bibliography for the Study of English and American Literature*, 4th ed. (1971)

Fernand Baldensperger and Werner P. Friederich, *Bibliography of Comparative Literature* (1950)

Donald F. Bond, *A Reference Guide to English Studies*, 2nd ed. (1971)

English Association, *The Year's Work in English Studies* (1919–date)

James D. Hart, *The Oxford Companion to American Literature*, 4th ed. (1965)

Sir Paul Harvey, *The Oxford Companion to Classical Literature* (1937)

————, *The Oxford Companion to English Literature*, 4th ed. (1967)

Lillian H. Hornstein, ed., *The Reader's Companion to World Literature* (1956)

Stanley J. Kunitz and Howard Haycraft, *Twentieth Century Authors* (1942; suppl. 1955)

MHRA [Modern Humanities Research Association] , *Annual Bibliography of English Language and Literature* (1921–date)

PMLA [*Publications of the Modern Language Association of America*], *International Bibliography* (1922–date)

Horatio Smith, ed., *Columbia Dictionary of Modern European Literature* (1947)

S. H. Steinberg, ed., *Cassell's Encyclopaedia of Literature*, 2 vols. (1953)

music   Willi Apel, *Harvard Dictionary of Music*, 2nd ed. (1969)

Theodore Baker, *Biographical Dictionary of Musicians*, 5th ed., rev. Nicolas Slonimsky (1958)

Sir George Grove, *Dictionary of Music and Musicians*, ed. Eric Blom, 5th ed., 10 vols. (1955; suppl. 1961)

The New Oxford History of Music, 10 vols. (1954–   )

Percy A. Scholes, *The Oxford Companion to Music*, 10th ed. (1970)

Oscar Thompson, *International Cyclopedia of Music and Musicians*, 9th ed., rev. Robert Sabin (1964)

Jack A. Westrup and F. L. Harrison, *The New College Encyclopedia of Music* (1960)

philosophy   James M. Baldwin, *Dictionary of Philosophy and Psychology*, 3 vols. (1901–1905; rev. ed. 1925; rpt. 1960)

Frederick C. Copleston, *A History of Philosophy*, 8 vols. (1947–1966)

Paul Edwards, ed., *The Encyclopedia of Philosophy*, 8 vols. (1967)

Bertrand Russell, *A History of Western Philosophy* (1945)

J. O. Urmson, ed., *The Concise Encyclopedia of Western Philosophy and Philosophers* (1960)

psychology   Horace B. and Ava C. English, *A Comprehensive Dictionary of Psychological and Psychoanalytical Terms* (1958)

Alexander Grinstein, *The Index of Psychoanalytic Writings* (1956–date)

Philip L. Harriman, ed., *Encyclopedia of Psychology* (1946)

religion John Graves Barrow, *A Bibliography of Bibliographies in Religion* (1955)

The Catholic Encyclopedia, 16 vols. (1913; suppl. 1917)

F. L. Cross, ed., *The Oxford Dictionary of the Christian Church* (1958)

John W. Ellison, comp., *Nelson's Complete Concordance of the Revised Standard Version Bible* (1957)

H. A. R. Gibb and J. H. Kramers, eds., *Shorter Encyclopaedia of Islam* (1953)

James Hastings, *Dictionary of the Bible*, rev. Frederick C. Grant and H. H. Rowley (1963)

Isaac Landman et al., eds., *The Universal Jewish Encyclopedia*, 10 vols. (1939–1948)

Herbert G. May et al., *The Oxford Bible Atlas* (1962)

The New Catholic Encyclopedia, 15 vols. (1967)

Cecil Roth, ed., *The Standard Jewish Encyclopedia*, rev. ed. (1962)

Robert C. Zaehner, ed., *The Concise Encyclopedia of Living Faiths* (1959)

science and technology C. W. and Hazel C. Besserer, *Guide to the Space Age* (1959)

International Encyclopedia of Chemical Science (1964)

Frances B. Jenkins, *Science Reference Sources*, 5th ed. (1969)

McGraw-Hill Encyclopedia of Science and Technology, 15 vols., 3rd ed. (1971)

Walter C. Michels, ed., *The International Dictionary of Physics and Electronics*, 2nd ed. (1961)

George E. Speck and Bernard Jaffe, eds., *A Dictionary of Science Terms* (1965)

C. F. Tweney and L. E. C. Hughes, eds., *Chambers's Technical Dictionary*, 3rd ed. (1958)

Universal Encyclopedia of Mathematics (1964)

Van Nostrand's Scientific Encyclopedia, 4th ed. (1968)

social and political science Jack A. Clarke, *Research Materials in the Social Sciences* (1959)

Henry Pratt Fairchild, ed., *Dictionary of Sociology* (1944)

Bert F. Hoselitz, ed., *A Reader's Guide to the Social Sciences*, rev. ed. (1970)

Jack C. Plano and Milton Greenberg, *The American Political Dictionary*, 2nd ed. (1967)

E. R. A. Seligman and Alvin Johnson, eds., *Encyclopaedia of the Social Sciences*, 15 vols. (1930–1934)

David L. Sills, ed., *International Encyclopedia of the Social Sciences*, 17 vols. (1968)

Edward C. Smith and Arnold J. Zurcher, eds., *Dictionary of American Politics*, 2nd ed. (1968)

Walter Theimer, *An Encyclopedia of Modern World Politics* (1950)

John T. Zadrozny, *Dictionary of Social Science* (1959)

Almanacs, Yearbooks, and Compilations of Facts

These volumes can be consulted for miscellaneous facts and statistics:

The Americana Annual (1923–date)
Britannica Book of the Year (1938–date)
Collier's Yearbook (1939–date)
Facts on File (1940–date)
Information Please Almanac (1947–date)
The New York Times Encyclopedic Almanac (1970–date)
The Statesman's Year-Book (1864–date)
Statistical Abstract of the United States (1878–date)
The World Almanac and Book of Facts (1868–date)
Year Book of World Affairs (1947–date)

Atlases and Gazetteers

Geographical knowledge can be located in:

Encyclopaedia Britannica World Atlas (1959)
National Geographic Atlas of the World, 3rd ed. (1970)
R. R. Palmer, ed., *Atlas of World History* (1957)
Leon E. Seltzer, ed., *The Columbia Lippincott Gazetteer of the World* (1962)
William R. Shepherd, ed., *Historical Atlas*, 9th ed. (1964)
The Times Atlas of the World, rev. ed. (1968)

Dictionaries

Dictionaries that you should consider owning for everyday reference are discussed on p. 61. For research into the origins and changing meanings of words, see:

A. J. Bliss, *A Dictionary of Foreign Words and Phrases in Current English* (1966)

Sir William A. Craigie and James R. Hulbert, eds., *A Dictionary of American English*, 4 vols. (1938–1944)

S. I. Hayakawa, *Modern Guide to Synonyms and Related Words* (1969)

Ernest Klein, *A Comprehensive Etymological Dictionary of the English Language*, 2 vols. (1966–1967)

A New English Dictionary on Historical Principles (also called *The Oxford English Dictionary*), 12 vols. and suppl. (1888–1933)

C. T. Onions, *The Oxford Dictionary of English Etymology* (1966)

Eric Partridge, *A Dictionary of Slang and Unconventional English*, 2 vols., 6th ed. (1967)

————, *Origins: A Short Etymological Dictionary of Modern English*, 4th ed. (1966)

Webster's New Dictionary of Synonyms (1968)

Harold Wentworth and Stuart B. Flexner, *Dictionary of American Slang* (1967)

Biography

Names can be identified and lives studied in the following:

Chambers's Biographical Dictionary, ed. J. O. Thorne, rev. ed. (1968)

Current Biography (1940–date)

Dictionary of American Biography, 22 vols. (1928–1958)

Albert M. Hyamson, *A Dictionary of Universal Biography of All Ages and of All Peoples*, 2nd ed. (1951)

International Who's Who (1935–date)

National Cyclopaedia of American Biography (1893–   )

Leslie Stephen and Sidney Lee, eds., *Dictionary of National Biography* [British], 63 vols. (1885–1901); reissued 22 vols. (1908–1909; suppl. to 1963)

Webster's Biographical Dictionary (1971)

Who's Who [British] (1849–date)

Who's Who in America (1899–date)

Quotations

Your best hope of tracking down an unattributed quotation lies with one of these sourcebooks:

John Bartlett and E. M. Beck, *Familiar Quotations*, 14th ed. (1968)

Bruce Bohle, *The Home Book of American Quotations* (1967)

Bergen Evans, *Dictionary of Quotations* (1968)

H. L. Mencken, *A New Dictionary of Quotations* (1942)

The Oxford Dictionary of Quotations, 2nd ed. (1953)

William G. Smith, *The Oxford Dictionary of English Proverbs*, 2nd ed., rev. Sir Paul Harvey (1957)

Burton E. Stevenson, ed., *The Home Book of Quotations, Classical and Modern*, 10th ed. (1967)

TAKING NOTES FROM READING

A typical library book or journal will be available to you for a few hours or days or weeks, depending on its importance to other borrowers. When you try to get it again you may find that it's on loan to someone else, or sent to the bindery, or even misplaced or stolen. Thus you have to be sure to get everything you need from the work on your first try, and your notes must be clear and full enough to be your direct source when you compose. Although it's always a good idea to keep the work before you and recheck it for accurate quotation and fair summary, you should assume that this won't be possible. Your notes should contain all the information neccessary for full references in your footnotes (pp. 360–370) and bibliography (pp. 370–372), and you should be quite certain that the notes are error-free before you let the book or article out of your hands. (For advice about finding a topic and thesis, organizing an essay, writing a first draft, and revising, see Chapter Two.)

Notes from reading, then, ought to be handled systematically to minimize the chance of error. Here are some tips about form:

1. Put all your notes on cards or sheets of equal size, for easy filing and rearranging (but see item 14 below).
2. Write in ink. Pencilled notes smudge when pressed against other notes.
3. Never put entries from different sources on one card or page, and never write on the back. Otherwise you will probably lose track of some of your work.
4. Include the call number of any book or magazine you've found in the library. You never know when you may want to retrieve it for another look.
5. Quote exactly, including the punctuation marks in the original, and check each quotation as soon as you've copied it.
6. Use quotation marks only when you're actually quoting verbatim, and check to see that the marks begin and end exactly where they should.
7. Be attentive to oddities of spelling and punctuation in quoted material. If, for instance, the original text omits a comma that you would have included, you can place a bracketed [sic], meaning *this is the way I found it*, at the questionable point in your notes; this will remind you not to improve the quotation illegitimately when reproducing it in your essay. But don't retain the [sic] unless it refers to an obvious blunder.
8. Supply page references for all quotations, paraphrases, and summaries.
9. Don't allow any ambiguities in your system of abbreviations. If two of your symbols mean the same thing, change one of them.
10. Distinguish between your own comments and those of the text you're summarizing. Slashes, brackets, or your initials can be used as signals that the following remarks are yours, not those of the author.
11. When copying a passage that runs from one page to another, mark where the first page ends: "*The district attorney is a vigilant enemy of crime in the / sheets*" (pp. 34–35). If you finally quote

only a portion of the excerpt in your paper, you'll want to know where it ended in the original.

12. Use a portion of the card or page to evaluate the material and to remind yourself of possibilities for further study. You might say, for example, *This looks useless—but reconsider chapter 13 if discussing astrology.*

13. Leave some space in the margin or at the top for an indexing symbol.

14. You may want to follow the practice of most researchers, who keep bibliography cards (usually 3 × 5″) in one system and content notes (usually 4 × 6″) in another. This enables them to see at a glance which works they've covered, and to avoid duplicating the bibliographic information when taking several separate notes from one source.

A typical bibliography card might look like this:

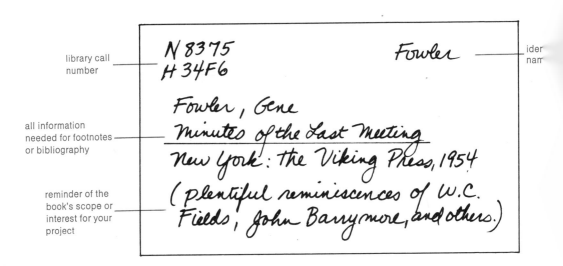

library call number

identifier name

all information needed for footnotes or bibliography

reminder of the book's scope or interest for your project

N 8375
H 34F6

Fowler

Fowler, Gene
Minutes of the Last Meeting
New York: the Viking Press, 1954
(plentiful reminiscences of W.C.
Fields, John Barrymore, and others.)

And a brief content note might look like this:

page reference — *Fowler, p. 103*

indexing key — *Cynical Realism*

context of quotation —

Remark after someone complained that an aspect of his will would make him "misunderstood and much disliked":

quotation —

" ' I've always been misunderstood,' he rasped. 'Besides, did you ever hear of a corpse complaining of unpopularity ?' "

personal comment —

(Not bad for illustrating Fields' morbid, sardonic quality. Cf. p. 223 – ref. to coffin vaults as "hope chests.")

EXERCISES

I. Describe how you would undertake library research on each of the following topics:

    a. The reception of Norman Mailer's book, *Marilyn*.

    b. Should abortions be automatically granted on demand?

    c. Pickett's Charge.

    d. How the Alaska Pipeline was approved.

    e. Recent advances in semiconductor memory systems for computers.

    f. The development of logical positivism.

    g. Beethoven's reputation today.

    h. Beethoven's childhood.

    i. The origin and evolving meaning of the word *wit* in English.

    j. Who wrote the line, "The proper study of mankind is man"?

II. Begin working on project b above. Copy out references to four *articles* you would read if you were to continue the project. Make your references full enough (including call numbers) so that the articles could be precisely located in the library.

III. Compile a bibliography (pp. 370–372) consisting of three recent *books* and three recent *articles* about the presidency of Franklin D. Roosevelt. Briefly state how you located the items.

IV. Acquire one of the items in Exercise III from your library, and make a sample *bibliography card* (p. 356) for it. Then write two *content notes* (pp. 356–357) about one passage. In the first note, *quote* the passage; in the second one, *summarize* it.

DOCUMEN14TATION

ACKNOWLEDGING YOUR SOURCES

Why Document?

For many people *footnotes* is a dirty word. When they see that a book or essay has abundant notes, they turn against it in advance. Surely the author must be "the footnote type," namely a person who hides behind his supposed objectivity, insisting on factual knowledge at the expense of feeling and opinion. Being at once dry, timid, and fastidious, the footnote looks like the perfect medium of communication for pedants. By despising footnotes in general, people sometimes believe that they're casting a vote for life itself.

This belief is partly a mental trick, a shielding of the ego against the humiliating assault of other people's learning. Yet there *is* such a vice as footnote-mongering. Footnotes can be used to fake, to boast, to sneer, and to filibuster. Writers who feel insecure about

360

their ideas sometimes develop a way of documenting every assertion, as if to turn to an authority after each sentence and ask, "Now didn't you tell me that?" Writers who can't handle their hostility sometimes demote it to footnotes, where they carry on savage quarrels with real and imagined opponents while their main text skips pleasantly along. Still others put their most challenging and important thoughts into footnotes, where they may seem less vulnerable to attack. The effect in all these cases — and the effect is at least half intended — is to keep readers from coming directly to grips with the argument.

But this says nothing about the usual and proper function of footnotes, which is to provide guidance for those who want it. If you as a writer have succeeded in provoking a reader's curiosity, he may wish to look at the books and articles you consulted — and to judge their reliability for himself. If your sources are reputable ones, your notes will not only render a service and pay a debt, but strengthen the effect of your essay as well. Any reader is bound to be more impressed by a reference to a standard work than by a claim that might, for all he knows, have been invented for the purpose of getting you out of a tight spot.

Plagiarism

There's another reason for providing documentation, and that is to avoid plagiarism — the taking of others' thoughts and ideas without acknowledgment. In theory a reader should be able to use your notes to track down all your borrowings and see whether you've handled them scrupulously, quoting and summarizing accurately and showing exactly where your own ideas end and someone else's ideas begin. In practice, of course, hardly anyone would be interested in checking your work so thoroughly. But the point of avoiding plagiarism isn't to escape being caught at it, but to refrain from being dishonest.

Sometimes a writer will commit unknowing plagiarism as a result of sloppy notetaking (pp. 354–357). He hasn't sufficiently distinguished between his own thoughts and the content of the book he was summarizing, and when he comes to write his essay he credits himself with a little more than his share of originality. Sometimes, too, a writer blunders into plagiarism through misunderstanding the rules of the game. He may think, for example, that a famous critic's opinion about a piece of literature is so authoritative that it belongs to the realm of common facts, and so he paraphrases it without acknowledgment.

What to Acknowledge

There *is* room for a measure of disagreement about what to acknowledge; but precisely because this is the case, you ought to make your documentation relatively ample. In addition to citing all direct quotations and paraphrases, you should give the sources of all borrowed ideas and facts that don't belong to general knowledge. That is, give a citation if you think that a serious person might disagree with your second-hand point or question whether it came from the most reliable source. You can casually mention how many people live in China, for example, and you can give your opinion that ecology is the most important issue in the contemporary world; but if you write about the way pig manure is recycled in Chinese communes, and if you haven't seen those communes in person, a reference is in order.

How to Document

A note, although it's the most common means of documentation, isn't always the most convenient or considerate one. If the reader has to keep skipping to your notes after every few lines of text, he's going to have difficulty concentrating on your essay itself. When most of your references are to one source, you can mention that fact in a brief statement or note, announcing that page references will be inserted parenthetically into the text (pp. 369–370). But you'll find that running away from notes can sometimes be clumsier than using them. It's better to refer your reader to a note than to stuff a sentence full of trivial data. Otherwise you will get clumsy effects like this:

- Marcuse's concept of alienation, as Alasdair MacIntyre maintains on pages 53–58 of *Herbert Marcuse: An Exposition and a Polemic* (New York: Viking, 1970), owes more to Feuerbach than to Marx.

All this information is necessary, but some of it is rhetorical dead weight. For a smoother effect the writer should get the merely technical data into a note, freeing his main text to pursue the argument:

- Marcuse's concept of alienation, as Alasdair MacIntyre maintains, owes more to Feuerbach than to Marx.[3] Furthermore, . . .

Substantive Notes

The purpose of most notes is simply to provide citations for quoted material and borrowed ideas. Occasionally, though, you can use a note to expand or qualify your main discussion itself. A point may strike you as worth making, yet rhetorically harmful to the flow of your argument. By placing it in a note, you give the reader a choice between reading it, skimming it, or ignoring it. If he wants to come to grips with your position in a critical spirit, the note is there to remind him that this idea hasn't been overlooked. And if his interest is more superficial, no great claim has been made on his attention.

Most often, a substantive note develops *from* a citation. The book or article being cited raises further issues that bear on your thesis in a challenging way. After giving the reference, you add a sentence or even a whole paragraph dealing with this challenge.

Bear in mind, however, that notes are supposed to remain subordinate elements. The time a reader spends poring over your notes amounts to a loss of his concentration on your central argument. If you find, in rereading a draft, that you've given disproportionate weight to commentary in the notes, try to condense the material as much as possible. Inessential chitchat should be deleted, and statements of key significance should be incorporated into the main essay. Your notes, when you've finished with them, should be clear and concise for readers who want to follow them, and unobtrusive for readers who don't. And there are ways (pp. 369–370) of offering all necessary citations while significantly cutting back on the total number of notes.

FOOTNOTE FORM

If you intend to write for publication, you should own a widely observed guide to all aspects of typescript form such as *A Manual of Style*[1] or *The MLA Style Sheet*.[2] Of course if you know that one magazine or press is going to print your work, you should present it in the style of that house. And you should note that scientific and technical writing follows other conventions than the ones I will describe here.

Placement and Numbering

The word *footnote* is loosely used to cover both a footnote proper, which is given at the bottom of the page on which the reference occurs, and an *endnote*, which is given in a consecutive series with all other notes at the end of the essay or article. Endnotes are preferred if you are submitting material for publication. In classroom work, depending on the preference of your teacher and the number of notes involved, you can choose either system or a combination of them:

Footnotes proper   For these, you must make sure to leave enough space at the bottom of each page to accommodate the references occurring on that page. (Sometimes you will have to continue a note on the bottom of the following page.) Five spaces below the text, and two spaces above the first footnote of each page, insert a ruled line one-third the length of a line of type. If you have no more than two or three references per page, you can identify them with asterisks: * for the first note, ** or † for the second, *** or ‡ for the third. But numbering by Arabic numerals is preferable: ¹, ², ³. You can use consecutive numbers throughout the essay or begin each page's notes from number 1.

endnotes   If you have many notes, or if some of them are quite lengthy, or if you are writing for publication, endnotes will serve you better than footnotes. Use one set of Arabic numerals and present all your notes in order after the main text (but before a bibliography, if any).

combined form   In some classroom essays you may find that you have both substantive notes (p. 362) and page citations, and you may want to make sure that your reader sees the substantive notes at the point where each reference to them occurs in the text. You can accomplish this by using footnotes proper for the substantive notes while putting the page citations into endnotes. Thus your substantive notes are marked by asterisks and given *on* the relevant pages, and the page citations are marked by consecutive Arabic numerals and given at the end. The ideal, here and in all aspects of form, is clarity and simplicity of effect without any sacrifice of needed information.

When writing for publication, you should double-space all notes and leave ample space between one note and the next. For classroom work you can single-space the notes and put double spaces between them.

Footnote numbers in your main text should look like this:

- Dr. Hyman shows a high regard for sex, if not for Latin, when he writes, "philanderer and philagyner discover a terrestrial 'peace that passeth all understanding' (*triste post coitu*)."⁴ But a few pages later . . .

Observe that the Arabic numeral is slightly elevated from the line, and that it isn't accompanied by any other punctuation such as a period or parentheses. It immediately follows all other marks except a dash that falls outside the quotation, as here:

- No aspiring philanderer or philagyner should overlook Dr. Hyman's penetrating remarks about "Trysting Place," "Trysting Time," and "Trousseau"⁵—and no one who has read them will soon forget them.

In general, footnote numbers should come after, not before, the material to be identified in the note.

Footnote form isn't an earthshaking matter, but as a courtesy to your reader you should adopt a widely recognized set of conventions and use them consistently. The following conventions are those recommended by the second edition of *The MLA Style Sheet:*

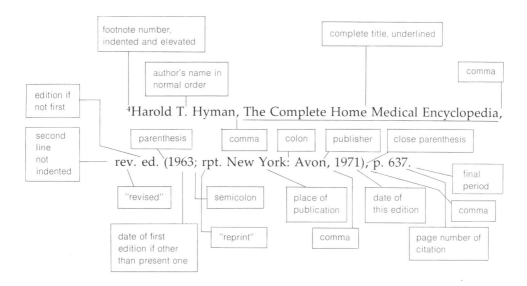

Information about the edition, date, place of publication, and publisher can be found on the back of the title page of the book you are citing. Note that several copyright dates may be given there, even if the book is still in its first edition. This means that some of the material in the book was copyrighted in earlier form. Locate the date of *this* edition, and look for an explicit statement of the first-edition date if this is a later edition.

Sample First Notes

books   Your first reference to a book should be fuller in bibliographical detail than all the subsequent ones (pp. 369–370). The following notes indicate some of the typical aspects of book citation in first references:

A FIRST EDITION:
   [1]Robert Langbaum, The Modern Spirit: Essays on the Continuity of Nineteenth- and Twentieth-Century Literature (New York: Oxford Univ. Press, 1970).

(If the same work appeared in your bibliography, you could shorten the footnote by dropping the book's subtitle.)

AN EDITED BOOK:
   [2]George Abbott White and Charles Newman, eds., Literature in Revolution (New York: Holt, 1972), p. 14.

(The publisher's full name is Holt, Rinehart and Winston, but *Holt* is sufficient.)

A BOOK EDITED BY
MORE THAN THREE PEOPLE:

   ³Frank Kermode et al., eds., The Oxford Anthology of English Literature,
2 vols. (New York: Oxford Univ. Press, 1973).

(The title page says that New York, London, and Toronto are the
places of publication. When more than two places are listed, you
need only supply the first.)

A PAGE REFERENCE
TO THE SAME BOOK:

   ⁴William Hazlitt, "My First Acquaintance with Poets," The Oxford Anthology of English Literature, ed. Frank Kermode et al. (New York: Oxford Univ.
Press, 1973), II, 705.

(Instead of giving the number of volumes as in note 3, you provide
the volume number of the passage being cited. With a Roman numeral for the volume number and an Arabic numeral for the page
number, there's no need to write *p.* before *705*.)

A TRANSLATION:

   ⁵Marcel Proust, Swann's Way, trans. C. K. Scott Moncrieff (New York:
Random House, 1928).

A LATER EDITION OF A BOOK
WITH CORPORATE AUTHORSHIP:

   ⁶Sunset Western Garden Book, 3rd ed. (n.d.; rpt. Menlo Park, Calif.: Lane,
1967), p. 79.

(The date of the first edition should come first in the parenthesis,
but this book gives no indication of when the first edition appeared;
n.d. means "no date." If the place of publication isn't given, replace
it with *n.p.* for "no place." Note that both the city and state—or in
some cases the city and country—should be given if the city isn't
widely familiar.)

A BOOK THAT FORMS
PART OF A SERIES:

   ⁷Thomas S. Kuhn, The Structure of Scientific Revolutions, International
Encyclopedia of Unified Science, II, 2, 2nd ed. (1962; rpt. Chicago: Univ. of
Chicago Press, 1970), pp. vii–viii.

(Kuhn's book is the second item in the second series issued by the
editors of the International Encyclopedia. The lower-case Roman
page numbers indicate prefatory pages.)

A BOOK REVISED BY SOMEONE
OTHER THAN THE AUTHOR(S):

   ⁸Edward F. Ricketts and Jack Calvin, Between Pacific Tides, rev. Joel W.
Hedgpeth, 4th ed. (1939; rpt. Stanford: Stanford Univ. Press, 1968), p. 295n.

(The cited passage appears in a footnote on page 295.)

A BOOK WHOSE VOLUMES WERE
PUBLISHED IN DIFFERENT YEARS:
⁹All quoted poems are based on the <u>Poetical Works of William Words-
worth</u>, ed. E. de Selincourt and H. Darbishire, 2nd ed., 5 vols. (Oxford:
Oxford Univ. Press, 1952–1959).

(The dates of the earliest- and last-published volumes are given.)

A PAGE REFERENCE
TO THE SAME WORK:
¹⁰<u>Poetical Works of William Wordsworth</u>, ed. E. de Selincourt and H.
Darbishire, 2nd ed., I (Oxford: Oxford Univ. Press, 1952), 217.

(The one volume being cited is indicated along with its date of publication.)

AN ESSAY PUBLISHED IN A BOOK:
¹¹Joan Riviere, "A Character Trait of Freud's," in <u>Psychoanalysis and
Contemporary Thought</u>, ed. John D. Sutherland (1958; rpt. New York:
Grove Press, 1959), pp. 145–149.

(The title of the essay or chapter belongs within quotation marks.)

A NOTE CITING
MORE THAN ONE BOOK:
¹² See Susan Isaacs, <u>The Nursery Years: The Mind of the Child from Birth
to Six Years</u> (1929; rpt. New York: Schocken, 1968); Géza Róheim, <u>Magic
and Schizophrenia</u> (1955; rpt. Bloomington: Indiana Univ. Press, 1962); and
R. D. Laing, <u>Self and Others</u>, 2nd ed. (1961; rpt. New York: Pantheon, 1969).

articles in magazines, Footnote form is slightly different for periodical publi-
journals, and newspapers cations, as these samples indicate.

AN ARTICLE IN A JOURNAL WITH CONTINUOUS
PAGINATION THROUGH EACH YEAR'S VOLUME:
¹³George H. Pollack, "On Time, Death, and Immortality," <u>Psychoanalytic
Quarterly</u>, 40 (July 1971), 435–446.

(Both the volume number and the page numbers can be given in
Arabic numerals, since they are clearly separated by the date of
the issue. Because the volume number is provided, *pp.* is unnecessary before *435–446*.)

AN ARTICLE IN A MAGAZINE WITH
SEPARATE PAGINATION FOR EACH ISSUE:
¹⁴Fred M. Hechinger, "Who's in Charge Here?" <u>Change</u>, Winter 1971–72,
pp. 26–29.

(If the paging starts anew with each issue, the volume number can be omitted. This eliminates the parentheses around the date, but it also means that *pp.* should be supplied.)

AN ARTICLE IN A JOURNAL THAT DOES
NOT IDENTIFY THE EXACT DATE OF EACH ISSUE:
[15]Richard P. Wheeler, "Poetry and Fantasy in Shakespeare's Sonnets 88–96," Literature and Psychology, 22, No. 3 (1972), 151–162.

(The number of the issue in the yearly series is given after the volume number.)

A BOOK REVIEW:
[16]S. K. Oberbeck, rev. of Reminiscing with Sissle and Blake, by Robert Kimball and William Bolcom, Newsweek, 30 Apr. 1973, p. 81.

(Note the preferred form for giving the date.)

AN UNSIGNED MAGAZINE ARTICLE:
[17]"Drugs That Don't Work," New Republic, 29 Jan. 1972, pp. 12–13.

A SIGNED NEWSPAPER ARTICLE:
[18]Peter Weisser, "Governor Reagan on Grass," San Francisco Chronicle, 29 Jan. 1972, Final Ed., p. 6, cols. 1–5.

(It isn't essential to give either the edition or the columns, but both can be helpful. Occasionally a story will appear in one edition of a day's paper and not in others. Note that the city where the paper is published isn't usually underlined.)

AN UNSIGNED NEWSPAPER ARTICLE:
[19]"Exxon Estimates 1st Period Profit Increased 43.1%," Wall Street Journal, 24 Apr. 1973, p. 8.

(The writer of this note has chosen not to give the edition and column numbers. Note that *Wall Street* is underlined as an essential part of the newspaper's name.)

encyclopedia entries

A SIGNED ENTRY:
[20]John Tasker Howard, "Yankee Doodle," Encyclopedia Americana, 1972, XXIX, 648.

(The publisher and place of publication needn't be mentioned in an encyclopedia citation. Note that Roman and Arabic numerals differentiate the volume and page.)

AN UNSIGNED ENTRY:
[21]"Know-Nothing Party," Encyclopaedia Britannica, 1971, XIII, 432.

pamphlets and bulletins

SIGNED:

[22]H. H. Koepf, Compost: What It Is/How It Is Made/What It Does, rpt. from Bio-Dynamics, No. 77 (Stroudsburg, Pa.: Bio-Dynamic Farming and Gardening Assn., 1956).

(Because pamphlets are hard to locate in libraries, any extra information about their origin should be supplied. The reader of this note could track down the magazine from which the pamphlet was taken or write to Stroudsburg for a copy.)

UNSIGNED:

[23]Dye Plants and Dyeing—A Handbook, rpt. from Plants and Gardens, 20, No. 3 (Baltimore: Brooklyn Botanic Garden, 1964).

dissertations

[24]Henry Morton Boudin, "The Ripple Effect in Classroom Management," Diss. Michigan 1970, p. 89.

Parenthetical References and Subsequent Footnotes

If you have many references to one book, your first and only footnote to it can look like this:

[1]Alex Comfort, The Nature of Human Nature (New York: Avon, 1968), p. 76. Hereafter cited parenthetically as Nature.

Then your next mention of the work in your main text, and similar references to it afterward, can take the place of footnotes:

• Human longevity has more than doubled since Neanderthal times (see Nature, p. 150).

If only one work by a frequently cited author is mentioned in your text, you can simply use his last name and the page numbers to identify your parenthetical references:

• (see Comfort, p. 150)

But don't test your reader's memory or patience; a fuller reference should be used if the work hasn't been mentioned in recent paragraphs.

A first footnote has to be detailed because a good deal of information is needed to distinguish one source from all others. Subsequent references can take most of this information for granted; they should be brief and simple.

Until recently, subsequent footnotes tended to be cluttered with Latin abbreviations, chiefly:

abbreviation	meaning
ibid.	the same title as the one mentioned in the previous note
loc. cit.	in the same passage as the one cited in a recent note
op. cit.	in the work cited in a recent note; but the page number of this passage is different (*op. cit.*, *p. 321*).

(For other abbreviations, see pp. 335–336.

These terms are increasingly being abandoned in favor of shortened references to the author and/or the title of the work, plus the page number. Now a reader, instead of having to ask himself which previous reference *loc. cit.* or *op. cit.* alludes to, can see at once what's intended:

[11]Hechinger, p. 27.
[12]Cf. Riviere, pp. 148–149.

A slightly fuller reference is useful if the reader isn't likely to recall at once what "Hechinger" and "Riviere" actually wrote, or if more than one item by the same person has been mentioned.

[11]Hechinger, "Who's in Charge?" p. 27.
[12]Cf. Riviere, "Character Trait," pp. 148–149.

Once you have established the author and title of a long poem or play, and have specified the edition you're using, you can cite lines by using a combination of Roman and Arabic numerals. The same form can be used in both footnotes and parenthetical references:

citation	meaning
Lear I.ii.56–59	Shakespeare's King Lear, Act One, scene two, lines 56–59
Aen. III. 201	Vergil's Aeneid, Book Three, line 201
P.L. IV. 32–33	Milton's Paradise Lost, Book Four, lines 32–33
II Kings iv. 6	The Bible, Second Book of Kings, Chapter Four, verse 6

(Note that the Bible and its books aren't customarily italicized.)

Bibliographies

A bibliography is a list of works that you've consulted, or that you recommend to your readers for further reference. Research papers, dissertations, and scholarly books typically contain bibliographies at the end, but in shorter or more informal writing they're less commonly seen. Apart from your teacher's preference, you can decide whether or not to include a bibliography by asking yourself whether your footnotes have given a sufficient account of your sources. If you want to show that you've taken account of unmentioned works, the extra effort of compiling a bibliography may be worthwhile.

Bibliography entries are always full, with complete specification of all information contained in the *first footnotes* above. The presence of a bibliography, in fact, gives you the option of shortening your first footnote references to the same works. In scientific and technical papers, which usually include bibliographies numbered by item, the main text refers parenthetically to those numbers, thus eliminating most footnotes:

• The work being done at Duke University on high-resolution proton beams (12) shows the extremely coherent and detailed nature of analogue resonances. In addition, the findings of Anderson (3) and Wigner (13) deserve comment.

Things aren't so efficient in the humanities, but if you do include a bibliography you can at least drop subtitles and publishers' names from your footnotes.

Most bibliographies follow the alphabetical order of the authors' last names, with anonymous items inserted in the alphabetical order of the first significant word in each title. When several entries by one author are listed, they are usually given in order of their dates of publication. Some bibliographies are divided by categories—for example, into *Primary Sources* indicating works *by* an author being studied and *Secondary Sources* indicating works *about* that author. The most useful bibliographies of all are those that include brief comments on the value of the separate items after each entry.

Like footnotes, bibliography entries should be double-spaced if you are writing for publication. Otherwise they can be single-spaced, with double spaces between the entries. The first line of a bibliography entry is not indented, while the second and all succeeding lines are indented five spaces.

The following comparison of a typical footnote and bibliography entry spells out the differences in form.

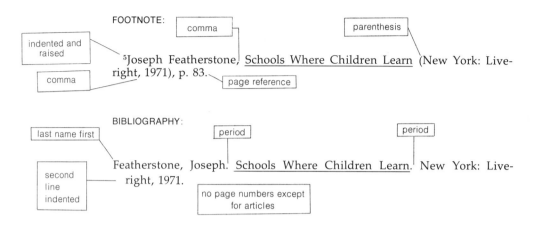

FOOTNOTE:

indented and raised

comma

parenthesis

⁵Joseph Featherstone, <u>Schools Where Children Learn</u> (New York: Liveright, 1971), p. 83.

comma

page reference

BIBLIOGRAPHY:

last name first

period

period

second line indented

Featherstone, Joseph. <u>Schools Where Children Learn.</u> New York: Liveright, 1971.

no page numbers except for articles

Here are a few more bibliography entries, which you can compare to the sample footnotes for the same works:

"Drugs That Don't Work." <u>New Republic</u>, 29 Jan. 1972, pp. 12–13.

Pollack, George H. "On Time, Death, and Immortality." <u>Psychoanalytic Quarterly</u>, 40 (July 1971), 435–446.

Ricketts, Edward F., and Jack Calvin. <u>Between Pacific Tides</u>. Rev. Joel W. Hedgpeth. 4th ed., 1939; rpt. Stanford: Stanford Univ. Press, 1968.

EXERCISES

I. If you made the following statements in essays, which ones would require documentation? What kind of documentation would be appropriate? Briefly defend your answer.

1. If people could only learn to love one another, the world would be a better place.
2. The "black hole" hypothesis, once generally dismissed, has been steadily gaining favor among astronomers in recent years.
3. To be or not to be: that is indeed the central question for anyone who experiences suicidal feelings.
4. There can be no denying the fact that industrialization and lung disease are inseparable twins; where you find the first, you are bound to find his grim brother.
5. The oppressed people of the world must often feel like those who cried out, "How long, O Lord, holy and true, dost thou not judge and avenge our blood . . . ?"
6. The first direct act of atomic warfare occurred at Hiroshima in August 1945.

7. Reasonable people may disagree over the wisdom of our policy toward revolution in Southeast Asia.

II. Write sample notes giving the usual amount of information about these sources:

1. An article by Barbara Bailey Kessel, called "Free, Classless, and Urbane?" and appearing in Volume 31 of the journal *College English*, published in March of 1970, on pages 531 through 540. The pagination of *College English* is continuous through each one-year volume.
2. A quotation from page 428 of this present book.
3. A book by Herman Ermolaev called *Soviet Literary Theories 1917–1934: The Genesis of Socialist Realism*. The book was published in 1963 by the University of California Press, whose offices are in Berkeley and Los Angeles, California.
4. A 1940 pamphlet issued by the United States Department of the Interior, Bureau of Indian Affairs, called *Navajo Native Dyes: Their Preparation and Use*. The pamphlet was published by the Government Printing Office in Washington, D.C.
5. A story by Philip Roth called "On the Air," published in Number 10 of *New American Review*, on pages 7 through 49. This magazine does not carry dates, and its pagination begins anew with each issue.
6. A two-volume book called *American Literary Masters*, edited by Charles R. Anderson and seven other people. The work was published in 1965 by Holt, Rinehart and Winston, whose places of publication are listed on the back of the title page as New York, Chicago, San Francisco, and Toronto.

III. For each of the following footnotes, write two subsequent parenthetical references (pp. 369–370). In each case, make your second reference more concise than your first:

[1]Thomas Mann, *Confessions of Felix Krull, Confidence Man* [*The Early Years*], tr. Denver Lindley (New York: Knopf, 1955), p. 18.

[2]Thomas Lindley, "Bichromate Printing," *Popular Photography*, Oct. 1973, pp. 124–125.

[3]Apicius, *The Roman Cookery Book*, tr. Barbara Flower and Elisabeth Rosenbaum (London and New York: Peter Nevill, 1958), pp. 152–157.

[4]A. S. Neill, *Summerhill: A Radical Approach to Child Rearing* (1960; rpt. New York: Hart, 1964), p. xxiv.

[5]"Desperate Journey: The Story of the Mexican Alien," *Focus*, Sept. 1973, p. 11.

[6]Margaret Atwood, *Surfacing* (New York: Simon and Schuster, 1973), p. 84.

[7]Sheldon Renan, *An Introduction to the American Underground Film* (New York: Dutton, 1967), pp. 250–251.

[8]Sabrina and Roland Michaud, "Winter Caravan to the Roof of the World," *National Geographic*, 141 (Apr. 1972), 435–465.

IV. Make sample bibliography entries for the items in Exercise II, placing the entries in normal bibliographical order.

NOTES

1. *A Manual of Style*, 12th ed. (Chicago: Univ. of Chicago Press, 1969).
2. *The MLA Style Sheet*, 2nd ed. (New York: Modern Language Assn., 1970).

A 15 SAMPLE PAPER

Because the research paper is usually presented as the last and tallest hurdle in a composition course, it is sometimes regarded with unnecessary awe. Students feel that their main purpose should be, not to write an interesting essay, but to prove that they've done a punishing amount of research. Thus the paper often has a fact-ridden, gloomy air. Emphasis falls primarily on the footnotes, and the reader finds himself yo-yoing continuously between the text and the notes. If several sentences go by without a footnote, the student feels that he's losing the name of researcher and slipping back toward the primitive days when he had to write "How I Spent My Summer Vacation."

A real research paper is simply an essay written on the basis of materials the writer has sought out and examined. It should of course have some notes, and it should also provide a bibliography at the end, especially if the argument rests on some reading that isn't indicated in the notes. But the essay itself needn't be dull or impersonal. Everything I have said about lively prose applies as much to a research paper as to other kinds of writing.

Perhaps the greatest risk you face in writing a research paper is the loss of your independent perspective. When you find a book or article that seems impressive, you may be tempted to begin quoting it at great length, allowing it to dominate your argument and distort the structure of your essay. The best way of ensuring that this doesn't happen is to choose a topic in which you've had a long-standing interest. The writer of the paper that follows, for example, though he didn't know in advance how he would explain W. C. Fields' humor, had followed Fields' movies for years and knew that he could come up with ideas of his own.

If you do find that a published work anticipates what you hoped to say, your first impulse may be to give up and begin looking for a completely new subject area (p. 21). But this is usually a wasteful overreaction. The reading you've already done with one topic in mind will alert you to several closely related topics, one of which ought to prove satisfactory. As you take notes, then, you should keep exploring ways of shifting the topic, either to resolve unanticipated difficulties or to make room for new ideas and evidence you may want to include. Before settling finally on one topic, you should review all possibilities together, looking for the best way to be original, challenging, and convincing. The majority of good research papers are about topics slightly different from the writer's first idea.

Thus the author of the sample paper began by thinking he would write about the character and opinions of W. C. Fields, but as his research progressed he saw certain obstacles in his way. A recent book, he learned, cast doubt on the authenticity of many of the "facts" he had wanted to use; he had trouble finding a thesis (p. 22) that would have broad interest; and he gradually realized that a paper about Fields' personality wouldn't deal sufficiently with his comic art. Eventually, however, the writer found a way of including some of his biographical observations.

Here are some of the writer's notes comparing the several topics he had thought of choosing:

CHARACTER AND OPINIONS

Rich material, great quotes — but F's grandson questions many of the anecdotes. Can't get solid thesis. NB: F's *comedy* is what makes him interesting.

VAUDEVILLE AND FILM

Good topic for originality: many people are unaware that F. stole movie material from his own career as stage clown. Plenty of evidence in Ronald Fields' new book. But old Larson would probably say this is too cut-and-dried, just rehashing what R. Fields has turned up.

F'S IDEAS ABOUT COMEDY

Allows discussion of films, and there's enough material in Monti, R. Fields, and F's own writings—esp. "Anything for a Laugh." But this would just be retelling. I need a *problem*.

WHAT'S SO FUNNY ABOUT F?

Looks good. Draws on best evidence for other topics, and focuses on F's nastiness. (Good because that's what makes him different.) NB: F arouses wildly different reactions; make sure to bring this out.

WHY DO WE LAUGH AT W. C. FIELDS?

by

M. J. Kane

Professor Larson

Film Criticism 86D

The writer uses a topic outline (pp. 28–30), showing the subordination of some ideas to others.

OUTLINE

Thesis: Fields' characterization as a doomed victim of American life allows us to laugh at his malice and cynicism.

  I. The Problem: How to Explain the Popularity of Such a Nasty Figure
       A. His popularity thrives
       B. Do we admire sheer aggression?
 II. Evading the Problem: The Attempt to "Humanize" Fields
       A. Emphasis on his sympathetic roles
       B. Unsuccessful "proof" of his gentleness
III. The Record Is Clear: Fields as Cynic and Champion of Meanness
       A. Biographical testimony
       B. His remarks about comic appeal
       C. Sadistic episodes in his films
 IV. The Problem Solved: We Laugh at a Ridiculous <u>Character</u>
       A. Distinction between isolated acts and a consistent character
       B. Fields as a defeated figure
             1. In appearance and manner
             2. In family and business
             3. In unfulfilled endings
       C. We laugh at Fields' pettiness, not his cruelty
       D. Fields gives us comic distance from his cynicism

WHY DO WE LAUGH AT W. C. FIELDS?

    In San Francisco in 1973, a portly man wearing a long
checkered coat, spats, white gloves, and a top hat strolls
down Market Street, puffing on a cigar and twirling a cane.
He is not in fact W. C. Fields, who died in 1946, but one
Ted Allison, who makes a living entirely by impersonating
Fields in advertising stunts. Wherever he goes he is
"surrounded by the inevitable clusters of people, every age
group, every color seemingly mesmerized by the curious magic
he dispense[s]."[1] It is the same magic that prompts thousands
to stand in line for "W. C. Fields Film Festivals," to buy
enormous posters of their idol scowling behind a poker hand,
and to trade improbable tales about his offscreen antics.
W. C. Fields, it seems, is alive and well, not only in San
Francisco but across the United States.

    This fact is by no means easy to explain. Fields was a
great slapstick comic, but he was only one among many performers
who successfully made the leap from burlesque to Hollywood. In
a contest of talent he would rank behind Charlie Chaplin and
not far ahead of Buster Keaton, Harold Lloyd, Laurel and Hardy,
or the Marx brothers. His comedy, furthermore, is offensive to

---

    [1]William Moore, "Following in W. C. Fields' Footsteps,"
San Francisco Chronicle, 23 July 1973, p. 14.

The essay begins with a "baited opener" (pp. 128–129)—a story that catches attention and gradually leads us toward the main argument.

Footnotes are placed at the bottom of the page where the reference appears. They could also have been placed consecutively after the end of the main text. See pp. 363–364.

2

Having caught our interest, the writer poses his problem.

many people and puzzling even to his devoted fans. What is funny about a pompous, malicious, disagreeable-looking fellow whose half-inaudible gags, in the opinion of one critic, combine "frustrated aggression" with "a hopeless expectation of audience disapproval"?[2] Do we think that sheer nastiness is funny?

The next two paragraphs consider, and reject, a suggestion that the problem doesn't exist.

The problem of justifying Fields has been around for a long time. Most people are reluctant to say that they enjoy seeing vicious behavior even in a movie, and some of Fields' commentators have denied that he usually appeals to such a taste. Thus, in a 1939 review of You Can't Cheat an Honest Man, Frank S. Nugent fumed: "Considering that he wrote it himself, Mr. Fields seems singularly ignorant of the qualities that have endeared him to his millions. His Larson E. Whipsnade, circus proprietor, is completely unsympathetic. He is a scamp, but not a loveable scamp; a blusterer who bullies for the sake of bullying and not to conceal a tender heart."[3] Although this in itself has a comical ring—surely, we tell ourselves, "a tender heart" isn't something we should associate with Fields —the reviewer was echoing a widely held belief that comic figures should be appealing. Indeed, we now know that Fields

---

[2]Raymond Durgnat, "Subversion in the Fields," Films and Filming, Dec. 1965, p. 43.

[3]Reprinted in Donald Deschner, The Films of W. C. Fields (New York: Citadel, 1966), p. 137.

3

himself was at least passingly affected by this idea. He
complained to the producer of You Can't Cheat an Honest Man
that important scenes of "pathos" had been cut,[4] and he wrote
to Mae West that My Little Chickadee (1940) ought to present
"just the two of us at the end of the picture with no attempts
at comedy or wise cracks from either of us. I think it will
leave a nice human, homey feeling in the audience's mind."[5]

These revelations are provided by a new book which is
itself an unconvincing effort to solve the Fields problem by
declaring that no problem exists. Fields' grandson, in
introducing his collection of letters and scripts, claims to
be presenting us with "a gentle man, a proud father, and a
loving grandfather,"[6] and his editorial remarks imply that
Fields' audiences simply recognized the genius of "The Great
One." Skimming W. C. Fields by Himself, we could almost
imagine that we were dealing with an ordinary citizen who
happened to be very good at making people laugh. Yet the
documents themselves, when studied apart from Ronald Fields'
enthusiastic notes, make quite a different impression. The
"proud father" hardly ever saw his son, who grew up to despise
him, and the "gentle man" shows a disagreeable temper on page

---

[4]W. C. Fields by Himself, ed. Ronald J. Fields (Englewood
Cliffs, N.J.: Prentice-Hall, 1973), p. 322.

[5]Fields by Himself, p. 366.

[6]Fields by Himself, Introduction, p. xiv.

Compare this note to the
bibliography entry for
the same book (p. 392).
Because a full reference
appears in the
bibliography, the
footnote is shortened.

A shortened second
reference (see pp.
369–370).

4

after page. Fields may have wanted some pathos in his scripts,
but neither his grandson nor anyone else can convince us that
he projected "a nice human, homey feeling" either in his life
or in his art.

The next two paragraphs rely heavily on quotation to establish support for the writer's view of Fields.

The Fields we see on the screen is, by and large, the one
we know from many biographical sources, and most reliably from
his mistress of fourteen years, Carlotta Monti. This Fields
is the pathologically suspicious, cynical man who once drawled
on election day, "Hell, I never vote <u>for</u> anybody; I always
vote <u>against</u>."[7] It is the man who scorned the jury system
because, in his view, "It is impossible to find twelve fair
men in all the world."[8] Again, it is the man who once defined
business as "an establishment that gives you the legal, even
though unethical, right to screw the naive--right, left, and
in the middle."[9] The Fields we know is epitomized in Robert
Lewis Taylor's story about how the aging star performed his
old pool-hall routine in one last movie for wartime release
in 1944. After the shooting "several people thanked him for
his fine patriotic effort and said how much good the scene
would do. He shook their hands with self-conscious pleasure,

---

[7]Quoted by Robert Lewis Taylor, <u>W. C. Fields: His Follies
and Fortunes</u> (Garden City, N.Y.: Doubleday, 1949), p. 275.

[8]Quoted by Gene Fowler, <u>Minutes of the Last Meeting</u> (New
York: Viking, 1954), p. 173.

[9]Quoted by Carlotta Monti with Cy Rice, <u>W. C. Fields and
Me</u> (Englewood Cliffs, N.J.: Prentice-Hall, 1971), p. 134.

5

went to the cashier and collected the $25,000 he had agreed
on, then shuffled off toward his car, whistling a soundless
tune, his eyes fixed on the distant horizon."[10] Some of these
stories may be inaccurate, but there are dozens of similar
recollections that can't be dismissed.

When Fields wrote and talked about the nature of his
comedy, "homeyness" was the farthest thing from his mind. He
asked Carlotta Monti to remember that "everyone has a percentage
of the sadist in him, even though infinitesimal. If I hit you
over the head with a club in public . . . I'd be arrested. In
a comedy act, it draws laughter."[11] Quarreling with script
writers (his favorite fish, he once said in reply to a question,
was "a piranha in a writer's bathtub"[12]) about whether he
should kick Baby Leroy in <u>The Old-Fashioned Way</u> (1934), he
remarked, "There is not a man in America who has not had a
secret ambition to boot an infant. They will love it."[13]
And in a magazine article Fields once had this to say:

> I know we laugh at the troubles of others, provided
> those troubles are not too serious. Out of that
> observation I have reached a conclusion which may be

**For a long quotation, the
writer omits quotation
marks and indents the
whole passage five
spaces.**

---

[10]Taylor, p. 85.

[11]Quoted by Monti, p. 66.

[12]Quoted by Monti, p. 68.

[13]Quoted by Alva Johnston, "Who Knows What Is Funny?",
<u>Saturday Evening Post</u>, 6 Aug. 1938, p. 43.

6

of some comfort to those accused of "having no
sense of humor." These folks are charming, lovable,
philanthropic people, and invariably I like them
--as long as they keep out of the theaters where
I am playing, which they usually do. If they get
in by mistake, they leave early.
   The reason they don't laugh at most gags is
that their first emotional reaction is to feel sorry
for people instead of to laugh at them. . . .
   I like, in an audience, the fellow who roars
continuously at the troubles of the character I am
portraying . . ., but he probably has a mean streak
in him and, if I needed ten dollars, he'd be the
last person I'd call upon.[14]

Turning to the films themselves, we find no shortage of

cruel, "sick" humor. The uncensored version of The Dentist

(1932), for example, contains an episode that looks provocatively

like a case of rape. In The Fatal Glass of Beer (1932) Fields,

alias the Northern trapper Snavely, notoriously announces that

he has eaten his lead-dog, who tasted "mighty good with mustard."

The movie ends with Mr. and Mrs. Snavely tossing their prodigal

son out into the Klondike snow, presumably to freeze. In You

Can't Cheat an Honest Man Fields knocks a woman down when no

one is looking and then tells her, for the benefit of the

gathering bystanders, that her husband should take her home

since he was the one who "got you drunk." And in The Bank Dick

(1940) Fields torments the bank examiner, J. Pinkerton Snoopington

after he has made him sick with heavily spiked drinks, by

conjuring up pictures of the heaviest, greasiest fried foods

Some of the research for this essay consisted of the writer's seeing old movies. Although some of the script lines were verified in books about Fields, no footnotes are required for them.

---

[14]W. C. Fields, "Anything for a Laugh," American Magazine,
Sept. 1934, p. 130.

7

he can imagine. The audience always howls with delight.

Thus we are brought back to our original question: if Fields' sadism is undeniable, must we accept it as the basis of his funniness? Perhaps so--yet I can't believe that matters are so simple. Consider Fields' own example of provoking laughter by hitting a woman over the head with a club in a comedy act. In such a case would we be laughing at a vicious assault, or rather at a ridiculous <u>figure</u> who expressed his rage without any of the restraints we ourselves would apply? Fields, we know, wasn't just a gagster but a student of character who placed a high value on consistency.[15] Although his fictional personality varies from one plot to the next, he does have an increasingly well-defined "self" that we hope and expect to meet in every film. It is this total character, not a few instances of shocking cruelty, that disposes us to laugh.

In order to define this character, let's begin by studying Fields' celebrated appearance and manner. Unlike most of his Hollywood contemporaries--Chaplin the tramp, Keaton the soulful outsider, the mildly retarded Laurel and Hardy, the peasant immigrant Marx brothers--he seems completely devoid of childlike

The writer restates his problem to indicate that he will now begin presenting his solution to it.

---

[15]He told Carlotta Monti, for example, that although Scrooge was his favorite Dickens character, "he fell from my good graces at the end of the tale." Carlotta asked why. "He reformed, that's what the blithering idiot did. He became benevolent. That was Dickens' only mistake! He allowed Scrooge to get out of character!" (Quoted by Monti, p. 40.)

A substantive footnote (see pp. 362–363).

8

innocence. He is not only grown up, but grown sarcastic as
well. His sarcasm, in fact, marks him as a more thorough
victim than any of his rival comedians: he is walking proof
that daily American life can strip away all illusions. His
shifty eyes indicate that he has long since learned not to
expect decent treatment. His bulbous nose identifies him as
a man who has been driven to drink. His spasmodic gestures
of self-defense, which prompted one critic to think of "the
crabbed helplessness of a teddy bear with arthritis,"[16] reveal
a frayed nervous system and a conviction that the worst is
yet to come. With his drinking Fields tries to blot out
humiliation; with his cheating he·tries to compensate for the
bad hand he has been dealt by fate; and with his grandiose
fibs he tries to insulate himself in fantasy. What we laugh
at is the image of a man who has been made grotesque and
preposterous without losing his itch to settle the score.

　　　Fields strikes us not only as a victim, but as a recognizably
American one who has to undergo the seemingly unbearable nuisances
of family and business life. Take the famous bedtime ritual in
The Fatal Glass of Beer, when mother, father, and long-lost son
exchange pseudo-helpful advice. "Good night, son, and don't
forget to open your window . . ." "I won't, Ma, and don't
forget to open your window . . . good-night, Pa, and you open

---

This article has been previously cited; hence the shortened second reference.

[16]Durgnat, "Subversion in the Fields," p. 42.

9

your window too, Pa. . . ." The advice escalates as all
three characters begin speaking at once, until the din is
finally halted by the slamming of the son's door. Any
attempt at civility within the family, Fields seems to tell
us, is destined to backfire; after all, it can't possibly be
sincere in the first place.

Or again, consider what happens in The Pharmacist (1932).
There Fields, having cut through a large square of three-cent
stamps to get the one in the middle that his grouchy customer
has selected, wraps the stamp in a huge paper bag after the
customer has decided against having it "sent," gives it on
credit when the customer produces an unchangeable hundred-
dollar bill, and then remembers to present his latest sales
gimmick, a gigantic souvenir vase. Before the scene is over
Fields has given away three vases without having made a
genuine sale. He calls to our minds every small businessman
who has to abase himself, not in the ever more distant hope
of getting ahead, but simply because the customer is king.

Even though some of Fields' movies have conventional "happy
endings," there are limitations on the happiness that can be
imagined for a hero like Fields. Chaplin, Keaton, and Lloyd
regularly "get the girl" when their sufferings are over, but
the very thought of Fields on a honeymoon is wildly farcical.
In My Little Chickadee (1940) he reaches for Mae West in bed and
gets--a nanny goat. A typical fate is his reward in The Bank Dick:

10

a limp "heartiest handshake," a calendar of "Spring in Lompoc,"
a minor job, and a renewal of his life sentence of henpecked
marriage and parenthood. We begin to understand what Fields
meant when he welcomed the viewer "who roars continuously <u>at</u>
<u>the troubles of the character I am portraying</u>."

In short, then, Fields is an extraordinarily defeated
figure who invites a certain scorn. Unlike the typical comic
hero, who wins our sympathy and our permission to break a few
rules before achieving his rightful success and happiness,
Fields is going to keep mumbling and snarling forever. He
doesn't even <u>want</u> us to take his side in his quarrel with the
world; all apparent friends are really enemies in disguise.
What he wants is to be left in peace (an impossible hope) and
to win a few cheap victories over the people and animals who
get on his nerves.

Those victories are funny, not because of their cruelty,
but because of their extreme triviality: Fields is so helpless
that he can only pick on the weak, the infantile, the senile,
even the blind.[17] The supreme Fieldsian gesture occurs in

---

[17]Fields' movies contain more vendettas than a casual viewer
might think. Thus in <u>The Bank Dick</u> he stops to "help" an old lady
and her chauffeur with their stranded car, and after one turn of a
screw the engine drops onto the street--whereupon Fields tips his
hat and strolls briskly away. The scene looks like a funny
accident, but Fields, in Robert Lewis Taylor's words, "told a
friend that the automobile skit had been taken from his own life.
'People were always offering to help me out like that, with about
the same results,' he said" (Taylor, p. 328).

11

The Barber Shop (1932), after he has taken a giant safety pin
from a baby, warning him that swallowing the open pin could kill
him. But when the baby then socks Fields with his milk bottle,
Fields hands him back the pin, still unsheathed. It is a moment
either of mad fun or of appalling bad taste, depending on your
idea of how far comedy can go; but in any event it illustrates
Fields' absurdly defensive survival tactics toward everyone,
including the newborn. Although some--not all--of his actions
are sadistic, what they really show is a fear of assault from
every quarter.

    "A thing worth having," Fields intones in one of his movies,
"is worth cheating for."[18] The sentence is a marvelous reversal
of Ben Franklin wisdom. With one part of our minds we may
secretly agree with it, but if we openly agreed, the humor
would disappear. What Fields does for us is to portray such
a spiteful, self-absorbed, implausible character that we can
easily distance ourselves from his cynicism, taking it as a
joke instead of as a serious philosophy. Like every great
comedian, Fields finally has only one message, that life is a
laughing matter. The laugh, we have seen, is on him--and
that's exactly where he wanted it to be.

> A striking quotation has been saved for the concluding paragraph.

---

    [18]Quoted in W. C. Fields, Drat!, ed. Richard J. Anobile
(New York: Signet, 1969), p. 53.

12

For bibliography form, see pp. 371–372.

BIBLIOGRAPHY

Agee, James. <u>Agee on Film: Reviews and Comments</u>. New York: McDowell Oblensky, 1958.

Deschner, Donald. <u>The Films of W. C. Fields</u>. Intro. Arthur Knight. New York: Citadel, 1966.

Durgnat, Raymond. <u>The Crazy Mirror: Hollywood Comedy and the American Image</u>. London: Faber and Faber, 1969.

_____. "Subversion in the Fields." <u>Films and Filming</u>, Dec. 1965, pp. 42-48.

Everson, William K. <u>The Art of W. C. Fields</u>. Indianapolis: Bobbs-Merrill, 1967.

Fields, W. C. "Anything for a Laugh." <u>The American Magazine</u>, Sept. 1934, pp. 73, 129, 130.

_____. <u>Drat!: Being the Encapsulated View of Life by W. C. Fields in His Own Words</u>. Ed. Richard J. Anobile. Intro. Ed McMahon. 1968; rpt. New York: Signet, 1969.

_____. <u>Fields for President</u>. Ed. Michael M. Taylor. 1940; rpt. New York: Dodd, Mead, 1971.

_____. <u>W. C. Fields by Himself: His Intended Autobiography</u>. Ed. Ronald J. Fields. Englewood Cliffs, N.J.: Prentice-Hall, 1973.

Ford, Corey. <u>The Time of Laughter</u>. Boston: Little, Brown, 1967.

Fowler, Gene. <u>Minutes of the Last Meeting</u>. New York: Viking, 1954.

Greene, Graham. Review of <u>Poppy</u> in <u>The Spectator</u>, 17 July 1936; rpt. <u>Intellectual Digest</u>, Apr. 1973, p. 29.

Johnston, Alva. "Who Knows What Is Funny?" <u>Saturday Evening Post</u>, 6 Aug. 1938, pp. 10, 11, 43, 45, 46.

Lahue, Kalton C. <u>World of Laughter: The Motion Picture Comedy Short, 1910-1930</u>. Norman: Univ. of Oklahoma Press, 1966.

Montgomery, John. <u>Comedy Films, 1894-1954</u>. 1954; 2nd ed. London: Allen and Unwin, 1968.

13

Monti, Carlotta, with Cy Rice. W. C. Fields and Me. Englewood
     Cliffs, N.J.: Prentice-Hall, 1971.

Moore, William. "Following in W. C. Fields' Footsteps." San
     Francisco Chronicle, 23 July 1973, p. 14, cols. 1-6.

Schickel, Richard. Movies: The History of an Art and an
     Institution. New York: Basic Books, 1964.

Sennett, Mack, with Cameron Shipp. King of Comedy. Garden
     City, N.Y.: Doubleday, 1954.

Taylor, Robert Lewis. W. C. Fields: His Follies and Fortunes.
     Garden City, N.Y.: Doubleday, 1949.

Zimmerman, Paul D. "The Great Debunker." Newsweek, 3 Apr.
     1967, p. 88.

4

 The Fields we see on the screen is, by and large, the one we know from many biographical sources, and most reliably from his mistress of fourteen years, Carlotta Monti. This Fields is the pathologically suspicious, cynical man who once drawled on election day, "Well, I never vote for anybody; I always vote _against_."[7] It is the man who scorned the jury system because, in his view, "It is impossible to find twelve fair men in all the world."[8]

[7] Quoted by Robert Lewis Taylor, _W.C. Fields: His Follies and Fortunes_ (Garden City, N.Y.: Doubleday, 1949), p. 275.

[8] Quoted by Gene Fowler, _Minutes of the Last Meeting_ (New York: Viking, 1954), p. 173.

ABOUT THE AUTHOR

Frederick Crews, Professor of English at the University of California at Berkeley, received the Ph.D. from Princeton University. Throughout a distinguished career he has attained many honors, including a Guggenheim Fellowship, appointment as a Fulbright Lecturer in Italy, and recognition from the National Endowment for the Arts for his essay, "Norman O. Brown: The World Dissolves." His writings include highly regarded books on Henry James, E. M. Forster, and Nathaniel Hawthorne, as well as the best-selling satire *The Pooh Perplex*. Professor Crews has also written the entry on Literary Criticism for the 1973 edition of the *Encyclopedia Britannica*, and has published articles in *Partisan Review*, *New York Review of Books*, *Commentary*, *Tri-Quarterly*, and other important journals.